4 25
c 4
cccc

(35- 19710) 4-26-65

AMERICAN BIOGRAPHY

A
HISTORY
OF
AMERICAN
BIOGRAPHY

1800-1935

*

by

Edward H. O'Neill

*

A Perpetua Book ∞

A. S. Barnes & Company, Inc.
New York

To
MY FATHER
and
MY MOTHER

PREFACE

THIS book is a history of biographical writing in America since 1800. It is also a record of the development of biography from a memoir, a eulogy, a reference work, to something which is as distinctive a form of literature as the essay or the novel. It was the remarkable changes that have appeared in methods and materials of life-writing in the last twenty years that suggested this study, for I think that the time has come to evaluate American biography for what it is worth. The old factual record gave way to the journalistic, psychological form. The post-war biography with its appeal to the emotions rather than to the intellect of its reader has run its course, and we now have, I think, a form and method which combine the best features of the old and the new. One of the purposes of this book is to show how biography has followed the trend of the times, gradually developing its method and broadening its scope. A century ago, little more than a generation ago, the huge books which passed for biographies of Washington, Lincoln, and the other great or near-great men of the country were studied by a few, but seldom read for themselves, for they had neither style nor method to recommend them. Many lives of this earlier type will be mentioned in the following pages, for they deepened the stream that is now running clear.

I have confined the material in this book to actual biographies, lives written or edited by someone other than the subject. Thus I have eliminated autobiographies, diaries, and journals, fascinating literature but outside the field of biography. The material is presented historically with as much criticism as could be included under the plan. In view of the fact that this is the first comprehensive study of American biography that has ever been made, I felt that it was necessary to present an historical and critical survey rather than a severely critical study of the form and the methods that have been used.

The material here presented is representative but does not attempt to cover the field in detail. In a book covering as large an historical and contemporary field as this, there are bound to be omissions. In some cases I may have overlooked an important book; in others I have deliberately omitted many books because they would have added nothing of value to the study or because they fall into types which are represented. My problem here was one of exclusion rather than inclusion.

The arrangement of the book is the best that could be made, considering the wide variety of the material. The general classification is a chronological development by subject, the exception being the chapter on modern biographers. Some of the divisions within the chapters are entirely arbitrary and were made to achieve some semblance of unity. No one is more aware of the deficiencies in arrangement than I am, but I could find no better method.

I regret that I was not able to treat the biographical writings of the seventeenth and eighteenth centuries in this book. Circumstances beyond my control prevented me from visiting distant libraries which have copies of the rare early writings. Inasmuch as I could not examine all of the material, I decided to omit all consideration of it, even though the principal biographers, Cotton Mather and Jeremy Belknap, were available.

The arrangement of the last chapter requires some explanation. Rather than open the body of the text, which was finished in January 1934, I chose to discuss the important biographies which have appeared since that date in one chapter, making page references to earlier books and to biographers who have been discussed in detail.

It would be almost impossible to name those who have assisted, consciously or unconsciously, in the preparation of this book. I have made some acknowledgments in the text; others are of such a tenuous quality that no definite acknowledgment can be made. More than to anyone else, this book owes its existence to Professor Arthur H. Quinn of the University of Pennsylvania. He encouraged an early paper on the subject; he gave me the benefit of his knowledge and advice during the preparation of the book; and he read the entire manuscript as I wrote it.

I am also indebted to Dr. Mark Longaker of the University of Pennsylvania, who likewise read the entire manuscript. His work and interest in biography made him an ideal critic, his sympathetic understanding of the problem involved in the preparation of this book, a kindly one. At this point I wish to remember the late Dr. Godfrey F. Singer of the University of Pennsylvania for the enthusiasm he brought to the reading of the earlier portion of the manuscript. For a critical reading of the proof I am deeply obliged to Dr. Ralph B. Allen of the University of Pennsylvania.

E. H. O'N.

Philadelphia
July 24, 1935

CONTENTS

CONTENTS

PART I

I

INTRODUCTION

MAN'S desire to preserve a record of himself is only less strong than his instinct to preserve himself. That desire has produced the allied arts of history and biography. Biography is, from the origin of the word, life-writing, or the record of an individual; history is the record of an age, a race, a nation. Biography and history have been commonly considered as synonymous terms, but they are not. Biography is a part of history, and history is frequently used as background for biography, but it is a simple matter to separate the two. Carlyle and Emerson believed that history is biography. Dryden, in his definition of biography, used the two terms as if they were interchangeable. Though we may accept Carlyle's and Emerson's definitions of history, we have gone farther than Dryden.

Someone has said that history is philosophy, teaching by example. In this idea can be found one of the germs of biography. Man has preserved a record of his ancestors out of respect for them and because their lives and deeds may serve as examples for present and future generations. These two purposes, the commemorative and the didactic, were for centuries the justification for life-writing.

The didactic purpose has always been very strong. It has produced the great majority of all the biographical writing in the world, but it has contributed very little to the literature of biography. On the other hand, the desire to commemorate his ancestors has led man to grope his way toward the portrayal and interpretation of personality. In the beginning he used stone and paint for his portraits, but they are not permanent media of expression. Time decomposes the stone and dims the paint, and copies of statues and portraits are never the same as the originals. The written word is permanent, for the original composition can be recopied or reprinted ex-

3

actly. How many statues or portraits have survived as long as Plutarch?

The permanence of the written word is only one of its advantages over other forms of art. The sculptor or the painter can present only one picture, can show his subject at only one period of life. The biographer can follow his subject from birth to death; he can show us his mental as well as his physical development; he can tell us, given the sources, what he said or did at any period of his life.

The history of biography is as old as the history of man. There are hundreds of biographies in the Old Testament. The Book of Ruth is an almost perfect piece of biographical writing, completely revealing her life and character in a comparatively short book. In the same manner but not to the same extent we get the story of King David from Samuel, and the stories of Solomon and Joshua from the books named for them.

It is, however, with Plutarch that biography as a distinct form of literature has its inception. Plutarch was a moralist and philosopher—he was one of Hadrian's tutors—and his *Lives of Noble Grecians and Romans* was written from the point of view of the moralist rather than that of the historian. Regardless of his many faults, he is one of the great biographers of the world, for he knew that portrayal of character and transmission of personality are the most important problems facing the biographer. His own words, which form the opening paragraphs of his *Life of Alexander,* are sufficient evidence that he was aware of the responsibilities of the true biographer:

It being my purpose to write the lives of Alexander the King, and of Caesar . . . It must be borne in mind that my purpose is not to write histories, but lives. And the most glorious exploits do not always furnish us with the clearest discoveries of virtue or vice in men; sometimes a matter of less moment, an expression or a jest, informs us better of their characters and inclinations, than the most famous sieges, the greatest armaments, or the bloodiest battles whatsoever. Therefore as portrait-painters are more exact in the forms and features of the face, in which the character is seen, than in the other parts of the body, so I must be allowed to give my more particular attention to the marks and indications of the souls of men, and while I endeavor by these to portray their lives, may be free to leave more weighty matters and great battles to be treated of by others.

Plutarch is not the only ancient life-writer who may be studied with profit today. Tacitus presents a real personality in his *Life of Agricola*. Agricola was the biographer's father-in-law and one of the great soldiers and administrators of the Roman Empire. The relationship between author and subject may have prevented Tacitus from portraying the whole career of his subject, but it did not prevent him from writing a life that is as complete, as clearly portrayed, and as individual as the average biography of today.

We speak of the journalistic, highly spiced, and scandalous type of biography as something new. It is at least as old as Suetonius. In his *Lives of the Twelve Caesars*, Suetonius collected every bit of scandal and gossip that he had ever known or heard of, and called the result biography. Just as the modern third-rate journalist turned biographer thinks that he knows what the public wants and produces a mass of lurid copy which is generally untrue in principle and in detail, Suetonius thought that the world was more interested in the vices of the Roman emperors than in their virtues. Suetonius has survived and his modern imitator has been successful because both supply that single element which attracts the average reader, intimate details of the lives of the great, the famous, or the notorious. Suetonius cared nothing about the politics, economics, or morals of his day; he was interested only in retailing the intimacies of the lives of the predecessors of Hadrian, whose secretary he was. With equal indifference to the important acts in the life of his subject, the modern scandal-mongering biographer collects and emphasizes only those facts which will attract the readers of the tabloids and true romances. The scarcity of such material as this had more than a little to do with Suetonius' survival. His modern counterpart will not be so fortunate. The scandal biography has never had a long reign—it has appeared at intervals between Suetonius' time and our own—and it has practically disappeared from modern American biography.

From the second to the eighteenth century there is little in the literature of biography that indicates any progress in the art. The great mass of medieval life-writing is pure hagiography and, as such, outside the realm of comment or criticism. It was written for the purpose of edification, and we assume that it achieved this purpose—at the expense of piously suppressing or falsifying the records of thousands of lives. Some interesting comments on the shortcomings of saints' lives may be found in the first chapter (page 12) of Miss Agnes Repplier's *Mère Marie of the Ursulines*.

Along the road to modern biography is an occasional milestone of one kind or another. Roper's *Life of Sir Thomas More* (c. 1557) is a charming commemorative essay. Sir Thomas More's *Historie of King Richard III* (c. 1515) is the first break in the line of hero-worshiping royal biographies. More attempted a critical interpretation of Richard III and presented a character which Shakespeare has made universally known. Sir Francis Bacon's *Historie of the Raigne of King Henry the Seventh* (1622), while primarily historical biography, points the way to a closer study of character than had heretofore been considered necessary. The whole history of English biography should be studied by every student of the subject. (See Part II of bibliography.) Such biographies as Izaak Walton's *Lives*, John Aubrey's *Brief Lives*, the various biographical writings of Defoe, and Johnson's *Lives of the Poets* contribute to both the literature and the art of biography. These and many others lead up to the high point of life-writing in England, James Boswell's *Life of Johnson*. Modern biography really begins with Boswell's *Life of Johnson*, for Boswell lifted life-writing out of the class of hack work and made it a form of literature as clearly defined as poetry or fiction. No one of the three forms has always remained pure, but, muddied at times, eventually each runs clear. The last decade has seen much mud in the biographical stream, but it is running clearer and stronger than ever before.

2

Man, being by nature an orderly creature, tries to define everything with which he comes in contact. It was not until the seventeeth century that any attempt was made to define biography. The word itself was first used in that century but not, as many have supposed, by John Dryden. It was he who gave impetus to a study of the form and formulated the first definition. "Biographia or history of particular men's lives" is not a very accurate definition, although it does give a certain individuality to the form. There have been innumerable definitions since then, each tending to a better understanding of biography as a specific type of literature. One of the best that we have is that found in the *Oxford Dictionary:* history of the lives of individual men as a branch of literature. A better statement is thus phrased: biography is a narrative of a man's life from birth to death. However, neither is adequate from my point of view, for the *Oxford* definition makes biography a part of history, which is not always true, and the second definition implies that biography is always a narrative. Modern biography has moved away from the simple narrative into the field of explanation and interpretation. My definition of biography is that it is the re-creation of a man as he really was, as he lived and moved and had his being. It is on the basis of this definition that I have judged the lives discussed in this historical study.

Biographical writing falls into two large classifications, narrative and expository. Narrative biography is a simple account, complete or incomplete, of a man's life from birth to death. It rarely attempts any explanation of the subject's career or any interpretation of his character. Historical biography, the memoir, the appreciation, the eulogy, and the panegyric are all forms of narrative biography. Washington Irving's *Life of Washington* is one of the best examples of narrative life-writing in American biography. There is an analysis of Washington's character in this biography, but it is an analysis which results from a narration of the facts of the life rather than from an explanation of those facts. In modern biography there is frequently a combination of narration and exposition, as in the case of such a book as Paul Van Dyke's *Catherine de Medici*. This book is primarily a history of France and Italy during the life and reign of Catherine de Medici; it is also a life of Catherine for, despite the preponderance of historical narrative, Catherine's character is completely delineated and she is always before the reader, in spirit if not in the flesh. The memoir and the appreciation are purely narrative accounts in which we see the subjects as the authors knew and saw them. Some of the finest things in the literature of American biography are to be found in these types, little masterpieces such as Professor Palmer's *Life of Alice Freeman Palmer* and Charles W. Eliot's *John Gilley*. The first is an intimate memoir by the subject's husband; the second is a sincere appreciation of a Maine fisherman and guide, whom his biographer knew for many years. The panegyric and the eulogy had their origin in the funeral sermon and the memorial discourse, and they have made little progress since then. These writings include conventional lives of national or folk heroes, candidates for public offices, and men who have been in public life though contributing little to the common good.

Expository biography adheres to the principles of chronology as strictly as does narrative biography, with some exceptions. It differs from the latter in that it seeks not only the facts, the events, the progress, and perhaps the decline of a life, but the explanation which lies behind the facts, the interpretation which will explain the progress and decline. It is a modern development in biographical writing and has been more highly cultivated in America than elsewhere, although certain phases of expository biography first appeared in the writings of Strachey in England, Maurois in France, and Ludwig in Germany. Each of these men brought something new to life-writing, something which, in their hands or the hands of their successors, has improved the general quality of, and interest in, biographical writing.

Expository biography may either explain or interpret the individual. In many instances it does both. The difference between explanation and interpretation is that explanation of a subject shows how a man acted, succeeded, or failed, while interpretation goes farther and shows why he acted, succeeded, or failed. If this difference is true, interpretive biography is the highest form of the art, for it presents the most complete picture of the subject; it is the closest approach to the re-creation of the man as he really was. In interpretive biography the writer is attempting to present not only the physical but the mental aspects of his subject, and it is in that attempt that many biographers stumble into the numerous pitfalls that line their paths.

There are many methods which the biographer can use to explain the life of his subject. Of these the best is to let the subject speak for himself wherever possible. If the biographer is fortunate enough to have a large amount of original source material in the form of diaries, letters, speeches, or public papers, and this material has some literary quality, then his task is comparatively simple. He can choose from that material the parts which will best serve his purpose and let the man speak for himself. Unfortunately it rarely happens that the diaries and letters of a public man or even a man of letters can be extensively used, for they are not always well written or in such form that they can be printed without a great deal of editing. One of the best examples of self-portraiture, not definitely autobiographic, in modern biography, is *The Life and Letters of Walter Hines Page*. Mr. Page was a born letter writer, and his correspondence through the years, particularly during the period when he was Ambassador to England, presents a more complete analysis of his life and character than any biographer could have made.

In the last twenty years biography, like every other form of literature, has made use of developments in modern science. There were psychologists in literature before the word came into use, but they did not consciously develop their work on psychological principles. It was not until the appearance of *Eminent Victorians* and *Queen Victoria* that the principles of psychology were definitely applied to biography, and these were the principles of abnormal rathèr than normal psychology. Psychology is the science of the human mind and its operations. It explains many of the problems which beset the biographer in his study of normal as well as abnormal people. It enables him to explain the driving forces in man which carry him to the heights of success and the depths of disaster. It enables him to explain why men are successful soldiers and unsuccessful statesmen, why they are liberals or conservatives in politics, why they become great or merely famous. It is the most valuable asset that the biographer has if it is used properly, for with it he can explain completely the man whose life he is trying to present.

Biography is, or should be, the study of personality, and the artistic biographer has the right and duty to use every legitimate device to explain and interpret his subject. If he is to be successful, he must so present the man or woman of whom he is writing that the reader will be able to follow the subject not on the printed page but in his imagination to the point where he actually knows that man and woman better than, or at least as well as, they knew themselves. One of the fascinations of biography is that the reader can know the great, the near-great, the famous, and the notorious of all time when their stories are unfolded by writers who are something more than mere chroniclers.

The methods which biographers use to bring these people to us are many. Some biographers can achieve their purpose by objective methods; others are more successful when using subjective methods. Carl Sandburg re-created the prairie years of Abraham Lincoln by literally absorbing everything he could find or hear about Lincoln. As far as such a thing is possible, he relived the years from 1809 to 1861, and, in my judgment, was able to see the Lincoln of those years as clearly as any biographer has seen him. On the other hand, Albert Bigelow Paine lived with Mark Twain for a number of years. He watched him; he listened to his talk; he took down what he said; and by these methods he was able to write one of the finest biographies in American literature.

Consciously or unconsciously, Sandburg and Paine drew heavily upon psychology, studying their subjects as completely as they could. Their purpose was to find the real man and present him as he actually lived. It may be that *Mark Twain* is not so complete as *Abraham Lincoln*, for there are circumstances and conditions which a biographer of a contemporary must respect. The incompleteness, assuming that the book is incomplete, does not detract from the art of Mr. Paine's technique. One may pick out dozens of books in this history that are excellent biographies because their authors not only knew psychology but knew how to use it to the best advantage that their subjects might be seen as they really were. It may be noted here that Katharine Anthony, whose biographies have been analyzed in the chapter entitled "The Biographers," was the first of the American biographers to use psychology as a definite method of approach to the study of personality.

The wide use of psychology in life-writing naturally led to the introduction into the field of biography of the derivative science, psychoanalysis. Psychoanalysis is a highly specialized form of abnormal psychology in which the sex element plays the dominant part. If we are to believe Dr. Sigmund Freud and his school, almost every act of man and every expression of the human mind stems from, or is affected by, the sex instinct. It is sufficient for our purpose here to point out that hundreds of so-called biographers have embraced Freudian psychology with open arms, for it opened the door to tabloid journalism in the field of biography. The psychiatrist or psychoanalyst searches for the abnormal that he may remove it and give the normal a chance to grow. The journalist-turned biographer or the more serious writer to whom psychoanalysis has become an obsession searches for the abnormal and uses it as the basis for his character analysis. The psychoses, the philes, the phobias, the complexes, the mental and moral aberrations are hunted down and pounced upon as the cat hunts down and pounces upon the unsuspecting mouse. General Grant had no idea that he was a zoöphile, nor did Nathaniel Hawthorne ever guess that he was an introvert. Herman Melville did not attribute his financial failure as a writer to the fact that he had an unhappy childhood; Edgar Allan Poe could not have imagined that he wrote *The Raven* because he had a diseased mind. These various Freudian complexes may have influenced the lives and works of the men I have mentioned—who knows?—but to make them the bases for biographical studies, as these were made in some cases, is to lose sight of the purpose of biography. Like the realist in fiction, the psychoanalytical biographer chooses only that material which will fit into the preconceived picture he has created. He does not see his subject completely, for the abnormal is only a part of any man. Certainly no man of the mental stature of those I have mentioned is completely abnormal. Psychoanalytical biography is unfair for this reason and because the biographers who use this method, regardless of their scholarship or ability, do not know enough about this complex study to handle it with real intelligence. Physicians who have spent the best years of their lives studying the eccentricities of the human mind hesitate to pronounce a definite opinion in the average case, while the occasional biographer who has read Freud's book on dreams or looked into a volume of Jung or Kraft-Ebing blithely damns the man who deviated in the slightest degree from the norm of the average American.

There is one other evil in modern American biography for which psychoanalysis is partly responsible; Lytton Strachey must bear the rest of the responsibility. This is the practice which has been termed "debunking." "Debunking" is merely a sensational method of finding flaws in the characters of great soldiers, statesmen, and writers, and attempting to drag them down from the positions that are rightfully theirs to the place where the reader can mouth that mighty platitude: "I'm as good as he is." Those of us who are interested in our fellow-men want to know wherein their minds and imaginations differ from ours rather than the fact that most men have stomach trouble or gout at some time in their lives. A writer who has a particular antipathy for some great or famous man should not use that man as a subject for a biography, for, disliking him, he cannot do justice to him. This is strikingly illustrated in the case of Paxton Hibben and his books on Henry Ward Beecher and W. J. Bryan. He despised both men, he set out to belittle them, and of course he succeeded. They were human and very fallible, but they had their good points. Hibben concealed or ignored all the good, and in so doing presented grossly unfair pictures of both men.

Both psychology and the later psychoanalysis (though it was not widely known at that time) were used by Gamaliel Bradford in the making of what he called psychographs. Mr. Bradford began his biographical writing in 1912 and continued it until his death in 1932. He was not a biographer in the ordinary sense of the word, for he rarely attempted full-length portraits. His method was to take certain characteristics of a man or woman and build his portrait around them. This method will be analyzed in a later consideration of his work. It is mentioned here because it is one of the variations of expository life-writing and a distinct contribution to American literature, if not to biography.

From the point of view of the reader, dramatic biography is one of the most interesting developments in modern life-writing. By dramatic biography I mean that method of presentation which develops the life of the subject in conformity with the rules of the construction of plays. The outstanding exponent of this method is Emil Ludwig, the German biographer and dramatist. Herr Ludwig was a dramatist before he was a biographer. He wrote plays with Napoleon and Bismarck as the central characters before he wrote their biographies, and he has stated that he sees lives of men only in terms of three- or five-act dramas. Ludwig has been widely imitated by American biographers but, unfortunately, his imitators had not his dramatic experience. The principal virtue of this dramatic biography is that it has movement and vitality which carry the reader along as the life unfolds. Ludwig's supreme achievement is his *Napoleon,* for there he had a subject and material which allowed him full scope. This method gives free rein to the writer's imagination. Ludwig seldom allowed his imagination to get the upper hand of his facts, but his imitators, in their desire to be dramatic, forgot that they were writing biography and filled their books with background, side issues, and irrelevant stories. These "lives" have a passing interest, as has the latest novel, but they are not biographies because they were written without plan.

The most pernicious form of modern biography is fictional biography. Fictional biography is not to be confused with biographical fiction, for the latter is a legitimate form of the novel, and is based on fact, while the former is an illegitimate form of biography and rarely has any basis at all. Fictional biography is a rewriting from secondary sources with the spaces filled in and interest aroused by products of the author's mind. The impetus for much of our fictional biography came from the same source as the impetus for much of the best in modern biography: Lytton Strachey. When Strachey wrote the last paragraphs of his essay on Manning and his biography of Victoria, he opened the doors to all sorts of biographical abuses. Neither of these passages is fiction; both are the products of a completely controlled imagination, based on an intimate knowledge of the lives and characters of the Cardinal and the Queen. The trouble began when men with far less background, less culture, and less knowledge of their subjects tried to do the same sort of thing. They went the master one better by substituting fiction for imagination. The workings of Queen Victoria's mind as she lay dying are qualified by a "perhaps"; the description of Cardinal Manning's cathedral church is an exact one. In place of the qualifying phrase, the "rewrite" school gives us pages of their subjects' thoughts and, in many instances, pages of conversations which can have no possible basis in fact, for there are no sources to support them. Cameron Rogers creates almost half of the book, *The Magnificent Idler, Walt Whitman,* and Arthur D. Howden Smith provides pages and pages of imaginary conversation in his *Commodore Vanderbilt.* In like manner the writers of this school describe the physical movements of their subjects, the clothes they wore, their modes of travel—though there is not a shred of evidence on which to support these imaginary pictures. The biographer may use his imagination to re-create his subject, but he may not supply details which are not in the records. He may construct an imaginary picture for the purpose of background or of heightening interest, but if he is honest, he will inform his reader that the picture is imaginary. The vogue for fictional biography has passed, along with the excessive and unfair use of psychology and psychoanalysis. All three have left their imprint on modern life-writing, and the biographer of today uses the results to the best advantage. An examination of the last three awards of the Pulitzer Prize Committee for Biography will show that we have passed from the stage of experiment and excess to a position where biography is one of the arts, not merely a book of reference.

There is one kind of biography that has been and is still used as a work of reference. This is the critical biography, the life of a man of letters, to which the term "literary biography" is frequently applied. This is not a very exact term, but it has come to be generally used and I have used it in this history. Until recently, critical biography could hardly be classed as true biography. It was largely a critical estimate of the work of a particular poet, novelist, essayist, or historian with a biographical introduction. Modern interest in life-writing and modern research have provided materials and reasons for revaluations of our principal writers. These modern critical biographies are, for the most part, complete life studies with the critical evaluations integral parts of the biographies. In the case of almost every writer, we can obtain a more complete understanding of his work if we know the story of his life. The work of a creative writer should not be interpreted solely in terms of his life, as some modern biographers have tried to do; but the facts of his life will often help us to understand the uneven quality of his work, its differences at different periods of his life, his choice of material, or the nature of his medium of expression. Such critical biographies as George E. Woodberry's *Life of Edgar Allan Poe,* Newton Arvin's *Hawthorne,* Raymond Weaver's *Herman Melville,* and Carl Van Doren's *Swift,* to name only a few, are distinct contributions to biography as well as to literary history and criticism.

3

Biography should be judged by the same fundamental principles of criticism as apply to the evaluation of any other form of literature. There are, however, certain standards which apply to biography alone. It must be true; it must be well planned and the plan completely developed; it must be a complete account of a life from birth to death; the subject must be of sufficient importance to justify the writing of a biography; and the biographer must be, as far as such a thing is possible, impartial.

"The value of any biography depends on its being true," said Samuel Johnson. If a biography is not true it is worthless. A reader can judge the truth of a particular life by his previous knowledge of the subject or by his knowledge of the biographer. If he lacks those bases for judgment he must depend on his intuition or on the good faith of his biographer. A biographer may be consciously or unconsciously untruthful. He may tell only part of the story, deliberately concealing important facts which reflect adversely on the reputation of his subject, or, because of deep-seated prejudice or actual ignorance of the facts, he may, without deliberate intention, present a partisan point of view. Every early biographer of Lincoln, except Lamon and Herndon, either falsified or evaded the question of Lincoln's religion. Practically every biographer of Grant has either weakly defended or evaded the question of the scandals that flourished during his two administrations. Senator Beveridge, in his *Life of John Marshall,* drew Thomas Jefferson as a complete villain because he was reared in, and was one of the leaders of, the political party which opposed everything for which Jefferson stood. Beveridge began his studies for *Abraham Lincoln* in the same frame of mind. Like the average American he believed that Lincoln had always been a great man. He found that the facts offered a very different interpretation. He was too honest to present an untruthful picture; he was too partisan to draw the inevitable conclusions from his facts. Consequently he confined himself to facts alone, letting the reader form his own judgments. In other words, Senator Beveridge chose to be truthful rather than artistic.

The question as to whether or not a biographer shall present his material in the form of a plain narrative, or whether he shall go into a detailed explanation and interpretation, is one which he must decide for himself. Some subjects are particularly suited to narration; others require explanation and interpretation because of their nature or their importance. We can pass judgment on the result, but we are not always in a position to know what problems the biographer had to face and what compromises he had to make. Matters of style and expression are distinctly relative, and should be judged accordingly. The best authority on a given subject may be least able to present a piece of finely polished literature. Here again our criticism must be tempered with justice. Occasionally we have an artist in biography, whatever the method, choosing a subject which is particularly interesting to him. Then there appear such lives as *Abraham Lincoln: The Prairie Years, President Eliot of Harvard, Sherman: Fighting Prophet,* and *The Scottish Queen.*

II

AMERICAN BIOGRAPHY

1800—1860

THE opening years of the nineteenth century in America were not particularly rich in any form of literature. Between 1789 and 1800 the United States of America were finding themselves, administratively and politically. Then in 1800 came a great political change. Thomas Jefferson was inaugurated President, March 4, 1801, and the Republicans, the common people, the people of the frontier, came into power. Everyone was politically minded. The Federalist party was rapidly disintegrating. There was strife between the parties and within the Federalist party particularly. Such conditions are not conducive to literature in any form. Some verse was being written, and novels appeared which have long since been forgotten. Few writers, however, turned to biography. It had not yet evolved from the ministerial panegyric.

Seventeenth- and eighteenth-century biographical writing in America came, with few exceptions, from clergymen. At the end of the eighteenth century the clergy was losing its power, and the separation of church and state was almost complete. Clergymen continued to write and to be read, but they could no longer lead public opinion. Politics and political writers had taken the place of theology and clerical writers.

The biography of the first half of the nineteenth century can be classified as clerical, literary, and political biography. Quantitatively, biographies with clergymen as authors or subjects exceeded those of the other two groups. The American Sunday School Union and the American Tract Society published thousands of panegyrics on the lives of the principal clergymen and pious laymen. They probably served their purpose—edification of the masses—but they added nothing to the fund of human knowledge or to the art of biography. It is hardly an exaggeration to say that the authors and subjects of this great mass of writing were practically unknown at the time of the publication of the books, and are entirely unknown today except to church historians.

A few of these books will illustrate the method and the value of almost all of this material. These examples are far above the average, for they concern men who were among the foremost clergymen and theologians of their day. The earliest book of this type was Thomas B. Chandler's *Life of Samuel Johnson,* published in 1805, but written some time before the American Revolution. Johnson was one of the most prominent clergymen of his day—the late eighteenth century—and this biography is a complete story of his life, though it is formless, voluminous, and somewhat laudatory. Despite these faults it is a good biography for the time.

Jonathan Edwards has been the subject of a number of biographies. One of the earliest and one of the best is that by Sereno E. Dwight, published in 1829 as an introduction to the *Works of Jonathan Edwards.* Dwight's book is much more than an introduction; it is a long and detailed account of Edwards' life and work, sympathetic and eulogistic in tone, as might be expected of an editor who was also a clergyman of the same denomination. Its principal fault is that common to all biographies of its type, excessive length, which is the result of the author's inability or refusal to apply any definite biographical standards to his work. Long passages of sermons and other writings are incorporated in the text where a sentence or a paragraph from the passage would prove the biographer's point. Admitting its faults, Dwight's *Life of Jonathan Edwards* is a valuable contribution to our knowledge of Edwards, if not to the art of biography.

William H. Channing's *Memoir of William Ellery Channing* (1848) is another example of an important book which discourages a reader because of its length. Because William Ellery Channing was the dominant figure in Unitarianism in the early nineteenth century, his biographer felt that he must include everything that the man said and did. When a memoir occupies three large volumes, it ceases to be a memoir. This book is really an autobiography with a very thin connecting narrative by the editor. Although we never lose sight of the subject—sometimes we wish we could—we have no clear idea of the great preacher when we have finished the book because we have heard too much and seen too little of him. It is an invaluable source book but a poor biography.

Ashbel Steele's *Chief of the Pilgrims, or, the Life and Times of William Brewster* (1857) illustrates another fault in biographical writing. This book is primarily theology and history, with occasional glimpses of William Brewster. Historical biography has a place in the history of life-writing, but it can be handled only by a biographer who is completely master of his material and is constantly aware that he must keep his subject in the foreground of his picture.

The faults that have been pointed out in these biographies are very common, particularly in the nineteenth century. They defeat the purpose of real biography: the re-creation of the man as he actually was. Furthermore, these books lack any distinction in style or manner. They are heavy, verbose, and frequently redundant. A biographer is required to do more than merely record facts. He must present those facts as attractively as possible. Lastly, he must know what to omit as well as what to include.

2

The first important figure in nineteenth-century biography is Mason Locke Weems, better known as Parson Weems. There are many who will say that he is neither important nor a biographer, and they may be right; at the same time he is one of the most remarkable and influential figures in American letters. In order to understand Weems and his books we must know something about him.

He was born in Maryland in 1752 and received as much education in the province as was available. We know very little of his early life before he began his travels. We know that he went to England to study medicine; that he returned to Maryland in 1776, but we do not know whether or not he had a medical degree. We know that he came under the influence of the Reverend William Smith of Chestertown, Maryland, first provost of the College of Philadelphia and the father of the Episcopal church in America; that he studied for the ministry and went to England again for ordination. He seems never to have been a very successful minister; toward the end of his clerical career he had no parish at all.

Parson Weems was interested in spreading practical moral knowledge, and wrote several pamphlets while he was a clergyman. They sold fairly well, and this success gave him the idea for the career he was to follow to the end of his life, which was to make him in his day one of the best-known men in the eastern and southern parts of the United States.

He became the first and the greatest of American book agents. He formed a connection with Mathew Carey of Philadelphia, the greatest book publisher in America at this time, and peddled Carey's books from Philadelphia to the Spanish province of Florida. He sold medical books, law books, sermons, books on theology, novels and, of course, his own tracts. On horseback and in a wagon, he traveled the abominable roads of the period from 1790 to 1825. He went everywhere and knew everybody; he would substitute in the pulpit or play his fiddle for a dance. Regardless of what he did, he always managed to work his books in somehow. As characteristic of America as Benjamin Franklin, Weems practised a great deal of what Franklin had preached.

It is not strange that this man should turn to writing what, in the absence of a better term, we must call biography. He knew the people of America as well as any other man living; he knew their mentality, their taste in reading, and most important of all, he knew how to write for the public. His first and most famous book was his life of Washington,

which will be discussed in Chapter VI. For its huge success
the author was perhaps more responsible than the subject.
The first edition of the Washington biography appeared in
1800, a few months after Washington's death, but the book
that we know appeared as the fifth edition in 1806.

Emboldened by his first success, Weems was ready to repeat it when the opportunity appeared. General Francis
Marion was the most famous of the Revolutionary generals
in the South. As a guerilla chieftain he had no superior; he
made life miserable for the British while they were in South
Carolina. His life was filled with adventure and the spirit
that we call romantic, and a whole legend has grown up
around his name in South Carolina.

General Horry, one of Marion's men, had been collecting
material for a life of his hero for many years. The General
was a soldier, not a writer; the material had reached enormous proportions, and he did not know what to do with it.
Finally someone suggested that he ask Parson Weems to assist
in writing the life. The Parson was only too glad to do it. He
took the material and, in the intervals when he was not selling books, fashioned it into what the title-page designated a
biography, but even the Parson himself admitted that it was
a historical romance. It took him a long time to write the
book, but it finally appeared in 1809, with General Horry
and Mason Locke Weems as co-authors.

When the General saw the book he did not recognize it;
he stormed and raged, but nothing could be done about it
then—it was published. The whole story of the collaboration
and the General's refusal to accept the book as his can be
found in Weems's correspondence, which has been published
within the last few years. The General had every right to be
offended; the General Marion of this book never lived; he
couldn't have. Weems did not care whether or not his Marion
was the real Marion. He intended to do for Marion what he
had done for Washington, to make a hero of him. There is
a moral purpose in everything that Weems wrote. This moral
purpose makes bad biography, but in this instance it provides

some interesting reading. It strikes us that Weems's reasoning was something like this: Marion was fighting in a great cause, he deserved to be a great man; he was a great man and could accomplish impossible feats of bravery against overwhelming odds. In the book he is a great man and does accomplish these things and is a hero. What more could a striving young country want than the example of Francis Marion, the "Swamp Fox"?

Of course the book was another success for Parson Weems and, incidentally, it helped him to sell his other books. He published two other "biographies," one of Franklin in 1817 and one of Penn in 1819. He was attracted to Penn by the latter's genuine piety and by his liberalism. The book cannot be criticized as a biography, but it is at least the tribute of one good man to another. Weems never attempted any research for his subjects; what he did not know he made up. There are passages in the life of Penn which Weems had lifted complete from his earlier books. A good idea is worth repeating; this seems to have been one of the Parson's maxims. His book on Franklin has even less claim to biographical recognition than the Penn biography has. With the exception of a few facts that everyone knew, the book is made up of a collection of Franklin's best maxims. These books on Penn and Franklin had not enough romance in them to make up for their lack of information; consequently, they were not so successful as the earlier lives.

These four "biographies" constitute Weems's claim to a place as a biographer. Again we say that he may not have been a biographer, but these books had a wider influence and reading than any other secular books of their day in America. Washington and Marion have not yet been stripped of the legends with which Weems covered them, and we know the maxims of Poor Richard far better than we would have known them, had not Parson Weems written his "biography" of Franklin.

We have no right to dismiss Parson Weems today without a hearing. More than one biography has been published in the last fifteen years that has as little basis of truth as have Weems's books. He is the literary ancestor of the fictional biographer, and, from the moral point of view, he has a better chance of having his literary sins forgiven or condoned. He popularized the biography of his day and he did it intentionally, for he knew then as we know now that we are essentially a nation of hero worshipers.

Not all of the early American biographical writers were romantic moralists. Some had a very accurate conception of what genuine biography should be. Among these was William Dunlap, a very important figure in the early American drama, both as playwright and producer. He had financial difficulties in his later years which forced him to turn to anything which would provide a living. As a biographer he is most commonly associated with the *Life of Charles Brockden Brown* (1815), the first professional novelist in America. As a matter of fact this book was not written by Dunlap and it can hardly be called a biography. The circumstances of Dunlap's association with the work can be best explained in Dunlap's own words from the preface:

The plan of these volumes and the proposals for their publication were laid before the public without the knowledge of the writer of the biography. Engagements having been entered into with the subscribers, the present writer has been engaged to fulfill them, but not until the selections for the first volume had been made and printed.

Dunlap felt obliged to carry out the original plan, with the result that the two volumes are made up principally of excerpts from Brown's novels and other writings. The biographical portion of the book is extremely meager, but it is still the best account of Brown that we have.

An earlier biography of Dunlap's will illustrate what he might have done for Brown, had he had the opportunity. The *Memoirs of George Frederick Cooke* were published in London in 1813. Cooke, an English actor who had spent some years on the American stage, was a personal friend of

Dunlap. During his last visit to America he asked Dunlap to be his biographer, and the latter consented. Cooke had written what he called a chronicle of his theatrical career, and had also kept a diary during the last years of his life. Dunlap uses this material extensively and successfully; he allows Cooke to speak for himself wherever possible, and the result is a remarkably good biography for the time.

There is a record of two other biographical works in which Dunlap had a hand, but I have not been able to find either of them. The first is the *Life of William Guthrie* (1796) and the other, the *Life of the . . . Duke of Wellington, by Francis L. Clarke. With Supplementary Chapters by William Dunlap* (1814).

3

Washington Irving, the essayist and short story writer, is a landmark in American literature. Irving the biographer has been unduly neglected. The probable reason for the neglect is that he produced his biographies in the period when "scholarship," meaning much detail, many footnotes, and endless theorizing, was in the offing. Irving was not considered a scholar, and his solid writing was given no more prominence than much of his lighter material. This was a serious error, because Irving is entitled to an important place in the history of American biography.

His first effort at biographical writing was a series of four essays on American naval heroes which appeared in the *Analectic Magazine,* of which Irving was the editor, during 1815–1816. These sketches of Captain James Lawrence, Lieutenant Burrows, Commodore Perry, and Captain David Porter are very short and as good as the average apprentice work in biography. He waves the flag and makes the eagle scream, but that was probably what the readers of his magazine wanted. The War of 1812 had just ended, and patriotism, in some sections, was still at fever heat. These men had performed valiant services in the campaigns against the

Tripolitan pirates and in the late war; therefore, they had to be given heroic stature. The principal fault of these sketches is careless writing, a fault of which Irving was seldom guilty. Periodical editing and proof reading were very carelessly done in those days; this may account for the more glaring errors in these sketches.

Irving's first long biography did not appear until 1828. In the winter of 1826 Irving was in Europe and was asked by Alexander Stephens, American Minister to Spain, to translate a volume of manuscripts relating to Columbus and the discovery of America which was about to appear. Irving went to Madrid intending to make the translation, but found such a wealth of material that he decided to write an account of Columbus and his voyages to America. He spent more than a year collecting and studying documents before he began to write.

A History of the Life and Voyages of Christopher Columbus (1828) is one of the best lives of Columbus that we have. We have learned a great deal more about Columbus than Irving knew, but Irving has seldom been found wrong. He developed a method for this book which he used for all of his later biographical writings. He made a careful study of his sources, digested the material, and then wrote his narrative. Scholars are inclined to scoff at this method because it eliminates footnotes and the rest of the critical apparatus. Irving was not writing for scholars and critics; he was writing for the intelligent reading public, which wants the results of scholarship rather than the methods.

Irving's *Columbus* is a full and rapid narrative of Columbus' life, his geographical studies, his attempts to secure aid for his project, his disappointments, his final success. The reader is carried along from one point to another with such ease that he feels he is actually with the Genoese. History and biography are so artistically combined that one is hardly conscious of the amount of history that is in the book or of the amount of research that went into the making of the book. This is historical biography at its best.

Some will say that there is too much history in the book. Columbus cannot be presented without a definite historical background. Others will claim that the book is too long. It requires space to present adequately the years of preparation and the period of the four voyages that Columbus made to America. It will be objected that there is too much of the romantic in the book. Columbus' whole life was one great romance, a vision and a realization of that vision.

While Irving was making his researches for Columbus, he came upon a great mass of Moorish material in the Spanish archives. The opportunity for using this material did not present itself for many years, but finally *Mahomet and His Successors* was published in 1849–1850. Even at this late date there was not much information in English regarding the great Arabian and his followers. Attracted by the romance of Mahomet's career and the religious and political empire that he had created, Irving told the story of the prophet's life from that point of view. In the preface to this biography Irving states that his material was incomplete, that he was too far away from the place where the man and his religion had their origin; consequently he filled out his narrative with the legends that had grown up in the twelve centuries since Mahomet's death. The result is a combination of fact and fiction, carefully separated, which is still good reading. This may not be the authoritative life of the founder of Islam, but it gives us the essential facts of his life in an atmosphere truly Oriental. That atmosphere was still prevalent in Spain, as Irving proves in the *Alhambra* as well as in this book. *Mahomet and His Successors* is a charming story, charmingly told and based on fact.

Irving's third important biography is *Oliver Goldsmith: a Biography* (1849). Irving had written two earlier versions of Goldsmith's life to accompany editions of his works. One was written in 1830, the other in 1840. When Irving began to collect his writings he realized that neither of the earlier accounts was adequate; furthermore John Forster had published his *Life of Oliver Goldsmith* in the meantime. Irving, without relying on Forster, made the *Life of Goldsmith* one of his finest works.

Irving was able to write a good biography of Goldsmith because he could understand the Irish genius better than any other man of his day. Their temperaments were much alike, and Irving's career might have exactly paralleled Goldsmith's, had he been born to the same position as was the latter. Both were wanderers, romantics, children of the eighteenth century who had turned their backs on rationalism, one to live in the world of the past, the other in a world of his own creation. Goldsmith was the greater creative artist, but the creator of Rip Van Winkle could thoroughly understand the creator of Parson Primrose; the creator of the *Legend of Sleepy Hollow* was in tune with the creator of *The Deserted Village.*

Irving varied his method a little in this book; in place of a historical background he built up a personal background, and one of the literary London in which Goldsmith lived and worked. We have excellent sketches of his contemporaries, of the booksellers, of the members of The Club. Again, Irving could do this because he was by nature of the eighteenth rather than the nineteenth century. As literary biography this book is the best of its kind that the early nineteenth century can show. As a life of Goldsmith it has not yet been superseded.

During his literary career Irving wrote numerous biographical sketches of contemporary Englishmen and Americans, such as Thomas Campbell and Washington Allston. He also wrote a long biographical essay for the *Biography and Poetical Remains of the Late Margaret Miller Davidson* (1841). This essay is typical of its kind, and in all probability was written at the request of the young lady's family.

Irving's last and most important contribution to biography was his *Life of George Washington.* This book will be considered with the other biographical material on Washington, but it can be said here that it will stand comparison with any biography of Washington written in the nineteenth century.

4

William Gilmore Simms was the most important man of letters in the South before the Civil War. Poet, novelist, editor, he finally turned to biography and published four lives in five years: a *Life of Francis Marion* (1845); *Life of Captain John Smith, the Founder of Virginia* (1846); *Life of Chevalier Bayard* (1847); *Life of Nathaniel Greene* (1849).

Simms's biographies are popular accounts of men whom he admired. They make no claim to original research, but they are based on facts as Simms knew them. General Marion had been the subject of numerous romances and at least one romantic biography; legend had built a story around the man, and when Simms published his factual narrative it did not receive the recognition that it should have received. The *Life of Francis Marion* is a sympathetic treatment of the career of the "Swamp Fox," but it tries to be accurate and fair; this is the reason it was not popular.

Simms handled the other subjects in the same manner. Smith's life seems to have been written to popularize Smith's adventurous career. Little was known of the man who saved the Jamestown colony from the fate of earlier settlements, and Simms endeavored to supply this want. Considering its date, this biography of Smith is excellent.

The *Life of Chevalier Bayard* was written because Simms greatly admired the man who has come down to us as the perfect example of chivalry and gentility. Simms was a romantic in his point of view, and he aspired to social eminence; Bayard was the exponent of what Simms wanted to be. It is natural that this should be the best of his biographies; it is a truism that a man can excel in that field in which his greatest interest lies. Simms considered this the best of his biographies, and time has justified his belief.

Simms called himself the editor of the *Life of Nathaniel Greene,* but his biographer, Professor Trent, believes that Simms was the actual author. The style and method of this biography prove Professor Trent's assertion. General Greene has a position second only to that of Washington in the military history of the Revolution, and this biography gives no more than a fair account of his life and career.

These biographical writings of Simms will always have a place in the history of American biography because of the prominence of the author. They are good, better than the majority of the lives of the times, but they are marred by faults common to all of Simms's works, turgid style and hasty writing.

There are numerous biographies by literary men in this period which are important largely because of the author rather than the subject. *The First White Man; or, the Life and Exploits of Daniel Boone* (1849), by Timothy Flint, is important in itself. Flint was a clergyman who spent a number of years early in the century in missionary work in the West. He was also a novelist and writer of verse. His long residence in the western country gave him an opportunity to observe and understand such men as Boone, and when he came to write the life—the first edition was published in 1833 with the title, *Biographical Memoir of Daniel Boone*—he was in a position to handle his subject intelligently. He knew and talked with Boone shortly before the latter's death. This personal contact gave him an opportunity to interpret Boone's character and personality. Flint's biography is still the best biography of Boone that we have.

James Fenimore Cooper's *Lives of Distinguished Naval Officers* (1846), *The Memoirs of Margaret Fuller Ossoli* (1852), by R. W. Emerson, J. F. Clarke, and W. H. Channing, and Nathaniel Hawthorne's *Life of Franklin Pierce* (1852) added nothing to the literary reputations of their authors. Cooper's book grew out of his studies for his *History of the U. S. Navy.* The lives are principally of men who were friends of Cooper during his period of service in the Navy. Emerson contributed the chapters on Boston and Concord to the memoir of Margaret Fuller. Hawthorne wrote the *Life of Franklin Pierce* at the latter's request when Pierce was nominated for the Presidency in 1852. They were classmates at Bowdoin, but Hawthorne knew little of Pierce's life as a politician in New Hampshire. He compiled the book from whatever material was at hand, keeping close to facts and commenting very briefly on Pierce's character and qualifications. In return for writing the book, Hawthorne received the consulship at Liverpool. To that period in Europe we are indebted for the *Marble Faun.*

In 1850 appeared an edition of *The Works of the late Edgar Allan Poe; With Notices of his Life and Genius.* The notices were James Russell Lowell's sketch of Poe, written at the latter's request in 1845, Nathaniel P. Willis' account of Poe's death, and the memoir of Poe by Rufus W. Griswold, Poe's literary executor. Griswold's memoir is an example of a deliberate attempt at literary libel and it is responsible for much of the false impression of Poe which still survives. In 1856 another edition of Poe was published, with a complete and conventional memoir of Poe by Richard H. Stoddard, a friend of Poe during his last years.

5

When we turn to the biographies of public men written in the first half of the nineteenth century, we find that they are, with a few exceptions, important for subject rather than for method. The most important figures in public life were politicians and statesmen, and the lives are either campaign documents or eulogies to prepare the public for the candidates. Consequently there is little in this period which can be termed genuine biography or which has any literary quality.

One of the earliest of the biographies of a public man, exclusive of the early Washington lives, is *Sketches of the Life and Character of Patrick Henry* (1817), by William Wirt. Wirt was a prominent Virginia lawyer and statesman, a man almost as well known as Henry himself. Mr. Wirt never knew Henry, but he knew and talked with many men who had known him. He collected a great mass of material in the shape of facts and anecdotes. He had no previous experience in any kind of writing, and he did not know what to do with what he had. He tried to choose and organize the most important matter, but the book as a whole is formless and unbalanced. For instance, it was not until the edition of 1841, long after Wirt's death, that chapter headings were given to the book; the original book was divided only into large sections. In spite of these serious defects the book is fairly good for the period. It is likewise characteristic of much of the life-writing that was to be done for the next fifty years.

The year after Wirt's *Sketches of Henry* appeared, William Temple Franklin published the first version of Benjamin Franklin's autobiography: *Memoirs of the Life and Writings of Benjamin Franklin . . . Written by himself to a late period and continued to the time of his death, by his Grandson: William Temple Franklin* (1818). The autobiographical part was totally incomplete; it would not be complete for sixty years, but that problem is not within the province of this study. The continuation is a factual presentation of the principal events of Franklin's later years, with little attempt at organization or careful treatment. The book, however, is historically important.

Another important figure of the Revolution, General Nathaniel Greene, was the subject of two biographies at this time. Charles Caldwell wrote the *Memoirs of the Life and Campaigns of the Hon. Nathaniel Greene, Major General in the Army of the United States* (1819); and William Johnson, *Sketches of the Life and Correspondence of Nathaniel Greene* (1822). Both of these books were inspired by the lack of consideration for Greene which characterized the books on the Revolution written during this period. Although there is not much choice between the two, Johnson's was the authorized biography, but Caldwell's is much more complete. Some years later George W. Greene contributed a life of his grandfather to Sparks's *Library of American Biography*. Having written it while in Europe, he did not have General

Greene's papers with him; later he expanded this sketch into a formal biography.

There were numerous real and folk heroes in the America of the early nineteenth century, and each received his share of biographical adulation. Perhaps the foremost was Andrew Jackson. From early manhood he was a hero in the West, and after each of his military exploits his heroic stature grew to legendary proportions. After the Battle of New Orleans his fame became national, and he was groomed as a presidential candidate, the people's President. The first campaign biography of Jackson appeared in 1817. It is always recorded as John H. Eaton's *Life of Andrew Jackson*. Eaton merely finished the book which Major John B. Reid had started. It is a campaign biography in the sense that it began the propaganda campaign which Jackson's friends opened at this time, a campaign which finally succeeded in 1828. Eaton was a fellow Westerner and a great admirer of Jackson. He was later a member of the Senate from Tennessee and a member of one of Jackson's cabinets. Eaton's book on Jackson is a typical campaign document. There is, perhaps, little in it that is not true, although the adulation is almost saccharine and it omits a great deal that might have been told. Jackson's early career is toned down; his legal knowledge is a little exaggerated; his dueling propensities are kept within the bounds of what the West considered necessary for a man of honor. Jackson's humble origin, his defense of the people against tyranny and oppression, his championing of the rights of the common man, his justice in the courts both as lawyer and judge (he had to decide cases on merit because he knew no law), his honesty, bravery, and personal character; all these things are carefully set forth in Eaton's *Life of Andrew Jackson* that the people in their wisdom might understand that true democracy would be safe only if Andrew was elected President of the United States. He was.

Eaton's biography was the source of every life of Jackson for nearly a half century. Why should anyone seek original material when a record of all of Jackson's virtues was at hand? From 1820 to 1860 biographies of Jackson continued to be written, published, and read, but almost all of them are the same—Eaton's facts in several different forms. Philo Goodwin's *Biography of Andrew Jackson* (1832) is one of the best of the later campaign lives, and Alexander Walker's *Life of Andrew Jackson* (1857) is an earnest attempt to present the man as he really was. It remains an attempt because it was written entirely from the sources that have been mentioned. Amos Kendall's *Life of Andrew Jackson* is an interesting fragment largely because Kendall was a close friend and a member of Jackson's "Kitchen Cabinet," which was composed of intimate personal advisers. Kendall's narrative stops with Jackson's victory in the Creek War, personal interests preventing the completion of the book. It would have been interesting, if nothing else, for few men knew Jackson as Kendall knew him.

There were almost as many condemnatory as there were adulatory biographies of Jackson. Many books were made up entirely of those phases of Jackson's career which Eaton had omitted. The campaigns of 1828 and 1832 were characterized by the most scandalous practices, on both sides, that American politics had experienced. Nothing like them would be repeated until the Cleveland-Blaine campaign of 1884. These examples of scurrility are interesting, but they add nothing to the literature of American biography.

Lafayette, Aaron Burr, and Thomas Jefferson were among the heroes of this period. Lafayette was an honorary citizen of the United States—his family still enjoys that honor—and he was considered a true American because of the assistance he rendered during the Revolution, and a true democrat because of his subsequent career in France. Biographies of Lafayette during this period are numerous but of little value, except that they indicate that Americans are not always unappreciative. These books appeared in comparatively large numbers when Lafayette made a visit to the United States in 1824, nearly fifty years after his first coming.

Jefferson and Burr, at one time friends and later bitter enemies, were the subjects of numerous biographies, which reflected either blind partisanship or implacable hatred. There is nothing of impersonal analysis or plain biographical narrative in these lives, or in any of the lives in this period. Politics was the dominant theme in public life. Every public man was open to praise or blame, and the biographies reflect almost blind partisanship and very frequently personal hatred. There is no early life of Jefferson that is worth mentioning, and only one of Burr, Matthew Davis' *Memoirs of Aaron Burr with Miscellaneous Selections from his Correspondence* (1838). Davis was a friend of Burr's, and he tried to create an atmosphere sympathetic to Burr without descending to mere eulogy. Later biographers of Burr were not so fair.

Henry Clay, Daniel Webster, and John C. Calhoun were the most prominent statesmen, if not the greatest, in the first half of the nineteenth century. They were exact contemporaries; all three were permanent candidates for the Presidency, which eluded their grasp; and they were the most influential men in the West, the North, and the South respectively. During the thirty years that they were potential or actual presidential candidates they were the subjects of many campaign documents and even serious biographies. Colton's *Life and Times of Henry Clay* (1845) is the best biography of Clay written before his death. It is not a campaign life, nor is it an authorized biography. Colton made independent researches for his work, and the result is a good book when one considers that it was written in the lifetime of the subject. After Clay's death, Colton brought the book up to date, and it is still one of the best books on Clay. Another important, although partisan, life of Clay is *The Life and Public Services of Henry Clay* . . . (1859), by Epes Sargent and Horace Greeley.

Webster was not so fortunate as Clay in his early biographers. Although there are a dozen or more early lives of Webster, none of them has any genuine biographical or literary value. The same may be said for Calhoun, although J. S. Jenkins' *Life of John Caldwell Calhoun* (1850), published in the year of his death, is a fairly impartial account of the great southern statesman.

There is an equal abundance of "biographical" material on the successful candidates for the Presidency during this period. Van Buren's campaign, which began in the middle of Jackson's second term, as was the custom in those days, was particularly bitter, largely because of Van Buren's connection with Jackson. Some half-dozen favorable campaign lives appeared, and almost as many which were decidedly unfavorable. Among the latter is one that is of particular interest because of its author. *The Life of Martin Van Buren, Heir Apparent to the "Government" and the Appointed Successor of General Andrew Jackson. Containing Every Authentic Particular by Which His Character Has Been Formed* (1835) is supposed to have been written by David Crockett, hunter, trapper, politician, congressman, and "hero of the Alamo." It is a sufficiently bad biography, from every point of view, to have been written by Crockett, who was practically illiterate, but I doubt if he contributed anything more than his name and some of the more scurrilous parts of the book. Crockett hated Jackson and sought to injure him through Van Buren. Everything that could blacken the character of either man is in the book. In this manner those who planned the book sought to further the candidacy of Hugh L. White and to blast Van Buren's chances. Actually, the book had little or no effect because it overshot its mark and was an object of derision rather than concern. It is interesting today because it shows the extent to which politicians would go to defeat a rival candidate, and because the spirit, if not the letter, has been followed in recent presidential campaigns.

Every presidential campaign brought forth and brings forth some striking examples of biographical effort. When the candidate is relatively unknown, as in the cases of William Henry Harrison, Zachary Taylor, and Franklin Pierce, the biographer says as little as possible; when the candidates are of the type of Garfield and Blaine, the biographer emphasizes one phase of the candidate's career and leaves the less savory episodes in the background.

As the nineteenth century advanced, the biographical field widened and the quality of individual biographies improved. Such lives as John P. Kennedy's *Memoirs of the Life of William Wirt* (1851) and H. A. Garland's *Life of John Randolph of Roanoke* (1850) exhibit a distinct advance in the art of life-writing. Kennedy was a prominent novelist and man of letters. His literary training enabled him to take a great mass of source material and fashion it into a biography which is excellent as biography and as literature. It seems old fashioned and somewhat prosy to us who have been reared on the Stracheyan method, but when it is compared with the products of its own time its superiority is obvious. Garland's book is equally good, but for a different reason. He had seen and heard Randolph in Congress and, although he did not know him personally, he knew many of his contemporaries and secured material from them. We know more about Randolph now than Garland did, but, historically speaking, his book is still good.

John Adams and his son, John Quincy Adams, and Jefferson were also the subjects of historical biographies at this time. In 1856 Charles Francis Adams published the *Works of John Adams . . . with a Life of the Author*. The first two chapters of the life were written by John Quincy Adams, and his son finished the book on the plan projected by his father. There is practically nothing of a personal nature in the biography, but it is still the best account we have of John Adams' public life. Josiah Quincy's *Memoir of the Life of John Quincy Adams* is in keeping with the conventions of the time; John Quincy never emerges as a man. Henry S. Randall's *Life of Thomas Jefferson* (1858) is a history of America during Jefferson's lifetime with an occasional view of Jefferson himself.

6

The Reverend Jared Sparks is the most important figure in early nineteenth-century American biography. A trained historian, he approached biography with the equipment for research and was the first American to study original sources for his biographical material. He made some serious mistakes, as we shall see, but his underlying methods were excellent.

Jared Sparks was born in Wellington, Connecticut, in 1789. Although his family was not in a position to educate him, he graduated from Harvard through the financial assistance of friends. He was later inducted into the ministry of the Unitarian church and was a pastor in Baltimore for four years. His interest in history and literature developed early, and in 1823 he resigned his pastorate to become editor of the *North American Review*. This magazine had fallen on evil days, but in the next seven years Sparks made it the most important and successful periodical in America.

Shortly after he became an editor he began to develop an idea for a history of the American Revolution which was to be primarily biographical. He intended to start with Washington, publishing his life and correspondence, and then to go on to the other important figures of the period. For five years he traveled in this country and Europe, visiting historical places and collecting material for an edition of the works and life of Washington. Another period of five years was spent in editing the material which he had collected and, in 1834, the first volume—Volume II of the *Works of George Washington* . . .—appeared. The final volume I of the *Works*, the biography of Washington, came out in 1837.

Meanwhile Sparks had published several other biographies. In 1827 he published the *Life of John Ledyard,* the famous American traveler. Ledyard's papers had been collected by a member of his family who intended to write a biography of him but never did so, the material being turned over to

Sparks for publication. In this book Sparks developed the
method which he was to follow in all of his writings. He got
as much first-hand information as he could, and verified his
source material wherever possible. Then he wrote the life
itself, using the subject's own words wherever they would
add to the truth or interest of the narrative. This is unquestionably one of the best methods of biographical composition and, while Sparks did not always achieve unity in the
narrative, he gave impetus to the development of biographical method. This book, a landmark in American biographical writing, was reprinted in Sparks's *Library of American Biography*. The next biography, the *Life of Gouverneur
Morris* (1832), was a part of Sparks's Revolutionary history.
It was published in three volumes, the first containing the
biography and the others, correspondence.

Between 1836 and 1840 Sparks published the *Works of
Benjamin Franklin; with Notes and a Life of the Author.*
As in the case of *Washington* this work was in ten volumes
with the available autobiography and a continuation of
Franklin's life in the first volume. Sparks now enjoyed the
reputation of being the foremost biographer and historical
scholar in America, his standing as a biographer having been
increased by the publication of the first series of the *Library
of American Biography* under his editorship. All of his work
was accepted at its face value, and the critics were unanimous
in their praise of the scholar who had gone to the original
sources for his materials, particularly the writings of Washington and Franklin. After 1840 Sparks did little writing or
editorial work, exclusive of the second series of the *Library
of American Biography*, which appeared between 1844 and
1847.

In 1847 Sparks was occupying the chair of history at
Harvard, to which he had been elected in 1839, and was
doing a great deal to further the study of history in general
and American history in particular. In this year (1847) there
was published the *Life and Correspondence of Joseph Reed*.

Reed was an important figure in the Revolution and a close friend and correspondent of Washington. The author of this biography published a number of Washington's letters which differed considerably from the same letters published by Sparks. Charges of altering the Washington papers were brought against Sparks by several Americans, but they were not pushed until, in 1851, Lord Mahon, an English historian, repeated the charges in his *History of England*. Sparks had to answer these charges, and he admitted that he had corrected grammatical errors, altered sentences, and even inserted sentences of his own in Washington's letters. He defended his actions on the ground that Washington had corrected and rewritten some of his letters before his death and that he had done nothing more than this. Of course, his defense was not accepted; his actions were indefensible, and his entire work was more or less discredited. What Sparks really wanted to do was to perpetuate the tradition that Washington never did anything wrong and that his letters were as perfect in their composition and expression as those of the most accomplished scholar. Furthermore, he toned down what he considered vulgar and removed whatever traces of anger he found in Washington's correspondence. In short, he desired that Washington be considered the prig that Weems's book had made him out to be. The whole affair, although it damaged Sparks's reputation too severely, had a salutary effect in that it prevented editors from mutilating source material for reasons of propriety. Sparks was not the only historical scholar who was doing this sort of thing, but he was caught. The "family" and "official" type of biography still suffers from various kinds of mutilation, but it can no longer be done in the case of public figures whose papers are open to public inspection.

The most important accomplishment of Sparks, either in history or biography, was the *Library of American Biography*. His purpose in projecting this work can be best expressed in his own words of the Advertisement in the first volume of the first series:

It is the design of this work to add something to the stock of our native literature in the department of Biography. The specimens here presented to the public will indicate, with sufficient clearness, the nature of the plan, and the manner in which it may be executed.

Our purpose is not to attempt the methodical arrangement or comprehensiveness of a dictionary, in which the number and proportional length of the articles are to be considered; but rather to select prominent names, to which opportunity and inclination may attract the different writers, and thus enable them to perform the task of a biographer with the more fidelity and interest in the subject. Hence the length and structure of each article will depend on the amount of materials accessible to the author, his judgment and taste in choosing from them, and his facility in narration.

The two principal objects to be attained, in biographical compositions, are accuracy as to facts and finish in the literary execution. The former demands research, the latter labor and skill. Biography is only another form of history; truth is the first requisite, simplicity of style the next. It admits of no embellishments that would give it the air of fiction; and yet its office is but half done, unless it mingles entertainment with instruction.

The plan of this work embraces the lives of all persons, who have been distinguished in America, from the date of its first discovery to the present time. . . . Each life will be prepared expressly for this work, except perhaps in a very few instances. . . . As the authors' names will be prefixed to their respective performances, the Editor will of course not hold himself responsible for any statements or opinions, except those proceeding from his own pen.

No clearer biographical creed has ever been formulated; unfortunately Sparks, as we have seen, did not adhere to his own standards. The plan of including the principal figures in American history was not followed. Cabot is the only early explorer in the *Library,* Captain John Smith the only early colonizer. There are sketches of Hudson, Marquette, La Salle, and Ribault. Later colonizers are represented by William Penn, General Oglethorpe, and the second Lord Baltimore.

The lives seem to have been chosen by the authors rather than by the editor.

The *Library of American Biography* was published in two series, the first in 1834–1838, the second in 1844–1847. The combined series contains sixty lives, written by thirty-six different men. The sixty lives occupy twenty-five volumes, which average about four hundred pages. Naturally, the biographies are very uneven in length and quality. Some are merely sketches; some volumes contain four lives; others only one. The quality is equally uneven. Some are obviously compilations; others are based on authentic sources and are carefully and well written.

Most of the lives are hardly worthy of serious criticism. The best biography of the series is the *Life of Cotton Mather* by W. B. O. Peabody. Mr. Peabody based his biography on the best sources, and he not only wrote an excellent account of Mather's life, but he analyzed Mather's character completely. No better biography of Cotton Mather has yet been written. William H. Prescott's *Life of Charles Brockden Brown* is not a life at all, but it is a very good critical memoir of the first professional American novelist. The accounts of Sir Harry Vane, Jonathan Edwards, Patrick Henry, James Otis, and General Oglethorpe are good, although all of them are uncritical and somewhat partisan. The long lives of General Greene, Commodore Decatur, and Lord Baltimore are histories rather than biographies. The life of John Eliot, Apostle to the Indians, is much more personal, even though it is as long as the others.

Sparks wrote eight of the lives in the *Library*, including the aforementioned *Life of John Ledyard*. His memoirs of Father Marquette, De La Salle, Pulaski, and Ribault are excellent though very short. He wrote longer accounts of Ethan Allen and Charles Lee. The former is frankly eulogistic, but even so it is far above the average of the series in method and the quality of the writing. He gives a very sympathetic account of Charles Lee, the English officer who entered the Revolutionary army. This is the Lee who was accused of treachery at the Battle of Monmouth and incurred Washington's wrath there. General Lee was later tried and acquitted of the charge of treason, but was dismissed from the army. Sparks is very fair to this man; in fact, he seems to favor him whenever possible, although there is little question that he was guilty of insubordination many times and was an enemy of Washington during the entire period of his service. Sparks treats Arnold very differently in his *Life and Treason of Benedict Arnold*. This is the only full-length biography that he wrote for the series. The first half of the book is concerned with Arnold's military career; the second half with his treason and its consequences. The whole book is unduly prejudiced and over-righteous in its tone. As Washington was the perfect hero, so Arnold was the perfect villain and traitor, and Sparks so writes that the treachery and villainy are evident on every page. There is as much special pleading against Arnold as there is for Washington.

Regardless of the faults and prejudices of the editor and his staff, the *Library of American Biography* is a landmark in the development of biographical writing in America. Sparks had knowledge and ability, and it is most unfortunate that he allowed his narrow moral and ethical standards to influence his sound scholarly judgment. He contributed a great deal to historical and biographical writing, and for that we should be thankful.

III

AMERICAN BIOGRAPHY

1860–1900

THE stream of literary biography continued to run very thin during the middle years of the nineteenth century. As the principal literary figures died, they were commemorated or embalmed in books large and small. Until the last quarter of the century there is scarcely an instance of a genuine attempt at a biographical or critical study of an American writer. Books there are, but they are either panegyrics or mere records, entirely devoid of method and generally lacking in interest. If the term "Victorian" implies a false standard for propriety and truth, this period may be called truly the Victorian age. Only the smiling aspects of a man's life were mentioned, and even these were described in such saccharine terms that the books are almost unreadable today.

The first book of any importance in this period is the *Life and Letters of Washington Irving* (1862), edited by Irving's nephew, Pierre M. Irving. This life is a very carefully edited account of Irving's career, told largely through his letters. Pierre Irving had possession of all of his uncle's papers which he used very skilfully to present such a picture of Irving as would carry on the legend that had grown up concerning him. Irving had been engaged to Matilda Hoffman, the daughter of Charles Fenno Hoffman, but she died before the marriage could take place. Irving never married, and the world believed that this tragedy of his early life was the cause of his bachelorhood. Pierre Irving's book intensified this belief by giving us the character of a lonely man constantly grieving for his lost love. This conception is entirely foreign to Irving's real character, and we know now that he was interested in several women during his life. A later book on Irving fills in some of the gaps in the *Life and Letters*, and there is in preparation a life of Irving which will be a genuine and accurate biography. Pierre Irving's book is, at this writing, still the most complete account of Washington Irving that we have. Despite the suppressions, it is both valuable and interesting. Richard H. Stoddard's *Life of Washington Irving* (1883) is a narrative biography based on the earlier book, and adds nothing to our knowledge of Irving.

The Life of William Heckling Prescott (1864), by George Ticknor, the *Life and Letters of Fitz-Greene Halleck* (1869), by James G. Wilson, and the *Life, Letters, and Journals of George Ticknor* (1876), edited by George Hillard and Anna Ticknor, belong to the same class of life-writing as does Pierre Irving's book. Ticknor was an old friend of Prescott's and performed a labor of love which is entirely appreciative and uncritical, although Ticknor was the foremost Spanish scholar of his day in America. Wilson's life of Halleck is entirely panegyrical and places this forgotten poet far above the position he had then and has now. The *Life, Letters and Journals of George Ticknor* is an improvement in method and material over the other books. Like Pierre Irving's book, it is almost entirely autobiographical. Ticknor was one of the earliest American scholars to study and travel in Germany, and his letters and diary entries during his European travels are fascinating reading.

Henry T. Tuckerman's *Life of John Pendleton Kennedy* (1871) is one of the best literary biographies of this period. Kennedy had an active life, not only in literature but in politics, and Tuckerman wrote a well-balanced book, giving each phase of Kennedy's career just the emphasis it needed. It is still the best biography of Kennedy that we have. William R. Alger's *Life of Edwin Forrest: The American Tragedian* (1877) is another excellent biography, complete and well documented. Both Tuckerman and Alger realized the responsibility of the biographer to tell the complete story of his subject, and each seems to have done this as far as he could with the material available. Few contemporary biographies are entirely satisfactory, for biography needs perspective in the same degree that history does.

As the nineteenth century drew to a close, the death roll of our men of letters rose. Bryant, Hawthorne, Emerson, Longfellow, Holmes, Lowell, and many others died between 1860 and 1900. The oldest of them, William Cullen Bryant, died in 1878. In 1879 George William Curtis published the *Life, Character and Writings of William Cullen Bryant,* a strictly conventional, appreciative memoir. In 1883 Parke Godwin, Bryant's assistant on the *New York Evening Post* and his literary executor, published the *Life of William Cullen Bryant* as the first two volumes of the standard edition of Bryant's complete writings. Godwin's biography is a good book from every point of view. In the first place his close association with Bryant gave him an insight into Bryant's character that the average biographer does not have. Secondly, Godwin was a professional writer, a trained journalist, and a man of some critical ability. Even though he was very close to Bryant, he could estimate him from an intellectual rather than an emotional point of view. Most of Bryant's creative work had been done before Godwin became associated with him; consequently he had some perspective for his literary criticism. Bryant was not only a poet; he was for years the dean of journalists in New York, a public figure of note, and, in his later years, in addition to his editorial work, he translated the *Iliad* and the *Odyssey.* All these phases of an active public and intellectual career Godwin handled so well that when we have finished this *Life of William Cullen Bryant,* we feel that we know the man as he actually was.

There have been two other lives of Bryant written since Godwin's appeared. John Bigelow wrote a short critical biography for the "American Men of Letters" series in 1896, and William A. Bradley, one for the "English Men of Letters" series in 1905. Both are short and primarily critical,

but Bradley's is superior both as biography and as criticism
to Bigelow's.

Numerous books on Hawthorne were published in the
first twenty-five years after his death. The most notable of
these early books was *Nathaniel Hawthorne,* written by
Henry James the novelist, for the "English Men of Letters"
series. It is a very disappointing book, for the reason that
James seemed incapable of understanding Hawthorne. If we
are to believe Mr. James, Hawthorne's art and genius were
stifled by his provincialism, his preoccupation with American
themes and American local characters. Mr. James intimates
that, had Hawthorne had the advantage of intercourse with
Europeans when he was young, he would have been a great
artist. This criticism is the result of a total ignorance of the
character and the mind of one of the truly great artists that
American literature has produced. The trouble with Henry
James was that he did not know that a man could live in
a small world and still be anything but provincial.

Nathaniel Hawthorne and His Wife (1884), by Hawthorne's son, Julian, is the usual family memorial. It is a
compilation of letters and journal excerpts which, quite
naturally, presents only one side of the picture. There is,
however, much material which has been used by later biographers. Moncure D. Conway's *Life of Nathaniel Hawthorne*
(1890) is a good short biography, emphasizing the personal
rather than the literary side of Hawthorne. The books mentioned are by no means the only studies of Hawthorne published during this period, but they seem to be the most
important.

The name of Ralph Waldo Emerson is frequently found
in lists of American biographers, but I have been able to
find no justification for the classification. Some people may
think that *Representative Men* is biographical in form, but
it is not. Montaigne, Napoleon, Shakespeare, and the others
in this volume are considered critically, and not biographically. The essay on Thoreau which Emerson contributed to

the *Atlantic Monthly* in 1862 may be considered a biographical essay, but it is more in the nature of a character study. Emerson tells us a great deal about the mind and soul of Thoreau, but very little about his life. Biography is primarily life-writing. *Plutarch* is another of Emerson's essays which approaches the biographical form, for it embraces the whole of Plutarch's life and all his writings.

Emerson was the subject of many biographies and studies after his death, some of which are important. The first one, *Ralph Waldo Emerson: His Life, Writings and Philosophy,* by George Willis Cooke, was first published in 1881, the year before Emerson died; the second edition (1900) is biographically complete. In his preface Mr. Cooke makes the statement that "the following pages are intended as an introduction to the study of the writings of Mr. Emerson. They are biographical only because light may be thrown on his books by the events of his life." Regardless of this statement, the book is a good, conventional biographical and critical account of Emerson's life and writings. A much better biography is James Eliot Cabot's *A Memoir of Ralph Waldo Emerson* (1887). Cabot was Emerson's literary executor and, in carrying out his trust, wrote an excellent biography. The best of the early lives of Emerson is Oliver Wendell Holmes's *Ralph Waldo Emerson* (1884). Written originally for the "American Men of Letters" series, it is a concise account of Emerson, combining biography and criticism in almost perfect proportions. Dr. Holmes was an exact contemporary of Emerson; he knew him intimately; and he was able to give a balance to his biography which stabilizes the enthusiasm of Cooke and Cabot. In addition to the purely biographical qualities of the book, it is noteworthy for its charm of style and manner, characteristic of all of Holmes's writings.

Dr. Holmes made one other venture into the biographical field with his *Memoir of John Lothrop Motley* (1879). Again he is writing of an intimate friend, but the work of the historian of the Dutch Republic was not so close to Holmes's heart as were Emerson's writings. Furthermore, Motley had spent many years abroad as writer and diplomat, and Holmes was not able to give such a complete account of Motley's later life as he did in the case of Emerson. Holmes makes an able defense of Motley's career as diplomat, and gives Motley's version of the trouble with President Grant which resulted in Motley's summary dismissal from his ministerial post in London. Holmes's book is a good contemporary account, but we need a modern interpretation of Motley and his work.

The last of the important literary figures of the nineteenth century died during the last twenty years of the century and, of course, books of a biographical nature followed close upon their deaths. In most cases they were either family or authorized biographies, with the characteristic virtues and faults of this type of biographical literature.

In 1886 Samuel Longfellow published the *Life of Henry Wadsworth Longfellow, with Extracts from his Journals and Correspondence.* In this first edition of two large volumes Samuel Longfellow assembled a huge mass of material concerning his brother's life and work, adding in 1887 a third volume of extracts from the journals and correspondence. This book is invaluable as source material, but it is not a biography. The editor had more material than he could properly handle. He simply printed what he thought should be printed, taking passages from all of the writings that best suited his purpose. There is a general chronological order in the book, but it lacks organization and unity. The material is almost entirely unassimilated, and there is little connecting narrative. In short, it is material for a biography rather than a biography itself. In 1891 a second edition, incorporating the material of the third volume into the text, was published.

S. T. Pickard's *Life and Letters of John Greenleaf Whittier* (1894) is exactly the same sort of book as Samuel Longfellow's life of his brother. In the same class, but somewhat better done, is the *Life and Letters of Bayard Taylor* (1884), by Marie H. Taylor and Horace E. Scudder. We are thankful that we have these books, but they represent a form of life-writing that defeats the purpose of true biography: the re-creation of a man as he really was.

Charles Edward Stowe's *Life of Harriet Beecher Stowe* (1890) and Mrs. Annie Fields's *Life and Letters of Harriet Beecher Stowe* (1897) belong to the same school of biography as those just mentioned. The first is merely a family record, entirely uncritical, and the second is a panegyric which places the author of *Uncle Tom's Cabin* among the greatest of authors, of women, and of benefactors of mankind. Such books as this of Mrs. Fields are, if not dishonest, certainly undistinguished by any sense of balanced judgment.

It is, at least, a relief to come upon such a biography as Herbert B. Adams' *Life and Writings of Jared Sparks* (1893). Professor Adams, a prominent historian of his day, has given us one of the most complete biographies written in the nineteenth century. In fact, it is too complete, for the details enumerated in the two fat volumes destroy the picture of the man that is there. Professor Adams wrote biography in the traditional manner of the nineteenth-century biographer, but he did not have a particularly interesting subject, and he treated it from a strictly impersonal point of view. This view is not conducive to literature in biography. Everything that a man said or did is not biographical material; the reader can become surfeited with the subject. This may be hypercritical, but a biographer must be master of his material and must be able to control it. Professor Adams seems to have lost control of his material time and time again.

A much better example of this type of scholarly biography is afforded by John T. Morse's *Life and Letters of Oliver Wendell Holmes* (1896). Mr. Morse, an experienced professional biographer, shows a much better command of his materials and achieves his purpose in a much simpler fashion than did Professor Adams. Perhaps the principal reason for Morse's greater success is that he writes from a personal and sympathetic point of view. Although this is apparently an authorized biography, it is neither eulogistic nor panegyrical. It is conventional biographical writing at its best or near it.

There are two other literary biographies of this period that illustrate the principle that a biographer must be interested in his subject. Professor Moses Coit Tyler, the historian of American literature, was not noted for the charm of his style, but in *Three Men of Letters: Berkeley, Dwight, Barlow* (1895) he seems to have found three particularly congenial subjects. Timothy Dwight and Joel Barlow were members of that literary group known as the Hartford Wits, and Professor Tyler has given us charming short biographies of these men and the parts they played in the development of American literature after the Revolution. George Berkeley was an English clergyman and the first English traveler to write a book on his experiences in America, which he visited in 1729. The nineteenth century can show nothing better in purely literary biography than this little book.

N. H. Chamberlain's *Samuel Sewall and the World He Lived In* (1897) is another excellent literary biography. Sewall's famous and priceless diary is, of course, the basis of the book, and Mr. Chamberlain filled in the background and chose his passages from the diary with rare judgment. The book is admirable in itself and even more admirable as an introduction to the diary.

2

The most important group of literary biographies published in the latter half of the nineteenth century were those written for the "American Men of Letters" series. Based on a similar series in England, this project was started in 1881 under the general editorship of Charles Dudley Warner, whose *Washington Irving* (1881) was the first volume in the series. About twenty-six volumes were published in some thirty years, when the series was discontinued.

This series was intended to provide short critical biographies of the principal figures in American literature, and the list is fairly complete, beginning with Franklin and coming down as far as Thomas Bailey Aldrich. There are some important writers missing—Charles Brockden Brown and Philip Freneau, to mention only two—but, on the whole, the collection is satisfactory. The books are small in format, and conciseness was made a necessity rather than a virtue. In some instances full treatment of the subjects could not be given, but the general plan was faithfully adhered to. These lives are excellent introductions to the authors included in the series. Naturally the books vary in quality, some because of paucity of material, others because of the choice of authors.

The second volume of the series was Horace E. Scudder's *Noah Webster* (1881), followed by F. B. Sanborn's *Henry D. Thoreau* (1882), both excellent books. Holmes's *Emerson* (1884) and Bigelow's *Bryant* (1890) have already been mentioned. All of these books maintained the high standard set by the first volume.

For various reasons, some of the volumes in the series are much more important than others. The first of these was Professor Lounsbury's *James Fenimore Cooper* (1883). This was the first attempt at a life of Cooper, for he had forbidden the publication of a biography. Miss Susan Cooper, his daughter, had published a volume of reminiscences, and this was the only biographical material available, exclusive of Cooper's own writings. In view of these facts, Professor Lounsbury's book is remarkably good. It is more critical than biographical, and the criticism seems to be a little unfair in its severity. Lounsbury set a very high standard, even for his own day, and Cooper suffers as a result. Furthermore, Cooper is judged by the poorest of his books rather than by the best, and some of Lounsbury's hypercriticism has persisted to the present day. He is particularly severe on the women in Cooper's novels, making the flat statement that they are able to do nothing except faint. The women in one of the earliest of Cooper's novels, *The Spy,* are sufficient refutation of Lounsbury's charge. He says that *Mercedes of Castile* is unreadable, and in his summarizing criticism judges Cooper by some of his less important European novels rather than by those which are distinctively American. Cooper should be judged by historical rather than by absolute standards of criticism.

Two of the very best volumes in this series appeared in 1885, Professor George E. Woodberry's *Edgar Allan Poe* and Professor Henry A. Beers's *Nathaniel Parker Willis*. Woodberry's book is the first intelligent treatment of Poe, as a man and a writer, that we have. It is genuine critical biography: its only fault is overconciseness, for which Professor Woodberry was not responsible. His later *Life of Edgar Allan Poe* is complete in every respect.

Professor Beers's *Nathaniel Parker Willis* is one of the best biographies of the series. It is a difficult matter to present adequately a second-rate writer; the biographer is very likely to be led into over- or under-emphasis. Beers steered a remarkably straight course, giving just the proper balance to the personal and literary phases of Willis' career. Willis was one of the leading writers of the day, and Beers makes us aware of that; Willis is practically unknown today, and Beers explains that. We know the reasons for his contemporary and later reputations, and we know Willis when we have finished the book. No biographer can accomplish much more than Professor Beers accomplished in this book.

Benjamin Franklin as a Man of Letters (1887) was written for this series by John Bach McMaster, professor of American history at the University of Pennsylvania. Professor McMaster brought to the writing of this book sound historical scholarship, a strong interest in the subject, and a keen literary appreciation. The book is the best short biography of Franklin that we have, and one of the best lives of Franklin of any type. The emphasis is, of course, on Franklin's writings, and the final chapter contains a brilliant account of a very complicated subject, the discovery and publication of the complete manuscript of Franklin's autobiography. The volume, as a whole, is one of the most important contributions to the series.

Equally important, perhaps, is Professor William P. Trent's *William Gilmore Simms* (1892). Simms was the most important man of letters in the South before the Civil War. Poet, novelist, editor, biographer, historian, and critic, he produced an enormous quantity of writing which is very uneven in quality. Professor Trent deals with Simms as he should be dealt with, as a hard-working man of letters who produced much more than he should have produced and, in so doing, relegated himself to a minor place in every field except that of the novel. Professor Trent was not unnecessarily severe in his criticism, for he realized that here justice must be tempered with mercy. This is the only biography of Simms that has been written, and I doubt if it could be improved upon today.

The later volumes in the "American Men of Letters" series are not so important as the earlier books and, in many cases, not so well done. The volumes on Taylor, Longfellow, Whittier, Whitman, Lowell, Parkman, and others are competent but by no means definitive. Edwin Mims's *Sidney Lanier* (1905) differs from most of the volumes in this series in that it is largely biographical rather than critical. The author was justified in this course because very little was known about Lanier at this time. He has since become better known and has been given his proper standing as one of the major poets of our literature. Harry Thurston Peck performed a valuable service in his *William H. Prescott,* by tempering Ticknor's panegyric with some well-considered though sympathetic criticism.

3

The first twenty years of the second half of the nineteenth century produced very few biographies of public men. In the first place the Civil War and its aftermath engaged the activities of nearly all men to the exclusion of everything else. We have seen that some literary biographies were written in this period, but they were comparatively few. Most of the elder statesmen had died before the Civil War; most of the political and military leaders were comparatively young men; there were few deaths among the really important men and, consequently, few occasions for the conventional biographical memorial of the day.

Campaign and military biographies are about the only forms of life-writing that were prevalent in this period. The campaign lives of Lincoln have been discussed in a separate chapter, and they formed the bulk of the campaign literature in the election of 1860. I have found only two campaign lives of Douglas and none of either Breckenridge or Bell, the other presidential candidates. They were Southerners and their campaign literature was probably circulated only in the South. There was little campaign literature in the election of 1864. Some additional material on Lincoln appeared, and there were some lives of General George B. McClellan, the Democratic candidate. After Andrew Johnson became President several biographies of him were published, the best of which was John Savage's *Life of Andrew Johnson* (1866).

During the Civil War and for many years after it the country was flooded with so-called "lives" of the heroes of the war. Practically every general officer in the Union Army was the subject of a "biography." It was rarely anything but a panegyrical compilation published after a great victory or for the purpose of furthering the promotion of the subject of the book. Most of them are so ridiculous that they are amusing. None of them is worthy of serious consideration on any ground. The stream continued for at least twenty-five years after the war, and each book proves that its subject saved the Union, not once but many times. Many of the biographies are in two volumes, an extravagant waste of paper and ink.

The Confederate biographies were not so numerous as those which poured forth from the presses of the North. The South had neither the time nor the money to eulogize its commanders, and politics was a secondary consideration during the war. Even after the war comparatively few biographies of the Southern leaders were written for many years. The three principal figures in the South were Robert E. Lee, Thomas J. (Stonewall) Jackson, and Jefferson Davis. General Lee was the subject of several biographies. None of them is of any particular value, although John Esteen Cooke's *A Life of Gen. Robert E. Lee* (1871) is important for his detailed study of the years of the Civil War. The biographical value of the book is lessened by the lack of balance between the war years and the years before and after the war. There are four or five other books on Lee that have the same fault. Cooke also wrote a military biography of General Jackson, which appeared in 1863, shortly after the latter's death, and a campaign biography of Samuel J. Tilden in 1876. Jackson was the subject of numerous biographies, largely because he was the idol of the South and because of the tragedy of his death. (In the confusion of battle he was mortally wounded by his own men.)

Jefferson Davis, as President of the Confederate States of America, was as much hated as he was admired, and the early biographies are about equally divided in their sympathies. None of them is of any particular consequence, but one at least is interesting because of the virulence of its attack on Davis in his official capacity. Edward A. Pollard's *Life of Jefferson Davis, with a Secret History of the Southern Confederacy* (1869) is a bitter attack on Davis and his conduct of the war. Pollard was a Richmond editor and a loyal Southerner; his attitude has been generally substantiated by modern historians and biographers of Davis.

With the exception of Lincoln, U. S. Grant was the most famous man in the United States at the end of the Civil War. Aided by Sherman and Sheridan, he brought about the military defeat of the South, and he was acclaimed the great hero of the war. I have examined twenty-five lives of Grant written between 1864 and 1900 and, with a few exceptions, they are all panegyrics. Fourteen of the twenty-five books were written as political propaganda during the campaign of 1868. Most of them are no worse than the average campaign biography, but some are actually sickening in their cant and hypocrisy. If these books are true, U. S. Grant was born to free the slaves from bondage, and to lead the Republican party of 1868 to a victory ordained by God. If these books are true, General Grant combined all the virtues of Galahad and Chevalier Bayard, and was saved from whatever vices these two knights may have had. There is an occasional gleam of intelligence in the midst of this mass of partisan writing in such a book as *A Personal History of Ulysses S. Grant* . . . (1868), by Albert D. Richardson. This is the best of the campaign biographies, for it gives a well-balanced view of Grant's early and private life as well as his public career.

The period of General Grant's Presidency, 1869–1877, was the center of the most scandalous era in American political and public life. Graft, corruption, and betrayal of public trust were commonplaces of the day and, although President Grant was personally honest, he condoned the very worst offenses and protected some of the worst offenders. I mention these things because it has been necessary for biographers to defend, condemn, or explain this phase of Grant's administrations. Some of his biographers have defended an indefensible position; some have condemned him without mercy; others have tried to explain Grant and have not succeeded. A characteristic defense of Grant is Frank A. Burr's *Original and Authentic Record of the Life and Deeds of General Ulysses S. Grant* (1885). According to these "authentic records," General Grant had a perfect and spotless career as general and President. It is difficult to understand how a book like this can be written unless under family supervision. Lives of Grant continued to appear almost every year, but none contributed anything new to our knowledge of the man or to the literature of biography. The best of this group was Hamlin Garland's *Ulysses S. Grant: His Life and Character* (1898). Garland, a popular novelist, became interested in the subject after he had been commissioned to write a life of Grant. After considerable travel and independent research, Mr. Garland produced a biography which attempted to present Grant as he really was. Had it not been for Garland's political bias favoring Grant, he would have been more successful with his portrait. He toned down the picture in several instances where the real truth should have been told. With all its faults, Garland's biography is the best one written of him in the nineteenth century and perhaps in the twentieth.

Every presidential campaign brought forth its quota of biographies of the leading candidates for the nominations and, later, of the two candidates for election. They are of value only in showing to what lengths politicians will go in order to win a national election. Little could be said about Hayes in 1876 because he was practically unknown, but William Dean Howells, the distinguished novelist, managed to write a campaign biography of Hayes which is far above the average. It added nothing to Mr. Howells' reputation as a man of letters, but it was a big improvement on his life of Lincoln and a welcome relief from the partisan doses that were and are administered every four years by the propagandists of the major political parties.

General Garfield, the Republican candidate in 1880, was beautifully whitewashed in several campaign lives. James M. Bundy's *Life of Gen. James A. Garfield* (1880) had, for the title of its first chapter, *Garfield's Noble Ancestry*. The chapter is a masterpiece of its kind and sets the tone for the rest of the book. The political hysteria that followed President Garfield's assassination is reflected in a number of books on him which were published later in 1881 and in 1882.

The unsuccessful candidates of this period, Seymour (1868), Greeley (1872), Tilden (1876), and Hancock (1880), had their share of biographies, but they were less partisan and less fulsome in their praise, because the Democrats, having nothing to lose and everything to gain, confined themselves to factual accounts of the lives and records of their candidates. The Democratic campaign documents were no better than those of the Republicans; they were simply less vociferous.

The presidential campaign of 1884 was one of the bitterest political fights ever waged in the United States. It was a campaign of vituperation, personal slander, and political hypocrisy: it was worse than the campaigns of either 1828 or 1928. Naturally the biographies expressed the mood of the campaign, and both sides were free with praise and blame. Cleveland was unknown nationally and had a perfect public record; Blaine had been in public life for nearly twenty years and had been involved in many of the scandals of what Mark Twain called the Gilded Age. The campaign lives, of course, were shaped to meet the exigencies of the time in each case. Nothing could save Blaine on election day, and he was defeated by a small majority.

James Gillespie Blaine was one of the great political figures of the last half of the nineteenth century. He was extremely popular throughout the country, but circumstances, partly political and partly personal, prevented him from achieving the ambition of his life, the Presidency. There were at least a dozen biographies of Blaine published before 1900, but not one of them attempted a truthful evaluation of the man who, like Henry Clay and W. J. Bryan, could carry audiences but not states. The most complete of the early lives of Blaine is Gail Hamilton's *Biography of James G. Blaine* (1895). This book cannot be trusted because the author, a member of the family connection, presented only the "more smiling aspects" of a career that had in it many dark spots. Every other early life of Blaine errs in the same respect, and it is only within the last decade that Blaine has appeared as he really was.

To complete the survey of the campaign literature of the period, it can be said that the lives of Harrison and those of Bryan and McKinley were in keeping with the tradition that had developed in political biography: say nothing in as many words as possible.

4

Almost every generation rewrites the biographies of the important and famous men of the country. New material, new points of view, and a better perspective attract writers to the great figures of the past. Washington, Lincoln, Jackson, Jefferson, Lafayette, Franklin, and many others were studied anew. In a few instances some improvement was made in method and style, but the majority of the biographies of these men were characteristic of the period, a panegyrical retelling of their stories without the slightest attempt to present the individual as he was or to tell the whole story of the life and career of any of them. A half dozen biographies of Jefferson, three or four of Jackson and Lafayette, and a group of single biographies of Revolutionary figures are among the representative biographical writings of the period. The books on Jefferson, Jackson, and Lafayette are unimportant, for they contribute nothing in material or method to biographical literature.

Franklin is the most important figure, biographically speaking, in this period. Including Parton's biography, more than a dozen books on Franklin appeared between 1860 and 1900. Not all were biographies, but practically all used the biographical method in developing the many phases of Franklin's career. The most important Franklin item was John Bigelow's *Life of Benjamin Franklin* (1874). Published originally in three volumes, this book contains the first publication of the *Autobiography* as written by Franklin and a very complete and excellent account of Franklin's life subsequent to 1757, which is the date at which the *Autobiography* ends. Mr. Bigelow was a man of letters, and while Minister to France negotiated the purchase of Franklin's original manuscript from a French family in whose possession it had been for nearly three-quarters of a century. After careful collation and editing, it was published with Bigelow's continuation, setting a new standard in biographical editing and writing.

Among the later important books on Franklin are Paul L.
Ford's *The Many-Sided Franklin* (1899) and Sydney George
Fisher's *The True Benjamin Franklin* (1899). Ford's book
is a series of essays on various aspects of Franklin's career,
while Fisher's is an attempt, in a single volume, to present
Franklin as he really was. It is interpretive biography of a
very high quality and is still one of the best biographies of
Franklin that we have. It has all the virtues and none of
the defects of modern interpretive biography. Ford's book
is not biography, but the brilliance of the individual essays
gives it a place with the best that has been written on
Franklin.

5

From the close of the Civil War to the end of the century
we occasionally come upon scholarship or attempts at
scholarship in biography. The materials for detailed study
of the Colonial and Revolutionary figures were becoming
accessible, and time had given a perspective which could be
used to advantage. The formal, scholarly biography of the
period was generally in two or three volumes, very stiff in
style, weighted with voluminous letters and diary entries,
and bristling with historical references. It was and is a monu-
ment to both author and subject, even though the subject
was frequently lost in the mazes of history and irrelevant
correspondence. The biographies to be mentioned in this
group by no means exhaust the list, but they illustrate the
good and the bad in this class of biographical writing.

The *History of the Life and Times of James Madison*
(1859–1869), by William C. Rives, is a striking example of
biographical scholarship carried to excess. The title indicates exactly the nature of the book; it is history and not
biography. In the three huge volumes Madison appears occasionally, but he is so completely surrounded by history that
his presence is hardly felt. This book belongs to that large
group of which we talk a great deal but seldom read. Wil-

liam L. Stone's *Life and Times of Sir William Johnson, Bart.* (1865) belongs in the same class although it is not quite so long, only two volumes, and the subject is more interesting to the average reader. Sir William Johnson was the feudal lord of central New York and one of the few men in America in the eighteenth century who knew how to handle Indians. He was the leader and adviser of the Five Nations for many years, and kept them on the side of the English.

There are three other examples of this "monumental" type of biography that are worthy of mention because of the importance of their subjects. Each has three large volumes; each is indispensable to a study of its subjects; and each is much too long. *The Life and Public Services of Samuel Adams* (1865), by William V. Wells, is really a history of the American colonies immediately before the opening of the Revolution, and of the famous Committee of Correspondence, organized and directed by the genius of Samuel Adams, rather than a biography of the famous agitator. The principal fault with this book, as with all biographies of the same type, is that it lacks proportion and balance. When we have finished a biography of this kind we may know a great deal about the history of the period in which the man flourished, but we know little or nothing about the man himself. The *Life of Nathaniel Greene, Major-General in the Army of the Revolution* (1867–1868) by his grandson, George W. Greene, is, in spite of its length, a fairly good biography. History is an essential complement to biography here because General Greene was one of the few great military strategists of the Revolutionary War and the greatest figure, always excepting Washington, to emerge from it. The book is too long, and it is partisan because of the relation of author and subject, and also because General Greene had been grossly neglected by early historians. He has since been given the position in our history which is rightfully his.

William W. Henry's *Patrick Henry: Life, Correspondence and Speeches* (1891) is a long and detailed account of the public life and career of the famous Virginian. The third volume of this book is composed entirely of correspondence which should have been, if it was to be used at all, worked into the text of the biography. This inability to organize and master material is one of the great faults of biographical writing when it is attempted by inexperienced people. The very sympathetic tone of the book is explained by the fact that W. W. Henry was Patrick Henry's grandson.

6

In 1879 Henry Adams began a great career as historian and biographer with the publication of the *Life of Albert Gallatin*. Adams had been interested in the early history of the United States, the financial history in particular, and his selection of Gallatin as the subject of a biography was quite natural. The famous Swiss was one of the greatest financiers and statesmen that America has produced, and his career gave Adams an opportunity to develop his ideas on the early history of our country, ideas which later grew into the classic *History of the United States during the Administrations of Jefferson and Madison*. The *Life of Albert Gallatin* is a very long personal, political, and historical biography. Even though it was Adams' first published book, it has the individualized style, the cultured background, and the somewhat ironical tone that characterized all of Adams' writings. If there is a serious fault in the book, it is its inordinate length, and that can be explained on two grounds: Gallatin's career was extremely full and varied, and Adams' interest in the man and the period was intense. Even though there is a great deal of finance, politics, and history in the book, one never loses sight of Gallatin. There is no question but that the book would be better if it were shorter, but Adams had not yet acquired that mastery of materials which was to make him one of the outstanding American historians. We are more than thankful to come upon this finished biographical work in the midst of a host of unorganized, undigested, uninteresting books miscalled biographies.

Benedict Arnold's name has been and still is synonymous with the word "treason." For almost a century he was condemned without a hearing as the arch traitor, a worthy associate of Judas Iscariot. We have always allowed our emotions to rule our judgments in public affairs, particularly where our patriotism has been concerned. Few writers even mentioned Arnold, and those who did, such as Jared Sparks, simply heightened the treasonable act and neglected to say much about his earlier career. Isaac N. Arnold in his *Life of Benedict Arnold: his Patriotism and his Treason* (1880) tried to present a more balanced picture of Arnold; he tried to write a biography and not an indictment. Although the author was a collateral descendant of Benedict Arnold, he tried to steer a middle course in his biography and he was fairly successful. The book is primarily a military biography with a discussion rather than a narrative of the treason and the events which followed it. Isaac Arnold was the first historian or biographer who made Peggy Shippen, Arnold's wife, a party to, or, at least, one of the reasons for, the treason. He had very little material on which to base this accusation, but he made out a plausible case against Mrs. Arnold, a case which has been greatly strengthened by later historians and biographers. This is not a good biography, but it is a competent book and looks toward a more intelligent and less hysterical treatment of some of the principal men and events in our history.

The men of the Revolution were being revived in increasing numbers as the nineteenth century advanced. Charles J. Stillé's *Life and Times of John Dickinson* (1891) is historically important, but it is not good biography. Dickinson was one of the most prominent figures in Pennsylvania before, during, and after the Revolution. He was a member of the Continental Congress and the author of *Letters of a Pennsylvania Farmer,* and, although he refused to sign the Declaration, was a staunch upholder of colonial rights. Stillé's book might have been much better, had it been better organized. As so often happens, he was overwhelmed by his material and produced a characteristic "life and times" which is neither one nor the other.

The last decade of the nineteenth century is particularly rich in biographical records of some of the famous men of the Revolutionary and early national periods. Most of these books are rather dull and commonplace accounts, filled out with letters, diaries, and state papers. They are important but uninteresting, and the usual method is that of the formal "life and letters" or "life and times" type. Among these biographies the best are the *Life of Paul Revere* (1891) by Eldridge H. Goss; *Life of Gen. George Rogers Clark . . .* (1896); *Life of George Mason* (1892), and *Life of Charles Carroll of Carrollton* (1898) by Kate Mason Rowland. These lives are all in two volumes and all are heavily documented. Mrs. Rowland's books on her kinsman, George Mason, and on Charles Carroll of Carrollton are more personal and better examples of biographic art than are the others. H. C. Merwin's *Aaron Burr* (1899) is a competent but uninspired study of one of the most romantic figures in our history. Alexander Hamilton was the subject of three biographies in this decade, all of which are conventional in method, Federalistic in point of view, and somewhat eulogistic in tone. Hamilton was a great man but not quite so important as some of his biographers would have us believe.

As a biography and as a historical document the *Life of Thomas Paine* (1892), by Moncure D. Conway, is a very valuable book. It is the first life of Paine which treats him justly and gives him his proper position as the one man whose personality and writings forced the issue of the American Revolution. His pamphlet, *Common Sense,* and his later essays aroused, inspired, and maintained the spirit of revolt in the colonies as nothing else did or could. Paine's later writings, *The Rights of Man* and the *Age of Reason,* were inspired by the French Revolution, into which Paine plunged as he had plunged into the American Revolution. Conway placed the man and his writings on a plane where they belong, among the greatest instruments of political and religious liberty that the world has seen. This biography is not easy reading, but in form and content it will take its place among the best of the century.

Equal in importance and superior as biographical literature is *Christopher Columbus . . .* (1891), by Justin Winsor. This is the most complete account of Columbus that we have, and it is a brilliant example of what historical biography can be in the hands of an expert. There is an almost ideal blending of history and biography.

7

The biographies of contemporaries of the period under discussion (1860–1900) are generally better in form and content than those of the preceding period. They are complete and correct, even though somewhat stiff and formal. The one great fault common to almost all of them is prejudice in favor of the subject, with the tendency to omit or distort facts which might reflect on the man whose life was being written. It was and is natural for a biographer to be sympathetic toward his subject, but when he chooses only those facts which will enhance the reputation of his hero and deliberately conceals others, then he is being untruthful. This method was the rule rather than the exception in the nineteenth century, with the result that few of the lives of the public men of this period can be accepted without reservation. If one is to judge these biographies, one must know something of the history of the United States in the nineteenth century.

Daniel Webster was the subject of at least six biographies between the date of his death (1852) and the end of the century. By far the most important of these was the *Life of Daniel Webster* (1870), by George Ticknor Curtis, Webster's literary executor. Curtis was a journalist, editor, and essayist, and was eminently capable of writing the authorized biography of Webster. The book is long and detailed and, while it may be heavy and somewhat dull, is historically important and the basis of all later books on Webster. Biographers of the great of the nineteenth century seem to have been over-awed by their subjects; they lost their usual style, their sense of perspective and, in many instances, their literary judgment. Curtis fared no better than many men of less literary prominence, and he left us an honest but somewhat prejudiced and uninteresting book. The other lives of Webster were either partisan defenses or very romantic and popular treatments of the man.

In the same class with Curtis' *Webster* is Samuel Tyler's *Memoir of Roger Brooke Taney, Chief Justice of the Supreme Court of the United States* (1872). An authorized biography, this book is complete but lacks any spark of inspiration, literary style, or interest. The facts are there, but it is a task to get through the book. Jacob W. Schucker's *Life and Public Services of Salmon Portland Chase* (1874), and Robert B. Warden's *Private Life and Public Services of Salmon P. Chase* (1874) are equally dull and partisan. We could name dozens of biographies of the last thirty years of the century which fall into the same group as those we have mentioned, but an enumeration of them would add nothing to the story of the development of American biography.

Among the major public figures of the nineteenth century was Charles Sumner, one of the most violent of the radical group in Congress during the Reconstruction Era. A member of an old Massachusetts family, a Harvard graduate, a man of learning and culture, Sumner was a fanatic on the question of slavery and, later, the political freedom of the Negro. He was a rabid Republican, and destroyed himself politically and physically for the party which eventually repudiated him. Personally honest, he not only condoned but commended the crimes committed by the carpetbaggers and scalawags in the South after the Civil War. I have tried to outline something of the man's character in order that the difficulties confronting his biographers may be understood. As a matter of fact, his principal biographers sidestepped the difficulties by omitting all facts and inferences that might adversely affect the character of their hero. The nature of Elias Nason's *Life and Times of Charles Sumner* (1874) can be best explained by a quotation from his preface: "The design of this work is to set forth in distinct relief the life, character, and public career of an accomplished scholar, an incorruptible statesman, and an eminent and eloquent defender of human freedom." This book was published in the year of Sumner's death, and probably it had his approval. Edward L. Pierce's *Memoir and Letters of Charles Sumner* (1878–1894) is a collection and compilation of almost everything that Sumner ever said or wrote. It is a source book rather than a biography; it is extremely partisan; and it is almost formless. Later biographies of Sumner have added nothing to our knowledge or understanding of the man. He had one of the most complex characters of any man in American public life, a character that requires not only industry but knowledge and genius for its proper interpretation.

8

Henry Cabot Lodge began his public literary career in 1878 with the publication of a biography of his great-grandfather, George Cabot. The *Life and Letters of George Cabot* is a long and apparently complete biography of an important figure in the early history of the United States and the Federalist party. Allowing for the party prejudice with which Senator Cabot was born and which was intensified with the years, this book is a good piece of work coming from a young man of twenty-eight.

In 1883, George Ticknor Curtis published the *Life of James Buchanan*. This biography has all the good and bad qualities of the author's *Webster* except that it is not quite so long and is a little more impersonal. In 1885 appeared another of those "monumental" works, *William Lloyd Garrison, 1805–1879,* by Wendell Phillips Garrison and Francis Jackson Garrison. Nothing was omitted from these four large volumes that had to do with Garrison's public life, and the whole of his adult life was public, very public. The man who was the heart and soul of the abolition movement in the North before the Civil War and whose paper, *The Liberator,* kept the agitation at a white heat among a sincere if small group of reformers is an almost ideal subject for a biography, but here, as in so many other instances, the compilers or editors were not able to master their material, so they printed the whole mass. The definitive biography of Garrison is yet to be written. Another reformer and fanatic had his life eulogized by F. B. Sanborn in *Captain John Brown, Life and Letters* (1891). This again is a compilation from a favorable point of view without any attempt at interpretation or even explanation. Most of these nineteenth-century biographical studies merely collected the material for later genuine biographies.

The presidential campaign of 1876 was the most dramatic of all our national elections, including that of 1932. The Republicans had been repudiated in the biennial election of 1874; there was general unrest in the country as a result of the panic of 1873; and the South was beginning to recover from the effects of the war and reconstruction. Neither party was able to nominate a popular candidate. Hayes was a compromise candidate after the convention was deadlocked between Grant and Blaine; Tilden was nominated by the Democrats because of his record as breaker of the Tweed Ring in New York City and as governor of New York state. Some mention has been made of the biographies of Hayes; in 1895 John Bigelow, the editor of Franklin's *Autobiography,* and former minister to France, published the authorized biography of Samuel Tilden. It is an excellent partisan biography; Bigelow was by this time an experienced biographer, and he made good use of the great mass of papers which Tilden had left. The book cannot be said to be extremely interesting, but it strikes a high note in political biography for its fundamental honesty. Bigelow's account of Tilden's election to the Presidency, and the momentous events which followed, is an almost inspired piece of writing, particularly for this period.

Miss Ida Tarbell had had some experience as a biographer before she wrote her *Life of Lincoln* (1900). She had acquired this experience in biographical writing from several earlier and shorter lives, including studies of Napoleon and Madame Roland. The life of Napoleon is a popular treatment of this apparently inexhaustible subject and the life of Madame Roland is an idealized study of one of the most famous women of the French Revolution. In 1896–1897 Professor William M. Sloane published his great *Life of Napoleon Bonaparte* in four volumes. I think that this biography is the best account of Napoleon that has been written by an American, and one of the best in the entire field of Napoleonic literature. It is largely historical and military, and the style is formal if not stiff, but these things are to be expected in a nineteenth-century life of Napoleon by a man who was essentially a scholar rather than a writer. Captain Alfred T. Mahan's *Life of Nelson, the Embodiment of the Sea Power of Great Britain* (1897) seems almost a complement of Professor Sloane's *Napoleon* in that Nelson is the only Englishman in the Napoleonic wars that can approach Napoleon as a romantic figure and as a military genius. Nelson was as great a sea strategist as Napoleon was a land strategist.

The last half of the nineteenth century was, as has been pointed out, a period of hero worship, smug propriety, and biographical white-washing. Not all biographers followed this trend, but the great majority did; those that did not, wrote or compiled books that are more remarkable for their omissions than for their contents. Some of the early divines and early leaders of New England were studied at this time with varying degrees of success. Robert C. Winthrop edited the *Life and Letters of John Winthrop* (1864). Mr. Winthrop made no effort to write a biography of his famous ancestor; he merely compiled a biographical record from letters and from the famous diary, known as the *History of Plymouth*

Plantation. There is some information in the compilation, but little interest. John Ward Dean published two memoirs of early New England ministers and writers: *A Memoir of the Rev. Nathanial Ward, A.M., Author of the 'Simple Cobbler of Agawam in America'* . . . (1868) and a *Memoir of the Rev. Michael Wigglesworth, Author of the 'Day of Doom'* (1871). I have not read either of these books, but they are said to be competent accounts of two of the most famous writers in colonial America.

There was a considerable interest taken in the Mathers, particularly Cotton Mather, during the nineteenth century. Cotton Mather's *Magnalia Christi Americana* (1702) was reprinted in 1820 and 1855. The edition of 1855 has a very inadequate memoir of Cotton Mather by Samuel G. Drake. In 1870, Delano A. Goddard published *The Mathers (Cotton and Increase) weighed in the balance . . . and found not wanting.* The title exactly indicates the nature and tone of the book. The first important life of Cotton Mather was Barrett Wendell's *Cotton Mather: Puritan Priest* (1891). Wendell was a descendant of some of the earliest New England settlers, an aristocrat by nature as well as by birth, and a defender of the old order in Massachusetts. This biography is a most sympathetic study; in fact it is a defense of Cotton Mather's life and writings. In this respect it is bad biography because the author started with a prejudiced point of view. Where he is unable to defend his subject he apologizes for him, and that is worse than a sturdy defense. *Cotton Mather: Puritan Priest* is well worth reading, but it can be accepted only with reservations. A. P. Marvin's *Life and Times of Cotton Mather; or a Boston Minister of Two Centuries Ago, 1663–1728* (1892) is a long factual account of Mather's career, with a good historical and social background.

Roger Williams was the subject of a number of biographies in the nineteenth century, the best of which is *Roger Williams, the Pioneer of Religious Liberty* (1894), by Oscar Strauss. This excellent account of Williams' stormy life and career emphasizes his great contribution to religious liberty in America. Williams believed in complete separation of church and state, and the right of every man to worship God according to the dictates of his own conscience. He was even tolerant toward Catholics and Jews, a position unprecedented in colonial America and one which probably attracted Mr. Strauss, a Jew, to the study of the life of the first great liberal in the United States.

Jonathan Edwards is one of the greatest ecclesiastical, philosophical, and literary figures in American history. He may be termed the last of the Puritans in that he was the last great minister who preached the literal doctrine of Calvin and the Old Testament. The best biography of him that we have is *Jonathan Edwards* (1889), by A. V. G. Allen. This is an excellent critical ,biography which portrays Edwards the man, as well as Edwards the minister and philosopher.

There is a great mass of ecclesiastical biography in this period, but the vast majority of it is of the pious or family type, written or compiled for the purpose of edification alone. There are, however, a few books in this group worthy of mention because of the importance of their subjects rather than for any value the books have as biographies. Octavius B. Frothingham's *Theodore Parker: A Biography* (1874) is a long and detailed account of the famous Unitarian clergyman and scholar. The author had excellent source material which he failed to use well; the result is a book which is badly organized and which fails to give us such a picture of Parker as we might have had from the hands of a competent biographer. The same charge may be brought against John Gilmary Shea's *Life and Times of the Most Reverend John Carroll, Bishop and first Archbishop of Baltimore* (1888). This book is the second volume of Shea's *History of the Catholic Church in America;* it is historical biography, and the subject is frequently lost in the history.

Joseph Smith, the founder of Mormonism, and Henry Ward Beecher, the famous minister and orator, were among the best-known figures in American religious life in the nineteenth century. Smith and his successor, Brigham Young, were the subjects of numerous biographies and studies, but without exception the books were written by either friends or enemies of the Mormons; consequently they are neither truthful nor valuable as biographies. Beecher was as much a figure of controversy as were Smith and Young. He was either idolized or hated; neither point of view makes for good biography. The favorable side is best represented by *A Biography of Henry Ward Beecher* (1888), by William C. Beecher and the Reverend Samuel Scoville. It is, of course, a family biography but it is fairly complete as to facts; the interpretation of those facts must be made by the individual reader. The unfavorable lives are negligible from any point of view.

9

James Parton can be rightly termed the first professional biographer in America. Jared Sparks was primarily a historian, and Washington Irving was much better known as a writer of tales than as a biographer. Parton wrote biography, either individual or collective, for more than thirty years.

James Parton was born in England in 1821 and was brought to this country at the age of five. The family settled in White Plains, New York, and Parton was educated there. As a young man he taught school for some time and then turned to journalism, apparently as a career. Horace Greeley was one of the great figures in American journalism of the period, and Parton believed that his life and career would make a good biography. This book, his first, appeared in 1855 as *The Life of Horace Greeley, Editor of the New York Tribune*. It is a typical biography of the period and shows no indication of what Parton was to do in the future. It must have been popular, for the third edition (1872) was much enlarged and revised. It was published, however, before Greeley was nominated for the Presidency. Some years after the great editor's death, Parton published the complete biography.

In the same year that the *Greeley* was published, Parton wrote a group of short lives which appeared under the title, *Captains of Industry*. This book contains sketches of the principal rich men of the country who, in Parton's opinion, had done more than merely accumulate money; it indicates that Parton's social and political ideas had been formed by this time.

In 1858 Parton published his first major work in biography, *The Life and Times of Aaron Burr*. Up to this time Burr had been considered almost as much of a traitor as Benedict Arnold, and those who had written about him refused to give him the credit that was his by right of his services as one of the most daring and distinguished officers in the Revolutionary War. It was Parton's purpose to present a fair study of Burr's life as a whole and not merely that part which followed his retirement, as Vice-President of the United States, in 1804. This is the first biography in which Parton used the method that was to make him the outstanding biographer of the later nineteenth century. In the preface he tells us that he read all that had been written on Burr, and examined original documents, wherever possible, before he began to write. It was interest in Burr that prompted Parton to begin the work, but he did not allow his interest to color his judgment. He neither excuses nor defends Burr; he merely tells the story of his life and tries to explain his actions by showing the kind of man he was. The question of Burr's treason to the United States has never been definitely settled. It is a matter of opinion whether or not he intended to set up an independent empire in the Southwest. This and the many other adventures in Burr's long life Parton treats as honestly as possible. As we shall see from the subjects of his biographies, Parton was a strong Democrat, and his sympathies naturally leaned toward the famous men of that party, particularly those who had not, in his estimation, been given their proper places in the history of the United States. The second edition of this biography, published in two volumes in 1872, contains considerable additional material in the appendices.

The publication of the *Life of Andrew Jackson* (1860) is the high point of Parton's career as a biographer. If such a thing is possible, James Parton was both a Jeffersonian and a Jacksonian Democrat. Jackson practised that which Jefferson preached so brilliantly. Jackson not only represented the "common people"; he was born and bred among them. At the same time, no man of his day was a more complete aristocrat than this same Andrew Jackson, even though he was of the frontier variety. He was not only an aristocrat, he was an autocrat whose word was law, and who enforced that law with the power twice given to him by the "common people."

The three volumes of Parton's biography tell the complete story of the man whom I have tried to characterize in a few sentences. From his birth in 1769 until his death in 1845, Andrew Jackson was constantly fighting somebody or something in defense of his personal honor (he was unusually sensitive even for his day), his country, or the principles for which he stood. Parton details almost every act of Jackson's life; he goes into the history of the Revolutionary and the Creek War, the War of 1812, the Seminole War and the acquisition of Florida from Spain, but we never lose sight of Andrew Jackson. His life between 1820 and 1845 is as minutely chronicled as is his early life. His campaigns for the Presidency and his two administrations are described as carefully and as well as his military campaigns. Parton visited every spot which played a part in Jackson's life; he examined his papers and the official archives at Washington; he mastered every source which would enable him to understand Andrew Jackson. It would be foolish to say that Parton wrote an impartial biography of Jackson. He had no intention of doing that; he intended to find the man who, in reality, lay somewhere between the eulogy of his friends and the invective of his enemies. He did find him and he recorded his findings as honestly as he could in the light of his sympathy for the man and his adherence to his political doctrines.

In spite of its length and detail, this is not a "life and times" book. Jackson is always in the foreground, and all other matters are discussed only insofar as they affect Jackson's life. Some may say that the book is too long; if we consider the diversity and richness of Jackson's life, that objection will be removed. Furthermore, it is written in the full and leisurely manner of the period. Readers in those days did not want to have their fiction, history, or biography condensed or digested for them; they were capable of digesting it for themselves.

Mention has been made of a number of lives of Jackson written before Parton's; others will be discussed in a future chapter. Parton's *Life of Andrew Jackson* is the primary source of all later books on Jackson, and I believe that it has not yet been superseded. It is one of the best biographies written in America in the nineteenth century.

Parton's biography of Jackson must have been a success, for he continued to publish long biographies along with the collective biographies which he seems to have written for popular consumption. His volumes of short lives were generally published by subscription publishers in Hartford, Connecticut; his larger biographies bear the imprint of some of the principal publishing houses in New York and Boston.

His second large work was the *Life and Times of Benjamin Franklin* (1864). This biography of Franklin, in two volumes, is a long and detailed account of the most famous and versatile American of the eighteenth century. Parton emphasized both the fame and the versatility; he was among the first of Franklin's biographers to give the proper importance to the latter's career as philosopher, scientist, and statesman. As the date indicates, Parton did not have the complete *Autobiography* at his disposal, but he made extensive researches into Franklin's later life, and his book is the best book on Franklin up to that time. It is interesting, well written, sympathetic in tone without being eulogistic. Parton always tried to find the man behind the legend.

In 1865 appeared the *Life of John Jacob Astor. . . .* This is, it seems, the first biography of Astor, and it is a very unfavorable one. Parton condemns Astor and his whole class because they accumulated fortunes through love of money alone and not with any intention of helping those less fortunate than they. One wonders if Parton would approve of the disposition of the Carnegie, Rockefeller, and other great fortunes of the present day. He would, at least, have written better lives of some of the architects of great fortunes than those that have appeared lately.

Famous Americans of Recent Times (1867) is Parton's best volume of collective biography. It contains biographical and character studies of the principal statesmen, financiers, and public men of the middle nineteenth century. Parton was interested primarily in the lives of his subjects but, in the course of a biography, whether long or short, he managed to analyze the individual's character or to explain the man through his acts. In 1869 he published two more popular collections, *People's Book of Biography; or Short Lives of the Most Interesting Persons of All Ages and Countries* and *Eminent Women of the Age; being Narratives of the Lives and Deeds of the Most Prominent Women of the Present Generation.* There is no doubt that these books were compiled to be sold by subscription agents throughout the country. They were intended to "edify and instruct as well as amuse." Neither has any claim to distinction unless it be that of diversity. The *People's Book of Biography* contains eighty sketches ranging from Jeanne d'Arc and Copernicus to Lord Byron and Father Matthew. *Sketches of Men of Progress* (1870) belongs to the same category as the volumes mentioned above.

It is natural that a biographer of Jackson should turn to the founder of democratic theory in America, Thomas Jefferson. Parton firmly believed in the political theories of

Jefferson; consequently, he was able to write a sincere biography. The *Life of Thomas Jefferson* (1874) may not all be true, but Parton believed it, and his honesty rings through the book. This life of Jefferson is very long, although not quite so long as that of Jackson. Jefferson had a comparatively quiet life; he did not serve in the Revolutionary War, and he was not a frontiersman. His life was spent in the midst of national politics and international diplomacy. We have no more complete biography of Jefferson than this and, allowing Parton the privilege of his political principles, none that is much better.

In his last single subject Parton followed, perhaps, lines that opened themselves while he was writing his life of Jefferson. The *Life of Voltaire* (1881) is one of the most interesting as well as one of the longest of Parton's biographies. A passage from the preface will explain Parton's purpose in writing the book: "I attempt in these volumes to exhibit to the American people the most extraordinary of Frenchmen, and one of the most extraordinary of human beings." There is no evidence that Parton ever visited Europe, so he must have obtained the material for this book from secondary sources. After all, Voltaire's life is written in his long list of histories, biographies, dramas, and poems, and there were numerous lives of him published before Parton's time. At all events, he wrote a good, straightforward biography of the great French sceptic which must have accomplished a great deal in introducing French ideas of intellectual and personal liberty to Americans.

Parton's last published volumes were again of a popular nature and were composed of short sketches. In his long biographies he set a standard of scholarship that has not been excelled. His recourse to sources, his balanced judgments, his efforts to be interesting without sacrificing truth, stamp him as one of the most important biographers in America. He was not a master of English prose, he was not a trained scholar or historian, he was not an impartial judge, but he wrote well, he had a genius for research, and he never consciously allowed his political or personal prejudices to warp his judgment as a biographer. We could do very nicely with a few Partons today.

There were numerous other writers in America at this time who published many books of a biographical nature. Mrs. S. K. Bolton was a voluminous writer who turned out such books as *Lives of Girls Who Became Famous, Lives of Poor Boys Who Became Famous.* Samuel G. Goodrich produced more than a dozen books of exactly the same type as those written by Mrs. Bolton. Various religious and social organizations continued the publication of biographical tracts which had been started in the early nineteenth century. Their purpose was to instill morality and patriotism into "young America." They were not concerned about either style or method in their biographies.

10

The "American Statesmen" Series was the most important group of political biographies published in America in the nineteenth century. Under the general editorship of John T. Morse, Jr., the series included practically every man of importance as a statesman up to the Civil War. The standard edition is in thirty-one volumes with twenty-eight subjects. A second series was started, but seems to have been discontinued after the ninth volume.

The purpose of the series was to present the public careers of the subjects chosen. In general this purpose was adhered to, although there is considerable diversity in treatment. In most instances the editor was particularly fortunate in his choice of authors. The editor wrote the biographies of John Adams, John Quincy Adams, Benjamin Franklin, and Abraham Lincoln. Each is an excellent piece of work, considering the limitation of space at the author's disposal. Each life was supposed to be confined to one duo-decimo volume, but in the cases of Washington, Lincoln, and Clay two were published. Even with two volumes Mr. Morse and Senator Lodge were compelled to compress their material on Lincoln and Washington; Carl Schurz's *Henry Clay* is longer than necessary.

It is both unnecessary and impossible to consider each of the lives in this series, but a word or two will be said about some of them. In addition to *George Washington,* Senator Lodge wrote *Alexander Hamilton* and *Daniel Webster.* The Washington biography, which is the best of the three, is discussed in the chapter on Washington. The other two are good political biographies written from the Federalist or modern Republican point of view. *Alexander Hamilton* is particularly partisan for the reason that Lodge was an intellectual and social as well as a political descendant of Hamilton. The Webster biography is more impersonal and, in a sense, more human.

Theodore Roosevelt wrote two of the volumes in this series, *Thomas Hart Benton* and *Gouverneur Morris.* Both were written when Roosevelt was a young man, and reflect his enthusiasms and the wide range of his knowledge. The book on Benton is a particularly sympathetic account of one of the great figures in Congress in the early nineteenth century. Benton represented Missouri in the Senate for many years, and he was a staunch defender of the frontiersman and the western expansion of the United States. As a young man, Roosevelt had spent a good deal of time in the West, and he was in a position to understand Benton's point of view. The biography of Morris differs very much from Benton's life. Roosevelt did not admire Morris particularly, but he presented a fair account of the man, giving credit where credit was due. Morris was one of the prominent politicians and diplomats during and after the Revolution. He was an extreme Federalist, a reactionary in fact, and Roosevelt, although a nominal Republican, never favored this wing of his party. Consequently, he was unable to understand Morris as well as he understood Benton. Both books are well written with that particular zest for life that is in everything that

Roosevelt wrote. We may not agree with the judgments, but they are at least stimulating.

Most of the volumes in this series are purely political in material and tone; that was their purpose, and the authors seldom attempted to present the man. Consequently Professor Moses C. Tyler's *Patrick Henry,* Daniel C. Gilman's *James Monroe,* and Professor William G. Sumner's *Andrew Jackson as a Public Man* stand out very prominently. In each case the author tried to infuse his book with the personality as well as the fame of his subject, and in each case he was successful within the limitations of space at his disposal. The best of the three is Professor Sumner's *Jackson.* While the book is mainly political and historical, we get a fair idea of the sort of man Jackson was in his later years and, what is even more important, the author points out what he conceives to have been the evils of Jackson's administrations. This is the first attempt at a fair criticism of Jackson and his administrations that we have. Parton intended to be critical, but his admiration for the man sometimes overbalanced his judgment of the executive.

The most personal of all these biographies are Allan B. Magruder's *John Marshall* and Henry Adams' *John Randolph.* Magruder's book on Marshall reflects the personality of the subject to an extent unusual in this series, and for this reason is one of the best biographies of the group. Henry Adams was an unfortunate choice as the biographer of John Randolph. Randolph was one of the strangest and most eccentric characters in American history. With an intellect brilliant but warped, with a power of oratory second to none in his day, with an unassailable social position and an utter contempt for most of his fellow-men, John Randolph of Roanoke was the terror of Congress for nearly half a century. He made himself the personal and political enemy of John Adams and John Quincy Adams, among many others. It was only natural that the son and grandson should welcome the opportunity to exhibit the brilliance of his irony on this really unfortunate man. Adams' book is cruel because it lays bare the idiosyncrasies of one who was not always master of himself. It is the essence of the concentrated spleen of three generations of Adamses who are as famous for their hatreds as for their intellects.

The other volumes in this series are, for the most part, competent studies of their subjects. Among those to which particular exception may be taken are Moorfield Storey's *Charles Sumner* and Samuel W. McCall's *Thaddeus Stevens*. Moorfield Storey was a prominent liberal of the later nineteenth and early twentieth centuries. He could not write a critical biography of Sumner without condemning the Senator from Massachusetts for his utter contempt of law and justice during the Reconstruction Era; therefore, he wrote a eulogy on Sumner's personal character, which he could honestly do, rather than a biography. McCall makes an open defense of Thaddeus Stevens for his part in the Reconstruction Era, a part much less defensible than Sumner's, for Stevens used his power for purely political purposes, while Sumner's fanaticism over the question of equal political rights for the southern Negro was the dominant factor in his actions.

The unfinished new series of American Statesmen included biographies of James G. Blaine, General Grant, John Hay, and William McKinley. Louis A. Coolidge's *Ulysses S. Grant* is a narrative account of Grant's life, with emphasis on his public career. Mr. Coolidge tried very hard to make a statesman out of Grant, but the material was lacking. The book is not, intentionally dishonest, but it certainly leaves a wrong impression concerning the success of Grant's administrations. A good and fair biography of General Grant remains to be written. Coolidge's biography was published in 1917, but it is considered here because it should have been a part of the original series.

This series seems to have inspired a number of other similar publishing ventures. In the last decade of the nineteenth century and the early part of the twentieth, numerous collections of short biographies appeared. Among them were the "American Crisis Biographies," a series concerned with the men who were identified with slavery before the Civil War, and the principal statesmen of the war and reconstruction period. Other series were "American Worthies," "American Men of Progress," "Men of Achievement," "Great Commanders" (military and naval biographies), and the "Beacon Biographies." The "Beacon Biographies" are particularly valuable for facts; they are very small and make no attempt at interpretation or criticism.

These series and others which we have not mentioned added little to the literature of biography. They were not intended to be complete lives; they were largely uncritical; and they were small in form. The majority were for popular consumption, although they are not particularly interesting or readable. They have a value, however, in that their publication indicates a growing interest in biography as a separate form. The reading public wanted to know more about the prominent men of the country, and were content for the time with these small contributions. The trend toward interest in biography for itself seems to have started.

IV

THE TURN OF THE CENTURY

1900–1918

THE early years of the twentieth century saw very little change in form or method in biographical writing. The formal "life and letters" or "life and times" was still the accepted approach in life-writing. This was particularly true in biographies of literary men, even when they purported to be critical. Few biographers thought of seriously challenging the positions of the principal American authors or of subjecting their writings to genuine criticism. Consequently, the majority of the lives of this period are valuable for their facts, but of little importance as interpretations of their subjects.

In 1901, Horace E. Scudder published *James Russell Lowell: a Biography*. This is a representative life of the period in both its good and bad points. A formal biography, it is the most complete account of Lowell that we have, but as criticism it falls far short of its mark. Mr. Scudder was one of Lowell's successors in the editorship of the *Atlantic Monthly*, and he seems to have been somewhat awed by the position of his subject. When we have finished the book, we know a great deal about Lowell, but we do not know Lowell himself. It is this failure to get at the man himself, to represent him as he really was, that makes these formal biographies uninteresting and incomplete. Mr. Scudder makes a feeble attempt at evaluating Lowell as a poet and critic, but his timidity or his reverence for his subject or his inability to judge Lowell's work results in eulogy rather than criticism. Ferris Greenslet's *James Russell Lowell: His Life and Work* (1905) is a much shorter and better book than Scudder's. It is good biography and fairly good criticism.

Mr. Greenslet also published a good critical account of Walter Pater (1905) and the *Life of Thomas Bailey Aldrich*

(1908). The latter is a particularly interesting and complete biography, sympathetic without being panegyrical. The criticism is not particularly valuable, but it is better than much of the criticism that was being written at this time.

In 1902, Professor James A. Harrison of the University of Virginia published the Virginia Edition of the *Complete Works of Edgar Allan Poe,* in ten volumes. The first volume is a complete biography of Poe and the last is a collection of Poe's letters, written between 1829 and his death in 1849. These two volumes were later published separately as the *Life and Letters of Edgar Allan Poe.* Professor Harrison spent many years on this edition, collecting much new material and editing the then known works from the original publications. The editor naturally obtained considerable new information on various phases of Poe's mysterious life, and his biography of Poe is an excellent narrative of the poet's career. There is little explanation or interpretation of Poe because the life was intended as an introduction to the works. As such it is admirable, and the whole work is the best edition of Poe that we have.

In the previous chapter, mention was made of Professor Woodberry's *Edgar Allan Poe* (1885). In 1909, he published a two-volume biography of Poe with the title, *Life of Edgar Allan Poe.* During the intervening years, a great deal more was discovered about Poe's life and work than Woodberry had known in 1885. The researches of Professor Harrison and others, including Woodberry himself, made possible a reexamination of the whole subject, biographically and critically. Woodberry was better fitted to be Poe's biographer than was any other man of his day in America, for he had made a lifetime study of Poe and his work. Furthermore, he had long experience as a teacher of literature and as a biographer.

The *Life of Edgar Allan Poe* (1909), is the best biography of Poe that has been written. Woodberry told the story of Poe's life as plainly and completely as possible. Beginning with his birth, he gradually makes his way through the vari-

ous stages of Poe's life, tearing away the legends, the prejudices, the hatreds that had grown up around one of the
greatest and certainly the most unfortunate of our great
writers. He neither praises nor condemns Poe as a man; he
merely tells us the sort of man he was and how he lived and
died. There is no psychological interpretation in this book,
no "debunking," no attempt to be clever at the expense of
the subject. Woodberry seems to have understood Poe better
than any other man who has written about him and, in understanding him, he pitied him and sympathized with him.
His account of Poe's vices is as complete as his account of his
virtues. Nothing is toned down, nothing overemphasized. It
is this sane balance that makes Woodberry's *Poe* the definitive biography.

The criticism in this book is of the same quality as the
biography. It is sane, balanced, and just. He points out Poe's
literary faults, such as the ornateness of his style, his literary
prejudices in his criticism, and at the same time gives him
credit for the greatness of his genius and the sweep of his imagination, and accords him that place as the first real critic in
American literature which is rightfully his. One of the outstanding qualities of this book, as a critical biography, is the
manner in which the criticism is woven into the life-story.
Each story, each poem is disposed of at the period when it
was written. In this way, we can see how Poe's mind grew
and changed as the circumstances of his life affected it. As we
read his life, we can better understand his habit of reprinting
old work in new volumes, of his preoccupation with a world
that never existed, of his predilection for death as a subject.
In short, the parallel study of life and work is the ideal
method in critical biography, and Woodberry is a master of
this method. Like every other book of the first class, Woodberry's *Edgar Allan Poe* must be read to be adequately appreciated, and it can be read easily. The style is simple and
smooth, and one subject moves into another almost imper-
ceptibly. One is hardly conscious that he is reading a narrative of one of the most complex and complicated lives in

American letters. Judging it from any and every point of view this is one of the best biographies that have been written in America.

Professor Woodberry's experience in biographical writing was very wide. In addition to the Poe biographies, he did a considerable amount of editing, and published several short biographies for popular series. *Nathaniel Hawthorne* (1902) is a very good short, critical biography, as is *Swinburne* (1905). *Ralph Waldo Emerson* (1907), written for the "English Men of Letters Series," is an admirable book of its kind and an excellent introduction to the study of Emerson.

There are numerous literary biographies of this period which are important because of author or subject rather than for any distinctive biographical qualities. Henry James's *William Wetmore Story and His Friends* (1903) is a two-volume memoir of an American artist and sculptor who lived the greater part of his life in Rome. James and Story were very close friends, and it was as a friend that James wrote the book. It is not good biography, for it is not well planned, and Mr. James did not know how to develop the life of his subject. There seems to be more James than Story in the book.

If there is any particular method in James's book on Story it is that of letting the subject tell of his life through his letters. If a man's letters, diaries, and papers have a definite literary quality, this is an excellent method, but Story's letters were not good enough to warrant the use that James made of them. Elizabeth Bisland's *Life and Letters of Lafcadio Hearn* (1906) is developed by the same method that James used, but it is an infinitely better book because Hearn's letters contain some of his finest prose, and that is saying a good deal. There is little pure biographical narrative in this book because comparatively little was known about Hearn at this time. The author, however, had access to all of Hearn's published letters from the time he came to New York until his death in Japan many years later. They tell their own story in a manner and style that make fascinating reading. Although Hearn was partially blind, he had an amazing power of observation and the ability to transfer his impressions, particularly those of the senses, to paper in such a way that the reader actually sees what Hearn saw. Two-thirds of the two volumes of this book is made up of letters from various parts of the United States and from Japan. They tell us a great deal about Hearn himself as well as about the facts of his life. By no means a complete biography, this book is still the best account of Hearn that we have. There have been several volumes written since 1906 on different aspects of Hearn's life, but no one is complete or satisfactory. A real biography of this great genius and strange man is badly needed.

Some other individual biographies of note in this period are: *Walt Whitman: his Life and Work,* by Bliss Perry (1906); W. J. Rolfe's *Life of William Shakespeare* (1904); F. P. Stearns's *Life and Genius of Nathaniel Hawthorne* (1906); M. A. deWolfe Howe's *Life and Letters of George Bancroft* (1908); and the *Life of James McNeill Whistler* (1908) by Elizabeth R. and Joseph Pennell. Each one of these biographies is a competent book, but none rises above the average either in form or method. Professor Perry's book is a good factual and critical account of Whitman and his work, and Stearns's life of Hawthorne is biographically complete but rather dull. Professor Rolfe's *William Shakespeare* is a voluminous book containing all "the facts, traditions and conjectures concerning Shakespeare's personal and literary history." The book would have been much better had it been half as long as it is, for Shakespeare frequently disappears under the masses of "traditions . . . conjectures . . . and literary history."

M. A. deWolfe Howe's *Life and Letters of George Bancroft* is an excellent account of the life and career of one of our first scientific historians. Bancroft was an important figure in public life as well as a prominent historian, and Mr. Howe produced a complete and well-rounded biography. In this, one of his earliest books, Mr. Howe shows evidence of the ability as a biographer that has made him one of the most prominent figures in this field of writing.

Mr. Howe produced a good conventional biography. Professor Wilbur Cross gave us two of the finest biographies in the language in the *Life and Times of Laurence Sterne* (1909–1925) and the *History of Henry Fielding* (1918). Professor Cross was for many years Sterling Professor of English at Yale, but the fact that he was an authority on the literature of the eighteenth century and the English novel would not indicate that he could write books like these; he is a genius in the art of biography.

His first life of Sterne, published in 1909, was a rather small book in which he told all that was known about Sterne, and contributed some admirable criticism of Sterne's writings. In the years between 1909 and 1925, Professor Cross did a great deal of research in Sterne and the England of his day, and when he published a new edition in two volumes— it is really a new biography—he produced the definitive life of "Yorick" and one of the great biographies of our literature. Wide and deep knowledge of literature, an exquisitely keen understanding of his subject, literary criticism at its best, and a perfect sense of humor are some of the qualities that make the *Life and Times of Laurence Sterne* great literature as well as great biography. It is one of the books that no lover of biography or of literature can afford to miss.

There is little to choose between the *Life and Times of Laurence Sterne* and the *History of Henry Fielding* (1918). The latter is longer than the former because Fielding had a more diversified career than Sterne and made a larger contribution to English literature. Few of the great figures in our literature are as well known as these two men because Professor Cross, following the standards set by Boswell, Lockhart, and Trevelyan, gave us their whole lives, their whole characters and, as far as it is possible for man to do, their whole minds. Carrying each man from birth to death, Cross sets down their stories with a method that is perfect and a style that is flawless. It is useless to add further praise; they must be read to be appreciated.

The *Life of James McNeill Whistler,* by the Pennells, is

one of the most interesting and charming books that have been written on the subject of Whistler. The collaboration seems to have combined Joseph Pennell's genius for art and art criticism with Elizabeth Pennell's understanding of human nature as embodied in the genius of Whistler. Both were close personal friends of Whistler, but they did not allow this friendship to color their portrait. The book is long and detailed, and every fact of Whistler's unique personality is presented in a kindly and what seems to be a true light. It must have been as difficult to write the biography as it was to understand the man.

Bret Harte was, in his field, as much of a genius as Whistler, but he was not so fortunate in his early biographer. H. C. Merwin's *Life of Bret Harte* (1911) was, for many years, the best biography of the famous short-story writer that we had. It has been superseded by a later book, but it is still a good book spoiled by a very bad arrangement of material. The biography is cut in half by the insertion of a long account of life in California before and during the time Harte was there. In this account, which is very interesting in itself, the author attempted to place and evaluate Harte's stories. He failed in both instances, for most of the places and people in these stories were located and lived only in Bret Harte's vivid imagination, and Merwin seems not to have been entirely aware of this. Had this section been made a part of Harte's life in California, the whole book would have been immeasurably better. The latter part of the book is biographically weak, for the author had little knowledge of Harte's later years and his life in England.

Merwin failed as a biographer because he seems not to have known what he wanted to do and that a biography, to be complete, must tell the whole story of a man's life. When Brander Matthews came to write *Molière: his Life and his Works* (1910), he knew just what he wanted to do and how it should be done. In the prefatory note he says: "In this biography, I have striven especially for three things: first, to set forth the facts of Molière's life, stripped of all the legends which compass it about; second, to trace his development as a dramatic artist . . . , and thirdly, to show his intimate relation with the time in which he lived. . . ." Just how completely Professor Matthews succeeded can be realized only by reading the book. This is a magnificent biography of the greatest of the French playwrights of the seventeenth century. The court of Louis XIV, the city of Paris, the people of France are all in this book with Molière as the dominant figure. Throughout the history and the criticism that is necessary in telling of the life and work of Molière, the latter is always where he belongs, plainly in sight of the reader. It is not an easy matter to write a biography of this size—it is very long—without, at times, losing sight of the subject, but Professor Matthews succeeds admirably. Professor Matthews' reputation as a historian of the drama, as a critic, as a biographer of distinction can rest on this one book; it is a masterpiece of literary biography.

There is one other book that deserves mention here although it is not a biography at all. *My Mark Twain,* by William Dean Howells, is a book which must be read if we are going to try to understand Mark Twain. Howells was his literary adviser and closest friend. This intimacy enabled Howells to write of Mark Twain as he did.

2

The second decade of the twentieth century was to witness a revolution in biographical writing before its close. Almost every important figure was to be subjected to the new treatment; some would emerge full bodied and would be given their proper place in the history of America; others would come forth mere wraiths of their former selves, having been drawn through the rolls of reality. It would produce some excellent biographies and some of no value whatever.

The decade opened, perhaps, better than it closed, for the publication of *Mark Twain: A Biography,* in 1912, marked one of the high points in biographical writing in America.

Albert Bigelow Paine was at that time, as he still is, a professional writer. In 1904, he had published *Th. Nast, His Period and His Pictures.* This is an excellent biography of the greatest, certainly the most influential, cartoonist that America has produced. The character and career of the man would be enough to provide an interesting book, but this one is further enhanced by reproductions of many of the cartoons that made Nast famous.

According to Mr. Paine, a casual remark of a third person, made soon after Paine met Mark Twain, suggested to him the idea of becoming Mark Twain's biographer. He broached the subject to the latter, it was enthusiastically received, and from that day until his death in 1910, hardly a day passed that the humorist did not contribute something to his biographer's material. Paine practically lived with Twain for the last four years of his life, and came to know him better, perhaps, than any other man had known him.

In the beginning, Twain began to dictate the account of his early life, but after some time gave it up and Paine had to get the facts of his career from his stories, which were numerous but not always accurate. In addition to this source, he had correspondence, speeches, and, more important than anything else, the books Mark Twain wrote, the great majority of which are at least partly autobiographical. With this material and the results of his own researches, Mr. Paine produced a biography more nearly like Boswell's *Life of Johnson* than any other life that has been written in America. It is literally the life of Mark Twain from his birth to his death. Three volumes of five hundred pages each are necessary to tell the story, but one never tires of it in the process.

Mr. Paine seems eminently fair in his delineation of Mark Twain's character. There are few men in America who have lived as fully and have had as varied careers as Mark Twain. He was a printer, traveler, Mississippi River pilot, miner and reporter in California, before he entered his long reign as the best-known author in America. All this and a great deal more is set forth in the *Life,* and if the author failed to present the complete man—we do not think he did, any more than Boswell or Lockhart did—no one can. Paine soon came to know every side of Mark Twain and endeavored to judge him for what he was. He has given us every side, every phase, every mental and moral turn, every good and bad point. He appreciated the innate fineness and coarseness of the man, and interpreted his life in the light of this understanding. With the abundance of his material, he was able to choose the best, most characteristic, and most illuminating of Twain's letters to make and prove his points of character. We see the born humorist, the inexperienced and prejudiced critic, the bitter satirist and cynic, and the faithful lover. We see just as much of the untrained, uncouth, and at times vulgar side of Twain's life as we see of his better nature. No man could be less biased in his treatment of a subject than Paine is in his treatment of this one.

Whether or not Mr. Paine used all his material and told the whole story of Mark Twain's life is a question that can be answered only by Mr. Paine or other writers who have investigated the subject. Mr. Bernard DeVoto in his excellent book, *Mark Twain's America,* repeatedly states that there is much manuscript material, left by Twain, that has never been printed or seen by anyone except the executors of the estate. That is probably true, but it is hardly possible that there is much in this unpublished material that could alter the character of Mark Twain from what we know it to have been. Mark Twain's later life was sad and bitter, and it does not require much imagination, knowing some of the comments on life and man that he did make, to picture what he may have written or said. In the *Life of Mark Twain,* we find such a complete representation of a remarkably complex character that we should not be surprised by anything that came from its pen. It would seem that a sufficiency is enough.

Woven into the text of the *Life of Mark Twain* is, of course, a great deal of criticism. In the cases of the great books, *Tom Sawyer, Huckleberry Finn, Life on the Mississippi,* and *Roughing It,* the biographer had to judge them on their own merits, using the accepted standards of criticism. The life they depicted was gone forever and he had to depend on his judgment and such knowledge as he could obtain from the treacherous memories of Twain and his contemporaries. No better criticism of the whole of Mark Twain's work has been written than that found in the three volumes of the *Life*.

In addition to those biographical and critical qualities which have been described, Mr. Paine's book has the additional merit of being well organized and well written. It seems almost to have written itself, for the narrative flows so smoothly that the reading requires little or no effort from the reader. This ease is the prime requisite of good writing. One of the finest features of this book is the arrangement and the selection of letters and documents. We have all the reasons for almost every act of Mark Twain's life, and most of them required reasons. As critical biography, as pure biography, Albert Bigelow Paine's *Life of Mark Twain* ranks and will rank among the best biographies in American literature.

Mr. Paine continued his work on Mark Twain by editing two volumes of letters and, in 1920, he published a *Short Life of Mark Twain*—an abridgement, though written anew, of the larger life.

In One Man's Life; Being Chapters from the Personal and Business Career of Theodore N. Vail was published by Mr. Paine in 1921. This seems to be an authorized biography of the business genius who developed and directed, for many years, the American Telephone and Telegraph Company. Developed by the same method that the author used in his *Life of Mark Twain*, this book falls far short of the latter because the material for a great book was lacking.

Mr. Paine's last important biography was *Joan of Arc, Maid of France* (1925). Perhaps the idea was suggested by Mark Twain's romance, *Joan of Arc;* Mr. Paine, however, wrote a strictly historical biography of the Maid. It is an excellent book and, though interest is sometimes sacrificed to historical reality, it is one of the best biographies of Joan of Arc in English.

The period between 1912 and 1919 was not very productive of biographies of men of letters of average or better than average merit. Carl Van Doren's *Thomas Love Peacock* (1912) is a narrative biography, with little criticism, of a prominent English novelist of the early nineteenth century. Hobart C. Chatfield-Taylor published *Goldoni; a Biography* in 1913. This is a long and complete life of the famous eighteenth-century Italian playwright. Based on Goldoni's *Memoirs* it tells the complete life-story of a man who considered himself an artist in matters of the heart as well as of the theatre. A good biography of one who has written his autobiography is generally an improvement on the latter, toning down its enthusiasms and filling in the blind spots which are present in almost every autobiography. Mr. Chatfield-Taylor renders these services in the writing of this excellent life, placed against the background of eighteenth-century France and Italy. One of the very best biographies of this period is *Edward Rowland Sill: his Life and Work* (1915), by William B. Parker. Sill was a poet and man of letters of more than average ability, and this critical biography places him just where he belongs in the history of American literature. To the quality of the book as biography is added a charm of style that makes delightful reading.

Julia Ward Howe, by Laura E. Richards and Maud Howe Elliott, was published in 1915. In the two volumes, Mrs. Howe's two daughters told, I presume, the complete account of her life. Mrs. Howe, in addition to being a writer and the author of the "Battle Hymn of the Republic," was prominent in public affairs, both municipal and national. She had a very full and interesting life, and it is well told in this book, but why *Julia Ward Howe* was awarded the first Pulitzer Prize in biography—the first award was made in 1917—I do not know.

It is not a particularly difficult matter to put together such a book as *Julia Ward Howe,* for a book of this kind is not and is not intended to be critical. It is quite another matter to write such critical biographies as did Professor George Harper in his *Charles-Augustus Sainte-Beuve* (1907) and *William Wordsworth; his Life, Works and Influence* (1916). The earlier book, written for the "French Men of Letters Series," is a short, critical account of the great French critic and biographical essayist. Necessarily short, it nevertheless gives us a complete picture of Sainte-Beuve from birth to death. The fact that Sainte-Beuve's published works occupy more than eighty volumes will give some idea of the preparation necessary for, and the difficulties involved in, the writing of such a book. It is, to say the least, the best introduction to Sainte-Beuve that we have in English, although it has been superseded by a later American biography.

William Wordsworth . . . is a much more important book than the one on Sainte-Beuve. The product of a lifetime of teaching and study, it is the most complete and the best biography of Wordsworth that has ever been written. Not only is this book a piece of genuine scholarship, but it is written in a style so simple, graceful, and smooth that it is fascinating to read as pure biography, quite apart from its critical value. Like every other great biography it presents the whole man and, while we may not agree with Professor Harper as to the importance of his subject or as to the quality of Wordsworth's poetry or his place in English literature, we must respect the author's point of view and judgments and credit him with having written one of the finest literary biographies in the English language.

In the same year that Harper's *Wordsworth* was published, there appeared a fragment of a biography by Professor Thomas R. Lounsbury: *Life and Times of Tennyson from 1809 to 1850.* Unfinished at Lounsbury's death, the book was prepared for publication by one of his colleagues at Yale, Professor Wilbur Cross. It was Professor Lounsbury's intention to explain the favorable and unfavorable influences working at the beginning of Tennyson's career. The fragment shows that it would have been an excellent biography of Tennyson's early life, had he been able to finish it.

This period (1912–1919) closes with two important books on two of the major figures in American literature, Henry David Thoreau and Joel Chandler Harris. The *Life of Henry David Thoreau* . . . (1917), by F. B. Sanborn, was the last of a number of books that Mr. Sanborn had written on Thoreau. It is a very long book and complete as to facts, but parts of it are almost separate essays on various aspects of Thoreau. As real, interpretive biography it leaves much to be desired; as a source of information it is invaluable. The *Life and Letters of Joel Chandler Harris* (1918) was written by his daughter-in-law, Julia Harris. It is good biography, particularly in view of the relationship between author and subject. It shows, in the development of his character, how this southern newspaperman could be the creator of *Uncle Remus.*

3

The lives of important clergymen and famous reformers frequently provide opportunities for biographers to display their skill and art. In most instances ministers, priests, reformers left either large quantities of published writings or masses of correspondence and diaries. The latter is particularly true in the case of Phillips Brooks, Episcopal bishop of Massachusetts and one of the best-known clergymen in the late nineteenth century. His authorized biography, *The Life and Letters of Phillips Brooks* (1900), was begun by his brother and completed by A. V. G. Allen, the biographer of Jonathan Edwards. This life, in three volumes, is very detailed, covering every phase of Brooks's varied life, but it is spoiled by lack of cohesion. If the journals and correspondence had been made definite parts of the biography, the book would have been better. Mr. Allen may have followed the plan laid down by the original biographer; if so, it is simply unfortunate that Mr. Brooks did not make a better plan for the book. In having interchapters of correspondence and journal entries, this biography shares the same fault that mars Dean Stanley's *Life of Thomas Arnold*. These two lives are striking examples of the misuse of invaluable source material.

Dwight L. Moody had a wider reputation in his day, as preacher and evangelist, than Brooks had in his, as a more conservative churchman. Moody did not subscribe to any particular denominational creed, but he was one of the most famous evangelists of nineteenth-century America. His official biography was published by his son, W. R. Moody, in 1900, and a completely revised and greatly enlarged edition appeared in 1930. Both editions are well-written accounts of Moody's life and work. Apparently complete, the book is interesting for the development of Moody's career and for its picture of life and religion in America in the nineteenth century.

Timothy Flint was one of the earliest workers in the field that Moody later cultivated so assiduously and militantly. His biography, *Timothy Flint, Pioneer, Missionary, Author, Editor, 1780–1840* (1911), by John E. Kirkpatrick, is an excellent book and a distinct contribution to the literature of western history and travel as well as to the religious life and activities of the western pioneer. Flint was a Presbyterian clergyman of New England when he decided to enter the missionary field in the western country. Ill health compelled him to return to the East several times, but in the periods of his missionary activity he traveled extensively through the Ohio and Mississippi valleys and the far south. His revivals were famous and attracted thousands of people who, in some cases, traveled hundreds of miles for a week of revival meetings. He wrote travel books and novels, and managed to do considerable editing of newspapers and periodicals. Mr. Kirkpatrick made admirable use of his sources and presented a faithful picture of this tireless worker against an historically accurate background of western life.

James, Cardinal Gibbons was one of the leading Catholic clergymen of America in the late nineteenth and early twentieth centuries. Archbishop of Baltimore and sole American cardinal for many years, Cardinal Gibbons exerted a tremendous influence in lay as well as clerical affairs among Protestants as well as Catholics. In 1911, Allen S. Will published the *Life of James, Cardinal Gibbons*. This is a very good biography, as far as it goes, but is incomplete because Cardinal Gibbons was living at the time of its publication. In 1922 Will published a new life in two volumes. This was an authorized biography, based on conversations with the Cardinal and on his private papers, to which Professor Will had complete access. This is not a revision or expansion of the earlier book, but an entirely new biography. In this very complete record of a long and busy life we have a picture not only of Gibbons but of the growth of the Catholic Church in America, which Cardinal Gibbons did so much to foster. We have also a picture of one of the highest dignitaries of the Roman Catholic Church as an American, first, last, and always. It was this independent American spirit that made Cardinal Gibbons a friend and adviser of politicians and Presidents as well as a great churchman. The author told the Cardinal's story with proper respect for the position of his subject, a keen appreciation of his qualities, and an unbiased judgment as to his accomplishments.

Churchmen of the past as well as the present were considered by biographers during this period. Among the best religious biographies of this period are: *Life and Letters of Martin Luther* (1911) by Preserved Smith, and *Martin Luther: the Man and his Work* (1911), by Arthur C. McGiffert. Both are excellent books, and the differences in them are in matters of theology and history, with which this study is not concerned. A third biography, *Martin Luther* (1917), is a popular treatment of the subject by Elsie Singmaster, the novelist. David S. Schaff took another reformer for his subject in *John Huss: his Life, Teachings and Death, after Five Hundred Years*. This is a very interesting and readable biography of a disciple of Wyclif who carried his teachings to Bohemia.

4

In the fields of public life and politics, biography made rapid strides during the early part of the twentieth century. Sincere attempts were made to get at the truth concerning the early and contemporary figures, with, of course, some exceptions. We no longer have so many eulogistic memoirs or one-sided "family" biographies. Disinterested, or at least unprejudiced writers, were working over the old materials and in many instances producing biographies which give an honest and fair portrayal of life and character. While it cannot be said that this period pointed definitely to the "new" biography, it did show a definite advance over the old apologetical or panegyrical type of life-writing. The fact that source materials, hitherto in the possession of individuals, were being opened to public examination had a great deal to do with the move toward more intelligent biography.

The heroes of the Revolution, the founders of the republic and the elder statesmen of the period before the Civil War were the subjects of many of these modern biographies. A. C. Buell wrote one short and three long biographies which are very good. *Paul Jones, Founder of the American Navy* (1900) is the first attempt at a complete biography of the great raider and fighter. More than a dozen lives of Jones had been written during the nineteenth century, but not one of them has any claim to recognition as good biography. Using all the published material and his own researches, Buell wrote a life of Jones which strips the legend and romance from him and shows him as a great man who performed almost incredible feats in spite of great obstacles. This biography also gives us a true account of Jones's life before and after the Revolution, and these are the most valuable parts of the book, for they show us the high-tempered, passionate man who was not always the acme of perfection which his eulogists would have us believe. Buell's *Paul Jones* is not the last word on the subject, but is a solid, well-written biography.

His second biography, like that on Jones, in two volumes,

was the *History of Andrew Jackson, Pioneer, Patriot, Soldier, Politician, President* (1904). This life of Jackson is concerned principally with his public life, emphasizing those phases which are mentioned in the title. Shorter than Parton's biography and lacking the narrative interest of that book, Buell's life is, excepting Parton's, the best up to that time. His third long biography, *William Penn as the Founder of Two Commonwealths* (1904), is the best life of Penn that has been written in America. Based on sound research, it tells the entire story of Penn's life in England and in America, and of the founding of the colony of Pennsylvania, a small part of which later became the colony of Delaware. It is, as far as one can tell, accurate, truthful, and complete. Buell's fourth life was a short biography of Sir William Johnson, the famous landowner and Indian leader in the colony of New York. While all of these biographies are well written, they lack any distinction of style and are not particularly interesting because Buell seems always to have sacrificed interest to truth, which, in the final analysis, is as it should be. Had Buell written twenty years later, he could have psychoanalyzed these subjects, as so many biographers were to do, but we doubt if he would have produced the solid work that he did produce.

A. C. Buell took some of our heroes for subjects; Charles Burr Todd tried to defend our so-called "traitors." *The True Aaron Burr. A Biographical Sketch* (1902) is an avowed defense of Burr and presents an able case but, as has been stated elsewhere in this history, it is impossible to arrive at any definite truth regarding the activities of Burr after he left the Vice-Presidency in 1805. Mr. Todd's book is, however, a welcome change from the prejudiced and flatly untruthful biographies of Burr that had been written by the "patriotic" school. The fact that Mr. Todd was a collateral descendant of Burr naturally influenced his point of view.

Todd's second biography is a much longer and more important book than that on Burr. *The Real Benedict Arnold* (1903) is a study of Arnold from an entirely new point of view. Instead of condemning Arnold without a hearing, the author tries to find the reasons for Arnold's treason, and he finds them in Arnold's wife and his own lack of character. The book is remarkably well done and if the premises are accepted the conclusions must be accepted. Mrs. Arnold's treason has been proved by later writers, historians as well as biographers.

John C. Calhoun, as the leading statesman of the South before the war, has been the subject of many biographies since his death. In 1903, G. M. Pinckney published his *Life of John C. Calhoun* in which he defended Calhoun and the extreme states-rights point of view of which Calhoun was the leading exponent. It is an interesting and well-written book, but it must be read with the author's thesis constantly in mind. William M. Meigs's *Life of John Caldwell Calhoun* (1910) is the best biography of the famous South Carolinian that has been written. Based on sound scholarship, it is as impartial as a biography can be. Meigs's purpose in writing this life was to try to explain Calhoun's life and politics and to place him among American statesmen. The calm detachment of the book, as well as its biographical and historical quality, places it among the best lives of this period.

The sanity and balance that characterize Meigs's book on Calhoun are frequently in evidence in the early years of this century. A striking example of this new method is C. F. Gettemy's *True Story of Paul Revere, His Mid-Night Ride, His Arrest and Court Martial, His Useful Public Services* (1905). This book, despite its subtitle, is mainly an account of Revere's career before, during, and after the Revolution. It puts the "Mid-Night Ride" in its proper place as a minor episode in Revere's busy life. Longfellow's poem, "The Midnight Ride of Paul Revere," has made Revere a folk hero, the man who, unaided, warned the "embattled farmers" of the coming of the British. As a matter of fact, Revere was not unaided, and his experience as an express rider made this particular ride just an ordinary night's work. The life of Revere as a patriot supporter, as silversmith, dentist, general artisan, is graphically and clearly set forth in this biography. We know the man by the time we have finished the book.

Andrew Jackson was as much of a folk hero in the West as Revere was in the East. We have seen that numerous attempts were made to write of him as he was, rather than as his friends or enemies thought he was. The most scholarly and least partial life of Jackson is John Spencer Bassett's *Life of Andrew Jackson* (1911). This book was the result of many years of study and investigation by Professor Bassett. He had access to the enormous mass of Jackson's papers and correspondence, and this material threw much new light on Jackson's career. In the first place, he presented Jackson as an individual rather than as one of the heroes of the nation. Secondly, Bassett was primarily concerned with Jackson's public life and told only enough of his private life to show the development of his character and certain phases of his private life that influenced his public career. The majority of the two volumes is concerned with Jackson, the soldier, the politician, the President, with the history of Jackson and his time rather than with the life of Jackson. Nevertheless, Bassett keeps his subject in the foreground, and the biography is not sacrificed to the history. As an impartial historian, Professor Bassett tries so hard to be fair that he exhibits, on the whole, a slight prejudice against Jackson. It is most difficult to write a cold, historical biography of such a man. He almost demands romantic treatment and that treatment Professor Bassett could not give. To anyone who wants the history of the United States during Jackson's life and the part that Jackson played in the making of that history, Bassett's *Life of Andrew Jackson* is indispensable. To anyone primarily interested in Jackson as a man rather than a historical figure, this book will not appeal; he must go to Parton or some of the new biographers.

If Mrs. Anna F. DeKoven had been capable of using Professor Bassett's methods, her *Life and Letters of John Paul Jones* (1913) would have been much better than it is. Her knowledge of Jones's life and career was by no means complete, and her enthusiasm for Jones and for early America was too strong. Having too little of one and too much of the other, she gave us a very romantic account of Jones, filling in the bare spots with what might have been or what she thought should have been the actions and reactions rather than that which really did happen. In short, the book is interesting but not reliable. Her background of American history is as deficient in spots as is her subject. The two volumes might well have been confined to one, had Mrs. DeKoven been content to tell John Paul's story as she knew it. Finally, the subject is not one that can be successfully handled by a woman who romanticizes war and sea fights; that may do for fiction but it will not do for biography.

Mrs. Laura E. Richards' *Abigail Adams and her Times* (1917), succeeded where Mrs. DeKoven's book failed, for the reason that she took a subject which she was capable of handling. Mrs. Adams, the wife of President John Adams, was the first mistress of the White House, and she left some memorable accounts of the difficulties she encountered in running the unfinished, cold, and bleak mansion. Abigail Adams was one of the great women of her time. We know more about her life than we do of the lives of thousands of other women of her day because she was a President's wife and because she was an excellent correspondent. She left very complete diaries and masses of letters, of which Mrs. Richards made excellent use. The biographer who is so fortunate as to have such source material as this, and is as skilful in the use of it as Mrs. Richards was is to be congratulated. As life-writing and history, *Abigail Adams and her Times* is an excellent book.

William Cabell Bruce, using the same method as Mrs. Richards, wrote *Benjamin Franklin, Self-Revealed* (1917). By allowing Franklin to tell his own story wherever possible the author was able to present a complete picture of one of the greatest men and certainly the most versatile genius in eighteenth-century America. Few men have written as much as Franklin; few authors have so closely studied the writings of their subjects in the light of their biographical significance as has Mr. Bruce. The magnitude of the task is matched only by the success with which the author achieved it. The *Auto-biography*, the *Bagatelles*, the political, economic, and scientific pamphlets, the public and private correspondence are used with a master hand. No man has used this biographical method with more skill or with a rarer perception of the values of the enormous source material than this biographer. Despite all the autobiographical material this is a genuine biographical and critical study of Poor Richard. Even though Franklin was particularly self-critical in his *Autobiography* and particularly careful as to details, his biographer has added a great deal to our understanding of Franklin during this period of his life. Even more important is the character, intellect, and genius of Franklin as developed by Bruce through the later writings. *Benjamin Franklin, Self-Revealed* was the Pulitzer Prize biography in 1918, and the committee honored itself as well as Mr. Bruce in making the award.

In 1922, Mr. Bruce published *John Randolph of Roanoke*. This two-volume life is the most complete and the best account of Randolph that we have. Based largely on new material, the book follows the same method that the author used in his *Benjamin Franklin*. Randolph left comparatively little of his own writings, but the author was able to draw extensively on those of his contemporaries, for Randolph was one of the most prominent and notorious figures in early American public life. A Virginia aristocrat and a Republican in politics, a brilliant mind with a twist in it, a great orator with a genius for invective unequaled in American public life, a bitter enemy and a staunch friend, a misanthrope with a wealth of kindness in his makeup, John Randolph was a unique as well as a great figure in American history and politics. Mr. Bruce has given us as true a picture of this strange man as we shall ever get, doing him full justice in every respect. There is one defect in the book, and that is that the larger part of the second volume is made up of essays illustrating Randolph's life and character. His personality was so strange and complex that it may have been impossible for his biographer to arrange the material in any other way. One of the most interesting features of the book is the severe and true strictures which the author heaps upon the earlier biography of Randolph by Henry Adams. With these lives of Franklin and Randolph, William Cabell Bruce has achieved a permanent place in the literature of American biography.

The "True Series" of biographies, started in the last decade of the nineteenth century, was continued until the end of the period under discussion. The purpose of this series was to present, in a single volume, the true lives of some of our principal public men as the authors saw them. The series was not entirely successful, for some of the writers presented their subjects in collections of character sketches rather than in unified biographies. Sydney George Fisher's *True William Penn* (1900) and *True Daniel Webster* (1911) are good short biographies, the one on Webster relying largely on G. W. Curtis' authorized biography. Joseph M. Rogers' *True Henry Clay* (1902) is a good personal and political account of Clay's career, and George Morgan's *True Patrick Henry* (1907) is an excellent interpretive biography, stressing the personality of Henry as it made and influenced his career. General Charles King's *True Ulysses Grant* (1914) is a straight biography of Grant, emphasizing, of course, his Civil War campaigns, while Cyrus T. Brady's *True Andrew Jackson* is a rather poor popular treatment in a series of essays.

That biography was becoming increasingly popular with the average reader may be seen from the numbers of short, romantic, or sensational lives that were being published in the first decade of this century. A representative writer of this type of biography was Alfred H. Lewis, the novelist. Between 1901 and 1909 he published *Richard Croker, Story of Paul Jones, When Men Grew Tall; or, the Story of Andrew Jackson,* and *An American Patrician: Aaron Burr.* These lives are about halfway between conventional biography and the fictionized biography of our own time. Based on second- or third-hand sources, they made no claim to biographical or literary quality, but were written for the average reader, interested in the lives of great or famous men. Such books as these often serve a good purpose, carrying readers on to a better class of literature.

5

Lives of Civil War heroes were being written and rewritten in increasing numbers in the twentieth century. Grant was still a popular subject, but no one of his biographers succeeded in producing anything approaching a definitive life. The most distinguished of the Grant biographies is Owen Wister's *Ulysses S. Grant* (1900). It is not a complete or a critical biography, but it does have the advantage of being well written.

W. C. Chase published the *Story of Stonewall Jackson: the Career of Thomas Jonathan (Stonewall) Jackson* in 1909, and Thomas Nelson Page, *Robert E. Lee: Man and Soldier* in 1911. Both are fairly good, their principal defects being the inability of their authors to write military history. I do not know Chase's profession, but Mr. Page was a novelist of the South, and while he had the imagination necessary to a novelist, he was not able to visualize and animate the great battles of the Civil War in which General Lee took part.

One of the most important biographies of this period is Oswald G. Villard's *John Brown, 1800–1859; Biography Fifty Years After* (1910). In this huge, exhaustive (and sometimes exhausting) life, Mr. Villard tells the whole story of John Brown from his birth to his execution as a traitor, at Harpers Ferry, Virginia. Mr. Villard has been for many years one of our outstanding liberal journalists, and naturally his is a sympathetic account of the famous abolitionist. This book is not partisan, neither is it a defense of Brown; it is merely a judgment, and a fair one, passed fifty years after the attack on Harpers Ferry took place. It seems to me that this is the definitive biography of John Brown, though it may not be the best from the point of view of interest and drama. Mr. Villard tried to tell the whole truth about John Brown, but he was not interested in dramatizing him.

Edwin M. Stanton and Thaddeus Stevens were fanatics, but their fanaticism took a different turn from that of John Brown. They were obsessed by a lust for power rather than for what they conceived to be justice. Stevens, particularly, was successful because of an almost demoniacal genius, not for leading men but for driving them and bending them to his will. Stanton would have done as Stevens did, had he had the opportunity and the ability. *Edwin McMasters Stanton, the Autocrat of the Rebellion, Emancipation, and Reconstruction* (1905), by Frank A. Flower, is supposed to be a biography; it is really an apology and defense in a series of character studies. Mr. Flower may have understood Stanton, but there is little evidence of that understanding in this book. This "misunderstood" man was a Democrat in Buchanan's cabinet and a Republican in Lincoln's. He did his best to betray both of them. He became a Radical before Lincoln's death; Lincoln knew it but kept him because he was an efficient Secretary of War. After the war he showed his true colors, becoming the willing agency for the impeachment of President Johnson. Stanton was a natural intriguer. On the other hand, he was a famous lawyer, a great administrator, and, as Secretary of War, performed inestimable service to Lincoln and the Government. Mr. Flower does not analyze his subject at all; he merely stretches his good qualities to the point of gross exaggeration and untruth. Furthermore, this book is entirely lacking in unity and is badly written.

Professor James A. Woodburn's *Life of Thaddeus Stevens* (1913) has the virtue of being well written, but that is its only virtue. This life is history rather than biography, and bad history at that. It is almost incomprehensible that a professor of American history could, in 1913, write such a book as the *Life of Thaddeus Stevens*. If he used any original sources, they were only those which would prove his case: that Stevens was a great man, one of the principal saviors of the Union, and a statesman. Historians and biographers, before and since Woodburn published this book, have proved conclusively that he was not a great man, a savior of the Union, or a statesman. He was a party politician of the lowest type, who gloatingly admitted that he would use any means to keep the Republican party in power. Professor Woodburn's book is bad history and worse biography, not only biased but also untruthful because his interpretation is not based on facts and his judgment is warped by partisanship. If a scholarly biographer cannot be trusted to state facts, we cannot expect any more of others.

6

The great financiers and railroad builders of the late nineteenth and early twentieth centuries were the subjects of some of the eulogistic biographies written between 1900 and 1918. The first one of any importance takes us back to the middle of the nineteenth century. *Jay Cooke, Financier of the Civil War* (1907), by Ellis P. Oberholtzer, is the biography of the greatest private banker of his day. Cooke was the financier of the Civil War, for he was the fiscal agent of the Government during the war, lending money himself and floating the various bond issues. He reaped the harvest during and after the war with the assistance of war contractors and politicians. The failure of the house of Cooke in 1873 precipitated the famous panic of that year. This and a great deal more is told by Mr. Oberholtzer. The principal fault of the book is that the author told only half the story, Cooke's half. The trouble with books of this type is that they make heroes of men who were frequently anything but heroes. Again only the "more smiling aspects" of their lives and careers are mentioned by their biographical apologists. Like the poor, this kind of biography is with us always and creates a false impression of our "great" men.

John Muir's *Life of Edward H. Harriman* (1912), Carl Hovey's *Life Story of J. Pierpont Morgan* (1912), and Joseph G. Pyle's *Life of James J. Hill* (1917) belong in the same class as Oberholtzer's *Jay Cooke*. They are interesting; they are inspiring to young Americans who wish to make fortunes;

they show how, in most cases, a poor boy can become a rich man; but they are absolutely unreliable. These four biographies were either authorized or endorsed by the families and friends of the subject. John Muir, Harriman's biographer, was himself a Wall Street operator; consequently he could interpret Harriman's career as a financial pirate and wrecker, as well as builder, of railroads in the conventional manner. Mr. Hovey's life of Morgan was certainly acceptable to the world in which he lived, and Mr. Pyle's book was authorized by the Hill family. All these lives are conventional biographies, complete as far as the average reader can tell, but, I repeat, they are untruthful in their omissions rather than their contents. This method of biographical writing is as old as biography; it is still being followed, and will continue to be used until human nature changes. Perhaps it should not be classified as biography, but placed in a special classification of apologetics. However, until this change is made, these books must be considered in any history of life-writing.

7

A large number of biographies of this period (1900–1918) belong to no particular group and will be considered here as good or bad biographies in themselves.

Carlyle once made a statement to the effect that a good biography could be written regardless of the importance of the subject. That statement, like so many of Carlyle's, is a little too sweeping, but we have examples in American biography which come close to proving the dictum. Charles W. Eliot, the famous president of Harvard, spent his vacations in Maine and came to know the people very well. In 1904, he published a little book titled *John Gilley*. It is hardly a biography and still it tells the story of this man's life. John Gilley was a Maine fisherman and guide for summer visitors. He had never been fifty miles from where he was born; he had no "experiences of life" yet he had a definite and, for him, complete philosophy of life. Dr. Eliot's character appreciation of this man whom, in some respects, he considered a great man, is a masterpiece of biographical literature in the real sense of the term. We get to know John Gilley mentally as well as physically, and we are compelled to admire this fisherman who had more wisdom than knowledge and who lived his life as fully as Eliot lived his. If this book does nothing else, it shows us that a biographer can make use of what seems to be a very circumscribed life, if he knows it well enough, and make of it a work of art, for *John Gilley* is a work of art.

George H. Palmer's life of Alice Freeman Palmer, his wife, is only a degree or two below *John Gilley*. Mrs. Palmer was President of Wellesley College and one of the most prominent women of her day, but her husband wrote of her as a woman and a wife. This small book is nothing but an appreciation, but it is done with such art and such objectivity that it will always have a high position in the literature of American biography.

Political biographies are far more numerous than biographies of educators or philosophical fishermen, and they are seldom particularly good biographies. Herbert D. Croly's *Marcus Alonzo Hanna: his Life and Work* (1912) is below the average, for it is neither well organized nor well written, and the biographical part is overshadowed by a history of the Republican party. Hanna was one of the party chiefs in the nineties, largely because of his own wealth and his ability to collect campaign funds from other wealthy men. He rose to political prominence first in Ohio and then in Washington when he placed William McKinley in the President's chair. One side, at least, of his career, the political, can be obtained from Croly's book if one has the patience to wade through it. Samuel B. McCall's *Life of Thomas B. Reed* (1914) is an intimate biography of a Maine politician who, as Speaker of the House of Representatives, brought about the greatest reform in procedure in the House that has ever been effected. The reform was an excellent one even though it was carried through for party purposes. This biography, by a fellow congressman and Republican, is very interesting and well done, but many phases of Reed's life and character are conspicuously absent. The whole truth is rarely found in political biographies.

Politics in the larger sense was the theme of the two biographies written by William Roscoe Thayer. Thayer was one of those fortunate people who can devote their lives to scholarship and literature. His principal interests seem to have been biography and Italian history. He wrote extensively for periodicals in addition to his longer studies in history and biography. His interest in Italy, and in modern Italy particularly, led him to make an intensive study of Cavour, the greatest of Italian statesmen and the man who succeeded in uniting Italy in the nineteenth century. Thayer's *Life and Times of Cavour* (1911) is a masterly presentation of the life of the statesman and his share in the unification of Italy. The two volumes contain more history than biography, but the nature of the subject made it inevitable that history should have a larger part in the book than biography. In spite of this fact, it is an excellent historical biography in which Cavour weaves his devious way through the diplomacy of nineteenth-century Europe to his goal. We learn comparatively little of Cavour's private life because life, to him, meant politics, the pitting of his intellect against the intellects of the greatest diplomats and statesmen of Europe. We cannot complain if we do not see as much of Cavour the man, as of Cavour the statesman. It was Cavour the statesman in whom Thayer was primarily interested. The organization and structure of the book are excellent, and the style is particularly well adapted to historical writing, being formal without being stiff.

Mr. Thayer was asked to contribute a life of John Hay to the new series of the *American Statesmen,* but a number of years elapsed before it was published in 1915. It was a very successful book because it was entirely different in form and style from the other lives in the series and because it presented the life of a rather unusual man. *The Life and Letters of John Hay* is, as a biography of a man of letters, an excellent book and captivates the average reader at the first reading.

The subject is interesting for himself. One of Lincoln's private secretaries, a poet in secret long before any of his writings were published, a newspaper man, novelist, co-author with John Nicolay of the *History of Abraham Lincoln,* politician, diplomat, and finally Secretary of State in the cabinets of McKinley and Roosevelt, Hay had the sort of life and career that must delight the heart of any biographer. To a man of Thayer's interests it must have been a particularly welcome subject, even though it was far different from anything that he had done. The response of the public was even more enthusiastic than Thayer could have hoped for.

Rereading, it seems to us, is the final test of the value of any book. Our interest and enthusiasm frequently get the better of our critical judgment on a first reading, but when we reread our critical faculty is dominant. In the case of biography, we frequently know nothing about the subject and read the book primarily for information. If, when we reread it, we have further information from other sources, we acquire a position from which to criticize more intelligently. Mr. Thayer's book does not stand up under rereading. It has all the original charm, but its method is open to serious criticism. In the first place, John Hay must have been an almost perfect man, if we are to believe his biographer. From the time he left Brown University until his death, more than forty years later, he seems never to have said or done anything that was not correct. He seems to have had an unfailingly sunny disposition and a permanent personal charm. He was engaged in all sorts of literary and business enterprises, and he always kept his sweet disposition. Marvelous man! Secondly, Thayer did not make the best use of his source materials. He seems to have used the letters which were published by Mrs. Hay, which she edited very carefully, removing almost all the proper names. Whether or not he had access to the original correspondence I do not know, but I think he did, for he states in the preface that he had suppressed names in letters and parts of letters because the use of them might possibly offend someone. This procedure is as misleading as untruth-

ful statements. Thirdly, Thayer's manner of using correspondence spoils its value and the unity of the book. Instead
of working the letters into the body of the biography he puts
them in separate chapters, frequently without comment. Hay
was a writer of more than average ability and his letters are
particularly good, but their effect is spoiled by the way in
which they were used or misused.

As a source of information on Hay and on America between
1850 and 1905 the book is very valuable. We get glimpses of
Horace Greeley, Henry Adams, Carl Schurz, Whitelaw Reid,
and a host of other political and literary figures of Hay's time.
In Hay's letters and diaries of the Civil War we get an amaz-
ingly human picture of Lincoln, for Hay lived in the White
House from 1861 to 1865. We are told much about the writing of the Lincoln book, some of which has been used in the
chapter on Lincoln in this study. We get a certain impression
of John Hay, his life and work, but we do not know him
completely, for no man has so little trouble with himself or
others as Hay has in the *Life and Letters of John Hay*.

*The Life and Times of Stephen Girard, Mariner and Mer-
chant* (1918) is the last important biography of the period,
and it is important chiefly for what it failed to do. This life,
by Professor John Bach McMaster, one of the leading American historians, is an historical and impersonal biography of
the first American merchant prince. There is entirely too
much history in the two volumes, and McMaster's effort to be
impersonal resulted in a book about Stephen Girard; he never
comes to life and it is almost impossible to imagine him as
ever having been alive. Scientific historians are seldom successful biographers, but this is an unusual case, for the author
wrote one of the most lively, fascinating, and interesting histories of the United States that we have. The biography is a
mine of information on Girard and on the American and
European history of his time. Even though McMaster had
been able to show us Girard as he really was, the excess of
history would have obscured the picture.

These last two biographies are examples of serious faults

in life-writing. They show that a biographer must try to be truthful above all, that he must have his material in a definite form, and that he cannot succeed unless he has not only opinions regarding his subject but feelings. There can be no purely scientific life-writing.

Emerson's *Journals* were published in ten volumes in 1909–1914. In Oscar Firkins' *Ralph Waldo Emerson* (1915), the *Journals* were used as biographical source material for the first time. There is so much of the real Emerson in the journals that they intensify and vivify the physical and the mental man. Mr. Firkins made excellent use of this new material, presenting Emerson in a new light. The book would have been much better if the author had adhered less strictly to the methods of conventional biography.

The majority of the biographies that have been discussed in the preceding pages give little evidence of the revolution that was so soon to change the trend of life-writing from the commemorative, the eulogistic, and the appreciative biography to the psychological, the psychoanalytical, and finally the best of modern biography as it is today.

PART II

V

THE BIOGRAPHERS' LINCOLN

ABRAHAM LINCOLN has been the subject of more biographies than any other man in the United States. They began with his nomination for the Presidency in 1860 and have continued to appear, and more will be written in the future. This "simple" man had so many sides to his character that he is an almost inexhaustible subject. The great majority of the Lincoln literature is not biographical in any sense of the word; much of it is not literature. There are, however, some thirty books which attempt to tell the story of his life, and it is the purpose of the present chapter to examine these books for the purpose of ascertaining their truths or falsehoods and their qualities as biographical literature.

Every life of Lincoln written before his death was based on material written by himself. As early as 1850, Lincoln had aspirations for the Presidency, and he had friends who were constantly and quietly working for him. His name was offered for the Vice-Presidency in the first Republican convention at Philadelphia in 1856. This gave added impetus to his ambition, and for the next four years the quiet campaign increased in range and intensity. He entered the senatorial campaign against Stephen A. Douglas in 1858 hoping to defeat Douglas, but willing to lose the seat in the Senate if he could strengthen his position as the Republican candidate for the Presidency in 1860. He was defeated in 1858 and he did strengthen his position for the battle of 1860. Late in 1859 one of his political friends, Jesse W. Fell of Illinois, persuaded him to prepare a sketch of his life for campaign purposes. This autobiography became the basis for the first campaign biographies that appeared.

When Lincoln was nominated at Chicago in 1860 no one knew anything about him. The original campaign sketch was used by Republican editors throughout the country. It did not satisfy John L. Scripps, editor of the Chicago *Tribune,* and he asked Lincoln to prepare another sketch. This second account is about three times as long as the first and was written in the third person. From it Scripps prepared a campaign biography, *Life of Abraham Lincoln. Tribune Tract, No. 6, 1860.* This material formed the basis for numerous lives which appeared immediately in Chicago, New York, and Boston. It likewise served as the source of all the biographies that appeared during the campaign of 1864.

Among the biographies of 1860 was the *Life and Speeches of Abraham Lincoln and Hannibal Hamlin* by William Dean Howells, later to become a famous novelist. At this time Mr. Howells was a reporter on the *Columbus State Journal* at Columbus, Ohio. He was commissioned to write the biography and, having no inclination to go to Springfield himself, he sent James Q. Howard to collect the material which he fashioned into a book. The life of Hamlin was written for this book by John L. Hayes. Howells' book was a good one as campaign lives go. It has added importance in that it was Howells' first published book, and he was rewarded for it by an appointment to the consulship at Venice, an office which he held for nearly five years. The many campaign lives of 1860 and 1864 are of no value, as biography, because they were purely political and were based on Lincoln's own material. Lincoln's death let loose a veritable flood of printed matter. The death of every public man in the United States is the occasion for numerous memoirs, eulogies, and biographies; we generally pay that homage to the dead which we denied to the living. This was particularly true in Lincoln's case. During the Civil War, he received at least as much condemnation as praise. His assassination opened the flood gates of hysteria and almost every literary hack turned out a "life." There were literally dozens of these lives, and they can be classified and judged in the light of their titles: *The Life and Martyrdom of Abraham Lincoln, The Martyr President, The Rail Splitter Who Became President,* etc.

There are at least three books that appeared during 1865

which deserve mention. One is the *Life of Abraham Lincoln* by Joseph H. Barrett. The author did not know Lincoln, but he admired him and collected all the available information concerning him. Barrett continued to publish books on Lincoln for more than forty years, and his researches were of considerable value to later biographers. This year also produced the first life of Lincoln by a woman, Phoebe A. C. Hanaford. Her book, *Abraham Lincoln, His Life and Public Services,* is nothing more than a fervid appreciation. In her treatment of Lincoln's mother, Mrs. Hanaford contributed a problem which has harassed many later biographers. She made Nancy Hanks a veritable saint, and by attributing almost divine powers to Lincoln gave his mother a position just a step below that of the Virgin. It was in this fashion that the life of Lincoln became so encrusted with legend that the excavations of the twentieth century have penetrated the surface only with great difficulty. The third important book of the year was Henry J. Raymond's *Life and Public Services of Abraham Lincoln;* . . . Mr. Raymond, the editor of the New York *Times,* was one of the most prominent Republicans in the country. He knew Lincoln during the years of the war and, as a trained journalist, carefully observed Lincoln during his many conferences with him in Washington. It was on this material that Raymond based his book. It really is not a biography at all—very little is said of Lincoln's life previous to his election—but Raymond did attempt a character study of the man as he knew him. The second volume of the work is filled entirely with speeches and correspondence. The books mentioned added very little to our knowledge of Lincoln and even less to the literature of biography, but Barrett and Raymond were at least pointing toward better things.

2

Josiah G. Holland published the first important early biography of Lincoln in 1866. Holland was an associate editor of the Springfield (Mass.) *Republican,* and something of a poet

and man of letters generally. An admirer of Lincoln, he decided to write a biography of the late President. He had not
known Lincoln, and he was not a politician; consequently, he
was able to approach the subject with a fairly open mind. He
went to Illinois and traveled over some of the Lincoln country. He interviewed William H. Herndon, Lincoln's law
partner, and secured a great deal of information from him
as well as from others. He returned to Massachusetts and
quickly wrote his *Life of Abraham Lincoln*. It is the first
serious attempt at an account and appraisal of Lincoln's life,
actions, and character. It is a simple narrative with no attempt
at interpretation. Holland frankly admits his admiration for
Lincoln, and that admiration is manifest, but not unduly,
throughout the book. The very nature of the book prevents
any extensive criticism of it, but it does contain one point of
view which has been the subject of fierce controversy among
later biographers. According to Holland's picture, Lincoln
was a Christian gentleman. Later biographers have proved
that he was neither a Christian nor a gentleman in the common meaning of these terms. We shall have occasion to mention these controversial problems in discussing some of the
later lives. Holland added a great deal to the legendary Lincoln, and he also gave us a good contemporary biography
written from the eastern point of view.

One of Lincoln's contemporaries in Illinois published a life
of the President in 1866. *The History of Abraham Lincoln
and the Overthrow of Slavery,* by Isaac N. Arnold, is the
first of a number of books on Lincoln which Arnold wrote.
He was a Chicago lawyer, a friend and admirer of Lincoln,
and an abolitionist. He had been a congressman during the
Civil War and was one of Lincoln's few loyal supporters in
the House. His first book was largely political and is colored
by his abolitionist views. His second book, *Sketch of the Life
of Abraham Lincoln* (1869), is more of a biography, and his
third book, *The Life of Abraham Lincoln* (1885), is a distinct
contribution to Lincoln biography. Arnold did not attempt
to present an orthodox view of Lincoln; he tried to tell the

story of Lincoln's life and career as he knew it. This book can be relied on as far as it goes.

Isaac Arnold was not a close friend of Lincoln; he was an admirer who collected Lincoln material for years after the latter's death. The next biographer was an intimate friend and special partner of Lincoln. He was with him for weeks on the circuit in Illinois, and he was an almost daily companion in the Washington years. Ward Hill Lamon was an Illinois lawyer slightly younger than Lincoln. He regularly traveled the circuit with him, was associated with him in many cases, and had a working agreement with the firm of Lincoln and Herndon which gave him the status of a special or limited partner. These intimate contacts had given Lamon an insight into Lincoln's life and character which no previous biographer had enjoyed. Shortly after Lincoln's first inauguration Lamon was made U. S. Marshal of the District of Columbia. In this office he was responsible for the maintenance of peace in the District, and also for Lincoln's personal safety until that responsibility was assumed by the War Department. Therefore, Lamon had an opportunity to see and study Lincoln at close range during the most important years of his life. Lamon was a man of intelligence and ability, and there is no reason to doubt his sincerity in regard to Lincoln and his friendship for him.

After Lincoln's death Lamon returned to Illinois and the practice of law. In all probability he read or saw some of the many books on Lincoln which were being published, and it is only natural to suppose that he thought of writing a life of him. He was on the ground; he had an intimate knowledge of the public and private life of Lincoln; and he was in a position to clear up many matters in connection with Lincoln's life in Illinois which were being misrepresented by his eulogists, apologists, and defenders.

It appears that Holland's book finally roused Lamon to action. He considered that it presented a false picture of Lincoln, and he decided to write a truthful biography. He began to collect material and put his own knowledge into concrete form. He purchased some of Herndon's papers to fill in the gaps in his own material. Lamon did not write the book which bears his name; he turned over his material to Chauncey F. Black, who did the actual composition under Lamon's supervision. The reason for Lamon's action has never been discovered; he may have felt unequal to the task of writing, or have been physically unable to do the work. However, he did assume complete responsibility for the book.

The Life of Abraham Lincoln; From His Birth to His Inauguration as President, was published in Boston in 1872. Its primary purpose was to controvert Holland's interpretation of Lincoln. It accomplished that purpose to the extent that it raised a storm of protest throughout the country, a storm that had its center in Springfield, Illinois. The spotless life of the national hero was besmirched by the touch of humanity; the god had feet of clay. Lamon had portrayed Lincoln as an ordinary Illinois country lawyer, a friendly, kindly man, a man who loved to tell stories which had their origin in the soil and their point in the fallible nature of man. He presented a man who was shrewder than his fellows, a born politician, a man eager for place and power. And finally, he showed a man who, in many of his personal habits, was anything but a gentleman, as we commonly understand the term; who, in Lamon's hearing, had repeatedly questioned the truth of the Bible and orthodox Christianity.

Lamon had intended to publish a second volume covering Lincoln's years in the Presidency, but the righteous publishers in Boston would have nothing more to do with the work, and the second volume was never published. The financial failure of the first volume had something to do with the publishers' decision as to the second volume. Many years later (1895), Lamon's daughter, Dorothy Lamon Treillard, edited the *Recollections of Abraham Lincoln, 1847–1865,* which contained most of the material which Lamon had intended to publish in the second volume of the biography.

The man who did the actual writing of Lamon's book had a great deal to do with the unfavorable reception. Black did not like Lincoln and, although he wrote under Lamon's supervision and used some of Herndon's manuscripts, he gave an unfavorable aspect to Lincoln wherever possible. It is an easy matter for any writer, particularly a biographer, to turn source material to his own purpose.

Regardless of Black's implications, Lamon's book was the most important life of Lincoln that had been written up to that time. The book is based on an intimate knowledge of the subject and on original source material. It is an attempt to portray Lincoln as a man, a lawyer, a politician, a potential statesman, from the point of view of a personal friend and legal associate, who had known him intimately for thirteen years.

The Lincoln books continued to grow with the years, and nearly all of them were of the same type, uncritical eulogies based on second- or third-hand information. Subscription books were very popular between 1865 and 1900, and more than one subscription publisher and his agents made small fortunes hawking a "life" of the Great Emancipator through the country. It had an honored place on the parlor table along with the Bible. Occasionally such a book as William O. Stoddard's *Abraham Lincoln: A True Story of a Great Life* (1885) or J. R. Irelan's *The History of the Life, Administration and Times of Abraham Lincoln* (1888) broke through the cordon of legendary lore that was so rapidly gathering. While neither of these books was of great importance, they were vast improvements on the average life. Both contained too much history for good biography; both carried on the traditional point of view, but they did not raise too high the pedestal on which their hero stood. Both Stoddard and Irelan were professional writers; consequently, they kept their enthusiasm within bounds.

3

While the glorifiers were about their work of saving the republic and the Republican party through the instrumentality of Lincoln's life and death, a middle-aged lawyer of Springfield was collecting every possible scrap of information concerning Lincoln from his birth to his death. William H. Herndon knew Lincoln better, and knew more about him, than any other man of his day.

William H. Herndon had known Lincoln by sight and reputation from the time he was a boy. He had seen him piloting boats on the Sangamon River; they slept in the same room when Lincoln first moved from New Salem to Springfield; Herndon heard Lincoln speak on all occasions and on nearly every subject that would interest people *in Illinois;* as a young lawyer Herndon followed Lincoln's career very closely. Finally, in 1843, Lincoln asked Herndon to become his law partner, and the partnership continued until Lincoln's death. Herndon idolized Lincoln but never idealized him. They were constant companions for seventeen years except for Lincoln's absence on circuit and a period of two years when he was a congressman. Both men had a great deal of intellectual curiosity; they discussed man, life, philosophy, religion, and politics endlessly. As Lincoln grew older he spent more time in the law office than he did at home. He was frequently there at seven in the morning and at ten at night, and they would talk, talk, talk. It was only natural that Herndon should come to know a great deal about Lincoln, his family, his home life, and even his thoughts. Again, it was only natural that from this intimacy Herndon should draw inferences regarding Lincoln's life that are not capable of proof and that are not in line with the Lincoln legend.

During their active partnership, Herndon kept the books for the firm and filed all the papers, personal and legal, that came into the office. Lincoln refused to do office work; that was the reason for the dissolution of his earlier partnerships with Logan and Stuart. Between 1861 and 1865 the two men corresponded occasionally, and Herndon carefully kept Lincoln's letters. Immediately after Lincoln's death Herndon began to collect material from every possible source. He interviewed people in Illinois, Indiana, and Kentucky. He wrote to others who were farther away, and he secured copies of Lincoln's letters whenever he could. He delivered lectures on Lincoln's life, including his religious views and his love affair with Ann Rutledge. These last two lectures brought down the wrath of the righteous; again their heaven-sent hero and savior was being traduced. Herndon continued to collect his manuscripts with the idea of writing a biography. The years advanced and the material accumulated until he despaired of ever doing anything with it. He aided Holland and Arnold in their researches and sold some of his material to Lamon. It was Herndon's statements on Lincoln's religion that Lamon quoted in his book.

During the eighties a young graduate of Knox College, Jesse W. Weiks, settled in Springfield and soon came to know Herndon. By this time Herndon was an old man, and not a very successful one. He still continued to practise law, but he was interested primarily in farming. With Weiks's aid he put his vast accumulation of material in order, made further researches, and finally the book began to take shape largely under Weiks's hand, for Herndon was by now incapable of sustained literary labor. The book was a collaboration of Herndon's mind and judgment and Weiks's mind and hand. Finally, in 1889, there appeared in three small volumes, published by Bedford, Clark and Company of Chicago, *Abraham Lincoln: The True Story of a Great Life*, by William H. Herndon and Jesse W. Weiks. A later edition edited by Horace White was published in New York in 1892. This edition had a few slight changes in it; it was reprinted in 1928. In 1930 the original text was reprinted under the editorship of Paul M. Angle, Librarian of the Illinois State Historical Society, to whose introduction I am heavily indebted.

As is the case whenever an important book on a great man is published, Herndon's *Lincoln* had a varied reception. The newspapers and the religious and patriotic magazines literally screamed in rage. The book was "infamous" and "obscene"; every billingsgate term in the rich vocabularies of the editors was invoked. Why? Herndon had stripped away the legend that had accumulated, and had presented a man instead of the demigod that had been created by the subscription writers, professional panegyrists, and politicians. He said some things that sounded unpleasant; he characterized Lincoln as an infidel; he said that Lincoln had loved only one woman in his life, and that woman was Ann Rutledge; he said that Lincoln had agreed to marry Mary Todd on January 1, 1841, and that he failed to appear for the wedding; he said that Mary Todd married Lincoln in November 1842 to spite him rather than because she loved him. He said many other things about Lincoln that were at least as important as these, but the penny reviewers neglected to mention them.

Herndon's *Lincoln* practically closes with Lincoln's departure from Springfield in January 1861. This is further evidence of Herndon's good judgment in using facts. He had no knowledge of Lincoln's life as President, and he refused to accept hearsay evidence in this case. As has been stated, he heard from Lincoln occasionally, but he knew little of what Lincoln was doing, and he very wisely closed his book with the interruption of their personal relations. Had he gone to Washington with Lincoln—he could have had any position he desired—he would probably have changed his mind on some of the subjects he discussed in his book, for the Lincoln of 1865 was a very, very different man from the Lincoln of 1861.

The more intelligent reviews throughout the country, and particularly in the East, accepted the book for what it was, the most important biography of Lincoln that had appeared. They gave reasonable judgments on the various parts of the book, endorsing this feature and questioning that.

A careful reading of Herndon's *Lincoln* will show the method by which Herndon developed his subject. His material falls into three classes: (1) Herndon's own knowledge of Lincoln obtained from the subject himself; (2) facts that Herndon investigated and found to be true; (3) facts that he obtained from others and accepted as true, or from which he drew inferences which were sometimes correct and sometimes incorrect. The material in the first class can be accepted because later researches have proved it to be true, and because Herndon was an honest and intelligent man who tried to tell Lincoln's life as it actually was. Furthermore, Herndon's facts, which were based on Lincoln's own memory and conversation, must be accepted as true. The second class of material is nearly always correct, as later researches have shown; the only serious errors are those made by Herndon's correspondents. He accepted this material as correct because he believed the people whom he interviewed and with whom he corresponded to be honest. It is only when Herndon is theorizing or drawing inferences that he is likely to be wrong. He thought that he could read character from the face; consequently, he would jump to conclusions because of a favorable or unfavorable impression made upon him by an individual. He did not like Mrs. Lincoln; he thought that she was responsible for Lincoln's sadness and melancholy; consequently, he gives an unfavorable impression of her in his book.

Herndon's entire book might be analyzed on the basis outlined above, but the analysis would prove no more than has already been indicated. Every subsequent biographer of Lincoln has used Herndon as the basis of his book, but no biographer has accepted all of his conclusions. Every serious biography is the life of one man from the point of view of another; it frequently is as revelatory of the author as it is of the subject. Despite Herndon's prejudices, mistakes, and unreliable inferences, his book is the most important single contribution to our knowledge of Lincoln's life. It is a book which everyone interested, not only in Lincoln but in biography, must know, for it contains nearly all the good and bad points of biographical method.

One frequently comes across a copy of Herndon's *Lincoln* in "rare book" catalogues and almost as frequently one finds the word "suppressed" used in describing the item. The first edition (1889) was not suppressed; it simply did not sell: that is why the book is a rare item today. The good people of America would not have such an iconoclastic book on their shelves (perhaps shelf is a more accurate word), and the book became a publisher's remainder. The New York edition of 1892 contained a few changes to conform to the genteel tradition; the changes were insignificant, but the statement that there were changes was enough to quiet the American conscience.

Another book on Lincoln was in preparation during the years that Herndon was working on his biography. It was to be a much more ambitious book than Herndon's, but it added very little to our knowledge of Lincoln, the man.

John G. Nicolay and John Hay were Lincoln's private secretaries during his years in the White House. Both were natives of Illinois, and both were great admirers of Lincoln. Nicolay was a lawyer in Springfield, and Hay was a law student there, at the time of Lincoln's election. Lincoln asked Nicolay to serve immediately after his election, and Hay became a member of the official family a short time later. Both men lived in the White House during the war, and they saw Lincoln at all hours of the day and night. This very close contact increased their admiration and affection for Lincoln to the point where they sincerely loved the great man, and that love colored their later judgment.

They planned to write a life of Lincoln immediately after the war, but circumstances were such that many years passed before they were able to begin the work. The whole story of the writing of the book is admirably told in William Roscoe Thayer's *Life and Letters of John Hay* (1915); consequently, I shall not go into the details here. The work first appeared in a series of articles in the *Century Magazine,* running for nearly five years, 1885–1890. In 1890 the material, expanded and to a certain extent unified, appeared as a book, *Abraham Lincoln, A History*.

The subtitle exactly describes the work; it is a history and not a biography. The ten volumes contain the history of the Civil War with Lincoln the dominant figure. The biographical parts of the history leave much to be desired. The reasons for this are numerous. In the first place, Lincoln was a hero to Nicolay and Hay, and they could see nothing wrong in the man and his acts either before or during the Presidency. Holding this point of view, they naturally told the story of his early life in the conventional form, omitting all controversy and all facts which did not contribute to the creation of the heroic figure. If we had only Nicolay's and Hay's account, we should be forced to the conclusion that Lincoln won the war almost unaided. This interpretation merely increased the heroic stature of the legendary Lincoln.

Even though Nicolay and Hay had wanted to present a true picture of Lincoln they could not have done so, for they did not have a free hand. The Lincoln papers were in possession of Robert T. Lincoln, the President's oldest son. By 1885 Mr. Lincoln had become a wealthy and prominent man, and he did not want the whole story told; he was particularly sensitive regarding his ancestors. For these and other reasons he compelled the authors to submit their manuscripts to him before publication, and he definitely decided what was and what was not to be in the book. Restrictions of this kind will prevent any biographer from doing good work; in this particular case they were fatal. *Abraham Lincoln, A History* presents a Lincoln minus the warts and the wrinkles, a Lincoln who is declaimed on his birthday, a Lincoln whom the subject would be the first to repudiate. On the other hand, the book is invaluable as a first-hand account of the war and what was going on behind the scenes in Washington. The authors had a free hand with the war chapters, and had they wished or been allowed to be as free in the narration of Lincoln's life, the book would be a much greater and finer work than it is.

There was one other biography of Lincoln published before 1900 which is worthy of consideration. In 1893 John T. Morse, Jr. published *Abraham Lincoln* as a unit in the "American Statesmen Series." Comparatively, this is a small book in two duodecimo volumes. The biography had to conform to the plan of the series of which Mr. Morse was the general editor. Even within its limits this is one of the best biographies of Lincoln that we have. It combines the personal, political, and historical phases of the subject without giving undue emphasis to any one of the three. Mr. Morse, as a professional biographer, merely used the material then in existence, giving it his own interpretation. He seems to have followed Herndon to a greater extent than any other biographer had done, and he used the material carefully. Morse's book is one of the few lives of Lincoln which give a complete record of his life. Not only is it complete, but the account of the war years is a connected narrative rather than a series of essays on various aspects of Lincoln and the war. This is something which no previous biographer had done and which few future biographers were to do. In this respect alone the book is valuable; furthermore, it is well balanced, and nicely attuned in judgment.

4

Morse's *Abraham Lincoln* is the last important life that was written in the nineteenth century. By the end of the century, the Lincoln literature had become enormous. There were books on his soul and his body, on his politics and his religion, on his genius and his scholarship, on his statesmanship and his "simple" greatness.

These books, with the few stated exceptions, created and maintained the myth and legend surrounding Lincoln. They were read by millions, who believed every word of them. Lincoln was the greatest man in the world; he had been born in dire poverty; he had secured an education despite almost insurmountable obstacles; he had been at the same time the simple country lawyer and the greatest living statesman from the time he attained his majority. Many of these books were written by hero-worshipers, fanatics, and hack writers, but most of them were inspired if not written by politicians. Lincoln became, not the hero of the Republican party, but its salvation. It achieved power with his election, power which it lost only twice, in 1884 and in 1892, between 1865 and 1912. There is little wonder that he was extolled and worshiped by the leaders and paid propagandists of his party; he could still make votes. On the other hand, it is almost inconceivable that three generations of Americans could be made to swallow the misrepresentations and lies that were issued in the form of biographies and histories. Lamon's book was a failure; Herndon was execrated as an iconoclast and an atheist. These men told the truth about Lincoln as they knew it, and their only faults were bad taste and an occasional long-drawn inference not warranted by the facts. Both the men and their books were ignored, and we must come to the conclusion that they were ignored intentionally by historians and biographers because the truth did not suit their purposes.

There is little to be said on the literary side for any of the books that have been discussed thus far. They were written in respectable English with no pretense to style or polish. Some of them are badly arranged as regards continuity; others are padded because agents had to have big books to sell. Morse's book is the most distinguished piece of writing on Lincoln that we have in the nineteenth century. His conciseness was made necessary by the nature of the series for which he was writing; his literary style was the result of experience and care.

5

The last decade of the nineteenth century received the backwash of the scandals which had inundated the country for thirty years before. The result was that every important movement and every important man of the last half of the nineteenth century was investigated in this and the next decade. To this period Theodore Roosevelt applied the ill-suited term, "muckraking era." The epithet was unfortunate because it carried with it a totally wrong idea of the purpose behind the investigations. They were prosecuted not merely to revive old scandals but to get at the truth of them and remove the cause.

Samuel S. McClure, the genius of the modern American magazine, was the moving spirit of these investigations. He came to the conclusion that the time had come to collect all the information obtainable concerning Lincoln from those who had been his contemporaries. The result would be a scientific account of Lincoln's career. To this end he gave Miss Ida Tarbell an unlimited assignment to prepare articles on Lincoln for *McClure's Magazine,* based on first-hand investigation. Miss Tarbell had written biographies of Napoleon and Madame Roland; therefore, her experience in biographical research was fairly extensive. Her search for material extended over a period of several years. She visited the scenes of Lincoln's life in Kentucky, Indiana, and Illinois; she corresponded with practically every person who had known him at any period; she published requests for information, letters, and manuscripts which would be of help in the preparation of her biography. In this way she collected a vast amount of material before she began to write the articles. The first series was published during 1895–1896; the second during 1898–1899. The material was supplemented and, to a certain extent, rewritten for book publication.

Miss Tarbell's *Life of Abraham Lincoln, Drawn from Original Sources and Containing Many Speeches, Letters and Telegrams Hitherto Unpublished,* appeared in 1900. It was the first attempt at a documented life of Lincoln. Naturally she used everything that had been published previously, but she relied principally on her own findings. Her method was an excellent one, but later investigators have found that some of her sources were not reliable. Regardless of this fact, she has a very important place among the modern biographers of Lincoln. She did what she could to tear away the mists of legend. She showed that Lincoln's father was not the shiftless, illiterate poor-white of the nineteenth-century biographies. Thomas Lincoln had been written down for the purpose of making his son greater by contrast. Miss Tarbell also pointed out that Lincoln was not the poverty-stricken child of legend; he was merely the child of his time and place. Millions of pioneer children had been reared as Lincoln was; he and they always had enough to eat and to wear, though the food was plain and the clothing homespun and homemade. His environment was as good as any frontier environment, and his opportunities no fewer than those of others in the same situation of life.

As Miss Tarbell moves into the period of Lincoln's maturity her evidence makes obvious the fact that Lincoln was a born policitian, that he played politics early and late, and that he did not appear suddenly as the Moses of the Republican party ready to lead it into the Promised Land. She casts doubt on Herndon's story that Lincoln failed to appear for his marriage to Mary Todd, January 1, 1841, by showing that no one in Springfield was aware of the intended marriage.

The instances pointed out indicate Miss Tarbell's methods and results. She gradually develops Lincoln's story to the end of the first period of his life, his election to the Presidency, substantiating her findings by documentary proof. Of course, the author could have gone farther in search of proofs, but she was a journalist engaged on a definite assignment which could not be prolonged indefinitely. The first part of her narrative is, with one or two exceptions, more accurate than any that had been published up to that time.

Miss Tarbell's account of Lincoln as President is not so complete or so unified as the first part of the book. It is a series of essays rather than a connected story of the life of Lincoln during the Civil War. Later biographers have had little more success with this period than Miss Tarbell. They either lose Lincoln in the history of the war or give us a series of disconnected accounts of his activities.

Miss Tarbell performed an inestimable service in publishing her life of Lincoln. She opened the entire subject to scientific investigation, proving the necessity of research into almost every act of Lincoln. She clarified many obscurities and suggested the lines on which later men would work. She destroyed the traditional Lincoln and built up the outlines of the man as he really was. As a contribution to the literature of biography, Miss Tarbell's book is of secondary importance; as a milestone on the path to a better understanding and interpretation of Lincoln the value of this book can hardly be overestimated.

6

There may have been just as many books written to belittle Lincoln as there were to praise and, later, to understand him. If there were, they have been successfully concealed, for I have been able to find only two books in the early period which are definitely hostile to Lincoln. *Truth is Stranger than Fiction; the True Genesis of a Wonderful Man* by J. H. Cathey, was published in Atlanta, Georgia, in 1899 and reprinted as *The Genius of Lincoln* in 1904. This book is based on a story that survived for many years to the effect that Lincoln was the natural son of a wealthy and cultured southern planter and that it was from his unknown father that he inherited the qualities that made him a great man. The falsity of this story has been definitely proved by Barton and Beveridge, but the story has persisted and may still be believed in some parts of the country. Stranger stories than this have been used for political purposes within the last ten years. In 1901 C. L. C. Minor published *The Real Lincoln,* which tells the same story with additional trimmings.

The twentieth century has produced almost as many lives of Lincoln as did the nineteenth, but the majority of them are of no importance in this discussion. A few, however, are notable for their value, interest, or unusual point of view. William Elroy Curtis' *The True Abraham Lincoln* (1903) is an excellent short biography, as are many of the other lives which were written for the series of "True Lives." The purpose of this book is to give a truthful, uncontroversial account of Lincoln's life. It pretends to no scholarship or original research; on the other hand it professes to be and is accurate and complete within its limits. In the same class with this is Brand Whitlock's *Abraham Lincoln* (1909) in the series of "Beacon Biographies." Written for the centenary of Lincoln's birth, this little book likewise disclaims originality. It is a simple retelling of Lincoln's story in the light of the latest investigations on the subject. Concise, charmingly written, and authoritative, it presents a sympathetic but not prejudiced picture of the man who was particularly the idol of Mr. Whitlock's generation in the Middle West. It is a contribution not only to the Lincoln literature but to the literature of biography.

It has been shown time and time again that a biographer can prove any point of view that he happens to take. He can so arrange and shade perfectly correct facts that any side of his subject may be made the dominant one. Denton J. Snider in his *Abraham Lincoln. An Interpretation* (1909) proves that Lincoln's character was formed by the great men whose lives he read and followed. When we realize that his principal biographical reading was Weems's *Life of Washington* and Eaton's *Life of Jackson,* augmented by parts of Plutarch, we may rightly question Mr. Snider's book. In T. A. Levy's *Lincoln the Politician* (1918) we have another thesis biography. In this interesting and, at times, incredible book we are shown how the Lincoln of, let us say, 1830 gradually developed those traits of national leadership which made him the leader of the North, not only in theory but in fact, from 1862 until his death. We can follow Mr. Levy very easily if, like him, we omit some of the steps in Lincoln's public career. Mr. Levy proves his case too, but his method is open to so much criticism that it is valuable only as an example of what should not be done if one wants to write a truthful book.

In 1922 Jesse W. Weik published *The Real Lincoln, a Portrait.* As will be recalled, Mr. Weik was Herndon's collaborator and amanuensis. In the years that followed the publication of Herndon's *Lincoln,* Weik continued to collect

Lincolniana until he had the most valuable collection of manuscripts in existence. From this vast material he developed a portrait of Lincoln in his private and domestic life which is invaluable. Very wisely, Mr. Weik did not stress the political and public side of Lincoln, because he was not so familiar with it. This book, admirable in conception and execution, is another of the major books on Lincoln. Its value is principally in its fidelity to realities, its avoidance of controversy, and its humanity.

Another biography of Lincoln appeared in the same year; a study which supplements Weik's book. In his *Lincoln; an Account of his Personal Life, Especially of its Springs of Action as Revealed and Deepened by the Ordeal of War,* Professor Nathaniel W. Stephenson presented a detailed character study of Lincoln. In addition to the literary quality of the book it is important because of the method which was adopted and successfully carried out. In the first place it presumes a knowledge of the facts of Lincoln's life, particularly the period before his election to the Presidency. Less than a fifth of the book concerns the latter period; the main part of it is concerned with the development of Lincoln's character as a man and a statesman from November 1860 to April 1865. We are shown the extent of Lincoln's ignorance of the actual condition of affairs in November 1860, his first attempt at conciliating the South, his groping and hesitancy during the first months of 1861. The author clearly demonstrates the terrible pressure that was brought to bear on Lincoln from all sides before inauguration and until April 14, 1861. Then we get an idea of the degree to which politics influenced, harassed, and bedeviled the weary man through 1861 and the early part of 1862. We see Lincoln's character changing, bending with the winds of politics and war until he finds himself, and from that time on we see the new, the great man emerging from the fiery ordeal. This book of Professor Stephenson's is one of the most important of all Lincoln biographies because it illuminates Lincoln in the period which few biographers have reached or handled successfully—the war years.

7

Rev. William E. Barton spent the majority of his adult years in the study of Lincoln. He knew more about Lincoln's ancestors, birth, and early life than any other man. At the time of his death he had one of the finest collections of Lincolniana in existence. Naturally Mr. Barton studied Lincoln's character, religion, and philosophy of life. We are not concerned with Barton's early books, *The Paternity of Abraham Lincoln* or *The Soul of Abraham Lincoln;* it is *The Life of Abraham Lincoln* (1925) that interests us.

He put into this book the study and researches of a lifetime; the result is one of the most important books on Lincoln that we have. Barton not only told the story of Lincoln's life, but he interpreted every phase of Lincoln as he understood it. We may not agree with his interpretations, but we must respect them because they are based on a thorough knowledge of the facts. Barton's judgment on Lincoln matters is nearly always correct, but he is more often wrong than right in regard to other men.

The method that Barton used in his life is a very effective one, particularly when the subject is as controversial as Lincoln is. He takes up one subject after another and traces it to a logical conclusion, and then dovetails another subject into the first and traces that. In this way, he disposes of Lincoln's ancestors, his early life, his early law career, his personal affairs in such a way that we have something definite and concrete on highly controversial matters. This is by no means the ideal method of writing biography, but it is suitable to this particular subject.

Mr. Barton's book is not easy reading; he had a vast amount of material and he used too much of it. He went into excessive detail regarding Lincoln's immediate and remote ancestors, quoting documents from, and conversations with, all sorts of people. He follows this method throughout the book with a consequent loss in narrative power which is not balanced by veracity. His reasons are very apparent; he had encountered so much falsehood regarding Lincoln that he determined not only to tell the truth but to prove it.

In many instances, Barton has said the last word on moot questions. No one can doubt Nancy Hanks's illegitimacy after going through the proof that Barton has marshaled, nor Barton's refutation of Herndon's story of the marriage that did not take place, for Barton proves that there is no record of a marriage license having been issued during the period covering January 1, 1841. In the same manner this indefatigable researcher tracks down fact after fact and either proves or disproves it or frankly states that the truth can never be known. No later biographer has added to Barton's facts, though others have arrived at different judgments.

Barton's second volume covering the last four years of Lincoln's life is less valuable than the first. Again there is the inability to achieve unity, and a similar inability to cope with the vastly extended horizon of the "man from Illinois." Barton treats every part as thoroughly as he can, but one is always conscious that each chapter is a separate essay. Even Lincoln disappears at times, and that is a cardinal sin of biography. The most valuable part of the second volume is Barton's account of the Gettysburg Address. Here he finally tracks down and refutes one of the most persistent of Lincoln myths, that the address was written on the train between Washington and Gettysburg.

One of the most remarkable features of this book is Barton's judgment on Edwin M. Stanton and Andrew Johnson. He persists in characterizing Johnson as a drunkard and as being generally unfit for the office to which he was elected. No intelligent man today accepts the Radical characterization of Johnson, not even the historians of the Reconstruction Era, most of whom have been Republicans. The only explanation for Barton's point of view is that he did not keep up with modern historical writing. The same explanation can be given for his attitude toward Stanton. In this book, Stanton is a hero and a much maligned man. The truth of the matter is that while Stanton was a most efficient Secretary of War, he was a tyrant and has been proved a traitor to Lincoln; his later treachery to Johnson is too obvious to need proof. These illustrations have been cited to show that Barton was so much interested in Lincoln that he failed to realize that more than a knowledge of Lincoln is necessary to interpret Lincoln.

As factual or narrative biography Barton's book is of great value; as interpretation it has serious limitations. It has added to our knowledge of Lincoln, but it is not a very valuable contribution to the literature of biography. Biographical literature as well as any other form of literature is something more than facts backed by proof, something more than interest in the subject, something more, even, than mere interpretation of character. That something is lacking in William E. Barton's *Life of Abraham Lincoln*.

Carl Sandburg was able to bring to the writing of *Abraham Lincoln: The Prairie Years* (1926), the imagination which Mr. Barton lacked. By imagination I do not mean that amazing ability to probe the thoughts and report the conversations of subjects in their graves long since; imagination in biography is the ability not only to understand and explain the subject, but the ability to live and move as the subject lived and moved. This is Mr. Sandburg's contribution to Lincolniana and the literature of biography.

Mr. Sandburg's method of writing biography is perhaps unique. He was born and reared in Illinois among the same group as that to which Lincoln belonged. He had heard of Lincoln from earliest childhood; he knew and talked to many people who had known Lincoln. He began to collect stories and anecdotes concerning this man who was not a hero to the people among whom he had lived; he was more, he was a man who had grown great. Year after year, Mr. Sandburg tells us, he collected material and thought about it. Finally, the time arrived when, steeped in Lincoln truth and fiction, he began to write.

It is in the presentation that Sandburg differs from most of Lincoln's biographers. He probably did as much research as Barton or Herndon or Weik; he probably weighed the controversial questions as carefully as any of the former writers did; but when he came to write, he put aside all the trappings of so-called scholarship and wrote his account of the "man from Illinois."

In the case of almost every previous biographer of Lincoln the reader is conscious of the fact that he is reading about a man; in Sandburg's book he lives with Lincoln because Sandburg had the ability to re-create Lincoln's life and carry his reader along with Lincoln and himself from Kentucky in February 1809 to Springfield, Illinois, in January 1861. There is no argument in this book, no refutation of previous facts, no theorizing, no footnotes or bristling appendices. Sandburg had finished with all these things before he began to write. The result is a narrative against a genuine background, a narrative which requires no interpretation on the part of the author because it is perfectly clear. The background is crowded with relatives, pioneers, country lawyers and politicians, women and children, courts, plaintiffs and defendants, everything and everybody that went into the making of the Lincoln of the prairie years.

The criticism has been made that the subject of this biography is Sandburg's Lincoln and not the real Lincoln. No two men see the same subject from the same point of view, and this is particularly true in the case of the honest biographer. From our previous knowledge of Lincoln we have no reason to suppose that Sandburg materially changed or invented the facts that he uses. He uses them in the light of his own judgment; from his knowledge of Lincoln, he decides whether or not such an incident is true. Thus, Sandburg accepts the story of the marriage that did not take place; he accepts it on the evidence that Lincoln's mind was in a turmoil for months after January 1, 1841, and because he feels that it is the sort of thing Lincoln might have done under stress of some great emotion. In every instance Sandburg has balanced facts against his knowledge of the man and has given us his results. He did not interpret Lincoln by poetic intuition; he interpreted him by sound knowledge and poetic imagination. Many people will question Mr. Sandburg's right to be considered a poet; many more will question his poetic treatment of Lincoln and his environment. No American biographer has more nearly approached the ideal of biography: the re-creation of the individual as he really was.

Sandburg accomplishes this much because he has not hesitated to put in the shadows as well as the light; the total exclusion of either of these phases of a man's life and character destroys the value of any biography. Furthermore, Sandburg took Lincoln just as far as he could see him clearly; when the latter left Springfield in 1861, the prairie years were in the past and Sandburg could no longer live with his subject. I do not know whether or not Mr. Sandburg plans to write of Lincoln in the White House; I do know that the method which makes *Abraham Lincoln: The Prairie Years* a great biography cannot be used in writing of the Abraham Lincoln of Washington.

8

Senator Albert J. Beveridge of Indiana spent the last seventeen years of his life in the composition of two great biographies, *Life of John Marshall* (1916–1919) and *Abraham Lincoln 1809–1858* (1928). Both biographies will receive consideration here because the writing of the first led to the writing of the second, and an explanation of his method in the first is almost necessary for a proper understanding of his method in the second. Taken together, they illustrate his development as a biographer.

When Beveridge was a young man reading law, he became interested in Marshall's career but could find no adequate biography; he promised himself that he would write a biography of Marshall if he ever had the opportunity. The opportunity came in 1910 when Beveridge was defeated for reëlection to the Senate. He began to investigate sources and collect materials, but political and personal affairs prevented any real work on the project for more than three years. In the beginning he thought he could tell the story in one volume; before he was finished he had four large volumes averaging nearly six hundred pages apiece. The first two volumes were published in 1916, the last two in 1919. A book of such length is not in keeping with modern ideas, but such was the quality of this book that it became a best seller and was awarded the Pulitzer Prize in biography for 1916. The judges certainly had no other choice.

The *Life of John Marshall* is the best legal biography that has been written in America, and will take rank with the best biographies in English literature. The greatness of the *Marshall* is in its thoroughness and in the conception of biography itself which Beveridge formulated and carried through. Mr. Claude Bowers in his *Beveridge and the Progressive Era* (1932) has given the whole story of Beveridge the biographer, as well as of Beveridge the politician, orator, and statesman. Beveridge came to the conclusion that the biography of such a public man as Marshall is a part of the epic of the nation, and as such must be placed in its proper setting. His book is plainly historical biography and he was successful, as few men are who attempt this form of biography, in keeping his subject always in the foreground. The *Life of John Marshall* is also the history of America from 1755 to 1835 as that history touched John Marshall; it not only touched him, rather he made a great deal of it between 1801 and 1835.

Beveridge read everything bearing on the period; he collected letters, manuscripts, law reports, everything that might have a bearing on Marshall. The completed work is a masterpiece of biographical, historical, and legal scholarship. It is very doubtful if anyone will ever add anything to our knowledge or understanding of the great Chief Justice of the

United States. The book is constructed like a piece of great architecture. Settled on a firm foundation of family and personal biography, Marshall strides through the Revolution, the early republic, to the Supreme Court and the decisions by which he was to make the Constitution something more than a "scrap of paper." Along with the public man we have the private lawyer, the genial gentleman, the father and husband. Nothing is omitted that will help us to see John Marshall as he really lived.

There is no question but that he is the ideal biographer who is absorbed in his subject. Beveridge was absorbed in this subject to an extent that blinded him at times. It can be said that Marshall's life could have been presented in half the space that Beveridge gave to it. He devoted four long chapters to the famous Virginia Convention of 1788 where Marshall was one of the leaders in the fight to ratify the Constitution. There is a long chapter on the French Revolution and its influence on America, and another long chapter on the assault on the judiciary at the time Marshall became chief justice. There are four more chapters on the famous Burr conspiracy trial at which Marshall presided. Beveridge defended these historical excursions on the ground that they were absolutely essential to a proper understanding of Marshall's political and legal positions. A strictly conventional definition of biography would exclude all the material mentioned above. It is true that Marshall's life could be told without it, but to remove it would remove some of the finest constitutional history that has been written in this country. Great books defy all rules.

The one serious fault in Beveridge's *Life of John Marshall* is political prejudice, and that is almost excusable. Born and reared in the Middle West, the son of a Union veteran, Beveridge was bound to be a Republican and he was one throughout his life, although his party allegiance was strained, if not broken, in the last years. Theoretically the Republicans were the lineal descendants of the Federalists, and Beveridge was writing of the greatest of all the Federalists. Furthermore, he made the founder of the Democratic party the villain of the piece. Early in the book Jefferson is the political opponent of Marshall and Beveridge; as the narrative develops he becomes Beveridge's personal enemy. This is decidedly unfair and mars an otherwise great book. I felt this prejudice when I first read the book, and the feeling increased on rereading. Beveridge's biographer, using Beveridge's own words, shows that he regretted the extremes to which he went in his condemnation of Jefferson.

There is another feature of Beveridge's first book that must be mentioned. He passed judgment on Marshall, Jefferson, and a hundred others who entered Marshall's life at one time or another. Beveridge here narrates an incident, marshals his evidence and then gives his own opinion. It must be admitted that in the vast majority of cases that opinion is honest and fair, and it is only in the case of Jefferson that he is definitely prejudiced.

Despite all that has been or may be stated regarding this book it is and will be the greatest legal biography in American literature. The style in which it is written is not particularly distinguished, but it is good writing. One is never in doubt as to Beveridge's meaning. He has a narrative power that is fascinating, even though it is a little heavy, and his ability to digest legal cases rises to positive genius. In those chapters on the Virginia Convention of 1788, on the Judiciary, on the Burr conspiracy trial, and frequently in those chapters dealing with the more important of Marshall's decisions, there is a swing, an intensity, even an emotional appeal that stamps Beveridge as a great writer in this particular field. As sometimes happens, biographer and subject met.

Beveridge's *Abraham Lincoln* is a magnificent fragment. The Senator died suddenly before he had completed the second volume. The publication of the book was undertaken by Worthington C. Ford, a distinguished historian and biographer and one of Mr. Beveridge's closest friends and associates.

Because of its unfinished state, *Abraham Lincoln* cannot

be properly evaluated. As far as it goes, it is the best formal account of Lincoln that we have. The narrative stops before the end of the year 1858. In its published form the book is divided into two parts, the personal and the political life of Lincoln. Beveridge had not made his general revision; consequently, the arrangement cannot be said to be his. I think that the final arrangement would have been similar to that of the Marshall biography, alternate sections of biographical and historical material.

When Beveridge had completed the *Life of John Marshall* he immediately began to think of another subject which he could treat in the same way and which would continue his political epic of America. Many of his friends advised him to write a biography of Roger Taney, Marshall's successor as Chief Justice of the United States. Beveridge rejected this subject for two reasons: he did not and could not have the interest in Taney that he had had in Marshall and, as Taney had been a Democrat in politics, Beveridge felt that he could not do justice to a man whose political principles were the very opposite of his own. Lincoln was Beveridge's choice because he felt that Lincoln had carried on the principles of Federalism and because he naturally admired the great man from the Middle West.

The account that Mr. Bowers has given us in his *Beveridge and the Progressive Era,* largely in Beveridge's own words, of the latter's studies for his Lincoln book and their results, is one of the most amazing stories in the annals of biographical research. The last three chapters of Mr. Bowers' book should be read by every student of biographical literature.

Senator Beveridge had the usual legendary conception of Lincoln when he began his researches. Here was a man who had been a leader in the national politics of the Republican party, a college graduate, a lawyer, and a leader of the progressive movement in American politics, and he was totally ignorant of the history of the country which he was trying to influence and of the party which he was trying to reform. He had a totally false conception of the man who had placed the Republican party in power and whose death and resurrection in legend had kept it there. It is incredible that such a condition could exist in 1920; it is also true.

Beveridge was amazed, bewildered, shocked as he plodded his weary way through the books, manuscripts, and newspapers which told Lincoln's true story. No one knew the true Lincoln; no one had even tried to present him; perhaps no one could tell the truth about this most enigmatical man. These and many other cries of despair came from Beveridge as he worked in Washington and pored over old newspapers in Springfield, Illinois. He had found a Lincoln of Illinois who bore no more resemblance to the Lincoln in Washington from 1862 onward than a caterpillar does to a butterfly. He had found a Stephen A. Douglas who was anything and everything but the Mephistopheles that had been painted by the wavers of the "bloody shirt" and the subsidized literary men of the Grand Old Party. He was sick and disgusted with the lies that had been broadcast by the so-called biographers and historians. Mr. Bowers' last chapters merely confirm what is very apparent in the text and notes of Beveridge's book.

This revelation entirely changed the nature of Beveridge's *Abraham Lincoln*. As we have it, it is the most complete collection of facts of Lincoln's life to 1858 that has been or will be written. He went into all the evidence and weighed that evidence in the scales of legal training. With all the evidence in, Beveridge accepted Herndon and the Weik manuscripts in almost every instance where there was a diversion of authority. The longer he worked the firmer became his conviction that Herndon's had been the only true account. So completely did he believe in Herndon that he even accepted the latter's version of the wedding that did not take place and his interpretation of Mrs. Lincoln and the home life of the Lincolns. After all, such things are matters of individual judgment.

When Beveridge came to the actual writing of *Abraham Lincoln* he must have realized that he could do only one thing; relate the facts and stop there. That is what he did; he gave us a factual account that surpasses any previous attempt. He did not need to explain or interpret his facts; they speak for themselves. He could not follow the method that he developed in Marshall; he had the courage but not the heart. Beveridge's personal and political feelings affected this book even more than they affected the *Life of John Marshall*. His political feelings prevented him from passing judgment on the Lincoln of, let us say, 1835–1860; his personal feelings prevented him from judging many of Lincoln's acts during the same period. On the other hand, he went much farther in his statement of facts than Herndon did, and then allowed those facts to speak for themselves.

Beveridge's *Abraham Lincoln, 1809–1858*, has superseded every factual biography that preceded it. He told the truth even if he did not tell all of it. It is impossible to theorize concerning the unwritten, but we can certainly believe that he would have illuminated the last seven years as no other man had done or perhaps will do. He would have studied President Lincoln as carefully as he studied Assemblyman Lincoln, Congressman Lincoln, Lawyer Lincoln, Mr. Lincoln. Maybe it is idle to talk of what might have been, but one cannot help regretting that Senator Beveridge was not able to complete his task.

9

It would seem that Senator Beveridge set forth all the facts of the early life of Lincoln and that later biographers will be interpreters rather than narrators. There are unplumbed depths in his later life, but they will be developed through character analysis rather than through new facts. Biographers have already begun to present Lincoln in the light of the facts of his life rather than through the facts. Raymond Holden's *Abraham Lincoln: The Politician and the Man* attempts such an evaluation of Lincoln. Mr. Holden's purpose was to show the gradual evolution of the ambitious politician into the great man and statesman. Using the facts at his disposal, the author builds up his character step by step, and when we come to the end of the book we know that we are in the presence of a great man, of a man who had potential greatness in him, potential greatness which pain and suffering and war brought to maturity. If one compares this book with any of the eulogistic rhapsodies that have been mentioned he will see how much more truthful such a book as this is and how much greater Lincoln is when he is stripped of legend.

This book of Mr. Holden's is admirable of its kind. Written for a series of popular biographies it is necessarily limited in its scope, but the desired effect is obtained. Based on sound sources and scholarship, written in a plain, smooth style, this book is one of the sanest and most truthful books that have been written on Lincoln.

We have already observed that a writer with a thesis, a prejudice—call it what you will—can so use facts that they will support his argument. This is strikingly illustrated in Edgar Lee Masters' *Lincoln, the Man*. When the book was first published, it created a terrific furor which was really only a tempest in a teapot. It has come to have one thing in common with Herndon's *Lincoln*, senseless abuse by the public. Within a day or two of its publication the "patriotic" pack was in full cry. The newspapers screamed their abuse; patriotic societies condemned it—unread; bookstores announced that they would not pollute their shelves with such foul carrion. What was the result? The book went into five printings in the month of its publication; it became the book of the day; it was supposed to be scandalous and the story of the scandal grew because few stopped to read the book; they read the reviews.

The truth of the matter is that Mr. Masters' book is simply an interpretation of Lincoln from a particular point of view. It is the judgment of one who is a southern Democrat, an unreconstructed rebel, although he was born, reared, and still lives in Illinois. The author believes that Lincoln did more harm than good; that he enslaved more people than he freed. This point of view may be wrong; in the opinion of many it is wrong, but it is entitled to an intelligent and critical reply. Waving the flag and the "bloody shirt" will not answer here; mature judgment must answer mature judgment.

Mr. Masters based his book on the most authoritative sources we have, Beveridge and Herndon. He disclaimed any attempt to present new facts; the novelty of the book is its interpretation of the facts. By skilful grouping, emphasis, and interpretation, Masters develops a Lincoln who was crafty in politics, a little dishonest and wholly opportunistic. He points out that Lincoln did not follow, as President, the principles which he laid down as candidate; that he advocated democracy and practised dictatorship; that he posed as a friend of the people and forgot them in Washington. All this and much more are developed in *Lincoln, the Man*. Mr. Masters' final judgment is that Lincoln was a selfish politician devoid of genuine principle and that he has no claim to the position which has been accorded him among the nation's great men. Again I say that this is one man's point of view which he has a right to adopt if he can maintain it. Mr. Masters' does not maintain it; he does not treat Lincoln fairly; and when he is not on solid ground he becomes hysterical. Hysteria of hatred is worse than hysteria of ecstasy; Masters' book falls to pieces before it ends. It is only another anti-Lincoln book which time will place properly.

In 1931 there appeared *Abraham Lincoln: a New Portrait*, by Emanuel Hertz. The first volume is made up of a series of essays; the second volume contains an undigested mass of source material. Mr. Hertz has added nothing to the biographical literature of Lincoln; the second volume, which I have not examined very carefully, may contain material of value to future biographers.

Don C. Seitz's *Lincoln, the Politician* (1931) is a new working of old material. It is an important book for the reason that it gives a complete and unified picture of Lincoln the politician, and politics were always uppermost in Lincoln's mind. It is a solid, well-written book and a valuable contribution to Lincolniana.

One of the late books on Lincoln, by an American, is William E. Lilly's *Set My People Free; a Negro's Life of Lincoln* (1932). The book is disappointing in the sense that it offers no new point of view. It seems to me that the Negro should have an impression different from that of the white man, that he should be able to illuminate his picture of Lincoln with some of the imagination and drama that represents the Negro's contribution to American literature. Perhaps I expected too much; perhaps Mr. Lilly wished to avoid anything that savored of the "new" biography. At all events, *Set My People Free* is just another life of Lincoln.

Two lives of Lincoln were published in 1933, Barton's *President Lincoln* in two volumes and Leon P. Clark's *Lincoln; a Psycho-Biography*. Neither has much historical or biographical importance. The Reverend Mr. Barton's book is not a life of President Lincoln, as he intended it to be. The last three chapters were left unfinished at his death and were completed by William H. Townsend, but this does not affect the book in any way. In the first place, *President Lincoln* is more history than biography. Secondly, it opens in 1858, a date much too early for a study of Lincoln as President. Barton, like every other biographer of Lincoln in Washington, seems to have been unable to unify his material. Lincoln appears only at intervals when Barton is not trying to describe or explain some phase of the war, at home or abroad. Barton was not a military or any other kind of historian; consequently, the book is almost a complete failure. In my opinion, it is less valuable than the second volume of the *Life of Abraham Lincoln* (1925).

The type of biography which Dr. Clark has given us had to come. His method of treating his subject is, of course, new in Lincoln biography, but it does not settle anything. According to Dr. Clark, Lincoln had a mother-love fixation, and this theory is used to explain the whole of Lincoln's life. He was attracted to older women because of it, and yet Ann Rutledge, a girl much younger than he, was the real love of his life. His moods, his melancholia, his inability to make decisions in early life, all these phases of his life and many others are explained by Dr. Clark on the basis of his original theory. This may be true, but it does not provide a satisfactory explanation of Lincoln's character for us.

We have come to the end of our survey of Lincoln as seen by his American biographers. We have seen the truth and the fiction develop side by side, with the latter dominant, for almost sixty years. But the real man has been developing under the hands of Lamon, Herndon, Stephenson, and Beveridge, and we are now in possession of most of the truthful facts of his life. There is little left to investigate in the early periods, but we still lack an adequate treatment of Lincoln as President. We can only hope for another Beveridge to complete the picture. Biographies of Lincoln will continue to appear; he will be reinterpreted, perhaps psychoanalyzed; we shall have more of the Masters type of book. Whatever we may have in the future, we can be certain that neither additional facts nor carping biographers can alter the position that rightfully belongs to Lincoln, a position equal to that of Washington.

Lincoln was always fond of Shakespeare, and *Macbeth* was perhaps his favorite play. That passage in *Macbeth* which he most frequently read aloud applies to the biographers' Lincoln as truly as it did to Lincoln in life:

> Duncan is in his grave;
> After life's fitful fever he sleeps well;
> Treason has done its worst: nor steel nor poison,
> Malice domestic, foreign levy, nothing
> Can touch him further.

10

Herndon's *Lincoln* gave a prominence, perhaps we should say a notoriety, to Mrs. Lincoln beyond that of the wife of any other President. She has been the subject of fierce controversy, of attack and defense; she has been the stumbling block in the path of more than one biographer. Her presence colored Nicolay and Hay's book; it prevented Senator Beveridge from getting permission to use the Lincoln manuscripts in the possession of her oldest son, Robert T. Lincoln.

In the last four years four books on Mrs. Lincoln have appeared; it is a question whether or not any one of them is, strictly speaking, a biography. Katherine Helm, the author of *Mary, Wife of Lincoln* (1928) is a niece of Mrs. Lincoln's, and the book is typical of family biographies. Honoré W. Morrow's *Mary Todd Lincoln; an Appreciation of the Wife of Abraham Lincoln* (1928) is more in the nature of an apology than is Mrs. Helm's book. Furthermore, Mrs. Morrow's book is a combination of fact and fiction, a combination which is fatal to true biography. *Mrs. Abraham Lincoln. A Study of her Personality and her Influence on Lincoln* (1932) by Dr. William A. Evans is a consideration of Mrs. Lincoln from a medical point of view, which is perhaps the only proper basis for an understanding of her life. Carl Sandburg's *Mary Lincoln; Wife and Widow* with a collection of letters edited by Paul M. Angle, is the latest contribution to a subject which will probably continue to grow.

VI

WASHINGTON: FALSE AND REAL

THERE have not been so many biographies of Washington as of Lincoln, but the myths and legends surrounding Washington were more numerous and tenacious than those which enveloped Lincoln. Washington was a hero long before his death; to the majority of people Lincoln was not. If we exclude a few radical Republicans and disappointed office seekers, Washington was loved and respected by the entire country in 1799; Lincoln had not the love, confidence, or even respect of a majority of the people in the North at the time of his death.

There was, of course, only one Washington as there was only one Lincoln, but Lincoln had such a complex character that even all modern biographers have not succeeded in giving us the whole man as he was. The real Washington has readily appeared under the hands of intelligent biographers, though not all of his modern biographers have succeeded in portraying him as he was. Most of his early biographers made him either a godlike genius who never made a mistake, or an insufferable prig. For the first interpretation we have to thank the professional patriots, orators, and writers and publishers of schoolbooks; for the second Parson Weems and Jared Sparks are largely responsible.

Mason Lock Weems published the first biography of Washington after his death. Weems was a professional bookseller by this time (1799), and he saw the practical possibilities of being first in the field. Washington died in December 1799, and sometime early in 1800 there appeared *A History of the Life, Death, Virtues and Exploits of General George Washington*. Weems had the inside track in many respects: he was in Virginia at the time of Washington's death; he had visited at Mount Vernon and had known Washington personally; finally, he knew what he wanted to do and he knew what the American people wanted to know about the greatest of their heroes. This first edition was a pamphlet of about eighty pages which recounted the principal facts and a few legends concerning Washington. The Parson covered the first twenty years of Washington's life in a page, thus plunging him into the French and Indian War rather suddenly. Later on he devoted three or four lines to Washington's courtship and marriage. The rest of the book told the story of Washington as general and first President of the United States. Touching only the favorable high spots, Parson Weems compiled a eulogy not unlike many that have been written since.

Weems's foresight was rewarded; the book sold extensively and more editions were called for. The author embellished his masterpiece gradually until he produced, in the fifth edition (1806), *The Life of George Washington, with curious anecdotes equally honorable to himself and exemplary to his young countrymen . . . by a former rector of Mt. Vernon Parrish*. It was the Washington of this book that America cherished for nearly a century and perhaps still cherishes with that supreme indifference to the truth which characterizes those of us who know what we want to know.

Parson Weems was never rector of Mount Vernon parish because there was no Mount Vernon parish; Truro was the parish in which Mount Vernon was located, and Weems was never rector of that parish. It was in the fifth edition that Weems introduced the cherry tree incident, the cabbage and the colt incidents. The cherry tree and colt stories were pure fiction, and the incident of the cabbages planted in the form of Washington's initials was lifted from an English biography written in 1799. It would be a waste of time to point out the innumerable fictions and lifted stories in this book, but one is constantly reminded of Washington when reading the other biographies that Weems wrote, for the same stories appear there. No one can say if these stories were original with Weems; he repeats them so often that he may have had a "writer's guide."

It is impossible to criticize this book from any point of view. "It is a condition, not a theory." We may condemn

Weems for his untruthfulness, but he is no worse than many writers of popular biography today, and his intentions were good. Weems wrote this "life" of Washington for the purpose of showing that honesty, truth, and justice are the primary virtues of great men. Washington was a hero in the eyes of most Americans, and Weems felt that their hero should be the essence of all that is good in human nature. He did not write his book for scholars and critics; he wrote it for the common man of the farm, the forest, and the frontier, and for his sons and daughters. Weems knew exactly what he was doing, fabricating an individual that could never have been born and reared in Virginia, but he knew, too, that those whom he wanted to reach would not stop to examine the truth of the portrait; they knew it was true. Psychology is a new word; Weems was a past master of the science that it represents.

Weems did more than invent myths with which to invest Washington; he wrote as much about the actual Washington as was known. Underlying the falsehood and the fact of the book is a strain of genuine patriotism that is honest and sincere and that contributed much to the real value of it. The stories at which we scoff served their purpose perhaps in training up a generation or two that had some respect for truth and honesty. Furthermore, there are descriptive and narrative passages in the book that rise far above the average writing of the time. Weems was a man of education and wide reading who could write well when he took the time. This edition of 1806 is superior in style to the earlier versions. The irony of the whole thing is that, as usual, the worst parts of the book survived and the best parts were soon forgotten. Perhaps the makers of hatchets, candy, and bridge favors have had as large a part in keeping alive the absurdities of the book as the moral that Weems succeeded in painting. At all events it continued to sell; it has been reprinted countless times. It was one of the few books that Lincoln read as a boy, and he said it influenced him; it must still be read, for a large edition has been issued within the last two years.

About the time that Parson Weems was putting his first edition of *A History of the Life, Death, Virtues and Exploits of General George Washington* through the press, John Marshall was thinking of writing his monumental life of Washington, a task that was to be one of the banes of his existence for the rest of his life.

During the winter of 1800, Bushrod Washington, one of Marshall's later associates on the Supreme Court, and a nephew of the first President, suggested the work to Marshall. The future Chief Justice had numerous qualifications for the task. He was one of the leading Federalists of the country; he had known Washington as intimately, perhaps, as any man had known him; he had been at Valley Forge throughout the winter of 1777–1778; and he was a Virginian. On the other hand, he was not an educated man, even for his own day; he read fiction and poetry, but we have no record of extensive reading in biography or history. He had never done any writing and was not temperamentally fitted for writing. When he first thought of the biography he was a busy lawyer; by the time he began the actual composition he was a busier jurist. (There is a fiction to the effect that jurists and college professors have leisure for study and scholarly research; good ones generally have not.) He had little time and less patience for the examination of the enormous mass of papers, private and public, left by Washington. If the biography is any evidence, he did not examine half the material. Finally, he knew nothing about biography as a form and was incapable of organizing and handling his material. In spite of all these things he was very much interested in the project, and soon agreed to begin the writing.

Both Bushrod Washington and Marshall were eager to do the book because they were in need of money, and they thought that this biography would find at least 50,000 purchasers, although they were told repeatedly that no more than 6,000 copies of any book had ever been sold in America. In those days books were sold principally by subscription, and canvassers went through the country for months before the publication of an important book. This procedure was followed in the case of Marshall's *Life of George Washington*, but the response was nothing like what the sponsors had predicted or even hoped for. However, they continued to be optimistic. Marshall was so optimistic that, before he had examined the Washington papers, he thought he could do four or five volumes, averaging five hundred pages, in a year. He was soon disillusioned.

Meanwhile negotiations with various publishers and printers were carried on and a contract was finally signed in September 1802, with C. P. Wayne, a Philadelphia publisher. At that time, Marshall had not written a word, had not finished his examination of the Washington papers, had not read the principal accounts of the Revolution that had been published. Nevertheless, Wayne sent out a large corps of subscription agents headed by Parson Weems. The response was not very prompt; neither was Marshall. His court work piled up; his material piled up; he was lost. Bushrod Washington tried to help him and there ensued an apparently endless correspondence among Marshall, Washington, and Wayne, the publisher. Marshall thought that the dignity of his office would be lowered if his name appeared on the title page; this was one of Wayne's principal selling points, and the name finally appeared. Marshall was asking advice from Washington, Washington was trying to appease the publisher, and the publisher was constantly demanding copy. Finally, some kind of order came out of chaos and the first two volumes of the *Life of George Washington*, by John Marshall, Chief Justice of the United States, appeared in the summer of 1804.

The first two volumes were a great disappointment to the subscribers and must have been, when he saw them in print, a disappointment to Marshall himself. In the first place they were badly printed and the typographical errors were legion. Marshall had been careless with the original manuscript and had had no time for proof reading. Errors of fact and of composition worried him—after he saw them in print.

The first volume opens with the voyage of John Cabot to

North America and closes with the French and Indian War, 1756–1763. In the course of more than six hundred pages Washington's name appears twice, in the description of the fight at Little Meadows (pp. 356–358) and in connection with Marshall's account of Braddock's defeat (pp. 368–371). This volume is really a detailed history of America from Cabot's voyage to the close of the French and Indian War. We have the settlement of the colonies, an excellent account of the witchcraft persecution in New England, the development of colonial trade and commerce, the various large and small wars in which some or all of the colonies were engaged, the French settlements in America and their encroachments on the English Colonies, and finally a detailed account of the war in which Washington gained the only military experience he had when he was elected commander-in-chief of the Revolutionary army. If the history had been interesting and well told Marshall might have been forgiven.

The second volume opens with Washington's birth, the first page taking him to the age of nineteen; on the second page he is again, as in Parson Weems's biography, thrust into the French and Indian War. This total lack of proportion is one of the most serious faults of the whole biography. Marshall seems to have had no clear idea as to what he intended to do, and he certainly had no outline of his material. Washington is continually thrust into the background, lost for pages and chapters, while the learned Chief Justice discourses on history, politics, and economics. Much space is given to the deliberations of the various congresses; Washington's assumption of the command of the army is dismissed in one or two sentences. The second volume closes with the attack on Trenton and the capture of the Hessian troops quartered there.

Volumes three and four, appearing at intervals of about a year, are very much better than the first two. Marshall took advantage of the public and private criticism of the earlier volumes and evidently took more care in the preparation of his manuscripts. The third volume carries the story to the end of 1779 and the fourth to the end of the war and Washington's return to Mount Vernon. Each of these volumes contained more than five hundred pages, in the first edition, and even in 1783, we have little more knowledge of Washington than we had before we began. On the other hand, there are some very good passages in these volumes. Washington's troubles with the army and with Congress, his struggles to keep the ranks filled and to pay the men, the Conway Cabal, the condition of the country during the war, these things and many others are very well described, but they are not the important constituents in a biography of Washington. Marshall was an officer in a Virginia regiment for nearly four years; he was at Valley Forge and took part in the battle of Germantown, and yet his accounts of these important phases of the war are far inferior to some of the accounts we have mentioned. Perhaps it was modesty that prevented him from doing justice to those sections describing the war as he actually saw it. Whatever the reason, the unevenness of these volumes is at times painfully obvious.

The fifth and final volume appeared in the fall of 1807. From every point of view this is the best of the five volumes. Its seven hundred pages cover the last sixteen years of Washington's life. The early part of the volume is pure history in which Marshall traces the development of political parties in the new republic and prophesies the future glories of the Federalist party. He was not much better as a prophet than he was as a biographer. To the student of American history, however, this discussion of the theory of political parties is invaluable. He takes Washington through the Constitutional Convention and his two administrations, losing him frequently and often completely in the discussions of national and international politics. We finally come to the end, and no matter how strong our interest in biography and history may be, we breathe a long sigh of relief.

The *Life of George Washington* was, of course, the subject of much discussion and difference of opinion. The Federalist papers and magazines did all they could for it, but they often damned with faint praise. The plain truth was that the book was a disappointment; it was not a life of Washington; it was not well written; and it was not interesting. Some of Marshall's kindest critics said that it was heavy. What the Republican (Democratic) periodicals said may be left to the imagination. Unfortunately, for Marshall and for Washington, the critics could generally substantiate their attacks. Marshall knew the value of the book because it was a source of worry to him for the rest of his life. He started to revise the biography immediately after its publication, although the revised edition did not appear until 1832. He managed to correct most of the printer's and his own mistakes. The second edition was in two volumes with the introductory volume printed separately, but those who have made a study of the two editions claim that very little was omitted. The second edition is in much finer print than the first.

If we try to summarize our criticism of Marshall's *Life of George Washington,* we find that it is only incidentally a biography. There are more history, law, and politics in the book than there is life-writing. If it does nothing else, it proves that a man must know his subject and be master of his materials before he can write an authoritative biography. Marshall thought he knew Washington; maybe he did, but the man never emerges from the period which, in reality, he dominated in the flesh and in the spirit.

John Marshall's *Life of George Washington* did not appeal to the average reader of his day because it was too long and contained too much that was purely historical and extraneous to the subject. One book, at least, attempted to separate the wheat from the chaff. *The Life of George Washington* (1807), by Aaron Bancroft, was intended to present the biographical parts of Marshall's book. In the preface, the author stated his purpose very definitely and the reasons for publishing such a book: that the original was too long and too expensive for the ordinary reader. This book is not an abridgement of Marshall; it is a rewriting on biographical principles. Except that it does achieve its main purpose, there is nothing distinctive about it. It follows Marshall very faithfully; its tone is the same and the writing is just as formal.

In the same year that Marshall published the last volume of his biography there appeared the *Life of George Washington . . .* by Dr. David Ramsay. Dr. Ramsay was a physician, a student of history, and a great admirer of Washington. His biography, a small book, is primarily an account of Washington's public life and has the virtue of confining itself to its subject. Its style is better than that of Marshall's book and, while it does place Washington on the usual pedestal, he is kept in the foreground of the picture.

Biographies of Washington continued to appear at more or less regular intervals during the nineteenth century, but there is little that can be said for most of them. They followed Weems or Marshall or both, and no biographer previous to Irving made any research into the mass of public and private correspondence of Washington except Jared Sparks, whose life of Washington has been discussed in Chapter II. James Kirk Paulding, the novelist, published a conventional life of Washington in 1835; it was issued as a volume in "Harper's Family Library" in the following year. It has the quiet, easy style of all of Paulding's writings, but it does not tell us much about Washington. Sparks's *Life and Writings of George Washington* (1835) continues the tradition of the plaster saint and intensifies the prig that Parson Weems created. Sparks published a separate biography of Washington in 1839. It is substantially the same as the last volume of the *Writings of George Washington.* There is one unique item of Washingtoniana in this period: Francis Glass wrote a *Life of George Washington* in Latin prose! I am unable to say anything about the contents of this book.

If we were to confine our biographical reading on Washington to those books written before 1855 we should have to believe that Washington was in all respects the perfect character. He had no vices; he had no temper; he was completely unselfish. He was a master of military strategy as well as of English prose. He could defeat armies in the field and diplomats in the closet. Is it any wonder that this legendary figure became so strongly entrenched in the American mind that modern historians and biographers are condemned—generally unheard—when they present their view of the man as he really was, a view based on unimpeachable sources? Myths die hard, particularly patriotic myths in America.

Washington Irving was the first biographer of Washington who investigated and used the existing sources for a life of Washington. He consulted the Washington correspondence in the archives of the State Department and he made excellent use of the published writings edited by Jared Sparks. This book had been in his mind for many years but circumstances prevented him from doing any active work on it until after he had retired from the diplomatic service. When he settled at Sunnyside, on the Hudson, he began the composition of this biography, but it was not finished until a few months before his death in 1859.

He intended to write a biography of Washington and that is what he did. Naturally, he was forced to retell much of the history of the Revolution and the early republic, but he told it always with Washington as the principal figure. There is nothing in the book that did not have some connection with Washington's career.

The first edition was published in five volumes, the first of which was finished early in 1855. Each volume averages about five hundred pages, and the whole work is very logically divided. The first volume ends with Washington's assumption of the command of the army, the second with the attack on Trenton, the third with the opening of the final campaign in the South, and the fourth with Washington's election to the Presidency. The chapters are as carefully worked out as the volumes; Irving knew just what he was going to do before he started.

A great deal of adverse criticism has been directed against Irving's biography. It has been called old-fashioned, conventional, partisan, and what not. It may be all of these things, but it is much more. In the first place it is, as far as possible, a straight narrative account of Washington from his birth to his death. There are, of course, deviations but only those that were absolutely necessary. Irving had the good fortune to live and write in a period when such terms as psychology, psychoanalysis, and psychography were unknown. He had no thesis to prove, no psychoses to probe, no fixations to unearth. Despite the lack of all these scientific aids he succeeded in presenting a biography that is essentially true, and truth is the primary requisite of any good biography. His analysis of his principal is very quietly done but it is there, and we know George Washington when we have finished the book. Much has been discovered and published concerning Washington since Irving's time, and consequently his book has been superseded, but it cannot be ignored either as biography or as literature.

Many critics have claimed that the *Life of George Washington* has not the charm of manner and felicity of style that characterize Irving's writings in general. That may be true; if so, there are good and sufficient reasons for the change. In the first place, Irving was an old man when he started the book; he was dying when he finished it. Secondly, this subject was entirely different from any that he had previously attempted. Washington Irving was a romantic by nature and he matured in the midst of the romantic movement. His previous biographies were concerned with romantic figures and, excepting Goldsmith, not a great deal was known about them when he was writing. In the case of Washington he was dealing with a very real subject, with a man who had been known by men still living; he had a mass of definite source material to which he was obliged to be faithful; and the importance of the subject stayed his hand and probably involved him in masses of detail which were necessary and which demanded a more sober style than that which he had been accustomed to use.

This book is not only a biography of Washington; it has brilliant sketches of practically every man of importance in America during Washington's life. Sometimes a paragraph, sometimes a page or two gives us a perfect miniature of the men with whom Washington came in contact. Irving also had a natural sense for history, and this biography can be rightly called historical biography because it combines, in almost ideal proportions, the history and the biography of Washington and his times. Some modern biographers of Washington would have profited by a careful reading of Irving's *Life of George Washington.*

One of Irving's principal purposes in writing a biography of Washington was to remove the false impressions created by Weems and Sparks. He was very successful in this phase of his work, considering the period in which he wrote and his great admiration for Washington. Readers of the mid-nineteenth century did not want the truth concerning their heroes; they wanted the traditional aspects of the great figures of the world told in genteel language. In spite of Irving's investigations and judgments, the genteel tradition persisted for at least forty years after Irving. I have found more than a dozen lives of Washington written between 1855 and 1895, and hardly one of them made any use of Irving's book.

In 1860 Edward Everett wrote a life of Washington for the *Encyclopedia Britannica.* Lord Macaulay had been asked to prepare this article, but the state of his health and his desire to concentrate his efforts on his *History of England* prevented him from carrying out the original plan. It was then decided to ask a prominent American writer to do the work, and Everett was chosen. Edward Everett was at this time one of the leading orators and men of letters in America, but one would never guess his nationality from reading his article on Washington. When his *Life of George Washington* (1860) was published separately, he wrote a preface in which he stated that his authorities were Sparks and Irving. The influence of Sparks is much more obvious than that of Irving. This short biography reflects no credit on either Everett or American scholarship. Edward Everett Hale's *Life of George Washington, Studied Anew* (1888) does not measure up to its title. If there is anything new in the book, it has escaped the attention of this writer.

Genuine scholarship and research were gradually making themselves felt in history and biography during the last decades of the nineteenth century. Very frequently interest was sacrificed to the impedimenta of scholarship, but occasionally there appeared a book which combined interest and scholarship without the trappings of the latter. One such book is Woodrow Wilson's *George Washington* (1896). Wilson was then a professor of history at Princeton, and had been engaged for a number of years in the preparation of his *History of the American People*. In all probability he felt the need of a life of Washington which would be based on history but would not be historical biography. This is the kind of book that Wilson wrote. Using heredity and environment, he developed Washington's character and achievements in such a way that, after finishing the book, we understand fairly well the qualities that made Washington the greatest individual force in the country. Wilson was not so much concerned with correcting previous conceptions of Washington as he was with presenting a true conception derived from a close study of a multitude of original sources. There is not so much of the purely personal in this as in some of the later biographies, for Wilson strove to present a great man against a proper historical background. One of Wilson's greatest assets was an apparently effortless style—achieved, however, only with infinite effort and patience—which makes his meaning crystal clear and which is a joy to read.

A revised edition of Henry Cabot Lodge's *George Washington* (1889) was published in 1898. Lodge wrote this book for the "American Statesmen Series," and it was one of the best of the group. Lodge was a good scholar, having been trained under Henry Adams and in Europe, but his scholarship could never overcome his extremely partisan view of politics. These books are striking and, if we look into the future, prophetically ominous. Both men wanted to present a truer Washington than had yet appeared. Lodge wrote a complete biography for the purpose of humanizing the plaster saint that was Washington; Wilson wanted to and did write of Washington from an entirely new point of view. Lodge wrote of Washington from a strongly Federalist point of view; Wilson's book has no partisan tone at all. Lodge developed Washington's private life as fully, comparatively speaking, as he did the public career; Wilson contented himself with those phases of Washington's private and public life which would illuminate and explain the man's character and actions.

If biography is primarily the re-creation of personality, of a man as he really was, then Lodge's book is a better biography than Wilson's because it is more complete and more personal. Lodge tried to correct the wrong impression of Washington that previous biographers had created and perpetuated, and he wrote from a definite personal and political point of view. Wilson wrote with as little personal or political point of view as any biographer could. Wilson's book is probably more truthful than Lodge's, being shorter, but Lodge's is more nearly the ideal biography.

Many of the books on Washington in this period were military biographies, such as Bradley T. Johnson's *George Washington* (1894) (Great Commanders); H. B. Carrington's *Washington, the Soldier* (1898); G. B. Smith's *Story of George Washington, Patriot, Soldier, Statesman* (1898); and M. H. Hancock's *Washington's Life and Military Career* (1902). Of these, Carrington's book is by far the best.

During the last decade of the nineteenth century, Worthington C. Ford published the best edition of the writings of Washington and followed this in 1899 with *George Washington,* a biography in two volumes. Mr. Ford made excellent use of his materials in writing this account of Washington's life from birth to death. In 1911 Mr. Ford published an equally good short life in the "Beacon Biographies."

Every biography should be a unified account of a man's life, but we sometimes happen upon books of a biographical nature which do not conform to this standard. Owen Wister's book, *The Seven Ages of Washington* (1907), is a series of character studies of Washington at various periods of his life. The table of contents reads: Ancestry—The Boy—The Young Man—The Married Man—The Commander—The President—Immortality. This is a decidedly unorthodox method and an unsatisfactory one, but it is reclaimed in part by Mr. Wister's ability as a story-teller and by the charm of his style. Paul Leicester Ford's *The True George Washington* (1909) is, paradoxically, a less unified piece of writing and a better biography than Wister's. Ford had more of the biographical instinct than Wister and had more experience in the fields of history and biography. Ford's book is distinctly a series of essays, but we know more about Washington physically, mentally, and morally from it than we do from Wister's.

The next book of any importance is William Roscoe Thayer's *George Washington* (1922). In his preface, Mr. Thayer states that his purpose was to humanize Washington. He did that as far as he went, but the book is short and impregnated with some of the genteel literary tradition that characterized the biographers of Thayer's generation. It will serve as a good introduction to modern biographical material on Washington.

The Thayer type of biography was dying out in 1922; the younger, the post-war generation of writers was coming to the fore, and the men and women of this generation turned the great men of the country upside down and inside out, not to understand them better, but to lay them open to the merciless scalpel of the psychopathic and the pseudo-psychopathic writer. *George Washington, the Image and the Man* (1926) by W. E. Woodward is one of the few "debunking" biographies of Washington that has been written. Mr. Woodward must be given credit for trying to get at the heart and soul of his subject, though he let too many things interfere with his biography. Mr. Woodward seems to have been thoroughly disgusted with the panegyrical and eulogistic outpourings on Washington and the grossly partisan history that had been written. Consequently, he spent so much time correcting previous books that he forgot that he was writing a biography himself. This book is very interesting, but it is not a biography of Washington. Washington is not the central figure; the center of the stage is divided between the mistakes of historians and biographers and a very interesting account of the American Revolution. Another serious defect in this book is its flippancy, which is a characteristic of the school of biographers to which Mr. Woodward belongs; it is intended to be humorous but becomes merely tiresome. In spite of its defects, the book was worth writing and is worth reading, for it combines the best and the worst in modern biography.

We have the new and the old constantly cropping up in modern biography. *Washington* (1927), by Joseph D. Sawyer, is a very conventional biography containing all the facts but entirely lacking in interpretation. The two volumes contain fifteen hundred illustrations, including two hundred and fifty portraits; this feature alone would give the book some value. The same conventional treatment may be found in Lorenzo Sears's *George Washington* (1932).

The best modern one-volume life of Washington is *George Washington* (1929), by Shelby Little. This is an excellent personal biography in which Washington is allowed to speak for himself wherever possible. The author was very wise in confining this study to the individual rather than in trying to portray the national hero. We have plenty of books of the latter type; the former are scarce. The skill and art with which the author wove narrative and source material into a smooth account are truly remarkable. Furthermore, the man who walks through this book—and he does walk through—is a very close approximation of the man as he really was. His faults and his virtues are given equal space; the result is a book that has admirable balance, perspective, and judgment.

John Corbin's *Unknown Washington; Biographic Origins of the Republic* (1930) is a unique item of Washingtoniana.

Mr. Corbin's purpose was to show a neglected side of Washington, that of the genuine statesman as he exhibited himself in the Constitutional Convention and as President of the United States. The book is a revelation, certainly to the average reader, of the intellect and statesmanship of this Virginian farmer and gentleman. It is a Washington item that should be read by every student.

Someone has said that everything comes to him who waits. We have waited more than a hundred and thirty years for a genuinely adequate life of George Washington. We have it, or shall have it, when Mr. Rupert Hughes finishes his biography of Washington. Thus far he has completed three volumes, bringing Washington's life up to 1781. At least two more volumes will be necessary to tell the whole story. The first and shortest volume covers the first thirty years of Washington's life; the second, fifteen; and the third, four. There is an afterword to each volume which should be read before the volume is read, for each afterword explains Mr. Hughes's methods and purposes.

In the afterword to the first volume of George Washington, Mr. Hughes states that he has been collecting material for this subject since 1900, although the first volume did not appear until 1926. It has been his purpose to strip Washington of all legend because he believed, and rightly, that a much greater man would emerge from the whitewash. He has justified that belief in the volumes that have been published, bringing upon himself a great deal of emotional and patriotic criticism in the process. Mr. Hughes uses the best possible method in his biography: he lets his subject speak for himself. Washington's papers are the most voluminous of those of any public man in America. The number of letters he wrote is almost incredible, in addition to his diaries, plantation accounts, and state papers. How a man so busy, so harassed as Washington was could write as much as he did is a mystery. In addition to all this manuscript material, Mr. Hughes read all that has been published about Washington, the British, and the Revolutionary War. He has proof for every controversial statement he makes, which can be examined in the notes and appendices. This is one biography where the mechanism of scholarship must be left exposed.

George Washington is completely revealed as far as Mr. Hughes has taken him. The first volume aroused a storm of protest from the various societies of the sons and daughters of the Revolution. I wonder what they think of Washington's opinions of the members of his army as expressed in the second and third volumes! That Washington should be represented as a lover of wine, of cards, of dancing, and of fine clothes was a sacrilege in the minds of those who had been raised on Weems, Sparks, and their followers. Mr. Hughes has Washington's own words for these and for countless other facts which he uses to re-create the man as he really was.

It would be a waste of time to itemize Mr. Hughes's "iconoclasm." That Washington did not rally the British forces at Braddock's defeat, that he had never been in a real battle until after he became Commander-in-Chief of the American army, that his failure as a strategist was balanced by the stupidity or cupidity of the British generals, that he never knelt in the snow at Valley Forge, as so many patriotic pictures would have us believe, are just a few of the items that Mr. Hughes straightens out in this magnificent book. No one has to believe Mr. Hughes even though he offers proof. Under his pen, George Washington emerges a colossally great man, the body, soul, and spirit of the American Revolution. He has lost his toga and halo, but he has gained the respect, admiration, and love of his intelligent countrymen.

The author has been as fair to the enemies of Washington and his cause as he has been to Washington. He gives credit to the British where they deserve it; he presents the real case of General Lee and his supposed treachery at the Battle of Monmouth; he tells the real story of the famous Conway Cabal and General Gates; he proves that General Howe was neither stupid nor lazy, for he had a definite reason for refusing to follow up his victories.

Mr. Hughes's method is the simple one of fact and proof;

there is no "debunking," no heightening of interest by fictitious methods. Those phases of Washington which cannot be
subjected to the light of truth are left where they belong, as
theories. In a style that is easy and yet admirably adapted
to the importance of the subject, Mr. Hughes is writing a
biography which will supersede all others, and which will
have equal value as biography and history. As is the case
with any great book, this *George Washington* must be read
to be appreciated.

What the future holds for Washington, as a biographical
subject, no one can say. We can say that no intelligent man
can write of Washington as did Weems and Sparks and Bancroft and their contemporaries. It is doubtful if any biographer will be able to tell us more about Washington than
Hughes has done; it is quite possible that an artist in prose
will be able to write a prose epic of the greatest man that
America has produced. Washington is our greatest man, and
Mr. Hughes's book proves it, because, without his dominant
spirit, his strength of character, and his spiritual force, there
would never have been a United States of America.

PART III

PART III

VII

THE NEW BIOGRAPHY

THE World War, which has been held responsible for much that is good and bad in our modern civilization, has had some effect on modern biography. Since the war most of us have looked at life and men from a point of view much different from that of previous generations. We have questioned everything, from God to government, and we have tried to see men and things as they are and were, not as we should like to have them. Our scepticism has not been irreverent; we have not been iconoclasts; we have been and are trying to seek the truth about the world and the people in it. It is no longer the fashion to accept authority; we must investigate for ourselves. Our fiction has gone beyond realism into naturalism and plain reporting; our poetry has taken on new and strange forms, some good and some bad; our drama has become the medium for examining and generally satirizing our social customs and habits; our biography has become creative or re-creative and sometimes, unfortunately, imaginative.

There are other reasons for our present interest in biography. The world has grown larger, and the machine age has made man much smaller than he was fifty years ago. Circumstances have made the average man stationary; he has neither the time nor the money to travel and meet different kinds of people. At the same time education, the press, the "movies" have aroused in him a desire to know the great men and women of the past. Modern life has made it impossible for the great majority to come in contact with many people; most of us live and die in a small groove of life. The fact that we may meet many people will give us little or no idea of who and what they are. It is doubtful if anyone knew Napoleon in his own day as we know him, for we can read at least six great biographies of the man. Man and woman can come to know each other only by living together. We turn to biography because we can live with a hundred men in a year, if we can read rapidly, and we get to know those men intimately.

Modern man is more conscious of himself than was the man of a century ago. He tries to find reflections of himself in the lives of great men and to act as they acted. That is why many men and women read biography. We may find that we are a combination of Leonardo da Vinci, Casanova, and George Washington. If we read sufficient biographies, we may be able to analyze and help ourselves, or find that we are great men, denied the opportunity to prove our greatness. These are only a few of the reasons for the present popularity of biography.

Biography has made more definite progress in the last fifteen years than has any other form of literature. Every branch of literature has been the subject of experiment; some of the experiments have succeeded, more have failed. Modern fiction, modern poetry, and modern drama are in various experimental stages, but biography has emerged and has taken on, not a new form, but a form that is the logical development of the various methods that have been tried since 1918. We have seen the rise of the psychological, psychopathic, and pathological methods in life-writing. We have seen the two or three volumes of life and letters reduced to a sketch, an analysis, or a psychograph. We have seen the biography of an earlier day rewritten in modern slang and scientific jargon. We have seen facts sacrificed to effect, biography made into fiction or plain falsehood. We have seen the "debunking" school pulling figures from pedestals and then breaking the pedestals. Some of the exhibitions were painful to many of us, but the operations eventually saved the patient. The journalist who imbibed enough psychology to use some of the terms showed us that biography cannot be written that way; the psychologist or psychiatrist who tried to intensify his subject with the method of the journalist showed that biography cannot be written that way. The more serious writer who started with a preconceived idea of his subject and used only that source material which would prove his case showed us that biography cannot be written that way. The critic, turned biographer and always judging the individual in terms of his art, showed us that biography cannot be written that way. In the chapters that follow, the various types of life-writing that have been mentioned here will be more fully considered. We shall find the old biography appearing at frequent intervals (every biographer of this period was not a psychologist or a "debunker"; some were writers) falling below or rising above the contemporary methods. It is the purpose of this section to try to evaluate the biographies, old and new, that have been so popular since the World War and to show where they succeeded or failed, wholly or partially, to live up to the fundamental principle of life-writing: the re-creation of the man as he really was.

The period between 1919 and 1935 was the most prolific in the history of biographical writing in America. At times, the demand seemed to exceed the supply. People became interested in the lives of soldiers, statesmen, scientists, novelists, poets, ecclesiastics, suffragists, reformers, prize fighters, not as soldiers, statesmen, scientists, and so forth, but as men and women. It is only when we are interested in people as individuals rather than as folk-heroes that we can write or read about them intelligently.

Apparently, interest in the great men and women of the past was not the only reason for the popularity of modern biography. The methods used had a great influence on the popularity, and these methods had their beginnings, at least, abroad. The year 1919 has been chosen as the beginning of modern biography because the greatest influences were published in that year and in 1918.

In 1918, Lytton Strachey published *Eminent Victorians,* a volume of biographical studies of Cardinal Manning, Florence Nightingale, General Gordon, and Arnold of Rugby. This was not Strachey's first book, *Landmarks in French Literature* having been published before the war, but it was the first book in which his particular biographical genius was noticed. It became a best seller here and in England, and he became the literary lion of the hour. The appearance of *Queen Victoria* in 1921 seemed to justify all the praise that had been heaped on *Eminent Victorians*. In *Books and Characters* (1922) Strachey published biographical studies, ranging from Voltaire and Sir Thomas Browne to Lady Hester Stanhope, that represent some of his best work in this field. *Elizabeth and Essex* (1928) merely enhanced his reputation as a biographer and stylist. *Portraits in Miniature* (1931) added nothing to Strachey's position, though the portraits are extremely interesting in themselves. Mr. Strachey's death in 1932 brought to a close a career that had really just begun, for he was only fifty-two years old when he died.

Strachey's methods are outside the province of this study of American biography, but some explanation of his influence must be given. While Strachey never set forth his theory of life-writing as completely as did Maurois or Ludwig, the preface to *Eminent Victorians* tells us as much as we need to know. The following passage seems to me to illustrate his purpose and his method: [1]

The art of biography seems to have fallen on evil times in England. We have had, it is true, a few masterpieces, but we have never had, like the French, a great biographical tradition. . . . With us, the most delicate and humane of all the branches of the art of writing has been relegated to the journeymen of letters; we do not reflect that it is perhaps as difficult to write a good life as to live one. Those two fat volumes, with which it is our custom to commemorate the dead—who does not know them, with their ill-digested masses of material, their slip-shod style, their tone of tedious panegyric, their lamentable lack of selection, of detachment of design? They are as familiar as the *cortege* of the undertaker, and wear the same air of slow, funereal barbarism. One is tempted to suppose, of some of them, that they were composed by that functionary, as the final item of his job. The studies in this book are indebted, in more ways than one, to such works—works which certainly

[1] *Eminent Victorians.* Harcourt, Brace & Co. N. Y. pp. vi–vii.

deserve the name of Standard Biographies. For they have provided me not only with much indispensable information, but with something even more precious—an example. How many lessons are to be learned from them! But it is hardly necessary to particularize. To preserve, for instance, a becoming brevity —a brevity which excludes everything that is redundant and nothing that is significant—that, surely, is the first duty of the biographer. The second, no less surely, is to maintain his own freedom of spirit. It is not his business to be complimentary, it is his business to lay bare the facts of the case as he understands them. That is what I have aimed at in this book—to lay bare the facts of some cases, as I understand them, dispassionately, impartially, and without ulterior intentions.

There is no question that Strachey's first books sounded the death knell of the two-volume panegyric, but that he wrote with no other intention than to lay bare the facts as he understood them is open to argument. It is sufficient to state here that *Eminent Victorians* and *Queen Victoria* gave him his position as the father of modern biography.

Lytton Strachey revolutionized biographical writing, for he approached biography from a new angle. He was not concerned with his subject's life as a whole, but rather those aspects of it that brought out the individual characteristics. Even in *Queen Victoria*, his only full-length biography, there are great gaps in the chronology because those years provided nothing new in characterization. Her birth, her accession, her marriage, and the length of her rule were the principal events of her life, the events which made the Victoria who gave her name to an age.

The subjects in *Eminent Victorians* are less fully treated, and *Elizabeth and Essex* primarily concerns Elizabeth in her middle years. Nevertheless we know Manning, Gordon, Florence Nightingale, Arnold, and Queen Elizabeth when we have finished these books, but we do not know them completely, and that is one of the faults in Strachey's method. He is inclined to show us only one side of the picture, the ironical side. As a portrayer of character, Strachey is unexcelled in modern times; as a true biographer he has limitations, but they were imposed by himself. He succeeded admirably in accomplishing the purpose he had in mind.

Strachey's art was developed through the choice of his subjects. In every instance he took an unusual individual, saturated himself with knowledge and then produced the essence of the material. Strachey chose his material as carefully as a novelist chooses his, for the commonplace, everyday life of an individual meant nothing to him. He arranged his material as a dramatist sets his stage, and achieved the same effects. When you have carefully chosen facts arranged with dramatic effect and handled by a master of the method who has a style as original as the method, you will have a work of art. When you have this method used by men who have not or cannot choose such facts, who have not the ability to dramatize as the master does, and who have not acquired a distinctive style, you will have something less than art.

Lytton Strachey was a man of wide and profound knowledge of history, psychology, and human nature. He knew what people wanted to know about the great and the famous, and he knew how to write. These requisites are lacking in many of his disciples and that is why their work falls so far below his. Strachey had a genius for irony, together with the ability to keep his ironic tone; most of his followers, in trying to imitate his ironic tone, descended to satire or invective, neither of which is successful in biography. Strachey seemed to take pleasure in trying to lay bare the inmost thoughts of his subjects, and always succeeded in showing their littleness even though they also had something of the great in their characters. His imitators, unable to probe into character and mind, sometimes became vulgar and more often untruthful. The trouble with Strachey's method is that it looks so easy and in reality is so difficult. Knowledge, culture, genius, and a peculiar mentality were combined in Strachey as they have been in no biographer who has tried to imitate him.

I have tried to explain Strachey's method and the reasons

for his success because he has been more widely followed in America than any other modern biographer. Many writers have learned much from him without succumbing to frank imitation; others have followed him slavishly and have failed for the reasons given. Many more have been inspired by his method and success to work out methods of their own, and these have generally succeeded. It is his influence rather than his method itself that has helped to raise biography to the position of an art.

Emil Ludwig has had a different influence on our biographical writing from that exercised by Strachey. Ludwig's purpose seems to be dramatic representation of life. There is more movement, more analysis of motivation, more desire to get at the whole man in Ludwig than in Strachey. Strachey, of course, had the dramatic instinct (we have only to read the famous last paragraphs of "Cardinal Manning" and *Queen Victoria* to realize this), but Strachey uses drama only for effect while Ludwig bases his entire method on dramatic principles. Strachey had developed his method by the time he came to write *Eminent Victorians;* if we follow Ludwig from his first long biography, *Goethe* (1919), through *Bismarck* (1924), to *Napoleon* (1925) we will see a steady development that reached its climax in the last-named life. Ludwig's reputation has suffered in England and America because *Napoleon* was translated before either *Bismarck* or *Goethe*. He has published a number of biographies which were written after Napoleon, but they do not show any improvement in technique. As a matter of fact, his popularity has led him to write too much.

It seems that Ludwig's work more nearly approaches the biographical ideal than Strachey's. Ludwig's biographies are full and complete; they carry us along with Goethe, Napoleon, and Bismarck; and we see these men in their successes and failures, in their periods of depression and exaltation. We see their characters develop, and we are able to judge whether that development is good or bad. We see the man as he was to himself and to others. And always there is life in terms of drama, and it is that dramatic method that makes Ludwig's books so interesting. They have not the distinction of style, the brevity, the irony that characterize Strachey's writings, but they have a fullness, a rapidity of movement, a reality that make for great life-writing. Ludwig's influence has not extended over so long a period as has Strachey's, but it seems to have had a marked effect on American biography, a more wholesome effect than the sometimes cruel irony of Strachey.

André Maurois is the third European who has influenced modern biography. Like Strachey and Ludwig he has contributed something new to life-writing. Strachey desired to reform biography; Ludwig has dramatized and vivified it; Maurois has made it, according to his own statement, a means of self-expression. Maurois has written extensively on the subject; his book *Aspects of Biography,* in which he states his ideas and beliefs in regard to biography as an art, should be read by everyone interested in life-writing.

Maurois' three important biographies are *Ariel, the Life of Shelley* (1923), *Disraeli* (1927), and *Byron* (1930). The first one exemplifies his fundamental principle that biography should be a means of self-expression for the author as well as an explanation and interpretation of the subject. The average person, knowing nothing of Maurois or his method, might consider *Ariel* a historical romance rather than a biography, and he would not be far wrong. It has all the appearances of a novel based on fact. It is not a complete record of Shelley's life nor is it an interpretation of Shelley's character. The method is too novel to be successful. *Ariel* was very successful in this country, but it had a very bad effect in that it tempted writers of biography to use conversation to heighten interest; and very frequently that conversation had no basis in fact. I believe that *Ariel* is largely responsible for the fictional biography with which we are plagued and which is totally untrue. Fictional biography differs from biographical fiction in that the latter is fiction based on fact while the former purports to be fact when, in reality, it is the product of the writer's imagination.

In his second biography, *Disraeli*, Maurois changed his method somewhat, adhering more closely to the conventional form, and the third, *Byron*, is completely conventional in form. As biography, *Byron* is infinitely superior to *Ariel*.

Maurois' method is very much the same as that of Strachey and Ludwig. He stresses character and personality rather than day-by-day events, which is as it should be. There is no reason to believe that Maurois' method is not his own, although he must have been influenced by the writings of the other men. His books are as interesting as Strachey's, as complete as Ludwig's, if we except *Ariel*, and they have the further charm of an excellent and individual style. I know of no better way of judging the comparative merits of these three biographers than to read *Queen Victoria, Napoleon*, and *Disraeli*.

There are other names prominent in the new biography such as Philip Guedalla, Harold Nicolson, and the American, Gamaliel Bradford. Each has contributed to the development of modern biography; Bradford has given us what may be called a new form. Of the other two, Guedalla has produced in the *Third Empire, Palmerston*, and *Wellington*, biographies which will have permanent places in our literature. This is particularly true of *Wellington*. In addition to these long biographies Guedalla has written a number of volumes of excellent biographical essays.

VIII

THE BIOGRAPHERS

THERE have been numerous writers in America who have devoted all their time to biography, or who have, at least, written numerous lives. The last fifteen years have produced a much larger group of writers who have specialized in biography, or have contributed, let us say, more than one biography. This chapter will concern itself with these professional biographers, and will consider them in the chronological order of their writings. To repeat, there is no definite line of demarcation between the lives written before 1919 and those that have been written since that time, but there is a definite influence of the New Biography shown in most of the biographies of the later period.

It is a striking commentary on the growing popularity and importance of biography that essayists, poets, novelists, teachers, and even scientists have turned to biographical writing. These workers in other fields turned to biography because it was becoming a distinct literary genre and because they felt the necessity of writing or rewriting the lives of important men and women in the light of modern methods, that they might tell the truth about their subjects.

It was certainly for these reasons that Miss Agnes Repplier wrote two of the three biographies which she has published. Her first biography, *J. William White, M.D., a Biography* (1919), is the life of a famous Philadelphia surgeon who was also something of a personality. Miss Repplier and Dr. White were intimate friends for many years, and this intimacy enabled the author to present a complete and well-rounded picture of her subject. In this excellent biography she has caught the spirit of the man as he lived and worked, and we know him at least as well as she did. Combined with the high quality of the book as biography, is that animated and cultured style of the best of our contemporary familiar essayists.

Ten years passed before Miss Repplier published *Père*

Marquette, a life of one of the greatest of the Jesuit missionaries in America. It is a masterpiece of condensed historical biography, admirably preserving the balance between history and life-writing. Our only regret is that the book is not longer, for we should like to know more about Father Marquette's early life. Miss Repplier was justified in condensing the early years, for her purpose was to tell the story of Marquette the missionary and explorer. A comparison of this book with Jared Sparks's essay on Marquette in the *Library of American Biography* will show the progress that has been made in biography in a century. *Mère Marie of the Ursulines; a Study in Adventure* (1931) is the best of Miss Repplier's biographies. It is more complete, it has more unity, and it was a more interesting subject for the author than the other two. Miss Repplier was educated by the Ursuline nuns, and she was naturally interested in the foundress of the order. In this book (p. 12), the author makes some very pertinent remarks regarding religious biography as it had been written for centuries. Her principal point is that we are interested in the personality of the man or woman who became a priest or a nun rather than in religion, piety, and theology. The fact that Miss Repplier had a particularly clear view of biography is one of the reasons why this book was instantly popular and why it can be classed among the best biographies that have been written in this particular field. The influence of the new biography is very evident in Miss Repplier's later books, but she has also maintained the high standard of the best in all biographical writing.

Don C. Seitz began his career as a biographer in the same year as Miss Repplier. His first biography, *Artemus Ward,* was published in 1919. Artemus Ward, whose real name was Charles Farrar Browne, was one of the most famous humorists of his day. Starting as a reporter, he gradually developed into what we call a columnist. He gave up newspaper work for lecturing, a field in which he was very successful. He traveled into almost every part of the United States and, at the time of his death, was having a huge success in London. Mr. Seitz presents a very complete account of Browne's life and character showing that he was much more than a humorist, he was something of a philosopher and an artist. This book is not only an excellent study of personality, but it is also a history of American life in the nineteenth century as reflected in the humor of Browne and his contemporaries in this field, most of whom are mentioned in the book. With the exception of Mark Twain, these early humorists, as well as most of the later ones, spoke and wrote in dialect, generally yankee, western, or southern, and devoted most of their lectures and writings to current topics. For this reason they are soon forgotten, and a book like *Artemus Ward* is needed to make us aware that we have a genuine tradition in humorous literature.

Mr. Seitz's second biography, *Joseph Pulitzer: His Life and Letters* (1924) is, perhaps, his best book, for he had a wide and intimate knowledge of the subject. The author was on the staff of the New York *World* for many years and was intimately associated with its famous publisher for varying periods. Knowing the man and his work, he was able to present an excellent picture of him. Pulitzer's career was like that of many other wealthy Americans. Starting at the bottom in St. Louis, he through sheer genius became one of the greatest newspaper publishers in America. Instead of recounting this career through its achievements, Mr. Seitz chose to develop it by delineating a personality that was unique. In this way we can see how Pulitzer was able to make the success that he did make and how that unique personality affected the entire organization that he developed. The author admired his subject very much, but he did not allow admiration to color his judgment. This biography presents all sides and phases of the man, a man as changeable as the wind. It is this kind of life-writing that makes the field such a fascinating one, for not all of us have the opportunity to come in contact with such a character as Joseph Pulitzer.

The third long biography had for its subject *Horace Greeley, Founder of the New York Tribune* (1926). In all probability, Horace Greeley was the greatest newspaper editor that America has seen. Innocent and shrewd, clever and at times colossally foolish, a born newspaper man, Horace Greeley left his stamp on American journalism. He founded the *Tribune* and made it the greatest newspaper of his day. It was carried along for some years after his death by the momentum he had given to it, but it finally lost its place as America's premier newspaper, and in the end was absorbed by the New York *Herald.* Greeley was the greatest of the generation of great editors, a group which included Raymond of the *Times,* the elder Bennett of the *Herald,* and Dana of the *Sun.* It was his personality and genius that made the *Tribune* the great force of public opinion that it was, particularly during the Civil War and until Greeley's death in 1872. All this and more is told in Seitz's biography, a straightforward narrative which seeks only to tell the truth about its subject. Only a professional journalist could write such a book and evaluate Horace Greeley as a man, an editor, and a great public figure. The fact that Seitz succeeded so well is indicative of his skill as a biographer.

The James Gordon Bennetts appeared in 1928. This is a very good account of the lives of the founder of the New York *Herald* and his son. The elder Bennett was primarily a reporter, and he gave the impetus to the modern newspaper which places emphasis on news rather than on editorial opinion. Bennett did everything he could think of to improve his news service; he went out to ships before they docked; he established the first Washington office that any American newspaper had; and he devised a hundred other schemes to get the news before his competitors got it. The result was that the *Herald* provided more news and wielded less influence than any other of the great newspapers of the mid-nineteenth century. The younger Bennett carried on the original plan. This book would have been much better if it had been confined to the elder Bennett, for his life was certainly as interesting as Greeley's. Perhaps there was less material available, or perhaps Mr. Seitz did not want to take the trouble to find it. Seitz's latest biography is *Lincoln, the Politician* of which mention has been made in the chapter on Lincoln.

In addition to these biographies Mr. Seitz has written two volumes of short studies, *Uncommon Americans* (1925) and *The "Also Rans": Great Men Who Missed Making the Presidential Goal* (1928). The first volume is a collection of factual and anecdotal sketches of famous Americans ranging from Joseph Smith and Lord Timothy Dexter to Mrs. Mary Baker Eddy and David Crockett. There are twenty-one sketches in the volume and all are interesting, for the people are uncommon. The sketches are well done, but are too short for the reader who wants more than a glimpse of a group of people that has no counterpart in any other country or at any other time in the world's history.

The second volume contains eighteen short biographies of the famous men, from Aaron Burr to W. J. Bryan, who were unsuccessful candidates for the Presidency. The essays are well done, in a journalistic manner, and are really valuable because many of these unsuccessful candidates are unknown, although they were prominent men in their day.

Mr. Seitz has achieved success as a biographer because he has confined himself to subjects with which he is familiar. His four principal biographies are of journalists, and his book on Lincoln stresses only that side of Lincoln's career which Mr. Seitz could best handle, and which he probably felt had been neglected or misrepresented by Lincoln's biographers. In all his books Seitz has used modern trends in biographical writing to the best advantage and has, without adding anything distinctive to the literature, given us uniformly good work.

Don Seitz used none of the mechanism of psychology which was becoming increasingly prominent in the early years of the third decade of the century. One of the leading exponents of the psychological method in biography is Katharine Anthony. When Miss Anthony published *Margaret Fuller: A Psychological Biography* in 1920, something definitely new was added to biographical method. This new method depends for its success on a sound and thorough knowledge of the principles of psychology and the ability to analyze character by those principles. Miss Anthony's book broke away from all the recognized standards, for she was and is interested, not in the facts of a life and their interpretation, but in unearthing motives which will enable us to understand the character and the actions of a particular individual. Margaret Fuller was an unusual woman; she said and did things that no other woman of her day would have dared to say or do. Miss Anthony asks why, and attempts to answer the question. In answering the question the author uses heredity and environment, Margaret's mental aberrations, her dreams, her hysteria and her suppressed emotions, her unusual education, which was supervised by her father, to explain the woman and her achievements.

This small book is a landmark in American biography. It disregards chronology and character development and says little concerning the part Miss Fuller played in the Transcendental Movement in America. Chronology means nothing to the psychologist. It is the abnormal rather than the normal which occupies the attention of this school, and Margaret Fuller's interest in transcendentalism was perfectly natural in view of her early training and her nature. There is little theorizing in this book, for Margaret Fuller put into her journals and other writings just the sort of material best suited to the psychologist. Miss Anthony neither condemns nor defends her subject; she merely analyzes her, and the analysis is the explanation of that complex character, Margaret Fuller. Some may say this method is good, some may not like it. Used as a means of developing the whole character of a man or woman, it is excellent; used alone, it places insurmountable limitations on a biographer because the unusual, the abnormal, is only part of the story. We may understand the subject of a psychological analysis, but we cannot truly know him or imagine how he looked or acted under normal conditions. The picture of a disembodied soul is hardly the stuff of good biography.

Miss Anthony's method was new when she wrote *Margaret Fuller;* when she wrote *Catherine the Great* (1925) she had more thoroughly mastered that method and had made it a much more flexible instrument of biographical portrayal. Catherine was a more stable character than Margaret Fuller and intellectually superior to her, although she did not have Margaret's genius. In this book the author looks for an explanation of Catherine's conduct as empress and woman, and she finds it in Catherine's early training and in the years when she was the wife of the Czarevitch, years in which she had to submit to every kind of humiliation and degradation. This explanation seems to be the correct one, for here again Miss Anthony had a wealth of material from Catherine's own hand—diaries, letters, and state papers. As a study of the woman who was, perhaps, the greatest of the "Autocrats of All the Russias," *Catherine the Great* is an excellent book, even though it does overemphasize her love affairs.

Miss Anthony's next biography, *Queen Elizabeth* (1929), falls below *Catherine the Great* because she tried to refine or distill both method and style. Queen Elizabeth was on the throne during the greatest period of English history—some say she made the period great—and her life was as full as that of any woman who ever lived. The author tried to tell the story of that life in a few hundred pages. She failed because Elizabeth's life will not permit such compression. She was only the central spirit of Elizabethan England, and to understand her life we must know more than a psychological analysis of one character, however good it may be, can tell us. *Queen Elizabeth* is no more than a disjointed account, based on secondary instead of primary sources. Even Strachey used only one period of Elizabeth's life in *Elizabeth and Essex* because he realized that her character was completely revealed at that time. We certainly cannot know Elizabeth if we depend only on Miss Anthony's book, and that should be the test of every first-class biography.

Marie Antoinette (1932) is Miss Anthony's latest biography and it is very good, although it does not equal *Catherine the*

Great. It is a complete study of the unfortunate queen, but it is a little too concise, a little too psychological, a little too bare in terms of humanity. It has the latest and what seems to be the best point of view in regard to Marie Antoinette's responsibility for the French Revolution, but it is lacking in the portrayal of a very human woman who was forced to live a very artificial life and was driven by circumstances to the frivolities and extravagances which helped to bring her house about her head.

Miss Anthony was one of the earliest psychological biographers but she has not developed with the times. Psychology alone cannot explain human nature. Man is a creature of circumstance as well as the master of his own destiny. A biography must show all the influences that have affected an individual; it will not be complete if it gives only one side of the picture. If a man or woman is historically important, we must have enough of the historical background in the book to make the subject real and human. That is the principal fault in the purely psychographical method; it uses nothing but the individual himself and he is rarely enough. Miss Anthony's books are well written and always interesting, but they fail to reach the highest standards in life-writing.

Napoleon Bonaparte is a greater figure in the world's history than Marie Antoinette; consequently, he has been the subject of innumerable biographies, social, political and historical, sympathetic and condemnatory, dispassionate and prejudiced. And still they come. Many were written by Americans in the nineteenth and early twentieth centuries; these have been mentioned in Chapters II and III. In 1921 there appeared the first of four Napoleonic biographies by Walter Geer. So far as I know, Mr. Geer has written on no other subject, but he has certainly exhausted this one. *Napoleon. An Intimate Biography* is, as the title indicates, a study of the personality and actions of the man as an individual. The author admires Napoleon very much, but he is not blind to his faults of character or errors of judgment. He tries to present a fair picture of Napoleon the man, the soldier, the statesman. He succeeds very well in view of the fact that, in his plan, the book is necessarily incomplete. In 1925 he published two more of the series, *Napoleon and Josephine; the Rise of the Empire* and *Napoleon and Marie-Louise; the Fall of the Empire*. They are admirable studies of Napoleon during these two periods of his life and of the influence his two wives had on his career. Mr. Geer believes that Josephine was the only woman Napoleon ever loved and that he loved her all his life. This is the generally accepted judgment on the question, but Geer emphasizes it by the manner in which he presents the married life of the two and their divorce. He is a strong supporter of Josephine, and occasionally he overlooks some of her indiscretions. This point of view is readily understandable to anyone who has read extensively on the subject. The second volume, in which Marie-Louise is the wife, is particularly good, for it gives her her proper place in Napoleon's life, the mother of his son. The fourth volume, *Napoleon and his Family; the Story of a Corsican Clan* (1927), was written to prove that the family, his brothers and sisters, were more responsible for Napoleon's downfall than he was himself. Whether or not we accept this argument, it is an interesting one and the author does full justice to it. These four books constitute as complete a record of the personal and family angle of Napoleon's life as there is in English, and are a distinct contribution to Napoleonic literature. They are written in an easy, informal style quite in keeping with the manner in which Geer chose to treat the life of Napoleon. There is, naturally, a good deal of repetition in the four volumes, but they never become tiresome.

Scholarly biography kept pace with the popular type in the New Biography era. There are no better examples of scholarship in biography than Lewis Freeman Mott's *Ernest Renan* (1921) and *Sainte-Beuve* (1925). The first is an excellent and complete study of the life and work of the great French Biblical scholar. The redeeming feature of the book is that it maintains a perfect balance between biography and criticism. Most critical biographies are biographies in name only, but Professor Freeman narrates Renan's life just as fully as he interprets his work. *Sainte-Beuve* seems to be an even better book than *Ernest Renan,* for it was the first complete account of the literary historian and critic in any language. It is much more complete than Professor Harper's book and a more complete criticism of Sainte-Beuve's work, for Freeman was not limited by editorial requirements. When we read the average critical biography with its two or three chapters of biographical facts and its five or six chapters of minute research into matters that are of little importance, we realize the superiority of such work as Professor Freeman has given us in his biographies. The point of emphasis is that they are biographies and not theses.

A different kind of biography, but of the same quality, is to be found in the Reverend Peter Guilday's *Life and Times of John Carroll, Archbishop of Baltimore (1735–1815)* (1922) and *Life and Times of John England, First Bishop of Charleston (1786–1842)* (1927). There is as admirable a combination of biography and history in these books as there is of biography and criticism in Freeman's writings. John Carroll was a member of the Carroll family of Maryland, and this connection gave him a definite social and political standing in Colonial and Revolutionary America. After the war he was created the first bishop and then archbishop of Baltimore, the primary Catholic bishopric in the United States. Father Guilday tells the story of Carroll's long and useful life against a background of American history in such a complete manner that the book is an invaluable source for historians of church and state in the United States. The *Life . . . of John England . . .* is a very complete account of Bishop England's career and of the history of the Roman Catholic Church in the South. Both books are very well written. If the history of the times occasionally overshadows the biography of the individual, it is unavoidable. The fact that this happens so seldom is a point in the author's favor.

One of the results of the Stracheyan influence on modern biography is the habit of using attractive and sometimes misleading titles for biographies or biographical sketches. *Eminent Victorians* opened the floodgates for such titles, which will occur again and again. One of the earliest of these in American biography is *Strenuous Americans* (1923), by Roy F. Dibble. No one can deny the aptness of this title, for the subjects of his very entertaining and graphic sketches certainly led strenuous lives. In these studies of Jesse James, Admiral Dewey, Brigham Young, Frances E. Willard, James J. Hill, P. T. Barnum, and Mark Hanna, Mr. Dibble picked a group of representative nineteenth-century Americans whose lives were interesting as well as strenuous. He was not able to give sufficient space to any one of his subjects, but he did make his accounts read well, which is, perhaps, all that he intended. A book of this kind, of no particular value in itself, often leads to a definite interest in some or all of the subjects. If it does that, it has accomplished something.

Mr. Dibble's first essay in biography was *Albion W. Tourgée* (1921). This is a short biographical and critical sketch of a northern "carpet-bagger" who became a member of the Supreme Court of North Carolina after the Civil War. He is best known, however, as the author of novels presenting the political and racial problems of the post-war South. Among these are *Bricks Without Straw* and *The Invisible Empire,* which are really studies in northern disillusionment, for Tourgée seems to have been an honest, though misguided, man.

Following *Strenuous Americans,* Dibble published *John L. Sullivan; an Intimate Biography* in 1925. This is a good, journalistic account of the "Boston Strong Boy," the most colorful of all our heavyweight pugilists. The fact that such a biography could be successful, for it was, is an indication of the popularity of biography in the last ten years. Sullivan's life was not one that requires skilful interpretation or any particular art in presentation; it had all the elements of ro-

mance in it, and these the author used to the best advantage.
For his next book, Mr. Dibble chose an equally romantic
subject, but one that was not exactly suited to his abilities.
Mohammed (1926) is a sketchy, popular account of the
founder of a great religion. It is not very accurate in fact and
totally lacking in interpretation. One cannot write of Mohammed in terms of John L. Sullivan.

M. R. Werner belongs to the same school of biographers
as Mr. Dibble, but the former is in the upper grades. He
has written three popular lives, and each one is good in its
class. His first life was *Barnum* (1923). This is a very interesting and accurate account of the great showman. For those
who have not the time or the inclination to read Barnum's
autobiography, *The Struggles and Triumphs of P. T. Barnum,*
Mr. Werner's book is an excellent substitute. His book is
based of course on the autobiography, and he made remarkably good use of his material. No book on Barnum can be
as interesting as his own account of his own career, for it is
as honest an autobiography as can be found. Werner did tone
down some of Barnum's enthusiasms, and he filled in the
spaces to complete the life record of one of our unique public
figures.

For his second book, Mr. Werner took a larger and much
more difficult subject. In *Brigham Young* (1925), the author
had to deal with three subjects: Mormonism; Joseph Smith,
its founder; and Young, its greatest prophet. Based on the
Book of Mormon and the published writings of Smith and
Young, this book is really a history of Mormonism with Brigham Young as its central figure. It would be impossible to
write the life of Brigham Young without introducing Joseph
Smith and the religion that he founded, because Young's
place in history was achieved only through Smith and Mormonism. There are figures in history who cannot be treated
exclusively as individuals, and Young is such a figure. Mormonism gave him the opportunity to become one of the greatest leaders and executives that this country has ever seen.

The author proves the necessity for his extensive background in his development of his central figure. The book deals very fairly with Young and with Mormonism, although it is difficult to steer a middle course in such a highly controversial subject. It will not be acceptable to Mormons, but neither will any other book on the subject be accepted by Mormons if written by a Gentile, because he cannot see their religion as they see it. It seems essentially true, and it is an important item in American biography and history.

Mr. Werner's third biography, *Bryan,* appeared in 1929. To an admirer of the "Boy Orator of the Platte" this book may seem unsympathetic; to a follower of Bryan it is probably blasphemous; to the disinterested student of men and history it seems a fair, although inadequate, account of a man who was a combination of folk-hero, prophet, demagogue, politician, and fanatic. A biographer of Mr. Werner's school cannot resist the temptation that such a subject as W. J. Bryan presents. If one does not try to penetrate below the surface in the character of a man like Bryan, one can hardly avoid indulging in the modern biographical pastime of "debunking." Even when the surface is broken there is little to show that Bryan was the great man that his idolaters would have us believe he was. Mr. Werner has not said the last word on Bryan, but he has given an interesting contemporary account. It will be for the biographer and historian of the future to strike a balance in his career or to dismiss him as a "sport."

Mr. Werner's work, so far, has been along the popular lines of life-writing. He has made no independent investigations; he has made little attempt at sincere interpretation of character; he has merely told us the stories of the lives of three famous Americans. His method was popular for a time, but it seems to have lost some of its force, for the best biography of today (1935) is turning to a more serious method of presentation. Attractive backgrounds and a novel method of approach are still virtues in biographical writing, but we are also demanding more care in writing and keener analysis than Mr. Werner has given us.

2

Whatever may be its faults, the New Biography has the virtue of drawing the best writers to its practice. Freed from the necessity of writing traditionally, men have turned to biography as an art as well as a means of telling the truth about famous or great men. The old method attracted few independent minds; the new method not only attracts them but leads them further than they had intended going when they started. The New Biography demands the reinterpretation of many of our statesmen and public figures because new light and new truths can be revealed to a reading public that has ceased to be entirely partial. When a man of superior intellect, of ability in research, sound judgment, and good taste turns to biographical writing the results are bound to be good.

Claude M. Fuess belongs to this class of modern biographers, and his art has developed steadily since the publication of his first biography in 1923. The *Life of Caleb Cushing* is a long narrative of a prominent statesman, jurist, and diplomat. It required two volumes for Professor Fuess to tell the story of a busy and varied life, and it is well told. The faults of this biography are faults common to new biographers who have more than enough source material. Professor Fuess was neither completely the master of his material here—for he gives us more detail than is necessary—nor had he learned that selection is one of the essentials of all art. Nevertheless, this life is worthy of a place beside the best of American political and diplomatic biographies. It was the least successful of all of Fuess's biographies because the subject was unknown to a large majority of people. The average reader of biography wants to know the lives and characters of those men who received notoriety as well as fame, rather than those who have achieved only fame.

In *Rufus Choate; Wizard of the Law* (1928) Professor Fuess seems to have chosen, or been given, a subject which particularly interested and suited him. Written for a series of popular biographies, this book is a little masterpiece. Rufus Choate was a famous lawyer and orator in the early nineteenth century; he was equally famous for his learning and his wit. The author managed to crowd into a small space everything that is essential to a complete picture and thorough understanding of the great lawyer. The charm of the book lies in its informality, an informality that makes the man essentially human without sacrificing any of the dignity that was his by nature and position. I emphasize this method because informality in modern biography so frequently leads to a patronizing or contemptuous point of view on the part of the biographer and to a false impression in the mind of the reader. This author succeeds in avoiding both these mistakes.

Daniel Webster appeared in 1930. This is biography— modern, classical, or whatever you choose to call it—at its best. In form and style, in method and execution, it conforms to every standard of biography and of literature. It will rank with Paine's *Mark Twain* and Beveridge's *Marshall* and *Lincoln* as one of the finest biographies in our literature. Daniel Webster is a difficult subject for a modern biographer because he can be belittled as easily as he can be given the place that is rightly his, the place of a great lawyer, a greater orator, and one of the greatest of constructive statesmen. *Daniel Webster* is primarily and always a biography, but it is also a part of the literature of constitutional history and American politics. There is no phase of Webster's brilliant career that is not fully treated, and no act of his private life, as far as that is known, that is omitted. Every incident, every phase is given its proper place and importance, and almost every act of the man is judged in the light of its circumstances and from the objective and impartial point of view of the biographer. The chapters on the famous lawsuits and debates in which Webster took part are as complete and as clear as the chapters on his private and personal life. Webster was a great man, a careless man, and a weak man. His character is an open book to the reader who finishes Professor Fuess's biography, and no one who starts it can lay it aside until he has finished it. Written in a style that is exactly suited to the subject, presented with a nicety of balance that is almost unique in modern biography, this life is the best account that has been or will be written of Daniel Webster.

Professor Fuess's latest biography is *Carl Schurz, Reformer* (1932). This life of the famous German is unusually complete and shows his development from a young radical, through his experiences in the Civil War and Reconstruction, to the point where he became one of the really liberal statesmen of his day and a powerful influence in the period of national housecleaning that followed the Gilded Age. This book is as fine a biography as *Daniel Webster* and is, perhaps, even more finely attuned to the personality of its subject than the earlier book. Webster's career was one of steady progress; Schurz's had more lights and shadows in it, and the biography is all the more remarkable in that we are sympathetic toward the man that Fuess re-creates because, though he made a serious mistake in lining up with the Radicals after the Civil War, he did his best to correct that mistake in later life.

With the exception of a biographical record of Amherst graduates, these four books represent Professor Fuess's contribution to life-writing in America, thus far. They have placed him in the first rank of American biographers, and there is every reason to suppose that Fuess will continue his work in the field he has chosen and which he has done so much to elevate.

As a biographer, Henry Dwight Sedgwick takes rank with the best in America. His first biography was a short life of Father Hecker, founder of the Paulist Fathers, published in 1898. This was followed by a life of Samuel de Champlain (1903) and *Francis Parkman* (1904) in the "American Men of Letters Series." He has also written books on Marcus Aurelius and Dante, but it was not until 1923 that he began his career as a modern biographer. Every one of the earlier books is good, particularly the one on Parkman, but they are not comparable to his later work. In 1923, he published

Ignatius Loyola; an Attempt at an Impartial Biography. It seems that this book is much more than an attempt; it is an achievement. The founder of the Jesuits is not an easy subject for a biographer. For centuries his life was obscured by legends, hatreds, and idealizations. There have been and still are great differences of opinion regarding Loyola among Catholic writers; consequently, it is surprising to find an American Protestant the writer of such an excellent biography as this. Very wisely, Mr. Sedgwick confined his book to the life of Ignatius and left the history of his order to others. The famous *Spiritual Exercises,* other religious writings, and his enormous correspondence form the basis for any life of the great Spaniard, and it is the skilful use of these sources to develop the character of Saint Ignatius that makes the book a work of art. Loyola speaks for himself wherever possible and, as we follow him from birth to death, we see and hear him as he lived. Not every man can explain himself, but Loyola knew exactly what he was doing and why he was doing it. The author so thoroughly understood his subject that he was able to extract from the vast sources just those parts of the writings which give a complete material and spiritual picture of the man. When we have finished this book we know the man, know why he suddenly turned to God for inspiration, and finally, we know a great deal about the origin and early development of the Society of Jesus. There is no controversy in this book, no judgment passed on Ignatius the priest, the theologian. It is concerned only with the narration of a great life and with the attempt to develop that life from the facts as we have them. Not the least important qualities of this book are its restraint and liberality. Its style appears to be as simple as its content, but both are the results of years of writing and study.

Cortes the Conqueror; the Exploits of the Earliest and Greatest of the Gentlemen Adventurers in the New World (1926) is, in some respects, complementary to *Ignatius Loyola.* Where Loyola set out to conquer a spiritual empire, Cortes planned the conquest of a material empire of gold, silver,

and precious stones. Both succeeded, both have gained immortality; it is a matter of opinion as to the value of their
respective conquests, though there can be no doubt as to the
higher significance of Loyola's quest. In *Cortes the Conqueror*
we have the fusion of the judicious biographer with the
capable historian. It was necessary to place Cortes in his historical background, for he is a historical figure as Loyola
is a religious figure. The difference in method in these two
books is only further evidence of Mr. Sedgwick's art. We
have as complete a picture of Cortes as we have of Loyola,
but it is a picture of a man in action, not knowing where
that action will carry him. Both of these Spaniards were great
men, with a difference, and it is because each of these lives
shows us the difference in the men that they are biographies
of the first class.

In *La Fayette* (1928), Mr. Sedgwick maintains the standard
which he established with *Ignatius Loyola* and *Cortes the
Conqueror*. He is as much at home in the France and America
of the eighteenth century as he was in the Spain of the sixteenth century. Again, there is here that combination of biography and history which enables us to understand the times
and their influence on Lafayette and to see Lafayette himself
as he really was. *La Fayette* is an impartial, a classical biography which shows us the whole man and the relative importance of his American experience in his long life and his
equally long fight for liberty. This is the first biography of
Lafayette that I have read which tells the whole story and the
whole truth about this citizen of France and honorary citizen
of the United States.

Mr. Sedgwick has written two other historical biographies,
Henry of Navarre (1930) and the *Life of Edward the Black
Prince 1330–1376* (1932). They are of the same quality and
texture as the earlier books and they have the same perfection
of method and simplicity of style. In 1931, the author published the one literary biography of his later period, *Alfred
de Musset, 1810–1857; a Biography*. The method used here
is very much the same as the method in *Ignatius Loyola*. It

is a simple biographical narrative of de Musset's life with comparatively little criticism of his poetry. In this Mr. Sedgwick seems to follow his natural interest in biography, which is the development of personality. He uses the poetry to illuminate de Musset's character, but he does not commit the fault of so many modern biographers, that of trying to explain the man in terms of his work alone. In this book, too, Sedgwick shows his inevitable good taste by putting de Musset's love affairs in their proper place. He does not slight them; he gives them the emphasis that they actually had, minor notes in the life symphony of a genius.

Taking Mr. Sedgwick's work as a whole, we find that he is one of the major figures in modern American biography. The evidence of his historical scholarship is obvious on every page of his writings. Not only does he know and understand history, but what is more important, he knows and understands men. In spite of the fact that he is a historical biographer, Mr. Sedgwick never allows history to obscure the figure of his subject. It is only by a study of his work that we can realize the time and effort that have gone into the making of his art. Such simplicity of style and method is deceptive because it seems so easy to do. If we look over Mr. Sedgwick's subjects, we discover that each man had a romantic career and that Mr. Sedgwick has been able to make that romance real to us. More than that no biographer can accomplish.

The difference between Henry Dwight Sedgwick and Professor Robert McElroy is the difference between a biographer who uses history as a means of explaining great men and a historian who tries to write biography using historical methods. Professor McElroy's *Grover Cleveland, the Man and the Statesman* (1923), is a conventional, authorized biography of a great man rather than a great statesman. We do not see much of the man because the author was more interested in politics and history than he was in human nature. It was Cleveland's honesty, courage, and tenacity of purpose that made him Governor of New York and President of the United States.

Because his biographer hastens over his early life and entirely omits some of the characteristic incidents of his private life which should have been explained, we are never conscious of the forces that made a great man of Grover Cleveland. We are no longer interested in merely the public life of a prominent man; we want to know the circumstances, accidental or otherwise, that brought him to his high position, and we want to know wherein lay his strength and his weakness. There is little analysis of character in this biography of Cleveland, and less real knowledge. Professor McElroy filled two large volumes with a history of the United States as it affected and was affected by Grover Cleveland. This sort of biography no longer satisfies us, for we are interested in personality when we read biography. Professor McElroy's second biography was *Levi Parsons Morton* (1930). This life, done in the same manner as the Cleveland book, is less interesting because Morton, Vice-President during Harrison's administration, was obviously a much less important man than Cleveland.

Thomas Beer has what Professor McElroy lacks, a biographical point of view and the knowledge that all subjects cannot be given the same treatment. In *Stephen Crane: A Study in American Letters* (1923), we have an excellent example of sympathetic, imaginative biography. Mr. Beer has told all there is to be known, at present, about Crane. It was certainly interest in the man's life and writings that led Beer to the writing of this book. His sympathetic interest did not blind him to Crane's many faults, but it did enable him to interpret Crane, putting in his own theories as theories, to account for the many inexplicable actions of Crane's life.

Hanna (1929) is a totally different kind of book from *Stephen Crane*. The author says it is not a biography. That is true, but it is a remarkable character appraisal of the man who made William McKinley President of the United States, and whom Walter Davenport, the cartoonist, immortalized in his cartoons, depicting Hanna as dressed in clothes patterned with the dollar mark. *Hanna* begins in the middle of Mark Hanna's life. Weaving backward and forward, it manages to include every characteristic that made Hanna what he was. A conventional, chronological account might have succeeded as well as Mr. Beer's method succeeds here. In this small book, the author not only succeeds in re-creating Hanna as he really was, but in giving an excellent running account of the history of the period, and the part that Hanna played in it.

In these two books Mr. Beer has contributed to the literature as well as to the art of biography; he has made brilliant contributions in the orthodox and the unorthodox manner.

M. A. De Wolfe Howe has been a prominent figure in biographical editing and writing for many years. His early book on George Bancroft has been mentioned, and some of his short studies will be considered in a later chapter. Mr. Howe's most prominent life is *Barrett Wendell and his Letters* (1924). This biography, which received the Pulitzer Prize in 1924, is made up largely of letters which tell almost the whole story of Wendell's life and career as Professor of English at Harvard, where he was a landmark for forty years. His letters are literature of a very high quality, and Mr. Howe used excellent judgment in his selection. The material in the book is, however, very selective and the character of Wendell seems to be incomplete. In 1929 Howe published *James Ford Rhodes, American Historian*. This is an interesting, charming, and very proper biography of the historian, probably written at the request of his family. Mr. Howe wove Rhodes's correspondence into the text in an admirable fashion, constructing a book that is all that an appreciative memoir should be. There seems to be something lacking in this book as there was in *Barrett Wendell and his Letters*. They are literary appreciations in two dimensions instead of three-dimensional biographies. All the good points of the subjects are stressed, but they seem to have had no faults. *Moorfield Storey* (1932) is written in the same strain, and all three books represent the old method of saying very little that is significant of the real man, and thus give a decidedly biased impression of men who must have had some faults.

3

The number of professional biographers increased as biography became more popular. Nearly all of them were disciples of, or were greatly influenced by Strachey, Guedalla, Maurois, and others. Some of these professional biographers tried to develop the ironic and dramatic qualities that made Strachey famous, and failed because they lacked his culture, his knowledge of human nature, and his style. Others, beginning in this strain, gradually developed a method and style of their own. Herbert S. Gorman belongs to the latter group. His first biography, *A Victorian American, Henry W. Longfellow* (1926), is a product of the Strachey school, done in extremely bad taste. It is flippant, deprecatory, and sometimes vulgar. Mr. Gorman seemed to think that ridicule and irony are the same thing. They are not. In trying to make Longfellow a ridiculous figure, the author succeeded only in making himself ridiculous. In his desire for informality, Mr. Gorman constantly speaks of Longfellow as Henry. I am not a hero worshiper, but I do think that there is a certain respect due to such men as Longfellow. In his criticism, the author uses *The Children's Hour, The Village Blacksmith,* and other universally known pieces of Longfellow as the standard by which he judges him as a poet. Whether or not this was intentional I do not know, but it does show that, in 1926, Mr. Gorman had much to learn about criticism. He said very little about the poetic qualities of *Paul Revere's Ride, The Courtship of Miles Standish,* and *Hiawatha,* and seemed entirely unaware of the sonnets of Longfellow. Mr. Gorman's method of procedure can be justified on the ground of a preconceived opinion of Longfellow, but no biographer may choose only those phases of a man's life and only that part of a man's work which will prove his thesis. If he does so, he is being false to himself and to his readers, and very unjust to his subject.

Hawthorne; a Study in Solitude (1927) was written by Mr. Gorman for the "Murray Hill Biographies." It is a small volume giving the principal facts of Hawthorne's life and some comment on his major writings. The tone of the book is set by the subtitle: *A Study in Solitude.* Mr. Gorman leaves the impression that Hawthorne spent the whole of his life physically and mentally isolated from the world, thus explaining the uniqueness of Hawthorne's work. Hawthorne lived and worked in the world and was thoroughly aware of the great changes and movements that were abroad in New England and the rest of the United States. It was only with the experience gained in the world that he was able to write *Mosses from an Old Manse, The Scarlet Letter,* and *The House of the Seven Gables.* It was only by looking into the souls of other men, as well as his own, that he perfected his art. Mr. Gorman would have us believe that Hawthorne's art was a matter of spontaneous generation, that it grew of and by itself. In representing Hawthorne as a recluse, the author gives us a picture entirely out of focus. The criticism in this volume is much better than in the one on Longfellow; in fact it is surprisingly orthodox.

Mr. Gorman went far afield for a subject in *Dumas, the Incredible Marquis* (1929). This is a very long and complete biography of a man whose own life was almost as romantic as his writings. In this book Gorman had an opportunity to display his talents, and he made the most of it. It is, at once, more and less conventional than either of the earlier books. The romance of Dumas' career could not help influencing his biographer, and the flamboyancy of Dumas' character allows his biographer to indulge in the fictional style popular at the moment. There is gusto and life in the book as there was gusto and a joy of life in Dumas. The book seems to be fundamentally accurate and true, even though the author does occasionally set his stage and move his characters imaginatively rather than accurately. On the other hand, there is no incident in the book that might not have happened. The character of such a volatile genius as Dumas is an almost perfect vehicle for the modern imaginative biography. Of its type, this life is very good because it re-creates not only the man but the immortal spirit that was in the creator of *The Three Musketeers* and *The Count of Monte Cristo*.

Mr. Gorman's latest biography, *The Scottish Queen* (1932), is much superior to anything else that he has done. Mary Stuart is one of the most difficult of all biographical subjects to handle, for no one can be entirely unprejudiced when writing of her. As far as it is humanly possible, Mr. Gorman has told her story without fear or favor, and has produced the best biography of the tragic queen that we have in English. The literature on the subject is enormous, but the author seems to have made the best use of the best of it. In writing a life of Mary, Queen of Scots, a biographer must pass judgment on widely divergent points of view. To some, Mary was an insincere, unfaithful woman and a bad queen; to others she was a victim of circumstances and a pawn in a great political game. Mr. Gorman does not adopt either point of view; he tries to explain the woman in the light of her character, of her difficult position, and of the history of the times. The queen, as Mr. Gorman sees her, was both weak and strong, indiscreet and sometimes reckless, but loyal to her class and her church. She was a very human and very beautiful woman, and the fact that she was human and feminine and beautiful helped to bring about her downfall. Her heart often ruled her head, and her passion sometimes clouded her judgment. She made many serious mistakes, and they were used against her when the proper time arrived. Her nature made of her life a tragedy, for, given her character, her end was inevitable. It is this tragedy, as Mr. Gorman develops it, that makes his book a biography of great importance. It is his interpretation of those conflicting passions and desires that enables us to see her as she really was, as a woman and as a queen. Some have made her all woman, others, all queen; Mr. Gorman saw her as both.

There were famous and great people in Mary's life, and Mr. Gorman fills in his canvas with lifelike, if not life-size, portraits of them. Her brother; her husbands, Darnley and Bothwell; her secretary, Rizzio; her worst enemy, John Knox; and her greatest enemy, Queen Elizabeth, live in this book as completely as Mary herself. These are the principal players in the tragedy of the Scottish queen, and each is given his proper place and importance. The extreme value of these secondary biographies will be realized by anyone familiar with the story of Mary's life.

As we have pointed out, there is a great change in Mr. Gorman's work from the flippant study of Longfellow to the distinguished biography of Mary Stuart. In the latest book there is a firmness of texture, an individuality of style, a mastery of material and method, and a soundness of judgment that are entirely lacking in the first biography. In short, Mr. Gorman has made remarkable progress in his art, and *The Scottish Queen* is entitled to a prominent position among the best of modern biographies. In one respect, however, Mr. Gorman has not yet thrown off the influence of the fictional school of biography. He still likes to set his stage, and there are numerous scenes in this book which can have no basis in fact. There is a picture of John Knox's first audience with the Queen of Scotland which is brilliant and, no doubt, it adds interest to the narrative, but it is a scene which Mr. Gorman imagined, for we do not know how Knox and Mary were dressed or how they actually greeted one another. This may seem carping criticism, but this imaginative re-creation of particular scenes is one of the evils of modern biography, for, if the writer imaginatively re-creates one part of the book, he may do the same for other parts and so destroy the truth which he has been at such pains to discover and express.

Just as Herbert Gorman endeavored to tell the truth about Mary Stuart, George S. Hellman endeavored to present true pictures of Washington Irving and Robert Louis Stevenson. In *Washington Irving, Esquire, Ambassador at Large from the New World to the Old* (1925), we have the best biography of Irving that has been written. There is little criticism in it, for Hellman was interested in the man and not the author. In the earlier books on Irving, particularly in the compilation by his nephew, he is represented as a charming gentleman who had never recovered from the loss of his first and only love, Matilda Hoffman. Mr. Hellman's book seems to indicate that Irving found more than one solace for his lost love, that he was on the verge of marriage on more than one occasion, and that the postponements and rejections were not on his side. He also presents the "Ambassador from the New World to the Old" in a mellow and genial light that is much more characteristic of the real Washington Irving than the impression that his earlier biographers created. Mr. Hellman is not "debunking" in this book; he is simply trying to get at the truth of Irving's life, particularly during the seventeen years that he wandered over Europe. Our only regret is that this book is not longer, for it is good biography, written with an engaging style.

In *The True Stevenson* (1925) Mr. Hellman embarks on another voyage of biographical discovery. In all previous lives of Stevenson nothing was said of the period of his young manhood when he was wandering around Edinburgh without interest or occupation. Mr. Hellman clears up this vagueness by showing that Robert Louis Stevenson was living a rather fast and loose life during this period, a life that was exhausting him physically, but giving him experiences on which he would draw heavily during his creative years. Robert Louis Stevenson was no different from other men, and there is no reason why his whole life should not be examined. The reputation of Francis Thompson or George Gissing did not suffer because of the facts of their private lives. Why should Stevenson's reputation suffer because he frequented the demi-world of Edinburgh at various times? No creative writer gets his material wholly from his imagination; his experiences of life are the foundation of his art. Stevenson's writings are not of the type that makes such experiences obvious, but no man who is ignorant of the world could have written some of Stevenson's stories. Stevenson wrote other books besides *Treasure Island* and *A Child's Garden of Verses*. *The True Stevenson* is even a shorter book than the one on Irving, but it is done in the same manner. Had Mr. Hellman incorporated his discoveries in a full-length biography, he would have been more successful.

Mr. Hellman based his books on known and newly discovered facts; Cameron Rogers wrote books on Walt Whitman and Robert G. Ingersoll, using a combination of fact and fiction. In an effort to make *Magnificent Idler; the Story of Walt Whitman* (1926), an interesting biography in the modern manner, Rogers, inadvertently perhaps, became a second-rate novelist. The book is smart and entertaining, but it is not biography. The title is misleading, for Whitman could hardly be called a "magnificent idler." The subject is moved here and there, now loafing by the sea, now riding the East River ferries, now enjoying himself driving an old Fifth Avenue omnibus. Whitman did do all these things, but Mr. Rogers has no evidence to prove that he did them at certain definite times, as the book indicates that he did. Furthermore, there are conversations, soliloquies, and thought processes which are made to appear real, but which can have no foundation in fact. They might have been, and if Mr. Rogers had used them as possible rather than actual, they could be accepted as part of his method. When we come upon such fictional devices as these we are inclined to doubt the truth of the whole book because one invention will lead to another, particularly when a writer desires to present a case in a certain light, as Rogers did in the case of Whitman. Mr. Rogers follows exactly the same procedure in *Colonel Bob Ingersoll; a Biographical Narrative of the Great American Orator and Agnostic* (1927). This is even a better example of fictional biography, and a more irritating book. It is sketchy, unanalytic, and totally lacking in distinction. It is the sort of thing that any competent newswriter could turn out in a few months. A display of scholarly apparatus is not necessary, but when intimate thoughts and conversations are reported as actualities it is well to know their sources.

Gallant Ladies (1928) shows the same penchant for attractive titles and second-hand material that the earlier books show. This book contains a number of very ordinary sketches of such lovely ladies as Mata Hari, Calamity Jane, Adrienne Lecouvreur, and Lola Montez. They represent exactly the sort of thing we find in the Sunday supplements. Books of this type are all too common in this period, for they sold well and neither author nor publisher concerned himself with quality.

Before publishing his latest book, *Cyrano* (1929), Rogers altered his method to a considerable extent. In this romantic biography of Cyrano de Bergerac, the great-nosed swordsman, lover, and writer of the days of Louis XIII and XIV, Mr. Rogers confined himself to facts, with a few exceptions, with the result that this is the best biography he has written.

Cameron Rogers violated some of the fundamental principles of biographical writing and failed of his objective; Paul Van Dyke disregarded at least one but managed to write a great book nevertheless. In the two volumes of *Catherine de Medici* (1922), Professor Van Dyke has given us a magnificent picture of the great Medici family, of Catherine, and of the times in which they lived. It is perhaps more history than biography, but over the whole book is the shadow of Catherine of France, who was the epitome of the family whose name she bore and of the age to which that same family gave their name. One might call this biographical history, for the book is a succession of pen portraits of the great of France and Italy. Professor Van Dyke was primarily a historian; this book is planned on a historical rather than a biographical method, but it is as great a biography as it is a history.

Professor Van Dyke's *Ignatius Loyola, Founder of the Jesuits* (1926) is true biography. Brilliantly written, it is a scholarly, unbiased, and sympathetic presentation of the man as he showed himself in his own writings. A comparative study of this biography and Mr. Sedgwick's life of Loyola will show little difference in their points of view and methods of approaching the subject. It is hard to say which is the better biography.

Professor Van Dyke's last biography was *George Washington, Son of his Country* (1931). This is not a full-length biography, for Van Dyke's purpose here was to try to explain the various factors in Washington's early life that contributed to the character of the General and the President. We may not agree with the author's conclusions, but we must admit that his method is the only true one in the case of such a man as Washington. The method is the same as that used in *Ignatius Loyola* and is admirably adapted to each subject.

Most of the young men who have entered the biographical field in the last fifteen years have, unlike the Van Dykes and the Sedgwicks, boldly plunged into the methods of the modern masters, without having done any preliminary work. In most cases they have become aware of their faults and have, without sacrificing the essence of the modern manner, adapted that manner to their own needs and the needs of the subjects. It would seem that Phillips Russell belongs to this class of modern biographers.

In his first biography, *Benjamin Franklin, the First Civilized American* (1926), Mr. Russell used the very latest devices in biographical novelty, writing a very interesting and entertaining book but not a life of Franklin. So much effort was expended on the subtitle that the main title was sometimes forgotten. The book is not very well proportioned because much more space is given to the "civilized" phases of Franklin's career than to his early life. It is in Franklin's early life that we find the index to his character. He did not change, he developed, but Mr. Russell does not make clear that development. There is one feature of the book that is irritating: Mr. Russell generally writes in the present tense, but occasionally he slips into the past tense; the whole book should have been written in the past tense. Lastly, the author does not know so much about the history of the eighteenth century as he should. Franklin was peculiarly a product of the eighteenth century, and without that background he cannot be completely understood. Despite the serious faults of the book, it is interesting and, to those who know the facts of Franklin's life, it gives a new point of view.

John Paul Jones, Man of Action (1927) is a much better biography than *Benjamin Franklin*. It is written in a simple, straightforward style that is an improvement over the "smart" style of Russell's first book. The story moves with a celerity that is characteristic of the man, and it is of excellent balance. The importance of this book lies in the fact that it gives a new and, apparently, a truthful characterization of John Paul Jones. It corrects the mistakes and idol worshiping that spoiled the biographies of Jones written by A. C. Buell and Mrs. Anna DeKoven. It makes Jones a great man in place of the pedestaled hero created by the earlier writers. He was a reckless, passionate, vain man more often than he was a hero. He was a man who always thought of himself first, except in the heat of battle. He was a natural gentleman, a lover of fine clothes and good living, a martinet on the quarterdeck, and a cavalier on shore. In short, he was of the stuff of which men are made, and the heroic legend is quite unnecessary. Mr. Russell's life of Jones is the best that has appeared, and it is not likely to be superseded very soon.

Mr. Russell seems to have found his own particular method in *John Paul Jones,* for he used the same method in *Emerson, the Wisest American* (1929). As Jones's world of activity was the sea, Emerson's was his mind and the New England of his day. In this biography of Emerson, we see him advancing his thinking from the point where he was an orthodox Unitarian to the point where he emancipated himself from all formal systems of religion and society. To a greater extent than any other biographer, Mr. Russell shows that Emerson was not a thinker but a man thinking. In spite of his activity of mind he was a citizen of New England, of Concord, outwardly conforming to standards while inwardly he had "hitched his wagon to a star." *Emerson, the Wisest American* is not the best literary biography of Emerson, but no other book on Emerson up to this time so completely re-created the man as this one has. Critical biographies are numerous, but biographies of the man are not. We can forgive Mr. Russell for not understanding the star gazer, the transcendental philosopher, for he has shown us the man as he gazed and philosophized.

It is to be hoped that Mr. Russell will continue his biographical writing, for his work has shown a steady development toward a method and a style that should produce even better things. It is difficult to realize that the same man wrote *Benjamin Franklin, the First Civilized American* and *Emerson, the Wisest American*. It speaks well for American biography that so many writers have, as Russell has, taken the spirit of modern biography and adapted it to their individual problems and subjects. As we advance toward the end of this period, we shall see that a desire for novelty and interest has been superseded by a desire for quality and interest. An interesting life, completely conceived and well written should be, of course, the ideal in the mind of every biographer.

This ideal never occurred to Paxton Hibben when he was writing *Henry Ward Beecher; an American Portrait* (1927) and the *Peerless Leader, William Jennings Bryan* (1929). These are classical examples of the psychological, "debunking" school of modern biography. Apparently, Mr. Hibben intended to make the characters of these men as small and contemptible as he possibly could, and he succeeded. Henry Ward Beecher was not a representative American of his day, and this book is not a portrait of him. The life of every man is made up of lights and shadows. Hibben was interested only in the shadows, and he made black spots of those shadows. Beecher was a famous member of a famous family; he was one of the best-known clergymen and writers of the later nineteenth century; he was a great orator and a dominating influence in American public life. He also was very human, a lover of praise and of the limelight. Perhaps he thought he was different from other men. He acted as if he did. Hibben took this side of Beecher and made it represent the whole man. There was a great deal that was good in Beecher, but Hibben carefully avoided the good. Nothing in the book can be accepted as truth, for there is so much in it that is blatantly false. Hibben thought he had Lytton Strachey's genius for irony; he had only a predilection for mud-slinging. The unfortunate factor in this study is that there was a basis for Hibben's point of view, but he also made the basis the superstructure.

Hibben used the same charming method in *Peerless Leader, William Jennings Bryan,* with an even more devastating effect, for Mr. Bryan had more vulnerable spots than the Reverend Mr. Beecher. If Mr. Hibben had personally planned Bryan's career and established his point of view of the world in general, that career and point of view could not have been more to his liking. He fairly revels in Bryan's emotions, absurdities, and crusades. He distorts every fact to suit his own purpose and produces a caricature instead of a character. I hold no brief for Bryan as politician or theologian, but I do think that a biographer should try to be fair to his subject. The time when personal invective passed for biography has gone, and if a biographer can say nothing in favor of his subject he had better leave that subject to a more temperate judgment. Mr. Hibben died before *Peerless Leader* was completed, and C. Hartley Grattan wrote the last chapters from Hibben's notes. They lack that rare talent for ditch-wading which was Mr. Hibben's only claim to fame.

William Marcy Tweed was a contemporary of Henry Ward Beecher, as notorious as the latter, but not quite so famous. In *"Boss" Tweed; the Story of a Grim Generation* (1927), Denis Tilden Lynch wrote a biography of Tweed, a history of the "Tweed Ring," and a commentary on American life and politics in the latter half of the nineteenth century. Mr. Lynch told a fascinatingly grim and sordid story in this book. He told the truth, but not all of it. No one could do that. The combination of biography and political history was unavoidable because Tweed's life, for twenty years, was so closely interwoven with New York politics that it is impossible to separate the two. A better separation could have been made, however, for more than half the book is made up of details which add nothing to our knowledge of Tweed. The writing is no more than good journalism, and Mr. Lynch used imaginative and fictitious methods too frequently. As biography *"Boss" Tweed* is mediocre; as social history it is invaluable, and not the least of its value is its fundamental truth.

For his second biography, Lynch went back to an earlier generation for *An Epoch and a Man; Martin Van Buren and His Times* (1929). This, like *"Boss" Tweed,* is an historical biography with less reason for the preponderance of history. It is not necessary to recount the details of state politics in New York during Van Buren's lifetime to write a life of the eighth President of the United States. He was a national rather than a local figure and should be treated as such. There are whole chapters in this book that have only indirect and slight connection with Van Buren, and they seriously impede the progress of the biography. A vast amount of research went into the making of this book, but only an expert in New York state politics can judge the accuracy of at least one-third of it. At this time, Mr. Lynch had not learned the art of omission. Except that it is written in a very modern style, this book differs little from the old-fashioned "life and times" biographies. Its only unity is chronology and its only virtue, industry. If we persevere we can get some idea of who and what Martin Van Buren was, and we get an occasional glimpse of character through the political haze, but we never come to see Van Buren as he really was, apart from politics. The style of this book shows no improvement over *"Boss" Tweed,* nor has the method improved.

Mr. Lynch did not repeat this mistake when he wrote *Grover Cleveland; a Man Four-Square* (1932). This is Mr. Lynch's best biography, so far, but it has many of the faults of the earlier books. In an effort to make this life interesting,

Lynch went to the extreme in the informal mode. Professor McElroy wrote a political biography of Cleveland and almost omitted the *man;* Lynch wrote a strictly personal life of Cleveland and laid more emphasis on his early and private life than on his public career. Both books lack balance, but we know Cleveland more intimately after reading Lynch's book than we do after reading McElroy's. *Grover Cleveland; a Man Four-Square* is a sincere attempt to explain the qualities of mind and character that combined to make Grover Cleveland one of the greatest of our Presidents, but it is marred by a lack of distinction in style and by those excursions into fiction which Mr. Lynch still considers necessary in modern biography. However, Mr. Lynch has broken away from the historical point of view and, when he has adapted modern methods rather than imitated them, he will do better work than anything he has yet written.

Although Mr. Lynch's biographies are long, no one of them is complete. This matter of balance and proportion is most important, for it determines the success or failure of biography as an art. *Trumpets of Jubilee* (1927), by Constance M. Rourke, is an illustration of this point. This volume contains short biographies of Lyman Beecher, Henry Ward Beecher, Harriet Beecher Stowe, Horace Greeley, and Phineas T. Barnum. Each of these biographies is complete, and each presents the subject as he or she really was. They are admirable in form and method, combining the best elements of the old and the new biography. A moment's reflection will show that each of these people was a trumpeter of jubilee, though in widely different fields. Two famous ministers, a famous novelist, a great editor, and a great showman. Where else but in nineteenth-century America could such a group have flourished and given force to what Miss Rourke calls jubilee? When we have finished this book we know the family that was said to be the most intellectual family in the America of its day; we know the man who urged young men to "go West and grow up with the country"; we know the man who developed that uniquely American institution, the circus. Miss Rourke's skill as a biographer is as evident in her choice of subjects as in her treatment of them.

Miss Rourke also wrote *Troupers of the Gold Coast; or, the Rise of Lotta Crabtree* (1928). The background of this book is the theatre of California during the gold rush of '49 and the decade that followed. Against this unique and colorful background is developed the story of the rise of Lotta Crabtree, one of the best-known actresses in America. The book gives a complete account of Lotta's life, but the emphasis is placed on her early career in California, a career the exigencies of which compelled her to become the versatile actress that she was. Tragedy and comedy, burlesque and satire were equally important elements in the repertoire of an early California company, and Lotta was able to do justice to each form. In addition to Lotta we meet the Booths, Edwin Forrest and his wife, David Belasco as a young producer, and a host of others whose names are unknown today. It may be said that there is more theatrical history than biography in this book, but, as has been noted before, it requires the exception to prove the rule. Lotta always remains the central figure of the book.

Charles Edward Russell shares, with Miss Rourke, the distinction of being able to write about people in widely different positions in life. His first biography was *Hero of the Filipinos, the Story of José Rizal, Poet, Patriot and Martyr* (1923). This is a really impassioned account of the life and death of one of the early advocates of independence in the Philippines. The author's sympathy for Rizal and his hatred of tyranny color the book to such an extent that it is a philippic against Spain rather than a biography of Rizal. A certain amount of sympathy and understanding is necessary, but too much is fatal to good biography.

In 1926, Mr. Russell published *Julia Marlowe, her Life and Art*. This is a much more temperate book than the first one, but it is not a good biography because there is too much art and not enough life in it. The early years of Miss Marlowe's life are covered too hastily and inadequately, for it is the formative years that generally determine the actions and character of a man or woman. We are interested in the actress and her art, but we would like to know more about the woman and her art. The style of *Julia Marlowe* is much superior to that of the *Hero of the Filipinos* and the tone is more quiet, adapting itself to the subject.

Mr. Russell's interest in the theatre and in music is at least equal to his enthusiasm for political and social reform. Proof of this is evident in *The American Orchestra and Theodore Thomas* (1927). This is an excellent biography of Thomas and an equally good history of American music. This book is another example of the necessity of combining history and biography when the occasion arises. Thomas' one interest in life was the development of symphonic music in America, and his biography had to be joined to the development of the American symphony orchestra. In writing this book, Mr. Russell proved his skill as biographer and musical historian, and he succeeded in giving the proper proportions to each part. *The American Orchestra and Theodore Thomas* received the Pulitzer Prize for Biography in 1927 because of its biographical quality and the American spirit which permeates it.

In his latest biographies, Mr. Russell has turned to history and politics for his material. *Charlemagne, the First of the Moderns* (1930) is a carefully constructed and interesting record of Charlemagne's life and reign. Based on the best ancient and modern writing on the subject, this biography is conventional in form and method and very modern in spirit. This combination always makes for good life-writing.

In *Haym Salomon and the Revolution* (1930) Russell attempted to tell the story of a little known but important financial figure of the American Revolution. Without the aid of this Jewish financier and patriot, Robert Morris could never have found the money that Washington needed to carry on the war. Salomon ruined himself for his country and he did not even receive its thanks. As a biography, this book is not particularly successful, for the material was too scant for a complete life, and the padding, of a historical nature, adds nothing to our knowledge of Salomon. The book is what we would call a successful failure, for Russell did the best he could with the material he had, and added the name of a genuine patriot to the American roll of honor.

The success of *Blaine of Maine; his Life and Times* (1931) is a matter of opinion. As a factual biography, it is all that could be desired. It is in the interpretation of those facts that there may be differences of opinion. Blaine was an anti-slavery man, a Radical after the Civil War, a party chieftain for many years, and once the nominee of the Republican party for the Presidency. He was a stalwart of the stalwarts in the Republican party; he was involved in several of the scandals of the Grant administrations; and he was the choice of the financial leaders of the party for the Presidency in 1884. On the other hand, he was one of the most popular men in post-Civil War America, for he was a great orator and an even greater campaigner. All these facts and many more are to be found in Mr. Russell's life of Blaine, but he always gives Blaine the benefit of a doubt although, in many of the questions arising out of Blaine's career, there is no doubt. In other words, Mr. Russell has taken a sectional rather than a national point of view in his interpretation of Blaine's character and actions, and he was largely influenced by Blaine's real or political attitude toward slavery. Today, *Blaine of Maine* cannot be accepted as the definitive biography of the "Plumed Knight."

If we consider Mr. Russell's work in its entirety, he deserves a prominent place among American biographers, for he has contributed six biographies, each one of which, despite its faults, is above the average, and one at least ranks with the best. If, in the future, he takes subjects which will not arouse his zeal for reform, he will probably repeat his successes of *The American Orchestra and Theodore Thomas* and *Charlemagne*. If he does not, he will probably write such competent and prejudiced studies as *Blaine of Maine*.

It is comparatively easy to understand the point of view of a biographer like Russell, and his reasons for presenting

what seems to be a one-sided picture of James G. Blaine. It is
much more difficult to understand how a modern biographer
can publish an authorized or official biography which deliberately omits anything which is unfavorable to the subject.
Anna Robeson Burr's *Portrait of a Banker; James Stillman,
1850–1918* (1927) is such a book. Instead of being an account
of the life and career of one of the greatest bankers and financiers of his day, it is merely a memoir of a man who had a
perfectly serene existence. We know that this is not a true
picture, for Mr. Stillman was one of the elder Morgan's
principal lieutenants and took an active part in the great
financial battles that were fought in Wall Street for forty
years before his death. If we are to believe Mrs. Burr, his life
was spent in a large and beautiful office where he quietly per
formed the administrative duties of the president of one of
the largest banks in the country. Mrs. Burr saw only the
finished product; she either could not or would not present
the man as he really lived. *The Portrait of a Banker; James
Stillman* is a study in still life, an exceedingly proper memorial to a man who may have been, at sixty-eight, the man
whom the author shows us. It would have been much better
for Mrs. Burr's reputation if she had declined such a commission as the preparation of this book evidently was.

Weir Mitchell: His Life and Letters (1929) is also an
authorized biography and another golden opportunity wasted.
This is a much more lifelike portrait than that of James Stillman, but it is very incomplete. His early life is fairly well
covered and his career as a great physician is sketched. Some
of the best of the family anecdotes are included, as well as
some of Dr. Mitchell's own stories. His position as a prominent Philadelphian is more than adequately handled; that is
relatively unimportant. The poet and the novelist are given
a decidedly secondary place because Mrs. Burr was either
unable or unwilling to go into that part of Dr. Mitchell's life
on which rests his principal claim to fame. He was a great
physician and neurologist, but fame of that kind is more or
less ephemeral; he will be remembered as a poet and novelist

long after his work in toxicology and mental pathology has been forgotten. A critical survey of the literary work of the physician would have greatly aided a more complete understanding of the man. In this book, Mrs. Burr lost the opportunity of writing a great biography of a great man.

Where Mrs. Burr wasted her opportunities, Henry F. Pringle made the best of his. Mr. Pringle, a journalist by profession, has given us the finest character study and one of the best biographies that the twentieth century has seen. *Alfred E. Smith: A Critical Study* (1927) is all that the subtitle implies. Written in 1927, it may have been an authorized campaign biography; if so, it is unique in that field of writing. Sketching in Governor Smith's early life with a few deft strokes, Mr. Pringle then goes into a detailed analysis of the political career and the character of the man who is one of the greatest public men of our day. When we have finished this book we understand why Alfred E. Smith was elected Governor of New York for four terms, why he has been and is the champion of unpopular causes. We understand how he became the great master of government that he is, and why he is the idol of the sidewalks of New York, and of many liberals in the United States. It is doubtful if any contemporary public man has been so thoroughly and completely analyzed as Governor Smith has been analyzed in this book. Not a move in his career has been omitted; nothing has been glossed over. If we knew as much about all our political candidates as Pringle has told us about Smith, we might be able to make more intelligent choices than we have been accustomed to make.

In 1928, Mr. Pringle published a volume of biographical and analytical sketches of some of the most prominent men in the country, under the title *Big Frogs*. The subjects range from Mr. Hoover and Jimmy Walker to Bernarr McFadden and Kenesaw Mountain Landis. Keen, incisive, and sound in judgment, these sketches represent the peak of journalistic biography. They were not intended to be profound, but they will be read for what they say and how they say it, long after the majority of the subjects have been forgotten.

Mr. Pringle made a definite and permanent place for himself in biographical literature when he wrote *Theodore Roosevelt* (1931). This is unquestionably the best biography of Roosevelt that has been written. Theodore Roosevelt is one of the many men in American public life who has been, and is, either greatly admired or greatly condemned. His biographers have been uniformly fulsome in their praise and lacking in their criticism. His letters and correspondence have been carefully edited, probably under family supervision, and no one, until Mr. Pringle took up the task, gave us a complete picture of Roosevelt as he really was.

Mr. Pringle's book is a masterly combination of personal, political, and critical biography. He had more material than any previous biographer, and made better use of it than any previous biographer could have done. As far as such a position is possible, Mr. Pringle approached the subject with an open mind. He neither condemns nor praises Roosevelt; he presents the facts and then gives his conclusions based on those facts. He analyzes Roosevelt as carefully as he analyzes Smith, at the same time maintaining his biographical position. We actually live with Roosevelt from the day he was born until the day he died. Throughout the long biography we see every action, every trait of character, and we do not need to depend on the author's judgments; we have sufficient material for our own. We see the young "silk stocking," the political reformer, the politician, and the radical. We see Roosevelt at home, in society, in the White House, on the battlefield, and in the political arena. We have judgments of himself and those more severe judgments of his friends and enemies. In short, we know Theodore Roosevelt better than anyone else, including himself, knew him. This is the test and the fascination of biography. This book approaches the ideal of life-writing as closely as any biography that I have ever read. In some respects this kind of biography surpasses the Boswellian type, for it is more complete and more objective. The fact that *Theodore Roosevelt* received the Pulitzer Prize for 1931 is only one indication of the quality of the book. Its style is in keeping with its form and method; it is a masterpiece.

It is seldom that a descendant of a biographical subject takes the position that Herbert Asbury does in *A Methodist Saint; the Life of Bishop Asbury* (1927). This book seems to present a very faithful picture of the founder of Methodism in America. It may not appeal to all Methodists or all Christians, for it is distinctly iconoclastic. Mr. Asbury tries to be fair, but his spirit of revolt against the precepts of this as well as all religious denominations leads him into the paths of satire and irony, though both are under control.

To a greater extent than *A Methodist Saint, Carrie Nation* (1929) shows Mr. Asbury's ability as a biographer. It is a sane and balanced treatment of a subject that could easily have been made ridiculous. Carrie Nation was certainly not an intelligent woman, but she had certain strong convictions, and an indomitable will carried her to a certain measure of success in her chosen field of prohibition. Step by step, Mr. Asbury carries the woman with the hatchet along her career of destruction and defiance of legal authority. Only occasionally does the author pass judgment, and then it is because he cannot restrain himself. Mr. Asbury shows us Carrie Nation as she really was, and presents a phase of social history that is as important today as it was in the late nineteenth century. Mr. Asbury's purpose in writing this biography is as obvious as his conclusions.

Carrie Nation illustrates the success that can be achieved by a modern biographer, using a subject that lends itself to modern treatment. Victor Thaddeus in *Julius Caesar and the Grandeur that Was Rome* (1927), *Voltaire; Genius of Mockery* (1928), and *Frederick the Great* (1929) offers striking examples of the worst in modern biography. These books contain practically every fault of modern biography, without a single redeeming virtue. Mr. Thaddeus combed the published material on these three men—there was no attempt at original research—and collected all that was low and mean and despicable in their characters and then added some imaginary spice of his own. They are bad fiction and worse biography, and the fact that they were published is even more remarkable than the fact that they were written. These books cannot even be called "debunking" biographies, for they appeal only to the tabloid reader of the day.

Mr. Thaddeus revels in the sordid because he thinks that that is what the public craves. Harold Lamb chooses the romance of "far-off things and battles long ago," for he knows that most of us have an insatiable curiosity for the reality of romance. In *Genghis Khan, the Emperor of All Men* (1927) and *Tamerlane, the Earth Shaker* (1928), Mr. Lamb has given modern interpretations of the lives and careers of two of the great conquerors and militarists of the world. In the careers of these men who appeared at the beginning of modern history, there is all the romance of the East, and the record of the beginnings of the great conflict between the East and the West, a conflict which has continued to the present day. The author has made the best of scant sources, separating fact from legend, without resorting too frequently to his imagination. It would seem that there is a certain license permitted to the biographer of such legendary figures as these, for Lamb repeatedly narrates situations of love and domestic life which can hardly have bases in fact, and yet they sound true and they may very well have been true. We are not admitting the right of a biographer to imagine scenes and actions; but we can understand the impulse that leads him to do so in such cases as these.

Like Harold Lamb, John K. Winkler turned to romance when he entered the biographical field, the romance of big business. In five years he has published five biographies, all written with the same tone and method. The first four are: *W. R. Hearst, an American Phenomenon* (1928), *John D; a Portrait in Oils* (1928), *Morgan the Magnificent* (1930), and *The Incredible Carnegie* (1931). The titles of these books indicate that Winkler was or is a newspaperman; they are perfect headlines. All are written in a spicy, journalistic style that appeals to the reader for whom many modern biographers write. The story is told as a newspaper story is told, human interest and news first, character development as an afterthought. There is nothing new or original in any of these books, except that the book on Hearst is the first complete life of the publisher that has been written. The sketches of Rockefeller, Morgan, and Carnegie are taken entirely from published material. This is a perfectly legitimate procedure, but, like many other members of this school, Mr. Winkler takes only those facts which will, in his opinion, prove interesting to the reader. Consequently, years are frequently summarized in a page because they provided no sensations which the writer could use.

After reading *W. R. Hearst, an American Phenomenon,* we can see that Winkler has had some connection with the Hearst papers. The life is an interesting journalistic and totally uncritical account of the developer of yellow journalism in America. Not only is it uncritical, but Mr. Winkler would have us believe that Mr. Hearst is a greatly misunderstood man, who has conferred innumerable benefits on the American newspaper reader. This book is interesting as a story—and no one of Winkler's biographies is anything more—of the development of Hearst and his idea of what a newspaper for the "common people" should be. Respect or admiration for his subject is one of the prerequisites of a good biographer, but he should be fair and present both sides of the picture. The "debunking" school does not subscribe to fairness. Mr. Winkler's method here is completely that of the "debunking" group, although his purpose is to show the external greatness of his subject.

The lives of Rockefeller and Carnegie are, in spirit as well as in method, of the "debunking" school. He holds them up to scorn and ridicule as examples of malefactors of great wealth. While the majority of people may agree with Winkler's conclusions, the methods by which he arrives at them are open to criticism. These are ledgers of life with all the entries on the debit side. We are told of the illegal means which they adopted to set up monopolies, control legislation, and thus acquire enormous power and wealth. His facts are unquestionably correct, but it is not necessary to hammer them home with cheap journalism, as Mr. Winkler has done. The "debunking" process of modern biography is very much like the "muckraking" methods employed in the early part of this century to expose the crooked politics of the country. Neither method is productive of the best results because it overshoots its mark and we read this sort of thing for its interesting features and forget to become aroused by it. Mr. Winkler has an aptitude for presenting characters, and we can watch Mr. Rockefeller, Mr. Carnegie, and their associates as they formed their monopolies, destroyed their competitors, and then became philanthropists. We can follow them in their careers, but we never get to know them because the author is so busy recounting their sharp practices that he has no time to show us how these men came to be what they were. Facts alone are not enough to make biography, for facts can be arranged to prove anything.

Mr. Winkler proves this statement in *Morgan the Magnificent*. A first reading leaves the impression that the same method has been used, but that the author has exercised some restraint and has given us a sounder book than those on Rockefeller and Carnegie. A rereading, however, shows that this book is written from a different point of view. It is a warmer, more human book than the others. Where Rockefeller and Carnegie were indicted for their business methods, the elder Morgan seems to be praised for his. It is a little difficult to understand this change in the author unless, for some reason, J. P. Morgan's career struck a responsive chord in Mr. Winkler. If we are to write the life stories of these three men in terms of the manner in which they acquired their power and wealth, there is little to distinguish among the three unless it be that Mr. Morgan merely supplied the ammunition for the oil and steel wars.

Mr. Winkler's latest book is *Woodrow Wilson, the Man Who Lives On* (1933). Here he has entered a new field, one not particularly suited to his methods. He has given us what he thinks is a sympathetic study of the great war President and greater idealist, but we learn nothing more than we already knew. The facts are relatively simple; it is the character of the man that requires a consummate artist for its presentation, and Mr. Winkler is not that artist. Because the material could not be adapted to his method, this is the least interesting of Mr. Winkler's books, and, in all probability, the least popular.

I have given considerable space to Mr. Winkler's writings because he is one of the best representatives of the journalistic "debunking" school of biographers. He is also representative of the "rewrite" school, but by no means the best. Books like these appeared in large numbers during the period under discussion and they did much to bring about a reform in biographical method and also did much to satiate the biography-reading public. A little novelty, sensation, iconoclasm is all right; too much brings revolt and a swing to other forms of literature. On the other hand, this kind of modern biography has a certain salutary effect in that it educates the reading public and leads it to better biographies.

Allan Nevins has one thing in common with John K. Winkler; he is a journalist by profession, but his methods and style are anything but journalistic. As an editor, historian, and biographer, Mr. Nevins is among the best-known men of letters in America today. He has edited the diaries of Philip Hone, John Quincy Adams, and James K. Polk, and has written several books on the American Revolution. Work of this kind is of the greatest value to a biographer, for it keeps him in touch with historical events and particularly with the lives and characters of public men.

Mr. Nevins' first biography, *Frémont; the West's Greatest Adventurer*, was published in two volumes in 1928. This long book tells the story of one of the most famous figures in nineteenth-century America and the history of the times in which he lived, making history himself. John C. Frémont was a natural pioneer and adventurer. A West Point graduate, he became a topographical engineer and did immensely valuable work in mapping the West. He was instrumental in taking the great territory of California from Mexico; he was a general officer, though not a very successful one, in the Civil War; and he was the first presidential candidate of the Republican party in 1856. This life of adventure and prominence Mr. Nevins has told in a fascinating manner against the background of the momentous history of the times. Not only does he tell the story of Frémont's life, but he so completely explains the man that we can easily understand his character and why he failed at the greatest moments of his career. This is the first biography of Frémont which approaches the subject from a disinterested, critical point of view, with a wealth of source material to sustain the biographer's judgments. It is in form and method the best type of classical biography, and the style in which it is written shows a complete understanding of the best in modern biography. This is not merely a life of Frémont; it is a re-creation of Frémont as he really was.

Henry White; Thirty Years in Diplomacy (1930), is a first-class biography of a second-class subject. Mr. White was an admirable character, a faithful public servant, and a credit to his country, but he was not a great man. Such is the biographical genius of Mr. Nevins that he makes us see Mr. White as a greater man than he was. When subject and author meet there is great art in any literary form, but it is only a real artist who can raise a mediocre subject to the point where it seems great. Mr. White's diplomatic career was distinguished but never prominent until, as a very old man, he was selected by President Wilson to be a member of the Peace Commission in 1919. Mr. Nevins makes the most of this opportunity as he does of every other opportunity which White's life affords, and so we know Henry White much better and more intimately than we know men who were much more important in the history of the United States. This is only an-

other instance of the fact that a biographer can create as well
as destroy the reputation of his subject. The use of letters and
official correspondence by Mr. Nevins in building up his narrative and in analyzing White's character shows that he is
here, as he was in *Frémont,* completely the master of his material. If the book has a fault, it is that it is too good, for
one often forgets White in reading Nevins.

Grover Cleveland; a Study in Courage (1932) is modern
biography at its best. It shows that a great subject will inspire
a biographer. Of the two previous lives of Cleveland, one is
political and conventional, the other is personal and decidedly informal. Mr. Nevins' book is as nearly perfect a
combination of the two as one could desire, and it is based on
a method and written in a style that exactly suits the subject.
Mr. Nevins saw Cleveland as a man who had courage, a courage that enabled him to perform some of the unpleasant
duties of his office as sheriff, to defy Tammany politicians
when he was Governor of New York, and to champion civil
service, tariff, and currency reforms when he was President
of the United States. This theme of courage runs through the
entire long biography, giving it unity, life, and spirit. Nothing in Cleveland's life is toned down, nothing overemphasized. Here, as in his other biographies, the author has made
excellent use of his material to explain the character of the
man, his actions, and the history of the time. There is considerable political and economic history in this biography,
and that history is made as clear as the facts of Cleveland's
life. Some really great biographies are difficult to read, but
Mr. Nevins' style has a clarity, a restraint, and a simplicity of
expression that leads one on to read and read until the book
is finished. The general editor of the "American Political
Leaders" has excelled his coworkers, and it is doubtful if any
of the future volumes will displace it as one of the finest political biographies of the century. Political biography is one
of the most difficult of all forms of biographical writing, for
it frequently becomes a treatise on politics and history instead of a biography. *Grover Cleveland; a Study in Courage*

received the Pulitzer Prize for Biography in 1932, and no one can seriously question the justice of the award.

Courage is a quality that takes different forms in different natures. The courage of Grover Cleveland is the highest kind because it is founded on morality and will; the courage of Simon Girty is of the lowest type because it manifests itself only when its possessor has the power behind him which will sustain his feeling of physical courage. Thomas A. Boyd, in *Simon Girty, the White Savage* (1928), has told Girty's story as it should be told, in a swiftly moving narrative of action. Simon Girty was a white man who became an Indian leader during the Revolution. He lived as an Indian, acted as an Indian acts, and added to the natural cruelty of the Indian that unnatural cruelty which seems to be the heritage of the white man. Mr. Boyd did not have to analyze the character of Girty; his actions spoke for themselves. He had that physical courage which has been mentioned, and it made him an Indian leader of unusual savagery and one of the most feared men of his day. In this biography Mr. Boyd has presented a phase of the American Revolution that has been overlooked or disregarded by most historians.

Mad Anthony Wayne (1929) is another life of a man of action, and Mr. Boyd has presented a brilliant picture of one of the great fighting generals of the Revolution. It is an excellent and complete account of Wayne's adventurous career, an account based on sound scholarship, a thorough understanding of Wayne's character, and a style that fits the dashing and headlong career of the commander of the Pennsylvania Line, of the hero of Stony Point, and the conqueror of the Indian allies of the British who tried to continue the war in the West after the Treaty of 1783. *Mad Anthony Wayne* is the best life of General Wayne that has been written.

Mr. Boyd continued his biographical studies of the Revolutionary period when he wrote *Light-Horse Harry Lee* (1931). This is not so good a biography as the life of Wayne, either because of lack of material or the author's inability to master what he had. The early part of the book is excellent, particularly in its study of Virginia life and manners in the eighteenth century and in the account of Lee's early personal and domestic life. Lee's career as a cavalryman in the American Revolution is clouded by a mass of detail, interesting only to the specialist, and this book was written for the general reader. The narrative clarifies and literally brightens toward the end of the book, which contains the account of the disillusionment and poverty of Lee's last years. Boyd performed a commendable service in rescuing the father of Robert E. Lee from obscurity, but he seems to have been unable to reproduce the romance that was the very essence of Lee's life, or to give him his proper place as one of the less great but unique figures of the Revolution. There is a further fault in this biography which seriously mars it: Boyd creates thoughts and actions which cannot be substantiated by facts. This fictional quality was not so apparent in his earlier books; it was perhaps an unconscious acquisition or a device to fill in the blank spaces in his narrative. Few biographers between 1925 and 1930 are immune from it.

John Stevens, a very important figure in the industrial and scientific life of the eighteenth century, was very little known until, in 1928, Archibald D. Turnbull published *John Stevens, an American Record*. Stevens was one of the American pioneers in steam transportation, both by rail and water, and the story of his career and those of his three sons, one of whom, Edward A. Stevens, founded the Stevens Institute of Technology, is a remarkable and immensely valuable chapter in American life. The book is primarily concerned with the elder Stevens and his inventions, but it is marred, as a biography, by a long and detailed discussion of the controversy between Fulton and Stevens over the priority rights in the invention of the steamboat.

Mr. Turnbull produced a much better biography in *Commodore David Porter, 1780–1843* (1929), for he had a more interesting subject. Porter was the naval hero of the War of 1812, and he also played a large part in the subjugation of the

Barbary pirates. He was a man of strong will and a violent temper, and as Turnbull unfolds his story we get a clear picture of a man who was a commander in fact as well as in name, and of a period when the captain of a war vessel was monarch of all he surveyed. Mr. Turnbull, a naval engineer, combines a thorough knowledge of ships and men of an earlier day with an engaging style. These two books are distinct contributions to American biography and history.

There are some men who cannot adapt themselves to conventional biographical writing and fail when they try to do so. *The Life and Times of Pieter Stuyvesant* (1928) by Hendrik W. Van Loon, is no more than a mediocre biography of the last, the most unusual, and the greatest of the Dutch governors of New Amsterdam. Stuyvesant is almost completely lost in the masses of Dutch and Swedish history which Van Loon tries to disentangle. If the book had been planned on a larger scale it might have presented both "life" and "times"; as it is it presents neither. Van Loon had too much material and failed to realize that a background must be clearcut if it is going to serve as a means of presenting such a man as Pieter Stuyvesant. We get some idea of the famous Pieter stumping along the cobbled streets of New Amsterdam, but we get only a slight conception of the character, the spirit of the old man. There is a golden opportunity here for someone to write a fine biography, for Pieter Stuyvesant's life is admirably adapted to modern biographical treatment.

Mr. Van Loon's second adventure into the biographical field is a book which may or may not be a biography, according to the individual point of view. I believe *R. v. R; Being the Last Years and Death of One Rembrandt Harmenszoon van Rijn* (1930) is one of the great biographies of modern times. Some may say that it violates every rule of biographical writing that has ever been formulated. It does violate every rule except one: the re-creation of a man as he really was. It is fictional biography: yes, glorious fiction, the fiction of reality. Rembrandt's life cannot be measured by any known standard, and his biographer took no more license than his

Maker. It is a combination of knowledge, imagination, and pure genius, so fused that the result is art—and it makes little difference how we classify it.

R. v. R. is patently fictionized biography. It purports to be the story of Rembrandt's life, set down, as he knew and learned of it, by an uncle of the editor (Mr. Van Loon). The uncle knew Rembrandt so well because he was his physician and most intimate friend; and knowing how great a man and artist Rembrandt was, he tried to tell the tragedy that was Rembrandt's life. This is fictionized biography, but it is also the closest approach to Rembrandt himself that we shall ever have.

R. v. R. is not only Rembrandt; it is Amsterdam, Holland, and Europe and America of the seventeenth century. There are literally throngs of people in the book, and we know all of them. We meet scientists with imaginations, and artists with a complete understanding of science as it then was, particularly physiological and physical science. We meet Descartes and Leibnitz, Rubens and Van Dyke. We live in the intellectually charged atmosphere of the European continent of the seventeenth century, and we can understand, a little, how men came to think and paint and write as they did in those days. The book is the spirit of the age, and Rembrandt van Rijn is the spirit of the book. Throughout this very long book, Rembrandt is never forgotten. His genius and art, his character, his work are the light, and also the reflections, of the century. There is nothing of the technical in this book which any intelligent reader cannot understand. One reader learned more about the reality of the seventeenth century from this book than from all the histories of the time that he has read. The things that make this book great may, in the minds of most people, make it absurd as a biography. That may be true; the fact that it is not only unorthodox but heretical is also true; nevertheless, this book is as much a revelation of the life of a man and his contemporaries as *Tom Jones* or *Henry Esmond*.

America has not yet produced a great painter, but she has

produced more than her share of religious fanatics. Of these, none is more interesting than Lorenzo Dow. Charles C. Sellers, in *Lorenzo Dow, the Bearer of the Word* (1929), has given us a remarkably good biography of one of the most famous itinerant preachers of the early nineteenth century. He was a master of the art of "camp-meeting religion," and his fame drew thousands wherever he preached. So great was his success that he went to Ireland to convert the Irish heathen to real Christianity; there is, however, a limit to every man's success. Mr. Sellers has not only given us a fascinating and excellent study of Dow, but he has contributed an important chapter to the religious and social history of America.

Mr. Sellers' second biography, *Benedict Arnold, the Proud Warrior* (1930), is the first attempt at a rational account of the man whose name is a synonym for traitor. Isaac Arnold tried to present an explanation of Arnold's treachery, but he did not analyze his character. This is where Mr. Sellers succeeds so well; he shows us a man who was by nature brave, impetuous, extravagant, careless, and vain. If we study this character as Sellers develops it, we can understand, at least partly, why Benedict Arnold betrayed his country. He was the moving spirit of the expedition to Quebec, and did more than his share to make that expedition a success. He aided Ethan Allen at the capture of Fort Ticonderoga; he fought as a private at Saratoga when his rank was not given the proper recognition. He was one of Washington's strongest supports in the early years of the war. For all this and more he received only belated recognition from Congress and wounds which incapacitated him for field service. Arnold lacked will power; he was careless about his accounts; he lived extravagantly; and he felt that he had not received proper recognition for his services. His grievances and the defects of his character were fertile soil in which the seeds of treachery grew for more than a year before that treachery was discovered. As Mr. Sellers points out, he paid for his treason, and he died a thoroughly miserable man. In this honest, searching life of

Arnold we get an explanation of his conduct which, while
it in no way excuses him, does enable us to see his life as it
really was, and to understand how he could reach the point
of treason.

Benedict Arnold, the Proud Warrior is a study of character; Allen Tate's *Stonewall Jackson, the Good Soldier* (1928)
is a study of war. This short biography of the great Confederate general is a military life with just enough personal background to round out the picture. Although written for a
popular series of biographies, the method is not suitable for
a biography of this sort because the general reader is not interested in an account of battles; he is interested in the man
who fought those battles. The battle scenes and movements
are brilliantly described, but we learn very little of the man
who planned and executed them.

Mr. Tate uses practically the same method in *Jefferson
Davis, his Rise and Fall; a Biographical Narrative* (1929). The
major portion of the book is concerned with Davis' Presidency of the Confederate States and his active leadership in
the Civil War. Mr. Tate is sympathetic toward his subject,
but this sympathy does not prevent him from pointing out
the numerous and serious mistakes that Jefferson Davis made.
He thought he was a military strategist and was constantly
interfering in the various campaigns. His most serious defect,
and the one that brought about his downfall, was pride. He
was blinded by it and was unable to see the inevitable out-
come of the war. He refused to accept advice, acknowledge
defeat, or alter the plans that he had made. The Jefferson
Davis of this book is a magnificent failure, and Mr. Tate
seems to have given him the fairest possible treatment. A comparative study of Raymond Holden's *Abraham Lincoln* (in
the same series) and Tate's *Jefferson Davis* will prove most
interesting from the point of view of biography and character. Like *Stonewall Jackson*, *Jefferson Davis* does not give the
complete history of the man, although the latter book is a
much better character study than the former. In all prob-

ability, the editorial policy of the series prevented a complete biography.

Biographies of soldiers and men of letters must be complete if they are to be read by the general public. Matthew Josephson was aware of this fact when he wrote *Zola and his Time* (1928) and *Jean-Jacques Rousseau* (1931). The former is one of the best literary biographies of modern times. Even those who know nothing of the school of fiction which Zola founded will find it interesting, for they will know the man and his work when they have finished this book. Mr. Josephson tells the whole story of Zola's busy and eventful life so that we can actually follow this Parisian through his career as journalist, playwright, and novelist. We see him engaged in the labor of collecting material for his novels and plays by observing, and living, as far as he could, the lives of the various classes of people he intended to describe in his novels, and the great "Rougon-Macquart" series embraces every possible class of French society. We see him at play and at work, but mostly at work, for he was tireless in his efforts to present life as he saw it. Josephson neither defends nor praises Zola the novelist; he merely tries to interpret his work according to his purpose and the success of his achievement. This, it seems to me, is the only proper method of criticism. Zola's friends and contemporaries are clearly sketched, and the journalistic and literary life of Paris re-created in a way that makes us feel as if we had lived in one of the most remarkable periods of French life and literature. Mr. Josephson has profited greatly from modern biographical methods, without becoming a psychologist, pathologist, or novelist.

Jean-Jacques Rousseau (1931) is a more scholarly book than *Zola*, for the subject demanded a great deal more research and a much wider field of study. It is, perhaps, a more important book than *Zola*, but it lacks the latter's interest. It is, necessarily, a study of French life and thought in the eighteenth century, and of Rousseau's economic, social, and educational theories. The life-writing is not slighted, but the man is frequently lost in the reformer. Mr. Josephson's style is a little heavier in this book, for it is quite natural for a writer to be influenced by his material. *Jean-Jacques Rousseau* is a long and well-documented study of the man whose writings had a tremendous influence on the French Revolution, as they had on French society. This biography is the best account in English of Rousseau and his work.

Biographies of writers, as we shall see in a later chapter, became increasingly prominent in the later years of this period, for many of the older generation were dying, and the time had come for a modern revaluation of the poets, novelists, and essayists of the past. Such a book as Professor Samuel C. Chew's *Thomas Hardy, Poet and Novelist* (1928) was a most welcome addition to critical biography. There is a great deal more criticism than biography in it, but, as it was written before Hardy's death and was based on published material and Hardy's writings, too much cannot be expected of it. It is an admirable account of Hardy's work and contains all the necessary facts of his life. Mrs. Hardy's long biography of the novelist gives little more concrete information than is found in Professor Chew's book.

Swinburne (1929) is a much better biography than *Thomas Hardy*, and is equally good criticism. The improvement is attributable to the fact that Swinburne had a more diversified career and that his work is much more personal than Hardy's. Hardy recorded his observations and thoughts in some of the best of modern English prose and poetry, while Swinburne's poetry was largely the outpouring of his nature and experience. Criticism is always improved by biographical knowledge, but it is not always necessary, even with some of the great artists, to have complete knowledge of their lives in order to evaluate their writings. This is certainly true of Hardy and Swinburne. One was an artist of the mind, the other, an artist of the senses.

There has been as much rewriting in the field of political and historical biography as there has been in literary life-writing. Some writers have ranged over the whole field; others have confined themselves to certain periods or certain types of men. Donald Barr Chidsey chose the England of Anne and George II for his first biographies; later, he entered the fascinating field of Elizabethan England. Mr. Chidsey's first book, *Bonnie Prince Charlie (Charles Edward Stuart)* (1928), is the life of the Young Pretender, the leader of the rebellion of 1745, which was the last attempt made by the Stuarts to recover the throne of England. This man has been a neglected figure in English history and biography, for most English historians and biographers have been Whigs or supporters of the house of Hanover. Chidsey has no political opinions on the subject of the succession; he is interested in telling the story of Charles Stuart and his wanderings, before and after the rebellion. This is a remarkably good first biography, for it tells an interesting story in a most engaging manner. It is not a scholarly book; it makes no claim to original research; there is not a great deal of character analysis in it; but somehow we get to know Charles Edward Stuart, to understand why he could lead a rebellion and why his defeat was inevitable; and, finally, we sympathize with this rather poor specimen of royalty, if for no other reason than that he was the champion of a lost cause. Prince Charles was anything but a great man, and the author does not try to make a great man of him. He succeeds in making him very real and very human. That is why we sympathize with him.

When Chidsey chose *Marlborough, the Great Conqueror* (1929), he chose a subject particularly suited to his talents. There have been numerous lives of Marlborough, but none has made the man's life and career as plain as this one of Chidsey's. There is as little history as possible in this life of one of the greatest of English soldiers, but it tells what sort of man Marlborough was, how he reached the position of the most powerful Englishman of his day, and of the part that his wife, Sara, Duchess of Marlborough, played in his career. In short, it is a chatty, informal account of Jack and Sara Churchill, Queen Anne, and those other contemporaries of Churchill who were his friends and enemies.

Chidsey pursues the same method in *Sir Walter Raleigh; That Damned Upstart* (1931) and *Sir Humphrey Gilbert* (1932). These half-brothers were equally famous in their day, but Gilbert's early death dimmed his memory, while Raleigh is still a romantic figure. His execution as a traitor, the legend of the cloak and Queen Elizabeth, and the romance of the man's whole life will always attract the attention of the world; for we are sentimentalists, thrill seekers, and Raleigh provides an excuse for tears and a reason for thrills. In his own day Raleigh was more hated than loved, for he was one of Elizabeth's favorites and he was not of noble birth. In his life of Raleigh, Mr. Chidsey has tried to give us the man as he really was, and it seems that he has succeeded. Raleigh was a great man in a world of great men, because he could do so many things well. As Mr. Chidsey points out, he was a poet of parts, a keen business man, a great soldier, and a greater lover of adventure. He was also his own worst enemy. His vices and his virtues are given equal importance, and if we weigh the facts, as Chidsey has weighed them, we are forced to admit with him that Raleigh was a brave man, an honest man (for his day), and one who helped materially to make the Age of Elizabeth the greatest period in English history. Americans have reason to remember Raleigh, for, with the vision of an empire builder, he persisted in his attempts to colonize America. None of his colonies survived, but he laid the foundations for the colonies that developed, even before his death.

Mr. Chidsey's biographies are good for at least two reasons: care in separating fact from fancy, and an interest in his subjects that makes his books eminently readable. Mr. Chidsey can be classed among the best of modern biographers because he is honest in the use of his materials. He tells us what are the facts and what the legends that have grown up around his subjects. He gives anecdotes and second-hand stories for what they are worth, and no more. He seldom heightens his picture by drawing on his imagination for what might have been, and he makes no attempt to dogmatize concerning the many points, in the lives of these four men, that never have been and never will be settled. As far as one can tell, his sources are those open to everyone and his narratives are based on those sources. Marlborough and Raleigh have not had a less prejudiced commentator than Mr. Chidsey.

Chidsey's biographies may not appeal to scholars of the two periods, but they were not written for scholars, and we must judge them from the author's purpose and not our own. In style, they are remarkable. While extremely modern in tone and manner, they are neither flippant nor fictional. They have a freshness of tone, a simplicity of expression that many an older writer tries to give, but fails. Chidsey is a young man, and only a young man can interpret a Raleigh or a Marlborough in terms of modern life. It is the youth, the gusto, the simplicity of these four biographies that give them their charm and their importance. Only the future can tell whether or not this young biographer will develop into the artist of which these books give promise.

4

The subject of rewriting in modern biography will be more fully considered in a later chapter, but it is worthy of comment here that almost every professional biographer between 1929 and the present has taken subjects which have received previous biographical treatment. There are numerous reasons for these restatements, but the most important one seems to be that both biographer and reader seem to feel the necessity for presenting old subjects in the light of modern method and with the additional knowledge that has become accessible.

Mrs. Dorothie Bobbé has presented modern versions of the lives of three women and one man prominent in early American life. Her first two biographies, *Abigail Adams, the Second First Lady* (1929) and *Mr. and Mrs. John Quincy Adams; an Adventure in Patriotism* (1930), were written for a popular series of short biographies. They are among the very best in the series, for they reveal the personalities of their subjects with a minimum of historical background. The analyses are most skilfully done and the judgments fair and accurate, particularly in the case of John Quincy Adams, the most complex character of all the Adamses. Both lives are written with grace and charm and a sound psychological insight, which is as much the result of sympathetic understanding as it is of patient research. Mrs. Bobbé gave the best interpretation of John Quincy Adams and his wife that was available at that time.

In *Fanny Kemble* (1931), Mrs. Bobbé has written a definitive life of the great actress and Shakespearean reader. Much longer than the earlier books, this biography is a very complete and equally fascinating account of Miss Kemble's public and private life. It is said of some conventional biographies that they read like novels, and this is true of this book, although it does not make use of any fictional or imaginative devices. She tells the story of the life as dramatically as it was lived, and there was both comedy and tragedy in the life of Fanny Kemble. Her English birth into a famous theatrical family, her training and her début on the stage, her successes in America and her unfortunate marriage are faithfully chronicled with an understanding and an enthusiasm that is communicated to the reader. The author must have lived, as we live, through those strenuous years when Fanny was achieving fame and fortune, happiness and misery in England and America. Fanny Kemble's separation from her husband, Pierce Butler, marks a definite point in her life, for it was then that she began the dramatic readings that took her through the whole of the United States and gave her a fame even greater than that which she achieved on the stage. This book is as important a contribution to the social and dramatic history of America as it is to biography.

Mrs. Bobbé had Miss Kemble's three volumes of memoirs and innumerable references in contemporary memoirs and biographies, in addition to her correspondence. Consequently, the foundations of this life are solid and based on the best possible information. Added to the truth of the book is a style that is mature, plastic, and dramatic, a style peculiarly adapted to the personality it portrays.

The art of biography lies, primarily, in the ability of the biographer to re-create the subject in his own mind, and to transfer that re-creation to the printed page so that the reader sees the man or woman as the writer saw them. Mrs. Bobbé did this in her biographies; Marquis James has been even more successful in his lives. *The Raven; a Biography of Sam Houston* (1929) is life-writing at its best. It is great narrative, great character analysis, and great history. It vitalizes a man, an era, and a phase of American life that has passed. To give a clear-cut account of a man who was a lawyer, Governor of Tennessee, an honorary member of an Indian tribe, a general in the Texas revolution, President of the Texas Republic, minister from Texas to the United States, and later Senator from the state of Texas is not an easy task; to carry the spirit and the character through his victories and defeats is even more difficult, but that is what Mr. James did, and only a small part of what he did. His knowledge of frontier life and character is remarkable, and even more remarkable is the fact that one forgets the tremendous amount of research involved, in the fascination of the book. Mr. James took Sam Houston as he found him, presented him as he actually was, retaining the romance, the misery, and the glory that came to Houston. The method of the book is that of all great biographies—plain narrative, vivid background, and masterly analysis, not only of Houston but of the host of minor figures in his drama, tempered with a balanced judgment that leaves the verdict to the reader, and expressed in a style that has the suppleness and the drama necessary to the telling of such a story. The Pulitzer Prize committee had no difficulty in choosing the best biography of 1929. This book is a further proof of the axiom that when a competent biographer has a great subject, his effort will be crowned with success. *The Raven* is not only a great biography, it is one of the important books in the literature of the frontier.

Mr. James justified the unanimous voice of the critics when he published *Andrew Jackson: Border Captain* (1933). Jackson's career was not different from that of Houston, but Jackson is a more difficult subject to treat because so much has been written about him. *The Raven* explored a virgin field. *Andrew Jackson* is the filtration of all that has been written concerning "Old Hickory," to which is added a decidedly new point of view. Parton was an ardent admirer of Jackson, who could see his faults as well as his virtues. Bassett was a historian, writing of Jackson as a public man. James is the character critic, trying to show Andrew Jackson as he was in love and war, in politics and business. We cannot judge this book as a complete biography, for it takes Jackson only to the fifty-fourth year of his life, a period when he believed that his public career was over when in fact it was only beginning, and that he could spend the remainder of his life as a wealthy planter at "The Hermitage" with his beloved Rachel.

As far as he has gone, James has given an entirely new interpretation to Jackson's character. Without detracting in the least from Jackson's patriotism, courage, and leadership, the author has shown us that Jackson acted always in his own interests, and the fact that those interests generally coincided with the interests of the state or the nation was of secondary importance. Jackson was honest and brave, but he was ambitious for wealth and power above everything else, and it was that ambition that made him a lawyer, congressman, judge, general, and business man. He was a faithful public servant, but he always had Andrew Jackson in mind. This interpretation does not affect Jackson's reputation; it simply provides a motive for his actions. Every man has a motive in life, and to disregard that motive, as so many biographers do, is to fail to understand completely the life of any great man. It would seem from this first volume—we assume that the work will be completed—that Mr. James will repeat, perhaps exceed the success that he made in *The Raven*. The border captain is completely realized; the President is yet to come.

Four writers who made their first appearance as biographers in 1929 chose European subjects in widely different fields. The most prolific of them, David G. Loth, has written four biographies of great figures in four different periods of history. *The Brownings: a Victorian Idyll* (1929) is a real biography of Robert and Elizabeth Barrett Browning, and their poetry is given a secondary place. The result is admirable life-writing, for Mr. Loth avoided the pitfalls that beset the path of the average Browning critic. Many people have tried to write about the poetry that they wrote; few have attempted the story of their own great poem, and it is here that Loth is so successful. It may be that their life had little to do with their poetry, but the idyll, for such it was, is worth telling for itself. No one, it seems, has so completely re-created the personalities of these two lovers, one of whom at least was a great poet, as Mr. Loth has done. With a simple and dramatic style, he has allowed us to live with Robert and Elizabeth through the years from their elopement to the end of the romance. We speak of them as Robert and Elizabeth because the author brings their lives so close to ours that we feel as if we had lived with them. He has done this without being either facetious or smart. He has simply used the best modern biographical methods as they should be used.

Lorenzo, the Magnificent (1929) is another excellent re-creation of personality, and a more difficult task than the first book. Lorenzo de Medici has always been a figure in history rather than a man, the apogee of the Italian Renaissance, the patron of the great painters, sculptors, and poets of the day. He was all these things, but he was something more—he was a man, and it is the man rather than the symbol that Loth presents. This is a closer approach to Lorenzo as he really was than any other biographer has given us. It is pure biography rather than biographical history, and it seems to be more readable than more complete accounts of the Medici are. It is Lorenzo de Medici, the Florentine, the banker, the politician, the statesman whom we come to know so intimately; the lover and patron of art is here, too, but subordinated to his proper place in the larger life of the man.

In *Royal Charles, Ruler and Rake* (1930), Mr. Loth makes a contribution to biography and history that has the accuracy of scholarship and the charm of good literature. Charles II is one of the many figures concerning whom there have been, until lately, only two opinions. He has been delineated as a good king or a bad king, but no conventional biographer ever tried to understand the man, to determine why he was good or bad, as a king or as a man. It has always been possible to find facts to support either point of view; those facts were collected and the result was called a biography. This bigotry is not confined to any particular nation. It is one of the fundamentals of human nature, but it has been more prominent in English and American literature than in that of any other country in the world. *Royal Charles* is just one example of the attempt that is being made by honest modern biographers to show us what men and women really were or are, instead of whitewashing or blackening their characters. Neither the Tory biographer nor the Whig historian has been fair to Charles II. Each has presented him in a fashion that Charles himself would have been the first to deride. As Mr. Loth tells the story, Charles is neither a great saint nor a great sinner. If we read this book carefully, we shall discover a man who was a clever politician, a statesman of ability, and a ruler who labored under the delusion that the word "subject" had a literal meaning. Charles's principal defects in character were lack of will power and indifference to everything but the pleasures of life. In *Royal Charles,* Mr. Loth analyzes the character of Charles II in a manner that enables us to understand the man, though we probably do not like him or admire him. Not only is this a strikingly good biography, but it shows the England and the London of Charles II as they really were, a nation and a city freed from the bonds of Puritanism, and going on a holiday with the man "who never said a foolish thing, and never did a wise one" at their head. The quotation is just one of many opinions which this biography has corrected.

Mr. Loth's latest biography is *Philip II of Spain* (1932).

Following the method and manner of his previous books, he has told the very complicated story of Philip, adhering as closely as possible to pure biography. Philip's life really encompassed the history of Europe in the sixteenth century, for the Spanish empire was at that time the largest empire in the world. The fact that Loth was able to write this life, using only a minimum of history, is indicative of his skill, his art as a biographer. In this short account there is a complete realization of the character and personality of the most powerful monarch of his time. This book is not so interesting as any of the preceding lives because Philip was not a great man in any sense of the word. He would have made an admirable chief clerk, he loved detail, and, if genius is "an infinite capacity for taking pains," he was a genius. He lived and died a Spaniard and his vision never extended beyond the boundaries of Spain, even though his soldiers were in America and the greatest of his fleets was destroyed in the English Channel and the Irish Sea. It was because he lacked vision that he lost his fleet and his successors lost America. It is this colorless, careful, quiet, pious, and intriguing man, whom Mr. Loth makes real in *Philip II of Spain.*

There are few biographers who choose as widely different subjects as Mr. Loth has chosen, and fewer who succeed as well as he has succeeded. All his books are based on sound biographical principles and each confines itself to the subject. Comparison of biographies of great historical figures is unfair; for some biographers make their subjects the centers of an epoch, while others confine themselves to the study of an individual. Mr. Loth belongs to the latter group and has accomplished his purpose, the re-creation of the life, character, and personality of an individual. With the possible exception of *Royal Charles* these books could have been made more interesting by the insertion of more detail, but the substantial portrait is there and detail is largely a matter of taste. *The Brownings, Lorenzo, Royal Charles,* and *Philip II of Spain* contain all that is important to an understanding of these very different people. Experience, perhaps, will broaden

Mr. Loth's canvas, but if a choice must be made between historical and personal biography, where the subject is interesting historically and personally, the personal method produces better life-writing.

In Fairfax Downey we have the exact opposite of that type of biographer represented by David Loth. Downey is as romantic in his biographical point of view as Loth is realistic, and he certainly chose the romantic hero when he wrote the lives of Sultan Suleyman and Richard Burton, the most picturesque of Turkish emperors and Levantine scholars. *Grande Turke; Suleyman the Magnificent, Sultan of the Ottomans* (1929) is a grand, romantic biography of a picturesque man and period. A contemporary of the great kings of the West, Philip II, Henry VIII, and Francis I, Suleyman was the greatest of the Ottoman rulers when the Turks were at the height of their power. He was a great man and a great soldier and ruler, living in the midst of Oriental splendor. The biographer of such a man can hardly restrain his imagination; there must be an irresistible impulse to add something of the *Arabian Nights* to such a biography. Mr. Downey did not entirely resist this impulse, and his biography is on the borderline between romance and reality. It seems to be fundamentally true, it is fascinating reading, but the background and embellishments are those of Sir Walter Scott rather than James Boswell. We must take such a book as this for what it seems to be worth, for it will appeal to some and be branded as fiction by others. Books of this type add little to the literature of biography, but they do add to our pleasurable reading.

Mr. Downey's *Burton, Arabian Nights Adventurer* (1931) is a real biography, with a romantic tinge. Richard Burton was one of the great adventurers of modern times, and it is impossible to consider him in a coldly realistic manner. Downey tried to present a fair analysis of the man; he at least told the truth about Burton's character, his difficulties with the English Government, and his writings. Earlier biographers were prejudiced either for or against the man; Downey

presented the facts as he understood them, and left many
questions, the truth of which could not be determined, to the
judgment of the individual reader. The plain narrative of
this great linguist, explorer, translator, and writer is worth
telling for itself, and Mr. Downey is a good story teller. It is
not necessary to analyze the character of every man who is
worthy of a biography; the narrative of his life is often sufficient. Mr. Downey's account of Burton's translations and
writing is short, for his version of the *Arabian Nights* is recognized as the best, and his *Pilgrimage to Meccah* has long
been a classic in travel literature. His other translations and
writings are equally well known, even the erotica that was
destroyed by Mrs. Burton after his death. *Burton, Arabian
Nights Adventurer* is a good piece of life-writing, for it at
least tries to portray the actual man.

In the course of this chapter we have had biographers covering many fields and individual biographers, such as Sedgwick, Werner, Gorman, and Loth writing on a variety of
subjects, but no American biographer has chosen such widely
different subjects as S. Guy Endore did when he wrote *Casanova; his Known and Unknown Life* (1929) and *Sword of
God: Jeanne d'Arc* (1931). Each is the best biography of the
subject that has appeared in English, and both are excellent
biographies *per se*.

Because of the memoirs which he left, Jacques Casanova
is one of the best-known men of the eighteenth century. He
wrote the memoirs in his old age, and, like all such writings,
they contain fiction intended as fact. Mr. Endore made a
thorough investigation of Casanova's life and writings, and,
using the memoirs as a basis, has written a full-length biography, filling in the spaces and checking the facts. Casanova,
by his own admission, was one of the world's great lovers and
adventurers. He went everywhere, did everything, and knew
everyone worth knowing in continental Europe in the eighteenth century. This is what his memoirs tell us, but his
biographer has toned down Casanova's own story, without
altering the character of the man or the spirit of the book. To

those who have read the *Memoirs of Casanova,* this book is indispensable; to those who have not, it will give a more complete picture of Casanova than he gave of himself. Mr. Endore, writing without prejudice, presents as much of the truth about Casanova as possible. The complete manuscript of the *Memoirs* will never be published. If it were, we should not understand the man more completely than Mr. Endore has understood and presented him. The author has preserved all the charm of the *Memoirs,* and has added an excellent style of his own. Of its type, this life has few equals in modern biography.

The Maid of France was as unique a personality as Jacques Casanova, and a much more controversial figure in history and literature. The literature concerning this girl, who died before she was twenty, has reached enormous proportions, but no better book on the subject has ever been written than Mr. Endore's *Sword of God: Jeanne d'Arc.* Until modern times, Jeanne was believed to be either a creature of the devil, or a saint. The Roman Catholic Church has accepted her as a saint and canonized her; it may very well be that there are people living today who believe that she was possessed by the devil. For centuries after her death the controversy raged until intelligent men began to take an objective rather than a subjective point of view as to men and things in this world. Doctors, lawyers, theologians, and novelists have written about her, and she has been declared sane and insane, guilty and innocent, a saint and a witch. Mr. Endore's book takes no point of view, but presents all of them. The volume is divided into two parts, the Narrative and the Discussion. In the Narrative, Endore tells the story of Jeanne as he found it in the original and secondary sources. The Discussion, the more important part of the book, provides a commentary on almost every bibliographical item and an explanation of the author's point of view regarding Jeanne's visions and subsequent actions. Mr. Endore does not force his opinion on the reader, but it is very evident that he believes and would have us believe in the divine mission of Jeanne. Even though we may not accept Endore's conclusions, we must admit that he has written an able biography, and that his patient research and complete discussion of the medical, legal, and theological phases of the subject offer the best basis for final judgment that has ever been given. It may be argued that the separation of narrative and discussion is bad method: it is the only method Mr. Endore could have used to present his case, without becoming dogmatic. He tries to achieve the fundamental purpose of biography: the re-creation of the individual as she really was. It remains for the reader to accept or reject the conclusions.

Robert P. T. Coffin found the subjects of his biographies in one field, Stuart England. *Laud, Storm Center of Stuart England* (1930) is a very readable life of that Archbishop of Canterbury who drove so many Puritans to America. Professor Coffin misinterprets Laud, for he tries to make him a literary man when he was only a fighting clergyman who gave his enemies the choice of conformation, prison, or exile. The author's preoccupation with Laud's literary side, which was negligent, spoils what might have been an excellent study of character. Coffin's second book, *The Dukes of Buckingham; Playboys of the Stuart World* (1931), is nothing but a collection of court gossip and spicy anecdotes which has accumulated around these favorites of James I.

Every biographer has the privilege of working out his own method for presenting his subject. Some are decidedly unorthodox; others are strictly conventional. James Truslow Adams is well known as one of the best of modern American historians, and his first biography is quite in keeping with his histories. *The Adams Family* (1930) is a group biography of five generations of the most famous political family in America. The Prologue tells of the American origins of the family, and the later sections present short but excellent studies of John Adams, John Quincy Adams, Charles Francis Adams, his sons and grandsons, including Charles Francis Adams, Secretary of the Navy in the Hoover cabinet. The biography of this family is told in the perfected style of all of Mr. Adams' writings, and he manages to give remarkably clear and correct character studies of each of the important members of the family. It is not an easy matter to give unity to such a work as this, but Mr. Adams did it successfully because he wrote of the family as he would write of an individual.

In 1932, Adams published a monograph on Henry Adams, the historian and author of *The Education of Henry Adams*. This small book was written as an introduction to the collected writings of Henry Adams. Financial conditions made such a project impossible at this time, and the introduction was published as a biography. As an introduction it would have been adequate; as a biography it leaves much to be desired. Few men could have written a better biography of Henry Adams than James Truslow Adams—he is not related to the family whose biography he has written—for he has the historical background and the literary distinction necessary to such a task. There is all the more reason for regret in that Henry Adams will be a literary figure long after his family has been forgotten. His *History of the United States During the Administration of Jefferson, Madison and Monroe* is a historical classic, and *The Education of Henry Adams* is one of the great books in American literature.

It is sometimes impossible to interpret a man completely. Henry Adams failed, with himself as the subject, and Vivian J. McGill succeeded only partially in *August Strindberg, the Bedeviled Viking* (1930). Mr. McGill seems to be a philosopher and he tried to present Strindberg's life and work from a philosophical point of view. The result is a mixture of philosophy and biography in which Strindberg frequently becomes lost in the midst of his own and the author's philosophy. Despite the faulty method, the figure of the Swedish dramatist emerges. Mr. McGill succeeded in giving us, in the book, the storm and stress that made Strindberg's life a great failure. In spots, this biography is difficult reading, for the author was never quite sure of his material or his interpretation. Some of the faults of structure and method may be attributed to the difficult subject; others are the result of a pseudo-philosophical style that is not suited to biographical writing, while still others are plain carelessness.

Schopenhauer, Pagan and Pessimist (1931) is a better biography than *August Strindberg*, for Mr. McGill wrote of the man rather than of his philosophy. It is a clear-cut biographical record in which we understand how Schopenhauer came to write as he did. This book will suit the man who wants to know Schopenhauer; it is of very little use to the student who wants an interpretation of Schopenhauer's philosophy. Before Mr. McGill can become a critical biographer he will have to adopt a method which will permit him to develop the character of the subject as well as the nature of his work.

In the course of this study it has been repeatedly demonstrated that the combination of history and biography is very often less successful than the combination of criticism and biography. Historical biography is successful only when the biography keeps the upper hand of the history. This was accomplished by Arthur Pound and Richard E. Day in *Johnson of the Mohawks; a Biography of Sir William Johnson, Irish Immigrant, Mohawk War Chief, American Soldier, Empire Builder* (1930). As biography, as history, as sheer romance, this is one of the best biographies of the century. Sir William is the feudal lord, the friend of the Indians, the faithful soldier of the king in this book as he was in life. To historical accuracy and scholarly analysis of character was added a facile and charming style that completely disarms the reader, after he has passed the formidable title of the book.

Mr. Pound alone published *The Penns of Pennsylvania and England* in 1932. This family biography is much less interesting than the earlier. It attempts to cover too much ground and it lacks the style of *Johnson of the Mohawks*. It is accurate and informative; but no member of the family emerges from the pages as a real man. It is a book about the Penns rather than a life of the Penns.

In reading modern biography, one constantly comes upon

extreme examples of the heavy and the light touch. The light touch frequently produces biographical fiction, as in the case of Byron Steel's *O Rare Ben Jonson* (1927). This is a good story, well told, but it is not biography. It is mentioned here because Mr. Steel's second book, *Sir Francis Bacon, the First Modern Mind* (1930), is in form a genuine biography. It is a brief and interesting account, but it adds nothing to our knowledge of Bacon's life, or to our understanding of his work. The author simply states that Bacon's was the first modern mind, and goes on repeating the statement in various forms. We get little conception of Bacon's real character, and there is no background at all. Mere statements are not enough in any biography, and they are certainly inadequate in the case of such a famous and complex character as Bacon. This book has no value at all, for it is beneath the notice of the scholar, and will give the general reader an entirely wrong idea of Sir Francis Bacon. I believe that Mr. Steel is a young man and that experience in life and in writing will bring a more stable method than either *Jonson* or *Bacon* shows.

Van Wyck Brooks was a young man when he wrote *John Addington Symonds* (1914). This little book is a biographical and critical study of a well-known English writer and Italian scholar of the late nineteenth century. It is a competent piece of work which was intended as criticism rather than biography, but it is mentioned here because it has some characteristics of biography. The next books of Mr. Brooks's, *The Ordeal of Mark Twain* (1920) and *The Pilgrimage of Henry James* (1925), are primarily criticism, but they contain sufficient facts concerning the lives of these writers to warrant their classification as critical biographies. As such, they prove the point that a writer with a preconceived idea of his subject can make actual facts suit his purpose. In both these books, Mr. Brooks's premises are incorrect and his conclusions are both incorrect and, to use a legal phrase, against the evidence.

It is, however, with Mr. Brooks's one genuine biography, the *Life of Emerson* (1932), that we are concerned. It is a masterpiece as biography, as criticism, and as literature. The method is unique, for we see Emerson's life as it passes through the mind of the author. It is as if Mr. Brooks had a photographic record of Emerson in his mind and we were permitted to watch the procession of photographs. It is as perfect a re-creation of an individual life as any I have ever read, and an equally perfect example of pure narrative biography, a form that is uncommon and rarely successful. We see Emerson as he lived day by day, and so clear are his actions that no explanation of them is necessary. The style is ideally adapted to the method, for it has a movement exactly in harmony with the movement of Emerson's life. The apparent simplicity of the method indicates hours of intense living with the works and the biographical records of the Concord seer. It is a method that would suit few subjects, but it is a perfect vehicle for Emerson's life story.

5

Gamaliel Bradford wanted to be a poet, a novelist, a playwright. He achieved a permanent place in our literature as the writer of a kind of life-writing which he called psychography. According to his own statement, he turned to this work after he had failed as a creative writer. Like so many other people, he seems not to have considered biography as a form of creative art. But he must have known that he had made a distinct contribution to the literature of life-writing.

Bradford wrote extensively on the subject of biography and his particular method. The most important of these writings are: "Psychography" in *A Naturalist of Souls* (1917, 1926); "Confessions of a Biographer" in *Wives* (1925); and "Biography and the Human Heart" in the volume bearing that title published in 1932. With this material available, it is not necessary to go into an extensive discussion of Mr. Bradford's method here.

Contrary to the general opinion, Bradford was not a disciple of Lytton Strachey. His first biography, *Lee the Ameri-*

can, was published in 1912, and his first volume of short studies, *Confederate Portraits,* appeared in 1914, while *Eminent Victorians* was not published until 1918. However, I think that Mr. Bradford's later work was influenced by Strachey.

Bradford began his career as a biographer in a more or less orthodox manner. *Lee the American* (1912) differs little from the conventional biography of the day. It is true that the author is primarily concerned with the development of Lee's character, but the same may be said of the average biographer. Furthermore, it was character rather than personality that made General Lee a famous and a great man. *Confederate Portraits* (1914) and *Union Portraits* (1916) are collections of conventional biographical essays on some of the more important military and civil leaders of the North and the South.

It was with *Portraits of Women* (1916) that Bradford began to develop the method which he later made famous. By this time he had come to the conclusion that the usual detailed record of a man's life from birth to death was tiresome, unsatisfactory, and inartistic. He had come to believe that we can best understand the individual by taking certain outstanding characteristics and building a portrait or, as he would call it, a psychograph, from them. By this method, a peculiar trait, an idiosyncrasy, a mental aberration, the ability to do a particular thing, becomes the core of a study in character. In the hands of such a literary artist as Mr. Bradford, this method provides interesting and provocative studies, but it does not produce biographies. We see only those particular traits which the author wishes to use, and those traits exaggerated far beyond their importance in the lives of the individuals under analysis. Psychography is inadequate for the presentation of a man as he really was; it frequently gives false impressions of its subjects. To anyone who knows the lives of Mr. Bradford's subjects, his studies are immensely interesting and often valuable. On the other hand, the reader who first encounters Mme de Sévigné, John

Donne, James McNeill Whistler, or Caesar Borgia in these volumes will know little more of the real person after he has read Bradford than he did before he started. This is the principal objection to the study which depends entirely on the analysis of character. Biography must be more than that if it is to satisfy any of its purposes.

Bradford's next three volumes, *A Naturalist of Souls* (1917), *Portraits of American Women* (1919), and *American Portraits* (1922), are fairly conservative analyses of some Europeans and Americans. In the American volumes he frequently reverts to the conventional biographical essay. It would seem that the psychograph is adapted to only one type of subject, the unusual or abnormal. When the subject has no distinctive peculiarity, it is treated conventionally.

Beginning with *Damaged Souls* (1923) and *Bare Souls* (1924), which are the finest examples of the art of psychography, Bradford's style and method took on a distinctly modern manner and tone, a change which was, I think, the result of Strachey's influence. The titles of the succeeding volumes, *Wives* (1925), *As God Made Them* (1929), *Daughters of Eve* (1930), *The Quick and the Dead* (1931), and *Saints and Sinners* (1932), clearly indicate that Mr. Bradford was competing with the biographers of the new school for an audience. There was really no necessity for competition, for Mr. Bradford's work is much the best of its kind that was written between 1914 and 1933.

It is impossible to itemize the subjects of Bradford's fourteen volumes of short subjects. He studied a hundred and fourteen men and women, ranging from Pliny to Henry Adams, from John Donne to Keats, from Ninon de Lenclos to Charlotte Cushman, and from Jane Austen to Catherine the Great. The majority of his subjects lived in England or America during the eighteenth and nineteenth centuries and were either writers or public figures. The amount of work that Mr. Bradford did for each subject is almost inconceivable. When he was preparing to write his study of Mark Twain he read the forty-four volumes of Twain's writings and all of the available biographical material. He did the same thing in the case of Henry James and, presumably, for every other writer whom he considered. His preparation for his historical studies was just as wide and just as thorough.

In addition to *Lee the American,* Bradford wrote three other long books, *The Soul of Samuel Pepys* (1924), *Darwin* (1926), and *D. L. Moody: Worker in Souls* (1927). These studies are constructed in the same manner as the shorter pieces. *The Soul of Samuel Pepys* provides the most complete demonstration of Bradford's method. Based on the immortal *Diary* of Samuel Pepys, this study is a mosaic of Pepys's soul. There is at least as much of Pepys's writing in the volume as there is of Bradford's. The latter picked from the *Diary* almost every passage which would help him to probe into the nooks and corners of Pepys's great and little soul. Of its kind, *The Soul of Samuel Pepys* is a masterpiece, but it is not a biography of the Admiralty clerk and secretary.

Darwin and *D. L. Moody* are lacking in the same qualities that mar *The Soul of Samuel Pepys*—completeness and vitality. *Darwin* is a study of Darwin's development as a scientist, but not as a man. *D. L. Moody* is a fascinating account of the greatest American evangelist of the nineteenth century, and of his musical partner, Sankey, but if there were other sides of these men's lives, Mr. Bradford has not revealed them.

In his search for souls, the psychographer frequently forgot that his subjects had bodies and a daily existence. It is this lack of humanity, of vitality, that makes Bradford's work a study rather than a re-creation of life. Bradford has given us nearly a score of interesting books; he has added something unique to American literature, but he has not made a permanent contribution to life-writing as I have defined and used that term in this study.

To my knowledge, Mr. Bradford has made only one disciple. Using Bradford's method, Edward C. Wagenknecht has written *The Man Charles Dickens; a Victorian Portrait* (1930) and *Jenny Lind* (1931). Both are excellent analyses of character, but—I must repeat—they are not biographies.

We do not know the lives of Charles Dickens and Jenny Lind after reading these books, though we do know a great deal about them. The distinction I have tried to make marks the difference between biography and books about people.

There have been many volumes of short lives, biographical essays, and character studies published in the last decade. All that I can do here is to indicate the nature of some of the more interesting and important books in this field.

One of the most popular volumes of this type was Will Durant's *Story of Philosophy* (1926). In a series of short studies written in a popular manner, Mr. Durant has given us accounts of the lives and works of the great philosophers from Plato to Benedetto Croce and John Dewey. As short biographies these studies are worth reading, regardless of their value as criticisms of philosophy. Professor Charles F. Potter, in his *Story of Religion as Told in the Lives of Its Leaders* . . . (1929), attempted to present the subject of religion as Durant presented philosophy. This is one instance where biography fails as a satisfactory medium. Religion is a continuous movement, and when it is presented in a series of sketches of the founders of the various faiths of the world, there are too many gaps in the story which cannot be closed.

One of the most interesting of our modern biographical essayists is Meade Minnegerode. His three volumes, *Lives and Times* (1925), *Some American Ladies* (1926), and *Certain Rich Men* (1927), contain excellent informal sketches of some famous and notorious men and women of the eighteenth and nineteenth centuries. The first volume contains studies of Stephen Jumel, William Eaton, Theodosia Burr, and Edmund C. Genet. Mr. Minnegerode has caught the spirit not only of his subjects but of the times in which they lived to an extent that we know these adventurers as well as we know the American ladies and the rich men of the later volumes.

The books mentioned must serve as an introduction to this form of biographical writing. Life-writing of this type is frequently interesting, but, except in the case of a Bradford, contributes nothing new to the literature or the art of biography. A more complete list of these volumes of short lives will be found in the bibliography.

IX

THE WORLD TURNS TO
BIOGRAPHY

IN addition to the field of professional biography, discussed in the previous chapters, there have been many excellent biographies written during the last fifteen years by poets, novelists, historians, and people who are not engaged in the profession of writing at all. Both the professional and the occasional biographer have been influenced by what are called modern methods of biography. In many instances the influence is quite obvious; in others it is not. Most of the professional biographers entered the field because it was profitable or because modern methods gave them opportunities which conservative life-writing forbade or discouraged. The majority of really good modern biographies, whether professional or not, have been written because the authors wanted to present truthful accounts of their subjects. That they did not always succeed, or succeed in the way they intended, was due to lack of method or ability, and in a few instances to bad faith.

This chapter and the next will cover the same period (1918–1933) that was covered in Chapter VIII, considering individual biographies according to subject and method. In this manner, the entire field of modern biography can be surveyed, including many lives which are interesting because of the subject, regardless of method. The present chapter will include the lives of novelists, poets, dramatists, and men of letters that have been written since 1918. The next chapter will discuss the remaining subjects in modern life-writing. The majority of these biographies are rewritings in the light of new material and modern interpretation. It has been said that every generation writes its own biographies. This is particularly true of the present generation, for it has new

methods and new points of view for the revelation and interpretation of character.

Among the best revaluations of older writers is William
Van der Weyde's *Life of Thomas Paine* (1925). This book
forms the first volume of the "Patriots Edition" of *The Life
and Works of Thomas Paine*. This is a better biography than
any life of Paine written in the nineteenth century, for it is
less controversial and more complete. Mr. Van der Weyde is
a great admirer of Paine, but his admiration does not blind
him when it comes to an analysis and interpretation of
Paine's character. The purpose of this biography is to explain the man and his work, and it gives us the complete
account of Paine's life and work before and after his experience in America. Most writers on Paine have given too
much space to Paine's work in America because they looked
at him from a provincial rather than a cosmopolitan point of
view. He was the voice of American independence, but he
was also the voice of English and French liberty. Added to
the excellent balance of the book, is a method that makes
Thomas Paine a real man rather than a legend, and a style
that carries us on along the rocky road that was Paine's.
This is not only an admirable introduction to Paine's writings; it is an excellent personal and critical biography.

Mary Agnes Best published *Thomas Paine; Prophet and
Martyr of Democracy* in 1927. This is an explanation and a
defense of Paine, but it is not entirely successful. A style that
is difficult, a defense that is spoiled by strident overemphasis,
and a compression of a large mass of material into an inadequate space combine to defeat the author's intentions.

Miss Best is too serious; Harold Kellock, in *Parson Weems
of the Cherry Tree* (1930), is too flippant. Mr. Kellock has
performed a valuable service in collecting the available information on Mason Locke Weems, Washington's first biographer, but he would have written a better book had he
restrained the impulse to make merry at the parson's expense.
This biography, with its occasional fiction and frequent
irony, is a typical product of the times. It is admitted that the

life and character of Weems lend themselves to this sort of delineation, but it belittles the writer as much as it belittles the subject. As a factual account of Weems's life, this is the most complete record that we have.

Claude M. Newlin's *Life and Writings of Hugh Henry Brackenridge* (1932) is, like Kellock's book on Weems, the first complete account of the subject. A biographical thesis, it has all the virtues and vices of this type of life-writing. It is accurate, complete, and rather dull. Every other statement is fortified with a footnote, many of which are unnecessary and make for difficult reading. On the other hand, the book is a unified piece of writing, with the life and the literary criticism closely interwoven. Brackenridge was a chaplain in the Revolutionary War, a politician, a lawyer and associate justice of the Supreme Court of Pennsylvania, and a novelist. It is as a novelist that he is best remembered, for he wrote *Modern Chivalry*, the first picaresque novel in American literature and a delightful satire on life and politics in the early republic. Dr. Newlin has done full justice to every phase of Brackenridge's diversified career. The background of Pennsylvania politics adds a great deal to the interest of the biography, though it would be a better book if there were less detail in it.

The early American drama and stage have attracted several writers into the biographical field. *The Life and Dramatic Works of Robert Montgomery Bird* (1919) is an interesting biographical thesis. Dr. Clement B. Faust has collected all the available biographical information on Bird and has contributed some excellent criticism on the romantic plays which made Bird famous in his day. This biography is a typical thesis, but it is the only complete account of Bird's career.

Bird wrote several plays for Edwin Forrest, one of the greatest of the early American tragedians and Shakesperean actors. In *The Fabulous Forrest: The Record of an American Actor* (1929), Montrose J. Moses had a brilliant opportunity of which he failed to take advantage. Forrest dominated the American stage for many years, raised it to a higher plain than it had previously occupied, and left the stamp of his personality upon it. It is the personality of Forrest that escaped Mr. Moses, leaving the book only the shadow of a biography, although it is interesting and valuable as dramatic history. The explanation of the failure of the book, as a biography, is that Mr. Moses is primarily a historian of the theatre and not a biographer.

Mr. Moses has some idea of what a biography should be. If we accept his one attempt at biography, Percy Mackaye has none at all. In *Epoch; the Life of Steele Mackaye, Genius of the Theatre, in Relation to his Times and Contemporaries; a Memoir by his Son* (1927), Mr. Mackaye has written everything and anything but a life of his father. The two volumes represent a compilation of genealogy, theatrical history, stage production and lighting, inventive genius; in short, they are a magnificent collection of source material. If there was ever a biographical memorial, this is one. It is a glorious shaft of tinted and veined marble; it needs only the hand of a sculptor.

All family biographies are not so formless as Mr. Mackaye's. When Susan Glaspell wrote the *Road to the Temple; the Life of George Cram Cook* (1927), she brought to that writing the best of her literary art, making this biography of her husband a thing of life and beauty. Because she shared his interests and enthusiasms, as well as his life, she was able to interpret the man as he really was. It must have been admiration that led her to the writing of this book, but it was much more than admiration that produced this intelligent and charming biography. There is nothing better of its type in American biography, and it will stand comparison with any literary biography of the day.

When we read such a book as Richard Lockbridge's *Darling of Misfortune, Edwin Booth* (1932), we can more readily appreciate Susan Glaspell's life of George Cram Cook. If Mr. Lockbridge chose his title before he began to write, he started out wrong and carried his mistake through to the end. He has used every trick and device of the "rewrite school" of biographers in writing of a man who needs nothing to illuminate the glory or darken the tragedy of his career. A great man and a great actor, Edwin Booth is an ideal subject for a biographer who can or will understand and interpret him. This is not the first biography of Booth nor will it be the last, but it is to be hoped that a man who knows the drama as well as the stage, who understands character as well as acting, who is a biographer and not a sensationalist, will undertake the task in the future.

2

Although Herman Melville died in 1891, it was not until 1921 that the first biography of him was published. For thirty years before his death and for more than ten years after it, Herman Melville was forgotten. Only one newspaper recorded his death, disposing of the man in a few lines in the obituary notices. He certainly deserved more than that, even though he had published nothing since *Piazza Tales* (1856). About 1912 his writings were "discovered" and he began to come into his own as one of the great romantic writers.

Raymond Weaver's *Herman Melville: Mariner and Mystic* (1921) was the first complete account of the author of *Moby Dick*. Mr. Weaver spent years collecting material for this biography, which is as complete a record of Melville's life as we shall ever have. After Melville's death, his wife destroyed his manuscripts and correspondence, for, like so many other wives of great men, she did not want the world to know the real man. However, Mr. Weaver and others have succeeded in re-creating Melville, with the aid of his own books and the correspondence that was left. Weaver's *Herman Melville* is a conventional biography of the best type. He tells the story of Melville's tortured existence as plainly as possible, letting Melville speak for himself wherever he can. His books form the basis of any biography of Melville, along with the few letters that have survived. Mr.

Weaver does not attempt any psychoanalysis of Melville's character; he tries to explain him in human and normal terms. Melville comes to life in this book, a young man in New York, a sailor, a whaleman, a writer who must tell his experiences, a literary failure who is bitter, not because his books did not sell but because the world could not or would not understand him, and finally a disillusioned old man who, failing to earn a living by his pen, accepted a post as customs inspector in New York. This is the Melville Mr. Weaver presents and the only Melville that ever existed. The criticism in this book is quite as good as the biography. The connection between Melville's life and writings is obvious to anyone who reads this life, but Mr. Weaver does not depend on the writings alone for his interpretation of character. Such books as Melville wrote are a combination of experience and thought, a combination on which a biographer can draw but which he cannot entirely depend. Mr. Weaver takes Melville's life plus his experience and writings and re-creates what he honestly believes to have been the real man. His method is the only sound one for such a subject as Melville, or Poe, or Hawthorne.

Mr. Weaver's life of Melville and his edition of the collected writings did a great deal to strengthen Melville's position in American literature, but it was not until seven years later that another biography appeared. Lewis Mumford's *Herman Melville* (1928) purports to be a critical biography, based on a psychoanalytical study of Melville and the relation between his life and his writings. Mr. Mumford is best known as a critic of American life and culture, and it is as a critic that he views Melville. The result is a very interesting book, but not a biography of Melville. In the first place, psychoanalysis alone will not interpret a character. It may help the living; it cannot re-create the dead, for it separates the individual into his component parts, explains and interprets some of them, but leaves the question of human nature unanswered. In the second place, Mr. Mumford carries his theories of Melville's actions to the point of absurdity. He has all the apparatus and the jargon of the scientist and, like the scientist, attempts to explain everything on the basis of his method. Thirdly, the author allows his imagination to direct Melville's actions, and he traces Melville's thoughts throughout his life, a feat that may be interesting but is inimical to truth. Finally, there is distortion of facts for the purpose of proving a preconceived point of view. Like every other biographer of the two men, he takes up the relations of Hawthorne and Melville at the time both were living near Lenox, Massachusetts. Mr. Mumford tries to prove that Hawthorne disliked Melville, and uses *Ethan Brand*, a short story of Hawthorne's, to make his point. Whether or not Ethan Brand resembles Melville I do not know, but I do know that *Ethan Brand* was written in the winter of 1847–1848, and that Hawthorne and Melville did not meet until the summer of 1850. Perhaps Mr. Mumford confused the date of publication, 1851, with the date of writing. The point of this is the oft-repeated statement that any biographer can sustain any point of view, if he so desires. Proof of this kind makes one suspicious of the entire book, creating in the mind of the reader a doubt as to judgment as well as facts.

If both of these biographies are read, one gets a fairly clear conception of Melville's life, the value of his writings, and the relation between what the man was and what he did. As biography, Mr. Weaver's is the better book, for it is a more sincere attempt to tell the story of a life. Mr. Mumford's criticism is immensely valuable and stimulating, making the reader want to reread Melville's books. It remains, however, for a future biographer to write a great book about a great man.

There is one phase of James Fenimore Cooper's life that is comparable to the whole of Melville's. He was as much misunderstood when he turned to public affairs as Melville was when he published *Typee, Omoo,* and *Moby Dick.* The misunderstanding affected Cooper's later career and made him an even more caustic critic of manners and politics in

America than he would ordinarily have been. At his death he forbade that any biography should be written, but his daughter Susan gave some biographical information in a collected edition of her father's novels. In 1888 Professor Lounsbury published his life of Cooper in the "American Men of Letters Series," a book which is more critical than biographical. Many years later a grandson of Cooper's published two volumes of correspondence, which opened the way for a complete biography.

In 1931, there appeared *Fenimore Cooper: Critic of His Times,* by Dr. Robert E. Spiller, the editor of a modern edition of Cooper's travel books. The subtitle indicates that the book was intended as a discussion of Cooper's career as a writer on political and social questions in America rather than as a novelist. In reality, the book is neither biography nor criticism, although it attempts to be both. Dr. Spiller apparently lost sight of his original purpose, for the early part of the book is purely biographical in form, while the latter part is a criticism of both the novelist and the citizen. It is true that many of Cooper's books and many of his prefaces to other books are concerned with the activities of Americans at home and abroad, but those novels which place him among the writers of great romances are free from any criticism of the times. Had Dr. Spiller confined himself to his original purpose, he would have given us a very interesting book, but when he attempted to join biography and literary criticism to his central theme, he produced a book which is inadequate as biography, incomplete as literary criticism, and indefinite as to its real purpose.

The first real biography of Cooper is Henry W. Boynton's *James Fenimore Cooper* (1931). Through the kindness of the present head of the Cooper family, Mr. Boynton had access to all of Cooper's papers. He made excellent use of them in presenting the portrait of the man who was quite different from the belligerent person of Professor Lounsbury's and Dr. Spiller's books. In this biography we have Cooper's complete life set down as he lived it. Mr. Boynton has corrected

many inaccuracies and misconceptions which have been perpetuated by literary historians, at the same time explaining
and interpreting the real Cooper. The best feature of *James
Fenimore Cooper* is that it is primarily biography and sec-
ondarily criticism. We have plenty of critical material on
Cooper, but we had no complete account of his life until
Mr. Boynton's book appeared. The story of Cooper's life
explains many problems which have bothered the critics,
for Cooper was a business man as well as a novelist, and his
business successes and failures frequently affected his writing.
Before he became a novelist, he was a partner in several
whaling voyages, and he added to his income in many other
ways. His books were successful, but he wrote more than he
should have or intended to, for, as his family grew and some
of his investments failed, he was compelled to capitalize his
success. Fenimore Cooper was neither the quarrelsome neigh-
bor nor the litigious aristocrat that most writers have made
him out to be. He was a genuine American who wanted to
see his country on the right path to greatness. Mr. Boynton
tells the entire story without resorting to any of the modern
devices of psychology or fiction. Cooper's life needed nothing to heighten the interest, for, although he was a man of
letters, he had a most spectacular career in America and in
Europe from the time of his expulsion from Yale until his
death. As a plain, straightforward biography, it is not likely
that Mr. Boynton's book will be superseded.

Cooper was one of the founders of the Bread and Cheese
Club, the stronghold of the Knickerbocker group of writers.
Among the members of this club was Fitz-Greene Halleck, a
poet and man of letters, most of whose writings have long
been forgotten. Shortly after his death in 1867, General
James Wilson compiled a memorial biography of Halleck,
which greatly overrates the author of *Marco Bozzaris*. Nelson F. Adkins' *Fitz-Greene Halleck; an Early Knickerbocker
Wit and Poet* (1931) is the first modern study of Halleck. In
this thesis biography, Dr. Adkins has written a history of the
period rather than a life of Halleck. The author has neither

point of view nor method; he simply puts down everything he knows about Halleck and his contemporaries. As the literary history of a definite period and group in America, the book is both interesting and valuable; as a biography, it is almost negligible.

In this period of rewriting, it was inevitable that Edgar Allan Poe should become the subject of various kinds of new biography. The dark spots in Poe's life and those which he intentionally darkened must attract the biographer who uses Freudian methods of character delineation. Poe also attracts the literary detective and the biographer who is looking for a sensational subject. There is so much that is mysterious and unknown in Poe's life that the desire to write about him is irresistible. The books on the various aspects of Poe's life and writings are legion, but only those which purport to be complete biographies will be considered here.

John W. Robertson's *Edgar A. Poe; a Psychopathic Study* (1923) is the first of four modern attempts at a biography of Poe. The subtitle of the book indicates Mr. Robertson's purpose and method. He took all the available information on Poe's life, and all of his writings, and attempted to judge them from a purely scientific point of view in an effort to explain the man that was Poe. The book contains a great deal of information—considerably more than Woodberry had —but it is not a biography and has little to show on the side of psychoanalysis. It does not solve the problem of Poe's personality, for there is too much necessary information which, it is reasonable to assume now, can never be obtained. Scientific analysis will not re-create any man, certainly not Poe. We may have theories of this and that incident, but they remain theories because of lack of proof. Such books as Mr. Robertson's are interesting to the Poe specialist, but to the educated reader of Poe who wants definite material on Poe's life that he may have some background to explain the works, they are worse than useless, they are confusing and frequently misleading. The scientific method will not produce good biography because it is too narrow.

Edgar Allan Poe, a Study in Genius (1926), by Joseph W. Krutch, is a more striking example of Freudian principles applied to life-writing than Robertson's book. Mr. Krutch bases the whole book on the eccentricities, mental aberrations, and physical deficiencies of Poe. If we are to believe Mr. Krutch, there was nothing normal in Poe; his genius was warped and his art completely decadent. Poe, according to this biographer, had a diseased mind and not an original one. Mr. Krutch makes the common mistake of trying to interpret Poe's work in terms of his life. Napoleon attempted the conquest of the world because he had a stomach-ache; Wellington defeated him at Waterloo because Wellington was an extrovert; Caesar became the first Roman emperor because he was an exhibitionist; Cleopatra conquered Caesar and Antony because she had "it." The fact that these people possessed qualities of character, good or bad, which raised them to fame seems never to have entered the minds of some biographers. Ambition and genius, experience and determination, intellect and personality are not capable of analysis in any kind of laboratory. Poe seems to have been created for the express purpose of providing clinical material for amateur psychiatrists. Psychoanalysis and psychiatry are helpful in the alleviation of nervous diseases; they are of little help in the re-creation of character and personality.

Mr. Robertson and Mr. Krutch failed to write biographies of Poe because they deliberately ignored human nature. They made clinical diagnoses of Poe and found that he wrote *The Tell Tale Heart, The Fall of the House of Usher, The Raven,* and *To Helen* because he had some kind of complex or phobia. The fact that he adapted the mechanism of the Romantic movement to his own genius and excelled his masters in the literature of the grotesque and the horrible because he was an artist as well as a genius, seems not to have entered their minds. These books are mental and physiological dissectings, not biographies.

Even though the studies of Poe by Robertson and Krutch are not true, they are interesting. Mary E. Phillips' *Edgar*

Allan Poe, the Man (1926) possesses neither virtue. It is a classic example of indefatigable labor culminating in chaos. It is absolutely impossible to read through these two volumes, for no attempt was made to digest the voluminous material or to formulate a method. The book is a veritable treasure house of information and has enormous value as source material. Future biographers will probably bless Miss Phillips for her researches, but modern readers cannot. If this book does nothing else, it proves that a biographer must have something more than material.

Hervey Allen's *Israfel: The Life and Times of Edgar Allan Poe* (1927) is the best life of Poe since Woodberry's. It is, as the title indicates, an account of Poe's life and the times in which he lived. Factually, it is as complete as any record of Poe can be. Mr. Allen used the material that has been placed in the Poe Museum in Richmond, along with all other available material, and followed Poe as closely as possible from birth to death. Mr. Allen's method is one that will appeal only to the specialist. He has examined every important fact in Poe's life, has marshaled all the evidence on both sides, and has then given his opinion as to the correct version. Using this method, he discusses at length Poe's relations with his foster parents, the Allans, his career at the University of Virginia, his enlistment in the army and his subsequent career at West Point, his marriage, his financial affairs, his various editorial employments, and the final mystery of his death. The book is too long and too controversial, for we frequently lose sight of Poe in the dissipation of the legends and lies concerning him. Mr. Allen would have been much more successful if he had left out the details of the various controversial points. In dealing with such a subject as Poe, notes and authorities are essential, but they should not be made part of the body of the biography, because they unnecessarily lengthen the book and confuse the reader.

Mr. Allen is a prominent younger poet and novelist and it must have been his interest in Poe's art that led to the writing of this book. For the reasons given above it is not an artistic nor an interesting biography, though it is a valuable one. He did what Miss Phillips was unable to do, organize his material into a work that has form and method. The critical chapters are the most interesting, and the criticism is good. It is a difficult matter to evaluate all of Poe's writing, giving to each part the place that it deserves, but it is not difficult to see in Poe one of the great artists in the short story and the inventor of the true detective story. As a critical biography, *Israfel* will have a secure place in American literature. However, the biography that will supersede Professor Woodberry's life of Poe is yet to be written.

Biographers are frequently handicapped by an excess of material and the importance of the subject, as in the case of Poe. Occasionally we come upon life-writing that makes the most of limited material. Thomas Holley Chivers is not a prominent figure in American literature, but he has some claim to fame in the fact that he was one of the few friends Poe had. Samuel F. Damon's *Thomas Holley Chivers, Friend of Poe . . . a Strange Chapter in American Literary History* (1930) is, regardless of the importance of the subject, an excellent biography. Its limitations are largely those of its neglected subject. Mr. Damon has revived if not re-created Chivers, making his life and work very real to us. Chivers was a minor poet who wrote some good things which the author has been careful to emphasize. The book is worth reading for itself and because of Chivers' connection with Poe.

Walt Whitman belongs to the New York literati of a somewhat later period than Poe and Chivers. Whitman and his poetry have been the subjects of innumerable books, biographical and critical. No one of them can be classed as genuine biography, for all the writers were prejudiced for or against the man and his work. The nature of Whitman's poetry is not our concern; we are interested in the life of the poet. Whitman had his Boswell in Horace Traubel, but the latter's *With Walt Whitman in Camden* is a collection of source material and not a biography. The first genuine biography of Whitman was *Whitman; an Interpretation in Narrative* (1927) by Emory Holloway. In addition to the biography, Mr. Holloway has published the best edition of Whitman's poetry. Mr. Holloway's biographical method is exactly described by the title. He tells the story of Whitman's life, interpreting his character and writings as he unfolds the narrative. Whitman is more subjective, more egotistical than most poets, and his life is of primary importance as the basis for criticism of his poetry. This biography is the most complete and certainly one of the sanest books that has been written on Whitman. We understand the man when we have finished this book, and the motives that prompted the writing of *Leaves of Grass*. Mr. Holloway is eminently fair to his subject, and his critical judgments are sound. *Whitman; an Interpretation in Narrative* received the Pulitzer Prize for Biography for 1926 because it is a great biography of the most characteristically American poet of the nineteenth century.

3

This period seemed to foster a particular interest in men and women of letters, with most of the biographers attempting new interpretations or rewritings in the modern manner. Longfellow, Emerson, Franklin, and Hawthorne were among those treated by the professional biographers. We have additional biographies of some of these men and lives of others who have received recognition for the first time.

Emerson. A Study of the Poet as Seer (1928) was written by Robert M. Gay for the "Murray Hill Biographies." This is a small book which is an admirable introduction to the work of Emerson. The author states his purpose very clearly in the preface: ". . . I have tried to confine myself to narrative and interpretation in the desire to persuade people, and especially young people, to read Emerson . . ." The author accomplished this difficult task with apparent ease, for he knew just what to include and what to omit. It is a book that will inevitably lead the reader to Emerson.

Not much larger than Gay's *Emerson* is J. B. Atkinson's *Thoreau, the Cosmic Yankee* (1927). It is a better biographical interpretation of Thoreau than Sanborn's book, for Atkinson is not only a lover of Thoreau but a lover of nature. Mr. Atkinson is a well-known dramatic critic, and he succeeds in making Thoreau a dramatic figure. We get to know Thoreau in this little book, for his entire life is packed into a pocket volume of not more than two hundred pages. It is this artistic compression and the author's ability in choosing his material that makes *Thoreau, the Cosmic Yankee* a little masterpiece. Sanborn's book on Thoreau is important for its detailed knowledge of Thoreau's life and writings; Atkinson's book is necessary to an understanding of the man who wrote *Civil Disobedience* and practised it.

Hawthorne is an apparently inexhaustible subject for the modern biographer. Each of his latest biographers has done a good book in a different manner. Lloyd R. Morris' *The Rebellious Puritan; Portrait of Mr. Hawthorne* (1927) is a personal biography, done from the psychological point of view. Morris tries to explain the rebel, the mystic, and the lover that was Hawthorne, and he seems to have succeeded. He is concerned entirely with the mind and character of Hawthorne, giving relatively little space to the writings except insofar as they explain the man. They are used only to illustrate the points of Mr. Morris' method. There is nothing new in this book except the explanation of Hawthorne's character on a psychological basis.

Newton Arvin's *Hawthorne* (1929) differs from Morris' book, emphasizing the critical rather than the biographical point of view. It is a good narrative biography in the modern manner. The criticism is particularly good because it is the work of a young man with modern ideas of criticism and a genuine interest in Hawthorne. It is the best critical biography of Hawthorne that we have, for Mr. Arvin has shown that

Hawthorne is a great artist, not primarily a moralist, and that his writings are as good today as when they were written. This book will not satisfy lovers of biography or hypercritics, but it will give the educated and intelligent reader a balanced portrait of the man and the artist.

Margaret Fuller and Bronson Alcott are two of the unique personalities of the Transcendental movement in New England. Margaret Bell tried to improve on Katharine Anthony's book in *Margaret Fuller* (1930). Miss Bell is entirely lacking in the knowledge of psychology and character analysis that has made Miss Anthony an important figure in American biography. Where her knowledge of facts seemed inadequate, she resorted to fiction, the result being a poor biographical novel. Apparently Miss Bell thought that she could put Margaret Fuller's thoughts into the form of the spoken word. No biographer can justifiably do that.

Honoré W. Morrow is a very good historical novelist and a writer of distinction. In the *Father of Little Women* (1927) she was more successful as a biographer than she was in her life of Mrs. Lincoln. She seems to have as much sympathy for Bronson Alcott as she had for Mary Lincoln, but she understands Alcott better. Bronson Alcott was the father of the family which Louisa May Alcott has immortalized in *Little Women*. He was also the most radical of the Transcendentalists, a man who had a new idea every day, but none of them ever approached practicality. He was a trial to everyone with whom he came in contact, for he neither could make a living nor would he try. Somehow or other, in telling the story of this communistic dreamer, Mrs. Morrow manages to make a man out of him, a feat not easy of accomplishment. Mrs. Morrow's method is the simplest kind of narration, with the emphasis on the good points of her subject. She does not overpraise him or excuse, but gives him credit for his efforts rather than his accomplishments. This is the only method that could make Bronson Alcott attractive.

The greatest American poet is the greatest mystery in American letters. While still a young girl, Emily Dickinson went into seclusion, seeing very few people outside of her family during the remaining thirty years of her life. During that time her inner life flowered in the finest body of poetry that we have. It is said that less than half of it has been published. It is fair to assume that something happened to Emily Dickinson which changed the whole course of her life and made her a great poet. What that something was has never been settled, though we have two theories and one hint by the three people who have attempted biographies of her.

The first published biographical record of Emily Dickinson, *The Life and Letters of Emily Dickinson* (1924) was written by Martha Dickinson Bianchi, her niece and the custodian of all her manuscripts. The life is merely a short sketch introducing a large collection of letters. In this sketch, Mrs. Bianchi leaves the impression that Emily had fallen in love with a married man in Philadelphia. Rather than break up his home, she gave him up and went back to Amherst to express her love in the only medium she knew, poetry. The man's name is not given by the author, but it is known that Emily was attracted to the Rev. Charles Wadsworth, pastor of the Arch Street Presbyterian Church in Philadelphia. Except for this veiled reason for Emily's seclusion, this sketch has no more biographical value than the usual family memoir.

In 1930 appeared *Emily Dickinson: The Human Background of Her Poetry* by Josephine Pollitt. Miss Pollitt is a staunch adherent of the tendencies in modern biography, for a large part of the book is made up of theories and imaginative re-creation of Emily Dickinson's life. The first part of the book is entirely untrustworthy. The poetess moves and has her being at the behest of her biographer. We are told the sort of coach in which Emily traveled to school, to Boston, and elsewhere. We are given her thoughts from the time she began to think until she left the world. I have said repeatedly that no biographer can give us these intimate mental and physical details because they cannot be proved. After this interesting section comes Miss Pollitt's explanation of the human background of Emily Dickinson's poetry. Miss Pollitt proves, to her own satisfaction, that Lieutenant Hunt was the man whom Emily gave up. Hunt was the husband of an intimate friend of Emily Dickinson's, who later became a famous novelist under the name of Helen Hunt Jackson. Emily met the Hunts in Washington when her father was a congressman. On their way home, she and her father stopped in Philadelphia, and it was on her return from this trip that the poetess gave up all social life. Miss Pollitt bases her theory on a novel which Helen Hunt Jackson wrote later, *Mercy Philbrick's Choice.* The heroine of this novel has been identified as Emily Dickinson; Mercy's career closely parallels that of Emily's, even to the tragic love affair. As a critical or personal biography, this life has little to recommend it, but it does show how far an idea can be carried if the biographer has the inclination.

The third attempt at an explanation of Emily Dickinson was written by Genevieve Taggard, a prominent American poet. As in the case of Miss Pollitt's book, *The Life and Mind of Emily Dickinson* (1930) propounds a new theory for Emily's seclusion. Miss Taggard bases her theory on what she claims to be unimpeachable evidence, given by one who knew Emily Dickinson and the man. According to this theory, Emily loved a young minister, the Reverend George H. Gould, who died shortly after he had become pastor of a church in Amherst. Miss Taggard's proofs are no weaker nor are they any stronger than those of Miss Pollitt. This explanation sounds more rational than the others, but it cannot be proved with the information we have. If we except the controversial point, this is, at present, the best biography of Emily Dickinson. Modern in manner, it never indulges in flights of imagination. Miss Taggard has carefully studied Emily and her writings, and the Emily of this book must be more nearly the real Emily than any other we have had.

Until we have all of Emily Dickinson's poetry and correspondence, as they were written, she will remain a mysterious figure. Her biographer will have to take her as she is and confine himself to her known life and poetry. There is enough material there for a character study and for an interpretation of her poetry. An unusual amount of space has been given to these books on Emily Dickinson for the purpose of showing that such biographical methods are futile. They satisfy no one and lack interest because of the nature of their method. Biography must be based on facts; interpretation of facts is for the biographer and the reader.

Sarah Orne Jewett lived almost as quiet a life as Emily Dickinson. Born in Berwick, Maine, she lived there for the whole of her life, taking occasional trips to Boston, New York, and Europe. The people of her country were the material out of which she molded some of the best stories, sketches, and character studies in American fiction. Francis O. Matthiessen had little biographical material for *Sarah Orne Jewett* (1929), but he made the best of what he had. This small book is an excellent personal account and critical evaluation of Miss Jewett's life and work. As the author points out, she was an artist in the field of short fiction and she knew her limitations. Such biographies as *Sarah Orne Jewett* contribute to our knowledge of American literature and our interest in the art of biography.

The latest biography of a New England writer is Albert Mordell's *Quaker Militant, John Greenleaf Whittier* (1933). As factual biography this book supersedes all other lives of Whittier. Of the earlier biographies, Underwood's was supervised by Whittier, and Pickard, the official biographer, married a niece of Whittier. Mr. Mordell has not only filled the gaps in these books, but he has added a great deal about Whittier that was previously unknown. In the thirty years since Carpenter's book appeared, we have increased our knowledge of Whittier's early literary and political career, and Mr. Mordell has made excellent use of that material.

Mr. Mordell has two main theses in his book, that Whittier's best poetry was written before the Civil War and that his bad health was largely the result of his chastity. Whittier never married. In support of his first thesis, the author shows that Whittier's most individual poetry was written in defense of freedom and against slavery. He further proves his point by quoting a considerable amount of unpublished poetry, written by Whittier in his early years. As Mordell points out, Whittier's fame rests on his New England ballads and legendary poetry, and on his narrative poems, such as "Snowbound" and "The Barefoot Boy." Without lowering the standard of this work, the author establishes the fact that the fiery poetry of the earlier period, "A Summons," "Massachusetts to Virgina," "Ichabod," and "Laus Deo," to name only a few, is the poetry that will give Whittier a permanent place in American literature and the literature of freedom.

Mr. Mordell lays particular emphasis on Whittier's love life, holding that responsible for certain characteristics and for his ill health. The question has been avoided entirely by all of Whittier's previous biographers, all of whom have left the impression that Whittier was a natural bachelor. Mordell explodes that myth by the use of correspondence and by quoting some of Whittier's unpublished love poetry. Then he goes on to show that throughout his life Whittier was attractive to, and attracted by, women. As he grew older he avoided marriage because he felt that he was not suited for it and could not keep a wife. This study in sex psychology is very interesting, but it has little or no bearing on Whittier's position as a poet of freedom or a poet of New England. It takes up too large a part of the book in comparison with its importance.

Mordell's criticism of Whittier's poetry is well balanced and fair. He gives him credit for being the greatest of our descriptive poets and proves that Whittier's poetry is more than mere rhyming. Most people know only those poems which become monotonous on repetition; they do not know the poetry which is as varied in verse form as that of any poet of Whittier's day.

The greatest fault of Mordell's book lies in its style. The writing is perfectly clear but has a deadly monotony that makes for hard reading. There is no lift, no movement in the entire book. It leaves us with the impression that we know a great deal about Whittier, but we do not know the man. Like so many biographers, Mr. Mordell is more concerned with matter than form, to the serious detriment of both. If biography is the re-creation of a man as he really was, then this book is not first-class biography.

Most of the eastern men of letters have been the subjects of thesis or conventional critical biographies, which contribute little to biography or literature. One example of this sort of biography is Pelham Edgar's *Henry James, Man and Author* (1927). A great deal is said about the author and his books, but very little about the man. It is difficult to write the life of such a man as Henry James, for his life was entirely intellectual. His biography can be written in a few pages; his real life can be found only in the books that he wrote. Those books were his life, though he put little life into them.

A much better book than Edgar's is C. Hartley Grattan's *Three Jameses; a Family of Minds* (1932). In this book Mr. Grattan presents short biographies of Henry James, Sr., William James, and Henry James, Jr. We can get a comparative perspective here of the three men, particularly the influence of Henry's father and brother on his own life and writings. Henry James, Sr. was a famous man in his day, a public figure and a leading Swedenborgian theologian. Although his beliefs did not affect either of his sons, he left the impress of his interest in the mind of man on William, and his prolixity on Henry. Mr. Grattan wisely made no attempt at a close comparative analysis, but he did give us the material for forming our own judgments.

O. Henry's life was as strenuous as Henry James's was quiet, but no good biography of the famous short-story writer has yet appeared. In Professor Alphonso Smith's *O. Henry,* we have a very sympathetic account of the writer, but lack of material or reticence left the book inadequate. *Through the Shadows with O. Henry,* by Al Jennings, gives us some concrete information and many anecdotes of William Sidney

Porter's life in Central America, in the Ohio State Penitentiary, and in New York. Jennings, one of the famous western bandits of that name, was an intimate of O. Henry's in Central America, later renewing the intimacy when both were prisoners in the penitentiary. After O. Henry had settled in New York, Jennings visited him, meeting an entirely different man from the one he had known. Jennings' book is good as far as it goes, but it presents only a part of O. Henry's life. In 1931 Robert H. Davis and Arthur B. Maurice published *Caliph of Bagdad; Being Arabian Night Flashes of the Life, Letters and Work of O. Henry*. This book started as a straight biography and ended in a series of disconnected anecdotes. The authors missed a golden opportunity, for they had one of the unique characters in American literature for a subject. We get some good stories about O. Henry and a fairly good account of his early life, but we do not get the biography that might have been written. The biographers depended on the published material, making no researches of their own. When their meager sources were exhausted they tried to pad the book with personal reminiscences, set down as they remembered them.

Isaac F. Marcosson lost an equally good opportunity in David Graham Phillips. Mr. Marcosson's *David Graham Phillips and His Times* (1932) is a stodgy, factual, uninspired account of a great journalist who became a famous novelist. The book seems to have been written to order. It presents nothing of the flavor of Phillips' life, and the books are passed over with only inadequate descriptions. A biographer who knows Phillips, his period and his books will produce a real life on this subject.

4

Appreciative and commemorative lives and memoirs constantly appeared in the midst of the new biographies. Such books as the *Youth of James Whitcomb Riley* (1919) and a later volume on his maturity, by Marcus Dickey, Waldo H.

Dunn's *Life of Donald G. Mitchell* (Ik Marvel) (1922), the *Life of Eugene Field; the Poet of Childhood* (1927), by Slason Thompson, and Vivian Burnett's *Romantick Lady* (Frances Hodgson Burnett); *the Life Story of an Imagination* (1927) belong in the same class; they are charming accounts of literary people. No one of these books represents the complete life of the subject, for in none of them is there any criticism of life or letters. Thompson's book on Field is the best of the group. They were fellow newspaper men and intimate friends. Thompson published a book on Field in 1906, but the modern life is much more than revision and amplification; it is a complete rewriting. There must have been more to Field's character than his biographer presents, just as there must have been more to Mrs. Burnett than the original of *Little Lord Fauntleroy* presents in this interesting study of his mother. These books are valuable as far as they go, but they give decidedly wrong impressions of their subjects to those readers who know nothing of the lives of these once famous writers.

The last four years have produced more than commemorative biographies of men of letters. There have been some sincere attempts at critical biographies, attempts which have succeeded in direct proportion to the objectivity of the writers. It is difficult to write objectively and impersonally of a living writer, particularly when the biographer is as greatly influenced by the subject as Dorothy Dudley was when she wrote *Forgotten Frontiers; Dreiser and the Land of the Free* (1932). With the exception of Burton Rascoe's sketch, this is the first attempt at a study of Dreiser's life and work. Its biographical sins are many and the writing is almost as chaotic as Dreiser's can be. Apparently Miss Dudley had a great mass of material, but she was unable to bring it under control. The book is really not a biography at all. Miss Dudley constantly wanders into the field of the development of realism in American fiction. Dreiser had a large part in this development, but it should have been given a definite place in the study. Instead, it sprawls over the whole book. A careful and persevering reader will learn a great deal about Dreiser, his work and the work of his contemporaries, but he will not know Theodore Dreiser as a man or an artist when he has waded through a book that was badly conceived and executed.

Professors Jacob Zeitlin and Homer Woodbridge succeeded in *The Life and Letters of Stuart P. Sherman* (1929) in just those phases of biographical writing where Miss Dudley failed, mastery of material, critical ability, and knowledge of their subject. The life of Professor Sherman is the best critical biography of the decade, for it combines genuine biography with excellent criticism. The collaboration seems to be perfect. Professor Zeitlin contributes the majority of the material, for he was a close associate of Sherman's during the seventeen years the latter spent at the University of Illinois. Sherman's early years, education, and early teaching are admirably handled by Professor Woodbridge. So uniform is the writing of the book that it is almost impossible to separate the material which each author contributed.

This long biography—it is in two volumes—tells the story of Sherman's life from his birth to his untimely death. We can watch the man grow from a young boy in Amherst, through his undergraduate years at Amherst College, his graduate work and early teaching at Harvard to the point where he decides to accept the offer to teach at the University of Illinois. It was while he was at Illinois that he did most of the writing on which his reputation as a scholar and a critic will depend. This work and his teaching are most ably interpreted by Professor Zeitlin. Throughout the critical account the daily life is presented with such skill and completeness that we feel as if we had lived with him and we can see him grow and change as teacher and critic. Several years before his death he became the editor of *Books,* the literary section of the New York *Herald-Tribune,* the position he held at the time of his death. He had become a liberal in his critical views by this time, and the reasons for the change in his point of view are explained, in part at least, by his biographers. As we finish the book we feel certain that we know Stuart P. Sherman as he really appeared to his closest associates. That is nearly as much as we can learn about any man from his biography when it is written by friends so shortly after his death. It is hardly possible that anyone will write a better biography of Sherman, though his final position as a critic may be more definitely settled by some future student of his work. It may be that his later critical attitude was affected by material interests, by a desire to free himself from the bonds of college teaching, but that will not affect the standing of *The Life and Letters of Stuart P. Sherman* as a critical biography of the first class.

The Pacific Coast has contributed a number of figures to American literature, the most important of whom are Bret Harte, Ambrose Bierce, and Frank Norris. Of these three, the best known is Bret Harte. Born in New York, he went to California after the gold rush, remaining there until 1871. His fame rests not only on the great short stories of his early period, but on the fact that his writings gave impetus to the local color movement in American fiction, a movement that has not yet died out, though its greatest vogue was in the last thirty years of the nineteenth century. *Bret Harte, Argonaut and Exile* (1931), by George R. Stewart, is the latest and by far the best biography of the creator of Colonel Starbottle. In the first place, it is true biography. Secondly, it presents a faithful picture of Bret Harte as he was in California, in Boston, and in Europe. The books on Harte by Petersen and Merwin gave an idealized picture of the man, the writer, and the state which he made famous in American literature. Mr. Stewart, writing in California, was able to give a true evaluation of Harte and his work because he took both the man and his writings as he found them and applied to them the best critical standards of character and of literature. The author proves that Harte was not the great artist that many would have us believe he was, but that he did write some of the best short stories in the world. It is not as criticism but as biography that this life of Bret Harte is important. The man himself is ever present, and Mr. Stewart enables us to understand the tragedy of his life. *The Letters of Bret Harte,* edited by Geoffrey Bret Harte, threw a great deal of light on Harte's life in Europe, and Mr. Stewart has made admirable use of them together with much material that is entirely new. It was Mr. Stewart's purpose to present Bret Harte as he really was. There is no question of his success.

Two biographies of Ambrose Bierce were published in 1929: *Ambrose Bierce; a Biography,* by Carey McWilliams, and the *Life of Ambrose Bierce,* by Walter Neale. The latter book is an appreciation of Bierce by an intimate friend who published his collected writings. There is nothing in it to distinguish it from a host of other similar appreciations. Mr. McWilliams' life of Bierce is good biography and good criticism. He traces, as well as anyone can, Bierce's life from his birth to his disappearance in Mexico in 1913. Not only does he give us biographical facts, but he succeeds fairly well in interpreting one of the strangest figures in American literature. In the interpretation of character the author shows the genius, the occasional artist, the cynic, and the born journalist that was Ambrose Bierce. Bierce is not a very important writer, but he is an interesting character, and the author has done his best to explain him.

Ambrose Bierce was a realist in life and a romantic in literature. Frank Norris was a realist in both. When he died at the age of thirty-two, he had produced a body of work which has had a profound influence on the American novel. He was the first real disciple of Zola in America. No one of his seven novels is a great book, but in *McTeague* and *The Octopus* he produced realistic novels which, had he lived, might have led to something much greater. Franklin Walker's *Frank Norris; a Biography* (1932) is a purely factual account of Norris' life. Mr. Walker missed a great opportunity in this book, for there are few modern American novelists more in need of biographical interpretation than Frank Norris. His life was short, but it was packed with adventure, a zest for living, and an artistic creed that was hardly realized at the time of his death. Lack of imagination, lack of understanding, and perhaps haste, made Mr. Walker's book a source rather than a biography.

5

Before 1919, there were comparatively few biographies of Europeans written by Americans. Those that were written were largely critical and were intended as introductions to the writings of famous English, French, and German men of letters. With the advent of the new biography, a definite interest in life-writing, and large bodies of new source material available, scholars, poets, and other men of letters began to study the lives as well as the works of the great writers of Europe. The new methods and new material gave writers an opportunity to show the real Rabelais, Shakespeare, Keats, and Erasmus. Not all were successful, but the occasional as well as the professional biographers proved that a knowledge of the humorist, poet, and scholar immeasurably aids the interpretation and appreciation of their work. A hundred readers of the tragedies of Shakespeare may have a hundred different points of view which may be clarified, explained, and substantiated by a good biography.

Innumerable books have been written on Shakespeare, many of which can be called biographies. American scholars have contributed their share to the biographical and critical literature on Shakespeare, with Horace White and William J. Rolfe the principal American biographers of Shakespeare in the nineteenth century. Modern research has added to our knowledge of Shakespeare to the extent that we have a fairly clear conception of the principal events of his life. Using the best of modern research, including his own, and his experience as a student and teacher of Shakespeare for many years, Professor Joseph Quincy Adams succeeded in writing the best account of Shakespeare's life and work that we have in English. A scholarly book, the *Life of William Shakespeare* (1928) is eminently readable, for it seems to have been Professor Adams' purpose to write a life of Shakespeare that will satisfy the general reader of Shakespeare as well as the specialist. This book is truly a biographical interpretation. Adams succeeds in explaining the various phases of the poet's life and their influence on his writings better than anyone else has done. This may be called a conservative biography, but it takes advantage of modern innovations that have made the new biography a field of creative literature instead of dull reference. The critical attitude of every Shakespearean scholar is a matter of personal opinion, but the author has succeeded in tracing, as far as possible, the parallel development of Shakespeare's character and work. As critical biography the *Life of William Shakespeare* stands alone in its field.

We do not know all about Shakespeare; until 1928, we knew nothing about Sir Thomas Malory, the author of *Morte d'Arthur,* one of the great prose romances in English literature. Edward Hicks's *Sir Thomas Malory, his Turbulent Career; a Biography* is the product of one of the finest pieces of research in American scholarship. It is a small book and there are large gaps in the biographical narrative, but it does help us to visualize the man who produced one of the few great books of fifteenth-century England. When we consider the difficulties under which Mr. Hicks worked, we must admit that this is a very fine piece of scholarly biography. It is not for the general reader but the specialist to pass judgment on *Sir Thomas Malory* as a critical biography. However, the student of biography may say that the author accomplished a great deal with comparatively little material.

There are parts of the life of Dean Swift that are as obscure as parts of the life of Sir Thomas Malory, who lived nearly three centuries before him. Jonathan Swift, poet, politician, prose writer *par excellence,* is one of the most difficult subjects in the whole field of biography. His letters and diaries are voluminous, and yet we do not and cannot know the man as he really was. Carl Van Doren's *Swift* (1930) is the best biographical study of Swift that has been written. Even this is incomplete, through no fault of Mr. Van Doren's, for, though it tells us how he came to be the man that he was, it does not succeed in re-creating him. So complex was Swift's character, so irrational his actions and thoughts, so concealed his real personality, that the biographer can only give us an incomplete picture of the man. In writing *Swift,* Mr. Van Doren used the only possible and, incidentally, the best biographical method in dealing with his subject. He allowed Swift to speak for himself wherever possible, thus making real much that would have sounded impossible if the biographer had attempted the narration or the explanation in his own words. Equally skilful is the manner in which Mr. Van Doren combined biography and criticism to form a unified narrative. By this method the author was able to show Swift's motives in writing *A Tale of a Tub, Gulliver's Travels* and the rest of the prose that has placed him among the greatest of prose writers in English. The many problems involved in the essays, the letters, and the diaries are examined and judgment passed on them. Mr. Van Doren's style is in keeping with his subject, plain, rich, and smooth. This life of Swift has every quality of great biography, including truth, and it will not soon be superseded.

Like Dean Swift, James Boswell is famous as the author of one book, *The Life of Samuel Johnson,* although both men wrote extensively. Boswell's *Life of Samuel Johnson* is the greatest and the longest biography in English. For more than a century Boswell was reviled, misunderstood, and underrated, for almost every literary historian followed Macaulay's opinion which he expressed in an essay on Croker's edition of Boswell's *Life of Johnson.* Editor, author, and subject were Tories. For that reason and because Macaulay still adhered to the moral and ethical standards of the Clapham sect in which he had been reared, he wrote one of the most bitterly partisan and grossly unfair biographical essays in English literature. Boswell's *Life of Johnson* is one of the many great unread but widely discussed masterpieces of English literature. Most of those literary historians who wrote of the book never read it, knew nothing about the author, and were incapable of understanding Boswell's method. Very few writers bothered to investigate Boswell for themselves, and it was not until 1922 that Professor Chauncey B. Tinker published *Young Boswell,* the first intelligent study of the greatest of all English biographers. Not only do we get an honest character study of Boswell in this book, but we also get some idea of the development of that biographical method that made the *Life of Johnson* one of the great biographies of the world. This excellent critical biography has been supplemented by Dr. Mark Longaker in his *History of English Biography in the Eighteenth Century* (1931). These two books give Boswell his proper place, as one of the great figures in English literature. A third important book on this subject is Harry Saltpeter's *Dr. Johnson & Mr. Boswell* (1929), a brilliant account, developed by the use of letters, of the relationship between these two famous men of letters, an account which helps us to understand how Boswell was able to write the *Life of Samuel Johnson.*

The scholarly biography has had numerous exponents in America during the last fifteen years. As an example of pure research, high enthusiasm, sympathetic treatment, and excellent criticism, Miss Amy Lowell's *John Keats* (1925) takes first rank. A distinguished poet herself, a leading exponent of the modern imagist poetry, Miss Lowell has left, in her two-volume account of John Keats, the definitive critical study of the man and the poet. Complete in every detail, exhaustive in its research and critical analysis of one of the greatest of English poets, it is a great book but not a great biography. In the first place it is too long, for Miss Lowell put into the book everything that she had discovered about Keats. A great deal of the material adds little or nothing to our knowledge of Keats. Selection is as necessary in biography as it is in any other form of literature. Secondly, Miss Lowell's criticism, excellent as it is, overshadows the biography. This is a common fault in critical biographies of writers. Most biographers of this type are more interested in a minute analysis of the man's work than they are in the re-creation of the man as he really was. Miss Lowell could have written an excellent biography of Keats with the material at her disposal, but she chose to write a book on Keats, his friends, his enemies, and his art. Keats constantly becomes lost in the labyrinthine analyses of the motives, the conceptions, and the finished products of his poetical genius. There is so much textual criticism, so much discussion of form and content of the poet's work that the book becomes dull as biographical reading. All of this is important and valuable, but it does not tell us much about Keats. It is because we are interested in Keats rather than in a highly technical discussion of his poetry that we wish to read his biography. To repeat, proportion is absolutely necessary in biographical writing, and it is because *John Keats* lacks that proportion that it is not a great biography in the sense that Woodberry's *Poe*, Paine's *Mark Twain* and Van Loon's *R. v. R.* are great biographies.

Walter C. Peck's *Shelley; his Life and Work* (1927) is a book very similar to Miss Lowell's *John Keats*. Its two volumes contain more material than *John Keats,* but it is a better biography because it has more unity and proportion. Like *John Keats*, it is the most complete account of Shelley that we have, and Shelley had a much more active and adventurous career than Keats. Both books are monuments of research and scholarship; both are definitive, both are invaluable for studies of their subjects or of early nineteenth-century English poetry, but they are not books that one would care to reread. They belong on the reference shelf rather than on the reading table. They will join that large group of unread but widely discussed books.

Franklin P. Snyder's *Life of Robert Burns* (1932) is based on the same sound research and scholarship as are those of Miss Lowell and Professor Peck, but it is less than half as long. It is an adventure in literary interpretation, for it is a life of Burns in terms of his poetry. This should have been the purpose of the authors of *John Keats* and *Shelley,* but they buried their subjects under masses of technical criticism. Professor Snyder is always aware that he is writing a life of

Burns, and everything else is secondary. There is an almost ideal balance between biography and criticism, a balance that makes for a better understanding of the man and the poet. Of the three biographies, the *Life of Robert Burns* is the most interesting and the best.

Snyder's *Life of Robert Burns* stands midway between the very long studies of Lowell and Peck and such a book as Professor Emery E. Neff's *Carlyle* (1932). This is a small book, but it contains the very essence of the life and work of Thomas Carlyle. Every biographer of a man of letters is drawn to his subject because he believes that there is no biography which does justice to the poet, novelist, or essayist in whom he is interested. Unquestionably, that was the motive which produced *John Keats, Shelley,* and *Robert Burns.* A similar motive led Professor Neff to write *Carlyle.* He believed that there was no adequate short life of Carlyle, and he has more than filled the deficiency. It may not appeal to the specialist, but, as a clear biographical and critical interpretation of a great and complex character, it has no peer When one finishes *Carlyle,* he knows the man as well, though not so completely, as if he had read the monumental work of David Wilson, which has just been completed in six volumes.

Continental as well as English men of letters have provided subjects for American biographers in the last ten years, and several continental writers have been the subjects of more than one biographer. Between 1928 and 1931, three books on Rabelais were published by American writers. In 1928, appeared the *Book of Rabelais* by Herman Fetzer, writing under the name of Jake Falstaff. This is an attempt to portray Rabelais as he would have written of himself. It is a lively and interesting book; its success and value are matters of opinion. *Francis Rabelais; the Man and his Work* (1930), by Albert J. Nock and C. R. Wilson, is a hero-worshiping biography. There is neither point nor plan to the book, for the authors failed entirely to explain why Rabelais was a great man and a great writer. Certainly there is an opportunity for an explanation of how the physician-priest came to write one of the great books of the world.

Samuel Putnam succeeded where Nock and Wilson failed because he approached the subject from the point of view of scholarship rather than hero worship and succeeded in presenting the soul and the spirit of the great Frenchman as well as analyzing the technique of his art. As a piece of scholarly interpretation, *François Rabelais; Man of the Renaissance; a Spiritual Biography* (1929) is a masterpiece. Mr. Putnam knows Rabelais and he knows the Europe in which Rabelais lived. The introduction to this biography is an historical and literary gem in itself. "A man of the Renaissance," Rabelais has to be placed against that background before his great satire can be understood. This is not an easy book to read, for Mr. Putnam delves deeply into Rabelais' character and the life of the day for his interpretation of the man, but to anyone interested in Rabelais, the Renaissance, or great literature, this biography is pure delight.

Another French writer who has come under the investigations of modern American biographers is George Sand. Two biographies of this once popular French woman novelist appeared in 1927. Elizabeth W. Schermerhorn's *Seven Strings of the Lyre; the Romantic Life of George Sand, 1804–1876* is a narrative biography in which the story of George Sand's life is told through the seven love affairs she had during her life. The method and the form used by the author seriously limit the scope of the biography. Narration permits no character analysis of the subject. The result is that we know the facts and incidents of George Sand's life, but we do not know the woman herself. There is too much of the story-book element in this biography for any detailed explanation of George Sand's life and work. The absence of any serious consideration of her writing may be explained on the ground that George Sand interests the modern reader as an unusual woman rather than as one of the most famous romantic novelists and playwrights of the nineteenth century, but the author failed to present a full and real picture of the woman. This failure is the fault of her form, for one cannot present a unified picture of a man or woman in a series of episodes.

Marie H. J. Howe pursued a different method in *George Sand; the Search for Love* (1927). It was Mrs. Howe's purpose not only to explain but to vindicate the life of George Sand. She succeeded insofar as eliciting sympathy for her subject is concerned, but she left her method open to serious criticism. In order to create an atmosphere of reality, Mrs. Howe used a great deal of dialogue in her book. She defends her use of it with the statement that every word in the dialogue is taken from the letters and journals of George Sand. In such a procedure the author always takes that which suits his purpose and gives to statements and passages meanings which were not intended. The fact that these are actual quotations does not mean that they are entirely true with respect to this particular book. Mrs. Howe's book is very interesting and very readable and is probably a faithful picture of the life and character of the woman who was George Sand, but its method cannot be recommended, for, regardless of its truth, *George Sand; the Search for Love* is on the border line between biography and fictional biography.

The art of modern biography can show few better examples than Ernest A. Boyd's *Guy de Maupassant; a Biographical Study* (1926). It combines good biography, good criticism, and good taste in equal proportions. One of the masters of the short story and an artist in general prose fiction, de Maupassant is also one of the tragic figures in literature. Mr. Boyd could have written a biography composed of equal parts of scandal and horror. Instead, he chose to treat de Maupassant as a great artist and an unfortunate man. In doing so he has fascinated us by the restraint, the charm, and the excellence of his study. A sane and truthful biography of de Maupassant was badly needed, for there is much in his writings that can be explained only by the facts of his life. It was for the purpose of explaining the life and writings of this unfortunate genius that Mr. Boyd wrote the book. That he succeeded as a biographer and a critic of de Maupassant, no one who has read it can deny.

There is little in the lives of some of our greatest writers that needs explanation. Boccaccio is in this class, for he put himself, unreservedly, into all of his wirtings. If this is true, such a book as Thomas C. Chubb's *Life of Giovanni Boccaccio* (1930) adds little to our knowledge of the subject. Boccaccio's writings need no interpretation, and his life was uneventful. Mr. Chubb has given us the facts of Boccaccio's life and some criticism of his writings. He has explained, particularly, Boccaccio's piety in later life, but it is hardly necessary to show that the author of the *Decameron* had a change of heart as he grew older. Nearly all men do.

The same Renaissance that produced Boccaccio nourished a greater scholar and humanist, Erasmus. A neutral in the great religious upheaval of the late fifteenth and early sixteenth centuries, Erasmus needed modern interpreters. He found two in modern America, Preserved Smith and John J. Mangan. The Reverend Dr. Smith, a church historian, wrote *Erasmus: a Study of his Life, Ideals and Place in History* (1923) because he believed that if the attitude of the great Dutch humanist could be explained, it would greatly help to clarify the religious and theological issues of the Reformation. *Erasmus* is a judicious, scholarly, and readable life of a man who will always be a subject for controversy. It is, necessarily, historical biography, but Erasmus is always in the foreground of the book. With the exception of a few chapters, this life is a simple narrative of Erasmus' career from birth to death. It is, as far as possible, neutral in its point of view. Erasmus lived and died a Catholic; at one time or another he leaned toward the Catholic or the Protestant side; he was claimed and disclaimed by both sides. He saw the evils of both sides and tried to bring about a reconciliation, but of course he failed. No man can be entirely unprejudiced when writing about Erasmus, but Dr. Smith was unusually successful because he approached his subject from a personal and historical rather than a religious point of view. This is the best short biography of Erasmus in English.

It has been frequently stated in this study that the best biographical method is to let the subject speak for himself wherever possible. Like everything else this can be overdone, not in frequency but in quantity. Dr. John J. Mangan's *Life and Character of Desiderius Erasmus of Rotterdam; Derived from a Study of his Works and Correspondence* (1927) is an example of too much quotation. The two large volumes contain more of Erasmus' writing than they do of Dr. Mangan's. The latter's admiration for the humanist frequently affected his judgment when he came to quote from the writings. At times there are whole pages of Erasmus, a great portion of which could have been omitted without affecting the point which the author was making. The principal objection to excessive quotation is that it unduly lengthens the book and makes for tediousness in reading. The fact that Dr. Mangan is a physician accounts, in part, for the length of the quoted passages, for many of them enable the author to interpret Erasmus on the basis of psychology. In spite of this defect, this life of Erasmus is a brilliant piece of scholarship as well as a brilliant example of psychology sanely applied to life-writing. The man who reads this book completely knows the mind of Erasmus, as far as any man can know the mind of another, as well as his life. No future biography of Erasmus can be more complete than this one is.

In the last few years we have had biographies of such widely different creative artists as Turgenev, Lope de Vega, Heine, and Ibsen. Avraham Yarmolinsky's *Turgenev, the Man—his Art—and his Age* (1926) is a competent piece of biographical writing, with the added distinction of having been the first biography of the great Russian novelist in any language. Angel Flores' *Lope de Vega, Monster of Nature* (1930) is a popular account of the Spanish playwright. There is too much fiction and too little criticism in the book to make it of much value.

That Man Heine; a Biography (1927) by Lewis Browne and Elsa Weihl is a better book than the title indicates, but its popular vein and the lack of harmony between authors and subject prevent it from being more than just another biography. Mr. Browne has lately published *Blessed Spinoza,* a popular treatment of the great Jewish philosopher. Adolph Zucker's *Ibsen, the Master Builder* (1929) is an excellent life of the great Norwegian dramatist, for it is done in the best modern manner.

6

The link between literature and religion in early America is a very close one, for practically all of the early writings in the New England colonies were either done by clergymen or by laymen for whom religion was the paramount subject in life. The ministers were particularly prolific in writings of a religious or theocratic nature, and the Mather dynasty, Richard, Increase, and Cotton headed the list. We have no modern life of Richard Mather, but his son and grandson are the subjects of biographies written within the last eight years. In 1925 Professor Kenneth B. Murdock published *Increase Mather, the Foremost American Puritan.* This is a valuable contribution to the literary and political history of New England in the late seventeenth century. Originally a doctoral thesis, the book is marred, as a biography, by the author's support of his thesis: "Increase Mather, the foremost American Puritan." Consequently we have, not a life of Increase Mather, but a statement and defense of his position as the leading Puritan of his day. The book gives a complete factual account of Increase Mather's life and work as minister and politician, but it lacks entirely any character study of the man as an individual.

When Ralph and Louise Boas were writing *Cotton Mather: Keeper of the Puritan Conscience* (1928), they kept in mind the fact that they were writing the life of a most unusual man rather than a history of his times. They presented a character study of the most famous clergyman in seventeenth-century America and a personality that was unique. Cotton Mather is an almost ideal subject for psychological treatment, and the authors made the most of their opportunities. This is not a scholarly biography; neither is it journalistic. It is a readable and fair presentation of the character of a man who could have flourished only in the Boston of the late seventeenth and early eighteenth centuries. It enables us to understand the man who wrote more than four hundred books and pamphlets, who was the leading prosecutor of the witchcraft persecutions and, at the same time, a member of the Royal Society. Some may criticize the book on the ground that it says little about his writings. The biographers were concerned with the man and not the author, and they succeeded in accomplishing their purpose. It remains for some future biographer to present a complete personal and critical study of one of the most learned men that America has produced.

Politically and religiously, the Mathers represented the most conservative element in New England. Roger Williams, their contemporary, was the leader of the liberals in politics and those who believed that church and state should be separate entities. His life in America was one long battle for political and religious freedom. Driven from Plymouth Colony, from Massachusetts Bay Colony, he succeeded in founding the Providence Plantations, which eventually became the colony and state of Rhode Island. Williams was the subject of numerous biographies in the nineteenth century and several in the twentieth. Emily Easton's *Roger Williams, Prophet and Pioneer* (1930) is a valuable book for its contents rather than its form. Miss Easton obtained considerable new source material, but she failed to use it to interpret her subject. Facts alone are not sufficient for a biography; they must be arranged in a manner that will permit interpretation on the part of the reader if the writer does not interpret them himself. In this book, for instance, there is a sixty-page introduction describing the London of Williams' boyhood, late Elizabethan London. It is interesting but it fails entirely in its purpose, to bring out the influence of this London on Williams' later development.

Roger Williams, New England Firebrand (1932), by James E. Ernest, is a much better book than Miss Easton's biography. While its tone is no less modern, it is a much finer piece of work. Ernest conceived and explained Williams as a genuine liberal, and proved his case. This is a much longer book than Miss Easton's, presenting a complete picture of Williams' life and work. It is also a book of better design and construction. Although both of these books are modern in method and contain new material, they have not, as biographies, superseded Oscar Strauss's *Roger Williams . . .* (1894), because they add nothing to his interpretation of Williams the founder of religious liberty in America.

Roger Williams was not the only rebel against the theocracy of the Cottons, the Mathers, and their followers. At least one woman dared to think and act for herself in religious matters. Like Roger Williams, Anne Hutchinson was banished from Massachusetts as a heretic, and a few years later she was the victim of an Indian massacre in northern New York. In 1930, three lives of this brave woman were published. Edith Curtis' *Anne Hutchinson; a Biography* is an excellent short, factual account of Mrs. Hutchinson's life. Helen Augur's *An American Jezebel; the Life of Anne Hutchinson* is an interesting book, but it is not a good biography. Mrs. Hutchinson was by no means a Jezebel; she was an intelligent, educated woman who believed that the individual had something to say about his own salvation. The second serious fault is Miss Augur's reconstruction of Anne Hutchinson's thoughts and conversations, for which there are absolutely no bases. Winifred K. Rugg's *Unafraid; a Life of Anne Hutchinson* strikes an almost perfect balance between the lives by Mrs. Curtis and Miss Augur. It is modern biography at its best, in that it combines truth and accuracy with the best in modern interpretation. There is nothing in the book which is not based on fact; Miss Rugg contributes only an explanation of Anne Hutchinson as she really was.

If all modern biographers confined themselves to biography instead of venturing into fiction and history, their work would be much more satisfactory. Unusual periods and unusual people are the downfall of more than one well-intentioned writer. In all probability, Henry B. Parkes intended that *Jonathan Edwards; the Fiery Puritan* (1930) should be a biography, but it is not. Written for a series of short biographies intended for the "general reader," it is an interesting account of the history of the time, in which the peculiarities of the period are stressed at the expense of the subject. It has always been a conundrum to me why so-called popular biographies either fail entirely to present the life and character of their subjects or else present them in the style and method of a primer or a ten-cent magazine.

Religion was in a state of flux in eighteenth-century America. Edwards represented both the old and the new. He believed that the religion developed by the Puritans of seventeenth-century America was the only true religion; he also believed that vitality and warmth were necessary for its preservation. He gave impetus to the emotional phase of religion which was to carry Protestantism in America to the extremes that it reached in the nineteenth century. John Wesley started a movement in England which was to flourish in America under the revival spirit that Jonathan Edwards advocated.

John Wesley was born and died in England, but his missionary work in America laid the foundations on which Bishop Asbury built the structure of Methodism. Wesley founded Methodism, and Asbury was his greatest disciple. Wesley is a most attractive subject for a biography, for he had an unusual personality and he provided in his journals a mine of biographical material which is by no means exhausted. Two Americans have written books on Wesley which are interesting but not exactly orthodox. Abram Lipsky's *John Wesley; a Portrait* (1928) is not a formal biography but rather a series of character studies covering the high spots in Wesley's life. As a study in personality, it is an excellent book.

John D. Wade's *John Wesley* (1930) is a much more ambitious project than Lipsky's study. Mr. Wade has a sincere appreciation of Wesley and his work and, at the same time, is aware of the abnormalities of Wesley's character. Using modern psychology tempered with restraint, and sincere appreciation, the author has proved that such subjects as John Wesley can be given dignified treatment in the modern manner. Wade's purpose is to try to explain the man who could move millions by his oratory, who could make converts by the thousands, who could organize and administer a new church at the same time that he was fighting for his own soul and his own domestic happiness. He did control himself, but he never succeeded in achieving domestic happiness. That the biographer succeeded in his task of interpreting Wesley must be evident to any intelligent reader of *John Wesley*.

Out of the welter of new religions, cults, and sects of nineteenth-century America there emerged two that have become a permanent part of the religious and social history of the country—Mormonism and Christian Science. Joseph Smith was the founder of Mormonism, and Mary Baker of Christian Science. Although Smith founded Mormonism, it was the executive genius of his successor, Brigham Young, that enabled this new religion to survive and develop. Smith was killed before the Mormons settled in Utah, but Mrs. Eddy lived to see Christian Science firmly established.

There have been many books written on Joseph Smith, Brigham Young, and Mormonism. Most of them were written by friends or enemies. M. R. Werner wrote an unprejudiced life of Brigham Young, and Harry M. Beardsley approached Smith from the same point of view in *Joseph Smith and His Mormon Empire* (1931). This is a complete narrative biography from his birth in New York to his death in Illinois. It is a narrative in the sense that the author has not attempted to analyze or interpret the character and personality of Joseph

Smith; he has merely told the story. Dramatization of such a figure is inevitable in these days, but the author has exercised really admirable restraint in view of the temptations that must have beset him. There are judgments passed by the author because he had to settle points of violent controversy between Mormon and non-Mormon writers; there is some imaginative detail which is justified, and some statements put into the mouth of Smith which are explained by Mr. Beardsley in his preface. In short, Mr. Beardsley has written a fundamentally true life of Joseph Smith, which presents the man as he really was. The ultra-conservative critic may question some of his methods, but they seem to have served their purpose. We have the author's word that there is nothing in the book that did not actually occur and for which he has not documentary proof. If we put *Joseph Smith and His Mormon Empire* over against the *Life of Brigham Young* (1930), by Mrs. Susa Gates and Mrs. Leah E. Widstoe, we can see the difference between impartial and prejudiced life-writing. Mrs. Gates is one of Brigham Young's fifty-six children, and one could hardly expect her life of her father to be either complete or critical. Prejudice either way is harmful, but deliberate suppression and misrepresentation of facts are dishonest. The reader of biography must judge for himself whether or not the writer is interested in truth or in propaganda. These two books are striking examples of each point of view.

Of the six biographies of Mrs. Eddy that have been published, one was suppressed, all available copies of another, together with the original manuscript and the plates, were purchased by friends of Christian Science, and a remarkably bold attempt was made to suppress a third biography by means of intimidation and boycott.

The first long biography of Mary Baker Eddy was Sybil Wilbur O'Brien's *Life of Mary Baker Eddy* (1908). This is the authorized life of Mrs. Eddy, published by the Christian Science Church. In 1909 appeared Georgine Milmine's *Life of Mary Baker G. Eddy and the History of Christian Science.*

Chapters from this book first appeared in *McClure's Maga-zine,* but were expanded for publication in book form be-cause of new material that had come to light. This biography gave an entirely different picture of Mrs. Eddy and Chris-tian Science. Soon after its publication, the plates and origi-nal manuscript were purchased, and the book has become very rare. The third important book on Mrs. Eddy was Adam Dickey's *Memoirs of Mary Baker Eddy* (1927). Mr. Dickey was associated with Mrs. Eddy for many years; he was a mem-ber of the Board of Directors of the Mother Church; and he was a faithful and ardent disciple. The memoirs were pub-lished three years after Mr. Dickey's death. Upon publication Mrs. Dickey was persuaded to withdraw the book, and all copies were recalled; consequently the two copies in the Li-brary of Congress, deposited there under the copyright law, are the only ones available in the American edition. We are told that this book is a most remarkable document, but I have not seen it and therefore can make no comment.

We now come to the first attempt at a complete and im-partial biography of the foundress of Christian Science and one of the most remarkable women in the nineteenth cen-tury. Miss Milmine's book is biographical, but it is not a unified piece of writing, for it is largely a compilation of facts with sworn affidavits substantiating those facts. Edwin F. Dakin's *Mrs. Eddy: the Biography of a Virginal Mind* (1929) is a complete, thoroughly documented and, I believe, truthful account of Mrs. Eddy's life and career. The fact that the officials of the Christian Science Church waged such a strenuous campaign against its distribution, although they neglected to point out any specific untruths, is presumptive evidence, at least, of its authenticity. It is the story of a woman who raised herself from obscurity to the position of a minor divinity in the eyes of her followers. All churches have been the objects of adverse criticism; few have taken the trouble to answer their critics; none has attempted, in Amer-ica, to question the freedom of speech in matters of judg-ment and proven facts. Mr. Dakin's book is good biography, judged by any standard, for he has limited his account to facts and their interpretation, and has shown Mrs. Eddy to be a remarkable woman, if not exactly a saint. To repeat what has been frequently stated in this study: we can judge the truth of a biography only on the basis of our knowledge of the subject and the author, and particularly on the honesty of the latter. A popular edition of Mr. Dakin's *Mrs. Eddy* was published in 1930. It contains a statement by the publishers regarding the attempt at its suppression. The statement was enlarged in an inserted pamphlet entitled *The Blight that Failed.*

Since Mr. Dakin's biography two other lives of Mrs. Eddy have appeared. Fleta C. Springer's *According to the Flesh: a Biography of Mary Baker Eddy* (1930) adopts the same point of view as that of Mr. Dakin's book, and it is written in much the same spirit. The Reverend Lyman P. Powell's *Mary Baker Eddy; a Life Size Portrait* (1930) seems to have been written to order, by the Episcopal clergyman, for the First Church of Christ, Scientist.

Before closing this record of American adventure into the very controversial field of religious biography, one foreign subject must be mentioned. Ralph Roeder's *Savonarola; a Study in Conscience* (1930) is the best life of the great Catholic reformer that I know of. Not only is it good biography, but it is unusually complete, for it gives Savonarola his proper position as a politician and a statesman as well as a religious reformer. It is a study of the politics and religion of the Italian Renaissance in the person of an honest man.

X

THE NEW BIOGRAPHY LOOKS
AT PUBLIC LIFE

DURING the last decade there has been a remarkable revival of interest in the lives of American political and military leaders from the Revolution to the Civil War. Some of this material has been discussed in the chapters on Washington, Lincoln, and the professional biographers. This chapter represents the remainder of the biographies of this period classified as to subject rather than author, for the majority of these authors have written only one biography. These biographies can be divided into three groups: first complete studies; modern interpretations; and popularizations. A great deal of valuable historical and biographical source material has been published or made available for study during the twentieth century. This material has attracted biographers because it offered opportunities for original lives or for complete re-examinations and re-interpretations of many subjects that had been untruthfully or inadequately treated in the nineteenth century. Of course the popularity of biography was a further incentive to the modern biographer. This is particularly true in the case of the so-called popularizers. In many instances authors of this type of biography were sincere in their attempts to produce a life of a soldier or statesman without the impedimenta of military strategy and politics, which have been stumbling blocks in the paths of many readers of biography. In all three types we see the influence of the New Biography with its psychological approach and its primary interest in the subject rather than the times in which he lived.

That the machinery of the New Biography may be adequate and inadequate, at the same time, is illustrated by Ralph V. Harlow's *Samuel Adams, Promoter of the American Revolution; a Study in Psychology and Politics* (1923). Professor Harlow attempted to psychoanalyze one of the main-springs of the American Revolution. In his effort to explain why Adams was one of the greatest politicians this country has produced, and why he failed as an executive and administrator, he unintentionally slights the genius in Samuel Adams, the genius that enabled him to keep alive the Committee of Correspondence, to maintain the spirit of agitation against the English Parliament which finally resulted in revolution. Samuel Adams was not the only agitator, but he was certainly the greatest. In this biography we get the impression that Adams was a failure. In that respect it is a poor biography, for it places emphasis where that emphasis does not belong. Had Professor Harlow resisted the temptation to psychoanalyze his subject, he would have written a much better book.

Samuel Adams is not so well known as his cousin, John Adams, for the latter was a statesman as well as a patriot. There are many short lives of John Adams, but as yet we have no complete biography of our second President, who was and is a very much misunderstood man. Samuel D. McCoy's *This Man Adams; the Man Who Never Died* (1928) is certainly not a contribution toward a better understanding of John Adams, but it does have some merit. It is what may be called a fantasy in biography which will have to depend upon the individual reader for its appeal. It is not fiction and it is not biography. It is biographical in that it purports to explain the character and personality of John Adams, and to show that the spirit of John Adams still survives in the country for whose freedom he risked so much. Some may not recognize that spirit in modern America; some may not see that Mr. McCoy has succeeded in showing that Adams bequeathed a heritage to the United States. At all events, the book is interesting and satisfies at least one of the requisites of good biography, the transmission of personality and a sense of the reality of the subject.

As a biographical subject, John Quincy Adams has fared little better than his father, John Adams, for it was not until 1932 that a real biography of him appeared. In that year Bennett C. Clark, United States Senator from Missouri, published *John Quincy Adams, "Old Man Eloquent."* Like his father, John Quincy Adams was condemned for certain peculiarities of his character which had little or no influence on his public career. A genuine statesman, a faithful public servant, a man of the highest integrity, John Quincy Adams was the greatest member of a great political family. From the age of thirteen, when he became an attaché of the American Mission to Russia, until his death, in the House of Representatives at Washington, at the age of eighty-one, Adams' life was that of a public man. Minister to Holland and England, Peace Commissioner after the War of 1812, United States Senator, Secretary of State, President of the United States, and congressman from Massachusetts, John Quincy Adams had little time to be a private citizen, but he was always an individual. It is this individual in public life that Senator Clark has given us, and he has enabled us to understand and respect this man who had no friends and a host of enemies because honor and honesty meant more to him than anything else in the world. "Old Man Eloquent" has come to life in this biography, and we leave it with the feeling that we have been living and fighting with a great man. A sound and thorough knowledge of early American politics, a definite point of view, a simple and forceful style, a complete understanding of the personality of his subject, are some of the qualities that Senator Clark brought to the writing of this biography. It is an outstanding personal and political biography, which combines the best qualities of the old and the new in life-writing.

There was little of what we call romance in the life and career of John Quincy Adams, but the American Revolution produced a number of romantic and picturesque figures. Among the best known of these are Anthony Wayne, Ethan Allen, Paul Revere, Benedict Arnold, and Aaron Burr. John H. Preston's *Gentleman Rebel; the Exploits of Anthony Wayne* (1930) is a popular treatment of one of the most picturesque of the Revolutionary general officers. Mr. Preston seems to have used all the available source material on Wayne, adding a little fiction and drama here and there where he thought it would do the most good. Here again we have a biographer setting his stage with the aid of his imagination and giving his hero dialogues which can have no basis in fact. This "creative" writing makes interesting reading, but it must be accepted only as imaginary background. The great evil of this method lies in the fact that the average reader, relying on the researches of the author, accepts these purple and vermilion patches as truth.

John Pell resorted to none of the modern tricks in biography when he wrote *Ethan Allen* (1929). This is an excellent life of the "Hero of Ticonderoga," Revolutionary commander, and pioneer. Taking advantage of all that is good in modern biography while confining himself to established facts, Mr. Pell has told a simple story of a complex character who was much more than a "Green Mountain Boy" and much less than his panegyrists would have us believe. He has given us a true and balanced biography illuminated by the greatest gift that any writer can possess—humor.

Ethan Allen had a brother whose fame rests on solid achievement rather than on romantic adventure. James B. Wilbur has told his story in *Ira Allen, Founder of Vermont, 1751–1814* (1928). The two large volumes of this heavily documented historical biography are invaluable as sources for the history of Vermont and the Allen family, but Mr. Wilbur forgot that he was supposed to be writing biography and not history. In extenuation it may be said that genuine historical biography is very rare.

The legends surrounding the life of Paul Revere are as tenacious if not so numerous as those enveloping the figure of Ethan Allen. If we accept the statements of our school histories, Paul Revere was a patriotic "midnight rider" who, alone and unaided, aroused the "embattled farmers" that they might fire "the shot heard round the world." Emerson

G. Taylor's *Paul Revere* (1930) succeeds in placing Revere in his proper position with respect to his patriotic duties and his daily life. Paul Revere was an expert horseman who had been for some years an express messenger between Boston, New York, and Philadelphia. His "midnight ride" was not made alone nor was it so extensive as Longfellow made it. (Poetic license often covers a multitude of factual sins.) Revere was a staunch, even an extreme patriot, contributing his services whenever he had the time. He was a jack of all trades and master of most of them, including dentistry. He was one of the finest silversmiths in America, and his pieces are cherished, not because he was ready "to ride and spread the alarm through every Middlesex village and farm," but because they are things of beauty, examples of the finest Colonial craftsmanship. To read such a life as Mr Taylor's *Paul Revere* is to feel that modern biography, despite its many transgressions, has come into its own.

Not many Americans know that, as a young man, Benedict Arnold was as patriotic as Paul Revere, the most trusted of General Washington's early lieutenants. The tragedy of his later years can be attributed to weak character, vanity, love of woman, and love of money. Several lives of Arnold have been discussed in this study. None of them is what one would term a dispassionate treatment. Neither are those of Oscar Sherwin and Edward D. Sullivan. Mr. Sherwin's *Benedict Arnold, Patriot and Traitor* (1931) is the best biography of Arnold that has yet been written, because he approached the subject with an inquiring, open mind, prepared to present the case as he found it. He shows just how Benedict Arnold changed from the man who was the backbone of the American attack on Quebec in 1775, the inspired leader, though he had no command, of the attack on Burgoyne at Saratoga, to the man who would have surrendered West Point to the British. The man's strength and weakness lay in his character, and it is in the analysis of that character, as affected by circumstances, that Mr. Sherwin succeeds in his difficult task of interpretation. Mr. Sherwin used facts alone to reach his conclusion, because it is only on the facts that Arnold can be explained.

The thesis of Mr. Sullivan's book, *Benedict Arnold, Military Racketeer* (1932), is exactly described in the subtitle. Before compiling this book, the author was engaged in the study of Chicago rackets and racketeers. He seems to have developed some sort of complex. I have diligently read my early American history, but I can find none of the specific charges that Mr. Sullivan brings against Arnold in his early career. Arnold was always careless about money; his official accounts were rarely correct. I imagine it was not an easy matter to keep accounts straight during the American Revolution unless one were a Washington. Someone must have told Mr. Sullivan that Arnold would fit in with his sociological and criminal studies, and he set out to prove it. A newspaperman can prove almost anything, given the necessity. General Arnold's financial and military transactions became shady only after his appointment to the command at Philadelphia and his marriage to Peggy Shippen. If we accept Mr. Sullivan's thesis, Arnold was born a racketeer. Further analysis of the book would be merely a waste of time. *Benedict Arnold, Military Racketeer* is dishonest, badly written, and totally misleading. It is an example of the havoc that deliberate distortion can work when used by a prejudiced writer.

We do not know so much about the life of Aaron Burr as we do about the life of Benedict Arnold. There are portions of Burr's career that never have been and never will be clarified. We lack the facts. It is this lack that permits biographers of Burr to construct their own theories and call them biographies. Burr is a much more romantic figure than Arnold. His career as an officer in the Revolution, as a New York politician, and as Vice-President of the United States in Jefferson's first administration provides excellent material for what may be called fictionized biography, biography that contains at least as much fiction as fact. Johnston D. Kirkhoff's *Aaron Burr; a Romantic Biography* (1931) is just the sort of book that attracts the average reader. It contains nothing that is new and much that is unreliable. It covers Burr's crowded life in leaps and bounds, giving only those parts of the life that will support the subtitle. In short, it is the worst kind of journalistic rewriting, for it has neither point of view nor truth to support it.

Where Mr. Kirkhoff's book is imaginative, Wandell and Minnigerode's *Aaron Burr: a Biography Written in Large Part from Original and Hitherto Unused Material* (1927) is entirely realistic. The nearest approach to it, in length, is James Parton's *Life and Times of Aaron Burr*. Parton's purpose was to present the whole story of Burr, to offset the hostile accounts that had been common up to that time (1858). Wandell and Minnigerode set out to defend Burr against his enemies. They accomplished their purpose at the expense of truth. Mr. Wandell spent his life in research on Burr; Mr. Minnigerode is a professional historian and biographer of the popular type. Both men could see only one side of the picture, presenting Burr as a great man publicly and privately, and ignoring Hamilton's public service that they might belittle the individual. This book, in my judgment, is a striking illustration of a prejudiced thesis worked out to a logical conclusion. I hold no brief for Hamilton, but I believe that biographers should not turn facts for the purpose of proving their case, as I think Mr. Wandell and Mr. Minnigerode did. Granting that every biography is the life of one man from the point of view of another, there yet remains the necessity of proving the truth.

Among the romantic figures of the American Revolution are Sir William Howe and the Marquis de Lafayette. The latter has been the subject of innumerable biographies, but the latest is certainly the best in English. Brand Whitlock has long been known as a novelist, historian, and biographer. He brought to the writing of *La Fayette* (1932) not only wide literary experience, but the advantage of years of residence in Europe as an American diplomat. These two large volumes cover every phase and feature of Lafayette's long and eventful life. Based on sound historical scholarship, written with a remarkable insight into the spirit of the French and of the period in which Lafayette achieved his fame, infused with the personality of the young, the middle-aged, and the old man who sacrificed so much for liberty, Mr. Whitlock's life of Lafayette is a masterpiece of historical and personal biography. The quality of the style of the book adds luster to the career of the subject and the reputation of the author. This biography is further proof that out of the combination of old and new in biography has come a distinctive form of art. If we do not know the red-haired boy of 1776 and the white-haired man of 1824 after reading this life, we shall never know him.

Bellamy Partridge's *Sir Billy Howe* (1932) is neither so ambitious nor so successful—within its limits—as Mr. Whitlock's book. As the title indicates, Partridge has a tendency toward smartness in his writing, a tendency that rarely accomplishes its purpose. Mr. Partridge broke new ground, for this is the first life of Howe by an American, and the best that has been written by anyone. It is concerned primarily with Howe's career as commander of the British forces in America during the Revolution. Its purpose is to explain why the distinguished strategist who won so many half-victories never tried to and never succeeded in putting down the rebellion against His Majesty, George III of England. The author achieves his purpose, and in doing so explains a phase of the Revolutionary War that was either ignored or suppressed by the patriotic school of American historians. Although there is a great deal of history in this biography, we never lose sight of the central figure, the man who was forced to accept the command of the American expedition, and who executed that command according to his idea rather than the ideas that emanated with such rapidity from Downing Street.

If some other general than Sir William Howe had been in command at Bunker Hill, at Long Island, at Brandywine, at Germantown, Thomas Jefferson might not have become

one of the American immortals. There seems to be no end
to lives of Jefferson, Washington, Lincoln, and many other
great Americans, but there must be definite choices for discussion. Among the Jefferson biographies of the last decade
are two that seem to be important. In *Jefferson* (1926), Albert
Jay Nock disclaims any intention of writing a biography;
he calls it a study. It is both, for it presents an interesting and
valuable picture of Jefferson separated from his background.
Mr. Nock analyses the personality of the man, the politician,
the statesman, and the philosopher. This is a portrait of an
individual rather than a biography. In that respect it is inadequate, by definition, but somehow or other we know
the mind of Thomas Jefferson when we have finished the
book. It complements any formal biography of Jefferson that
has been written. Gilbert Chinard's *Thomas Jefferson, the
Apostle of Americanism* (1929) is a book somewhat similar
to Nock's. Although Professor Chinard is a Frenchman, he
has resided in the United States for some time and has a
remarkable understanding of the county and its great men.
His book on Jefferson is a long mental biography and a good
one. Without using any of the tricks of modern psychological
life-writing, he has penetrated into the very essence of Jefferson's thinking. It is not a very logical picture, for Jefferson
was not always a logical man, but it does show the mental
processes in operation. It may not be a formal biography, but
it is a complete picture of the thinking Jefferson, and Jefferson was a thinker rather than a doer.

John Randolph of Roanoke and Thomas Jefferson had
one thing in common: both were Virginians. Gerald W.
Johnson in *Randolph of Roanoke; a Political Fantastic* (1929)
has given us a brilliant short biography of one of the greatest
orators, statesmen, and eccentrics that America has seen. The
one fault of this popular life is that it overemphasizes Randolph's eccentricities and the tragedy of his life. This overemphasis was probably in conformity with the editorial policy
of the series to which it belongs, for most of the books in
the series are of the same type. With this exception, which

may bulk large in the minds of some critics, Mr. Johnson does full justice to the man, the orator, and the statesman. To anyone who has neither the time nor the inclination to read William Cabell Bruce's great biography of the same subject, this is an excellent substitute.

To the same series Mr. Johnson contributed *Andrew Jackson: an Epic in Homespun* (1927). Written earlier than the Randolph, it is an equally good short biography, and it is popular only in the sense that it is terse and eminently readable. Mr. Johnson understood and admired Jackson without being a hero worshiper. That is why he could write such a good short life. David Karsner had the same qualifications and wrote as good a book in *Andrew Jackson, the Gentle Savage* (1929). Mr. Karsner admired Jackson, but he did not let his admiration affect his judgment. A little longer than Johnson's book, this biography is more concerned with character than with events. In interpretation, it is the best of the shorter lives of Jackson. It has all the attractiveness of modern life-writing and few of its faults. Its style would have been improved had Mr. Karsner used the historical present and future less frequently or more consistently than he did. These two books on Jackson show what can be done with a great subject when the author's space is limited.

Daniel Webster is as popular as Jackson with modern biographers. A number of his biographies, the best of them, have been discussed, but there are three in the last decade, exclusive of Professor Fuess's great book, that should be mentioned. Elijah R. Kennedy's *Real Daniel Webster* (1924) is neither real nor is it Daniel Webster. It is impossible to realize that a modern writer can still wield the whitewash brush with such a heavy hand. A campaign biographer of the Gilded Age could not have produced a more fulsome eulogy than has Mr. Kennedy. This book appeared at least seventy-five years too late. Allan L. Benson's *Daniel Webster* (1929) is a modern version of the same type of biography. Mr. Benson had a double purpose in writing this life: to dramatize Webster's life and to defend him against his enemies. The drama goes beyond the original in many instances, while the defense is unfortunate, to say the least. Mr. Benson brings up all the old charges against Webster and either dismisses or condones them. This biography has little to commend it from the literary point of view, and the judgments are entirely unreliable. Mr. Benson would have fared much better as a biographer of Webster, had he let sleeping dogs lie.

The Godlike Daniel (1930), by Samuel Hopkins Adams, appeared at the same time as Claude Fuess's *Daniel Webster*, which was unfortunate for Mr. Adams' reputation as a biographer. Mr. Adams is a famous journalist and popular novelist. He combined these two gifts and wrote *Godlike Daniel*. The fundamental outline of the biography is true, but the details are frequently what Mr. Adams thought they should have been rather than what they actually were. He does not attempt any defense of Webster's less virtuous habits and practices; he glories in them. The book is very interesting, but it is not biography, and it is not dependable.

2

In the chapters on Lincoln and the professional biographers numerous figures of the Civil War and the Reconstruction Era were discussed. Lives of famous men of this period continue to appear, throwing new lights and shadows on the heroes of the North and South. There is now a sufficiently clear perspective for the sincere biographer to approach his subject from a historical instead of a hysterical point of view.

One of the most difficult tasks for a biographer is to make a mediocre and colorless subject interesting. Roy Nichols accomplished this task when he wrote *Franklin Pierce; Young Hickory of the Granite Hills* (1931). No one ever intended to make Pierce President of the United States; he was the consequence of a compromise of despair in the Democratic party. Country lawyer, political general in the Mexican War, Democratic "boss" of New Hampshire, and, by the same token, congressman and Senator of the United States, Pierce was the least fitted of any of the prominent Democrats of the time to occupy the White House. His one redeeming feature was that he had no fixed opinions on the slavery question, although he leaned toward the South. In a closely woven narrative, complemented by keen interpretation of political events and sharp analysis of character, Professor Nichols presents Franklin Pierce as he really was, and gives him his proper position among the men who have achieved the Presidency. In view of the difficulties surrounding this subject, I think that *Franklin Pierce* is one of our finest political biographies.

Although he died before the Civil War began, John Brown will always be associated with the struggle between the North and the South. Villard's *John Brown* is the most authoritative book on the subject, but later lives have given us more informal accounts and provided different points of view. Hill P. Wilson began to study the life and career of the famous abolitionist in the firm conviction that Brown was not sufficiently appreciated. After a thorough study of all the material on the subject, Mr. Wilson came to the conclusion that Brown was nothing but a common adventurer engaged in a battle for money. That is the theme of *John Brown, Soldier of Fortune; a Critique* (1913). It is a little difficult to accept Mr. Wilson's interpretation. There may be some truth in it, but the picture he presents is so one-sided that it defeats its own purpose. John Brown was more than a soldier of fortune, if he was one at all. In Robert P. Warren's *John Brown; the Making of a Martyr* (1929), we have another side of the picture. Mr. Warren, writing from the southern point of view, makes Brown a fanatic for self-glorification. At the same time the author shows a sympathetic interest in Brown's mentality. He tries to explain the man by an analysis of his acts and the peculiarities of mind that prompted those acts. Warren's biography is more objective than Wilson's, and less biased. Neither book, in my opinion, provides a wholly satisfactory explanation of John Brown. Perhaps some future artist in biography may reduce the weight of Villard's book without sacrificing its essential truth.

General Grant is still a fascinating subject for biographers, and, like John Brown's, his life is open to numerous interpretations. William E. Woodward's *Meet General Grant* (1928) is the first really modern study of Grant, and it is by no means successful. In this biography as in *Washington, the Image and the Man,* Mr. Woodward has made use of every device of modern biography. Acceleration of movement, imaginary conversations, the jargon of Freudian psychology, and an apparent desire to belittle the man rather than to place him where he belongs, are some of the defects in this life. There are so many vulnerable spots in Grant's armor that the temptation to shoot at them may be irresistible, but it defeats the purpose of the biographer, if that purpose is to re-create a man as he really was, by one method or another. If that is not the biographer's purpose, then he should not classify his book as biography. Despite the faults that have been mentioned, *Meet General Grant* is the nearest approach to a true picture of the great militarist that we have. The definitive life of Grant remains to be written by someone who will take the man as he finds him and explain, without derision, the tragedy as well as the glory of his life and his career. We had to wait a century and a quarter for a true biography of Washington; we may have to wait nearly that long for a truthful interpretation of General Grant. His career as a soldier and military strategist has been the subject of two modern books, John F. C. Fuller's *Generalship of Ulysses S. Grant* (1929) and Arthur L. Conger's *Rise of U. S. Grant* (1931). Both are strictly military studies and add nothing to our knowledge or interpretation of Grant's character.

The two generals who were Grant's chief supports in the campaign that closed the Civil War have been the subjects of studies by modern writers. In 1931, Joseph Hergesheimer published *Sheridan; a Military Narrative.* If we except such a book as *Swords and Roses,* which is nostalgic romance rather than biography, *Sheridan* is Mr. Hergesheimer's first venture into the biographical field. *Sheridan* is not true biography; it may not be good military biography, judged by purely military standards; but it is good writing. Hergesheimer does what few military writers can do, he makes one see the battles, the men, the horses, and all the paraphernalia of war as they were in the actual battles. As literature this book is good; how much better it might have been had Mr. Hergesheimer chosen to tell the real story of Sheridan before, during, and after the war!

In *Sherman, Fighting Prophet* (1932), Lloyd Lewis has completely re-created the man who broke the back of the Confederacy, the man who is generally acknowledged as the greatest tactical genius, military strategist, and fighter that the Civil War produced. Like Grant, Sherman hated war; that is why he fought so mercilessly and planned so savagely. He wanted a quick ending. Against a background of characteristic rather than romantic frontier life, the author builds up the picture of the boy, the youth, the man. In business, which he liked, he was a failure; in war, he found the expression of his personality. Unable to make a living in 1862, he was General of the Armies of the United States in 1868 and could have been President of the United States. Using every effective biographical method, letting his subject speak for himself wherever possible, not only writing Sherman's life but living it, Mr. Lewis has given us one of the best of modern biographies and a life of William Tecumseh Sherman that will not soon be superseded. It will take a place with Beveridge's *Lincoln,* Fuess's *Webster,* Pringle's *Roosevelt,* and Nevins' *Cleveland* as an example of the best that has come from the incredible marriage of convention and revolt in biography.

We have no good full-length biography of any southern soldier or statesman. Many explanations of this serious lack may occur to the reader, and anyone may be correct. Some southern writers have attempted short popular lives of Davis, "Stonewall" Jackson, and others, but apparently no Southerner has yet acquired the perspective that will permit a full and truthful picture of Albert Sydney Johnston, Joseph E. Johnston, or Thomas J. ("Stonewall") Jackson. Numerous books on General Lee have appeared in the last decade, including *Marse Robert, Knight of the Confederacy* (1930), by James C. Young, and *Lee of Virginia; a Biography* (1932), by William E. Brooks. The first-mentioned is a charming book in which Lee is, literally speaking, the hero. The second is a competent account from a strictly southern point of view. Douglas S. Freeman has just published the definitive life of Lee, a discussion of which will be found on p. 356.

The less important generals of the Confederate Army have fared better than Lee and Jackson. J. E. B. Stuart, whose reputation as a handsome man was equaled only by his fame as the greatest cavalry leader of the Confederacy, perhaps of the Civil War, has found a most sympathetic biographer in Captain John W. Thomason, U. S. M. C. Captain Thomason has written a spirited account in *Jeb Stuart* (1930), but his attempted impartiality is sometimes smothered by his wholesome admiration for the romantic soldier whose career he is presenting. Eric W. Sheppard's *Bedford Forrest: the Confederacy's Greatest Cavalryman* (1930) is an excellent military biography of the great leader of the irregulars in the South. A natural cavalryman, even if he cannot claim the title which the author gives him, General Forrest was a raider who struck fear into the hearts of all Unionists who lay in the path of his sudden and terrible forays. Furthermore, he had a personality that was as forceful as it was unique. That personality is given greater emphasis in Andrew M. Lytle's *Bedford Forrest and His Critter Company* (1931), a much more personal biography.

There has been a revival of interest in the life and character of Jefferson Davis in the last decade, a revival that has produced three biographies of the President of the Confederate States of America. Professor H. J. Eckenrode's *Jefferson Davis, President of the South* (1923) is a scholarly account written from the southern point of view, which means that it is a rather heavy appreciation. Judge Robert

W. Winston's *High Stakes and Hair Trigger; the Life of Jefferson Davis* (1930) presents a very fair picture of the leader of the Confederacy. The title of the book explains the author's point of view, bringing out much of Davis' character and the significance of his position. Elizabeth B. Cutting's *Jefferson Davis, Political Soldier* (1930) is the best of the three biographies, because of its balance and objectivity. Davis was a political soldier, and to him may be laid many of the disasters of the Confederate Army. It is possible, as the author points out, that the result of the Civil War might have been somewhat different, had President Davis left military affairs in the hands of the leaders he chose. He was a West Point man, and although he had been out of the army for many years, he constantly interfered in the military plans of his commanders. A good full-length life of Davis remains to be written. In *Varina Howell, Wife of Jefferson Davis* (1927–1930) Eron O. Rowland has embalmed Mrs. Davis in a sentimental biography, done in the best ante-bellum style.

Some of the greatest men of this period have been neglected by modern biographers until very lately. Among them are Alexander H. Stephens and Andrew Johnson. The former is the subject of a short biography, *Little Alec; a Life of Alexander H. Stephens* (1932), by Eudora R. Richardson. Mrs. Richardson has written a charming and interesting book which gives us a fairly good idea of the man who was Vice-President of the Confederate States of America. There is opportunity for a later biographer to expand and develop the source material so that we may know all about the man who, despite almost incredible physical handicaps and equally incredible political opposition, never admitted defeat.

Andrew Johnson is a much more important figure in our national life than was Stephens or Davis or half a hundred others who have come under the pen of the biographer. For sixty years he was a political and social outcast relegated to the limbo of forgotten presidents such as James K. Polk, Millard Fillimore, and Franklin Pierce—but for a different reason. He had no southern tradition behind him and he was hardly recognized as a man in the North. It is rather remarkable that the principal writers on American history for fifty years after the Civil War were Republicans or wrote in the Republican tradition. It was not until the modern school developed some twenty years ago that the "bloody shirt" ceased to wave over modern American history. Read any large history of the United States by historians who flourished before the Great War, and it will be readily seen why President Andrew Johnson was a "forgotten man." Fortunately for us three men have had the courage and the ability to tell his story.

The first attempt to do justice to Andrew Johnson appeared in 1928 when Judge Robert W. Winston published *Andrew Johnson, Plebeian and Patriot*. In a book that is scholarly, as impartial as a first biography of this kind can be, Judge Winston set down the facts of the case for the first time. This is not the New Biography, for the author had neither time nor, I suspect, inclination for the various "-ologies" that had become part and parcel of modern biographical equipment. In a simple narrative that speaks for itself, Judge Winston told the story as he found it *in the records*. Andrew Johnson emerges from these pages as an orator, a statesman of the first rank, and as a defender of the Constitution, which his enemies almost succeeded in destroying that the spoils of office might remain in their hands and that they might sow the soil of the South with salt. To those who read this book intelligently it must have been a revelation, for it exposed a conspiracy against the law of the land unparalleled in our history before or since. Judge Winston did this without raising his voice.

Judge Winston's life of Johnson is long; Lloyd P. Stryker's biography is much longer, for he included much of the detail which the earlier biographer condensed. *Andrew Johnson: A Study in Courage* (1929) contains more than eight hundred pages and is the most complete account of Johnson's administration that we have. In his effort to vindicate the policy which President Johnson pursued through the four years

that he was in the White House, Mr. Stryker sometimes oversteps the boundaries of sound judgment. The President's
enemies were not quite so black as the author painted them,
and the President's path was not quite so straight as Mr.
Stryker marked it. The tone of the book is a little strident,
constantly warning us that we must be careful in our ac-
ceptance of the whole of the defense. Despite the excess zeal
and biased judgment, it is a good biography. Mr. Stryker
is a partisan, but he gives a source citation for every statement in the book which might be doubted. There are nearly
fifty pages of bibliography and citations. The facts cannot
be avoided, though the conclusions from some of the facts
must be denied.

The third biography, George Fort Milton's *Age of Hate;
Andrew Johnson and the Radicals* (1930) is the best and
should be the definitive life of Andrew Johnson and the
history of the years 1865–1869. Mr. Milton has a better style
and a more effective method than either Winston or Stryker.
Milton's account is less hysterical than Stryker's, for it combines the latter's research and scholarship with an objectivity
that admits of no injustice. It is impossible for any biographer
of Johnson to be impartial, but Milton is the most successful of the three. These three books are necessarily historical
biographies, for the history of Johnson's battle in defense of
the Constitution and his rights as President of the United
States is more important than the facts of his personal life.
Mr. Milton manages to get more biography into his book
than either of the others, because he was more fortunate in
the choice of his method, more skilful in the handling of
his material, and more objective in his judgment.

These three writers, together with Claude Bowers in his
Tragic Era, have done a great deal to clarify the unsavory
atmosphere that surrounded the Reconstruction Era for so
long. They have placed Andrew Johnson where he belongs,
among the great Presidents and the great men of the United
States. They have explained why it was necessary for Lincoln
and Johnson to run on the Constitutional Union ticket in 1864

rather than on the regular Republican ticket, and in telling Johnson's story they have shown what might have happened to Lincoln, for Johnson was trying to carry out Lincoln's plan of reconstruction.

3

In the field of American history the frontier has become an increasingly important subject because of the tremendous effect it has had upon the development of American civilization. Daniel Boone, David Crocket, Stephen Austin, Sam Houston, Simon Kenton, John Frémont and a host of other pioneers and frontiersmen were the subjects of biographies of many types during the nineteenth and twentieth centuries. The earlier lives contained almost as much fiction as fact; they were romances in every sense of the word. Modern biographers have worked over these romantic books, extracted the truth from them and, aided by modern methods of research, have produced biographies which combine good history with good life-writing. It is impossible to write of these men without introducing the history that they made.

In *Simon Kenton, his Life and Period, 1755–1836* (1930) Edna Kenton, a descendant, has written an excellent biography of one of the first men to penetrate the land beyond the mountains, the southern frontier of the Revolutionary period. With a method that is primarily biographical, an excellent historical background, and a style that is admirably adapted to her narrative, Miss Kenton has told of the life and times of Simon Kenton with a charm, a smoothness and rapidity of movement that leaves little to be desired in this form of biography.

One of the remarkable features of modern biography is the fact that, in dozens of instances, three and four writers have published lives of the same man within a few years, each one differing from the other in method and form. I am unable to give a satisfactory reason for this phenomenon other than the increasing interest in biography itself. Between

1927 and 1930, four lives of George Rogers Clark were published, only one of which was of the popular type. The first, Temple Bodley's *George Rogers Clark; his Life and Public Services* (1927), is an example of classical biographical history. As such it is very well done, but we never get very close to the man himself. We are interested in the "public services" of any important American; we are more interested, however, in the sort of person he was, and those phases of character which enabled him to accomplish the deeds which raised him above his contemporaries. We do not find much of this personal element in Temple Bodley's life of Clark. This lack, together with an excess of historical footnotes, detracts from the quality of *George Rogers Clark* as pure biography. James A. James's *Life of George Rogers Clark* (1928) is another life of the young empire builder which is spoiled, as biography, by too much history. We continually lose sight of Clark in the mass of historical narrative, the progress of the American Revolution in the Northwest. Background is necessary in a biography of such a man as Clark, but here we have entirely too much.

Discounting Lowell Thomas' *Hero of Vincennes: the Story of George Rogers Clark* (1929), for it is only a rewriting in a popular vein, the best life of Clark is Frederick Palmer's *Clark of the Ohio; the Life of George Rogers Clark* (1929). This is the best life because it is the most complete re-creation of Clark as he really was. Palmer gives the best account of Clark before and after his famous march into the Northwest which resulted in the capture of Vincennes and the acquisition of the vast territory north of the Ohio. We get to know the young man, his temper and spirit; we see the still young man surmounting every obstacle in the path of his magnificent march to Vincennes; and we are able to understand the trials, physical and mental, that beset him then and later, and made him an old man before his time. Mr. Palmer, as is every real biographer, is interested primarily in the man. This interest gives him an insight into character and personality which is ignored by the historian who uses a man as the pivot on which to turn his history. Mr. Palmer's biography of Clark will appeal to the scholar as well as to the reader whose interest is primarily biographical.

The pioneer and frontiersman is usually thought of and presented as being a shaggy creature in buckskin, generally taciturn, and illiterate when he does speak. He is ordinarily pictured as a man who lives alone and fights alone, whose physical courage is responsible for his fame. This picture is sometimes true, but there are exceptions. Stephen F. Austin, "Father of Texas," was an exception. Professor Eugene C. Barker's *Life of Stephen F. Austin* (1925) is the story of a most unusual pioneer. A man of education, culture, and innate refinement, Austin settled what is now the state of Texas and was a true pioneer, although he had no notches on his "trusty" rifle and he probably never wielded a bowie knife. The whole turbulent story of the settlement of Texas is told by Professor Barker in this excellent biography. It is of necessity historical, but Stephen F. Austin is always in the foreground. Such a combination of scholarship, biographical consciousness, and good style is rarely to be met with even in the best of modern biography.

It is inevitable that the romance of the frontier should be treated romantically by some biographers. They simply cannot resist the temptation to heighten the interest of their narratives by dramatic and other modern devices. George Creel has given us a highly dramatic narrative in *Sam Houston, Colossus in Buckskin* (1928). There is no question that he has caught the romantic spirit inherent in the personality of the great Texan, but he sometimes oversteps the boundary of even imaginative biography. A comparison of this book with Marquis James's *The Raven; A Biography of Sam Houston* will demonstrate the legitimate and the illegitimate in modern biography.

Stanley Vestal keeps on the side of the angels in *Kit Carson, the Happy Warrior of the Old West; a Biography* (1928). This is an excellent life of the famous Indian fighter whose name is synonymous with all that is fascinating and unusual in frontier life. The author has re-created the greatest of the scouts with a method and a style that have the swiftness of movement characteristic of Kit himself. In striving for the result that Vestal obtained, Frazier Hunt adopted a style and manner in *Custer the Last of the Cavaliers* (1928) that are too rapid and too modern for more than a glimpse of the real Custer. Perhaps this book should be classified as fiction rather than biography.

Billy the Kid is a name that is as familiar to students and readers of western history as is the name of Kit Carson. Billy was one of the most notorious desperadoes in the Southwest although he was killed, by his first biographer, before he was twenty-one. In 1882 Pat F. Garrett, the sheriff who killed Billy the Kid, published the *Authentic Life of Billy the Kid*. Even in its modern form, edited by Maurice G. Fulton in 1928, it is a fascinating account of a Dick Turpin who lacked Turpin's humanity. Walter N. Burns's *Saga of Billy the Kid* (1926) is a straight, factual account of this terror of early New Mexico. Mr. Burns does not pass judgment on his grim facts. For this reason alone, the *Saga of Billy the Kid* is a good biography and a valuable social document. The same may be said of Robertus Love's *Rise and Fall of Jesse James* (1926).

It is quite in character with the West that this account should close with a biography of one of its greatest men. In *Stephen J. Field, Craftsman of the Law* (1930), Carl B. Swisher has given us an unusually good biography that tells a story that could have happened only in America. A miner in California in his early days, Fields later became a Justice of the Supreme Court of California and an Associate Justice of the Supreme Court of the United States. Justice Fields has a unique position in American jurisprudence. On the California bench he created most of our mining law which he so brilliantly interpreted when he became a member of the United States Supreme Court. Mr. Swisher's biography is primarily legal, but it also presents the strong character and personality of this man who could make law because he alone of his colleagues knew what it should be.

4

Between 1870 and 1900 the country was flooded with books on famous and notorious public men. These books were called biographies. In reality, most of them were composed of extravagant or untruthful propaganda, designed to further the political careers of the subject. Every Republican candidate for the Presidency from Grant to McKinley, excepting James G. Blaine, was a veteran of the Civil War, as were several of the Democratic candidates. The latter had no chance, for it seems that the Republican party won the Civil War. Some of these memorials and campaign lives have been mentioned in Chapter III; the others are not worth mentioning. It was not until the third decade of the twentieth century that these Presidents and politicians were made the subjects of critical or quasi-critical biographies.

One of the most ambitious modern political biographies is Theodore C. Smith's *Life of James Abram Garfield* (1925). In these two large volumes Professor Smith has written a history of the United States between 1830 and 1880 as well as a life of Garfield. This book is the definitive life of Garfield, but one wonders whether or not the biography is not more important than the subject. The author tries to be critical and impartial in his judgment of Garfield's life and character, but he seems to have been a little awed by the fact that Garfield was President of the United States. Garfield's political career was no better than that of the average politician of the Gilded Age; his adherence to the Republican party during that period, including his activities in the impeachment of President Johnson, in the Crédit Mobilier scandal, and in the Hayes-Tilden election case, are open to serious criticism, but his biographer always gives him the benefit of the doubt. Professor Smith had access to all of

Garfield's papers and he may be right in his judgments, but some of them are against the weight of historical evidence. In my opinion, Garfield emerges from these pages a greater man than he really was because his biographer judged him from the historical rather than the biographical point of view.

Robert G. Caldwell's *James A. Garfield, Party Chieftain* (1931) is a more truthful interpretation of Garfield than that of Professor Smith. Garfield was a party man first, last, and always. Privately he regretted much of the activity of the Republican party from the close of the Civil War until his death, but publicly he gave it his strongest support. In other words, Garfield was a typical political opportunist. Caldwell strikes a balance between the man and the politician in Garfield, pointing out what he did and what he failed to do. Garfield was neither a great nor an important figure in our history, and he does not deserve a more important place than Caldwell has given him.

Mr. Caldwell's book is one of a series of biographies of public men that was begun about three years ago. The "American Political Leaders," under the general editorship of Allan Nevins, promises to be an extremely valuable collection of lives and an important contribution to the literature of American biography and history. Unlike the "American Statesmen Series," it permits each writer to handle his subject in his own way. Some of the biographies are entirely political; others more nearly approach the ideal of pure biography. Some are much longer than others, not because of the importance of the subject but because of the variety and richness of biographical material and the innate interest of the subject. Of the seven volumes thus far published, two have been discussed in Chapter VII: Fuess's *Carl Schurz* and Nevins' *Grover Cleveland*.

Thomas B. Reed, Parliamentarian (1930), and *John G. Carlisle, Financial Statesman* (1931), by William A. Robinson and James A. Barnes respectively, are two volumes in this series that deal exclusively with the public careers of their subjects. Both are excellent books of their kind, but they lack the completeness of full-length biographies.

The publication of "American Political Leaders" opened with *Rutherford B. Hayes, Statesman of Reunion* (1930) by Hamilton J. Eckenrode, assisted by Pocahontas W. Wight. In his preface Professor Eckenrode states that Miss Wight wrote the early chapters of Hayes's personal biography. This statement absolves him from the ridiculous, unfair, and bigoted tone and expression of the first quarter of the book. Apparently, Miss Wight is unaware that guerilla warfare is outlawed, and unwilling to believe that the Civil War is over. Her strictures on the North and the Union almost succeed in destroying what is an otherwise excellent book. Professor Eckenrode's treatment of the politics and statesmanship of Hayes is eminently fair and just. There is, as the author points out, no question that Samuel J. Tilden was elected President of the United States in 1876 and that the election was stolen from him in Florida, Louisiana, and probably in South Carolina. However, Professor Eckenrode proves conclusively that, all things considered, it was to the best interests of the country that Hayes was named President in March 1877, for Tilden might not have tried and could not have succeeded in withdrawing the Federal troops from the southern states which were still "out of the Union." Generally speaking, the author gives Hayes his proper place as the Republican statesman who began the cleansing of the Augean stables of the Reconstruction Era. In his attitude toward the South, toward economy in government, toward civil service reform, Rutherford B. Hayes gave impetus to the progressive movement in America, and that impetus is still being felt. The fact that he failed to secure most of the reforms that he sought, that he declined to run again in 1880 because he knew he could not be nominated stamps him as a man who was greater than his party. Hayes was not among the greatest of our Presidents, but his latest and best biographer shows that he deserves a much higher position than he has heretofore been given.

The latest volume in this series is Tyler Dennett's *John Hay, From Poetry to Politics* (1933). John Hay is best known as Secretary of State in the cabinets of McKinley and Roosevelt. He was not a politician, and he was hardly a statesman; he was a diplomat by nature, and as a diplomat he accomplished a great deal in the seven years that he sat at the right hand of two Presidents. Mr. Dennett's biography of John Hay is better than William Roscoe Thayer's *Life of John Hay*, for it is more honest and a more complete interpretation of the man. Although Mr. Dennett presents a better picture of Hay than Thayer does, his book is top-heavy, for more than half of it is the history of the foreign policy of the United States during the seven years that Hay was at the head of the Department of State. The first part of the book is excellent and fascinating biography, but we frequently lose sight of John Hay in the latter part, because of the author's inordinately detailed account of American foreign policy from 1897 to 1904. The reason for the lack of balance in the book is the fact that the author was formerly historical adviser of the State Department. We should, however, be thankful for what we have, for the first part of this book completely interprets an unusual American public man and a very complex character. *John Hay* demonstrates that there can be very good biography and equally good history within the covers of a single volume, and that a good biographer can impair the quality of his own work by overemphasizing a relatively small period of a man's life, regardless of its importance.

Whitelaw Reid was a contemporary and an associate of John Hay. Both were on the staff of the New York *Tribune* under Greeley, and both held diplomatic posts. When Reid became the owner and publisher of the *Tribune,* John Hay contributed occasional pieces and was always ready to advise the publisher. Unlike Hay, Reid was active in the councils of the Republican party, and his paper was its staunchest supporter after the Mugwump campaign against Grant had failed in 1872. Royal Cortissoz in his *Life of Whitelaw Reid*

(1921) has given us an interesting account of Reid's career
as publicist and politician. In the two volumes of narrative
Cortissoz included everything of interest in Reid's life without comment or judgment. As in the case of nearly every
biography written by a friend, it is decidedly uncritical and
partial. It is one gentleman's view of the life of another
gentleman.

Nathaniel W. Stephenson was equally observant of the
amenities in *Nelson W. Aldrich; a Leader in American
Politics* (1930). It is a very well-written but very partisan life
of a "big business" advocate in politics. It is rather strange
that such an excellent biographer of Lincoln should write
a book which, because of its partisanship, is untruthful. Perhaps Mr. Stephenson had not a free hand in the use of materials or their interpretation. That is the only explanation
of a biography which presents a reactionary of reactionaries
as a "leader in American politics." In the period of the late
nineteenth and early twentieth centuries, when the Senate
was generally known as the "Millionaires' Club," Senator
Aldrich was the Republican floor leader and absolute master
of the Senate until the Progressive movement reached the
point where he felt it necessary to retire. If we accept, as
Aldrich's biographer seems to, the Hamiltonian system of
political philosophy, then Mr. Stephenson's portrait of
Nelson W. Aldrich may be accepted, even though it is a
portrait in two dimensions.

Nelson W. Aldrich was one kind of political boss;
Richard Croker was another. Like Mr. Aldrich, Croker, boss
of Tammany Hall, aspired to social recognition and received
a certain measure of it—in England. Theodore L. Stoddard's
Master of Manhattan; the Life of Richard Croker (1931) is
aptly titled, for Croker was "Master of Manhattan" for nearly
a generation. Mr. Stoddard's account of Croker's rise from
the position of a gangster on the East Side to that of ruler of
New York, although he never held public office, is a fascinating and thorough study of American politics as it is, now
and forever. Croker was the last of the great bosses in New

York politics, and one of the last in America. We have bosses now, but they are puny creatures compared to Croker, Quay, Penrose, and Aldrich. Although this biography is largely a study of party politics in New York City, the author is constantly aware of his main purpose, the writing of a life of Richard Croker, and he keeps his subject always in the forefront of the picture—where he rightly belongs. For this reason Stoddard's *Master of Manhattan* is a better biography than Denis Tilden Lynch's *"Boss" Tweed*.

Politics makes strange bedfellows. It would be almost impossible to find two men more unlike than Richard Croker and W. J. Bryan. However, they were both Democrats, and Bryan needed Croker and Croker needed Bryan in the presidential campaign of 1900. They became friendly and spoke well of one another. John C. Long tells this and many another political story in *Bryan, the Great Commoner* (1928). This is a very sympathetic account, almost a defense, of William Jennings Bryan. In a straightforward narrative, tempered with a little explanatory criticism, Mr. Long tells the story of Bryan's life and career. Nothing is omitted, but those phases of Bryan's character which Werner and Hibben emphasized and overemphasized Long either explains favorably or dismisses. It may be that this biography gives a fairer interpretation of Bryan than either of the other two, but even here there are facts and conclusions which will seem unfair to the admirer of Bryan, and judgments which will seem weak to his critics. This was the first biography of Bryan published after his death, the lives by Werner and Hibben appearing the next year, which may account for the sympathetic point of view. The definitive biography of Bryan is yet to be written. When it is written we shall probably find that the real Bryan lies between the Bryan of Long and the Bryan of Werner and Hibben.

The career of Theodore Roosevelt has been interpreted from every angle, but most of the writers have been friends or disciples of the "Rough Rider." Even an enumeration of these books would not further the purpose of this history, but there are two that are worth mentioning here. In 1920, Joseph Bucklin Bishop published *Theodore Roosevelt and his Time, Shown in his own Letters*. These two volumes constitute a eulogistic appreciation of Roosevelt, with the material drawn largely from his own letters. The book achieved its purpose, but it failed as good biography because the author was too close to his subject in time and spirit, and because Roosevelt was not a good letter writer.

Walter C. McCaleb's *Theodore Roosevelt* (1931) is the first attempt at an objective study of Roosevelt. It appeared in the same year, but several months before Henry Pringle's *Theodore Roosevelt*. A comparison of the two books will show that McCaleb, with the same material at his disposal, failed to present and interpret Roosevelt as completely as Pringle did. It may be that again the personality of the subject captivated the biographer before he could assume a purely objective point of view. Pringle's masterly work excepted, McCaleb's life of Roosevelt is the best that we have.

There have been numerous books written on the subject of Woodrow Wilson. Some have praised him, some have condemned him, some have merely chronicled the events of his life. Limiting the field to those that have appeared since his death, there are four books that may be considered. Robert E. Annin's *Woodrow Wilson; a Character Study* (1924) is the only one of the four that has a distinctly hostile tone. It merely presents a decidedly adverse view of President Wilson without any direct evidence to substantiate it. To counterbalance this unproved indictment, we may turn to Josephus Daniels' *Life of Woodrow Wilson* (1924). This is not a biography at all, but merely a frank and fulsome eulogy. It has, however, the merit of being honest in its purpose, which is more than can be said for Mr. Annin's book.

A third book on Wilson also appeared in 1924: *Woodrow Wilson, the Man, his Times, and his Tasks*, by William Allen White. This book is not quite so ambitious as the title would indicate, but it seems to be the best short account of Wilson that has yet appeared. Mr. White is one of the most prominent Republicans in the country. In view of this fact it is all the more surprising that this book should present Wilson as it does. Beginning with the President's ancestors, Mr. White attempts to explain the mind and character of one of the world's great idealists. Considering the date of the book, it must be admitted that the author succeeded, as well as any man could at that time, in interpreting the complexities of character that went to the making of the war President.

Every important man has an authorized biographer selected by himself or by his family. A short time before his death, President Wilson chose Ray Stannard Baker as his official biographer. Wilson left the largest collection of papers ever accumulated by a President, and these were turned over to Mr. Baker by Mrs. Wilson in January 1925. The first two volumes of *Woodrow Wilson: Life and Letters* appeared two years later. In a lengthy introduction to the first volume, Mr. Baker explains the nature of his material and the method to be followed in the writing of the biography. In 1931 the third and fourth volumes were published, and at least two more will be necessary to complete the task.

If we may judge from the volumes published, Mr. Baker has written a typical authorized biography. Generally speaking, it is a narrative of Wilson's life into which the biographer seldom obtrudes a judgment. Some explanations of certain events are given, but they are strictly within the bounds of official life-writing. We learn something about President Wilson, but we are seldom able to reach the spirit and core of the man. I believe that Mr. Baker began to write before he had properly digested his great mass of source material. A letter or statement of 1921 might well explain the Wilson of 1870, or 1880, or 1890. Mr. Baker has not, I think, given himself a free hand, for there are many still living who must be considered by Wilson's official biographer. There is so much that took place between 1912 and 1920 that is, in the light of our present knowledge, inexplicable, that Mr. Baker cannot possibly present a complete picture of Woodrow Wilson as President.

Mr. Baker's book is the official life of Wilson, but it is not the definitive biography. This century may not see a definitive biography of Wilson, for much that is shrouded in secrecy must be brought to light before the whole truth about Wilson and the World War can be known. In my judgment, Mr. Baker is doing the best he can to preserve the contemporary opinion of Wilson. He is somewhat awed by the importance of his subject, and, in spite of his declaration to the contrary, he does not feel free to criticize him. Some later biographer will, and when all the testimony is in we shall see Woodrow Wilson stand forth as one of the world's great men, not for what he accomplished but because he had a vision and followed it.

Early in his first administration, President Wilson appointed Walter Hines Page as Ambassador to England. Page and Wilson had been students together in the early days of Johns Hopkins University, and they had remained friends in later years. As Wilson advanced in his chosen profession of teaching, so Page advanced in the world of publishing, becoming editor of the *World's Work,* a partner in Doubleday, Page and Co., and one of the leading publicists in America. All this and a great deal more has been told by Burton J. Hendrick in the two volumes of the *Life and Letters of Walter Hines Page* (1922). A third volume, published in 1926, contains the letters from Page to Wilson during the World War. The Pulitzer Prize biography for 1922, Hendricks' life of Page, is one of the outstanding American biographies of the twentieth century because Hendricks allowed Page to tell his own story as far as possible. Walter Page was one of the great letter writers of his day. Mr. Hendricks chose the best and most illuminating of these letters, which, connected by excellent explanatory and narrative passages, tell Page's story better than anyone else could possibly have done. In this instance the biographer revealed himself as the ideal editor. In 1929 Mr. Hendrick published the *Training of an American; The Earlier Life and Letters of Walter Hines Page*. This book, which received the Pulitzer Prize for 1929, is an amplification of the earlier chapters of the first volume of the *Life and Letters of Walter Hines Page*. Mr. Hendrick used the same method here that he used in his earlier book, and achieved an equal success.

In his books on Walter Hines Page, Mr. Hendrick has proved himself an able editor; in his biographical histories, Claude G. Bowers has succeeded in the use of a more difficult method of biography. Perhaps he was unconscious of the fact that he was approaching the field of biography in *Jefferson and Hamilton, Party Battles of the Jackson Period,* and *The Tragic Era*. These books are not biographies, but they contain dozens of admirable character studies and biographical sketches. In his latest book, *Beveridge and the Progressive Era* (1932), Mr. Bowers has become a political biographer in place of the former political historian. This book is a life of Albert J. Beveridge and a history of the Progressive movement in which Beveridge was one of the most prominent figures. Based on the best modern methods in historical and biographical writing, Mr. Bowers' life of Beveridge is one of the best political biographies of the present century. In its field, it is excelled only by Beveridge's own books on Marshall and Lincoln.

When we have finished *Beveridge and the Progressive Era,* we know Albert J. Beveridge as he was from birth to death, and we know the history of that movement in American politics which, starting in the early years of the century, has striven valiantly, if unsuccessfully, to bring a sense of personal responsibility for the welfare of the country to the rank and file as well as the leaders of the Republican party. In addition to the complete story of Beveridge's life and career, there are in this book dozens of biographical sketches ranging from David Graham Phillips to Nelson W. Aldrich and Robert M. La Follette. It is a magnificent panorama of

American life and politics from 1895 to 1927. For the student and historian of biography, the last three chapters of Mr. Bowers' book are the most interesting. In my own case they substantiated the opinions I had formed regarding Beveridge's methods and purpose in writing his *Marshall* and *Lincoln*. They explain and illuminate the paths Beveridge trod in his search of material. They leave no doubt that Albert J. Beveridge is the foremost legal and political biographer in American literature. Anyone who studies American biography must acknowledge his debt to Senator Beveridge and, in turn, to his biographer, Claude G. Bowers. My chapters on Lincoln and Washington have been enriched by facts from Mr. Bowers' life of Beveridge.

5

The period between the Civil War and the World War witnessed the rise of some of the great fortunes of the United States. The stories of the lives of John Jacob Astor, Commodore Vanderbilt, Jay Gould, Daniel Drew, and James Fisk, Jr., are almost incredible, as are those of a later generation, Rockefeller, Carnegie, Mellon, and others. Much has been written concerning all of these men. The earlier generation was praised by contemporary biographers, and the men who have been named above were held up as examples of frugality and business ability. The next generation was advised to follow in their footsteps and to profit by their examples. Many faithfully followed the advice.

The first creator of a great American fortune was John Jacob Astor, merchant, fur trader, and real-estate man. Astor was a business genius, a human adding machine, the first great manipulator of land and stock values. At his death in 1848 he was the richest man in America, and the Astor fortune has continued to grow. There have been only three lives of the elder Astor written, one of which is a business history rather than a biography. James Parton's life of Astor was decidedly hostile, in the manner of the mid-nineteenth century. Arthur D. Howden Smith's *John Jacob Astor* (1929) is equally hostile, though written from a more modern point of view. Mr. Smith's book is a good narrative account of Astor's life. Astor's character is developed by his actions, and Smith's judgment, like Parton's, is that the great merchant was morally blind to the consequences of his insatiable desire for money and financial power. He has had successors, but no other rich man in America has had less comfort and pleasure than the first of the Astors had.

The third account of Astor and his fortune is Kenneth W. Porter's *John Jacob Astor, Business Man* (1931). In these two large volumes, the author gives a detailed history of the manner in which Astor accumulated the millions that made him the greatest merchant and the greatest landlord in the New York City of his day.

It was not until the period of the Civil War and its aftermath that men of Astor's financial acumen again appeared. They made and lost their fortunes in railroads and stock speculation instead of trade and real estate. The great quartet of financial pirates was composed of Daniel Drew, James Fisk, Jr., Jay Gould, and Cornelius Vanderbilt. To speak in modern terms, the first three were "bears"; Commodore Vanderbilt was always a "bull"—and in more ways than one. Modern biographies have done full justice to these men and their activities.

The earliest account of this group is Bouck White's *Book of Daniel Drew* (1910). This is biographical fiction in which Drew tells his own story. Drew indicts himself, time and again, as a hypocrite, a liar, and a thief. It required little effort on the part of the author to construct this book as he did, for he had plenty of material.

Although Arthur D. H. Smith's *Commodore Vanderbilt; an Epic of American Achievement* (1927) is classed as a biography, it has little more title to that classification than has Mr. White's novel on Daniel Drew. Narrative in form, it contains as much fiction as fact, for the author neglects to mention any of the sources on which he may have drawn for his dialogue. Despite this serious fault, *Commodore Vanderbilt* is the best account we have of the founder of the Vanderbilt fortune and the builder of the New York Central Railroad. Vanderbilt was as unscrupulous and as lawless as his antagonists, but he was never a hyprocrite. He had vision and imagination, two qualities which are essential to success in any walk of life. His biographer wanted to present the man as he really was. There is no doubt that he succeeded, but he might have succeeded equally well had he not been tempted to indulge in the fictional method of biography that was so popular at the time he wrote this book. A comparison of *Commodore Vanderbilt* and *John Jacob Astor* will show that Mr. Smith can write real as well as fictional biography.

The only modern account of James Fisk is Robert H. Fuller's novel, *Jubilee Jim: The Life of Colonel James Fisk, Jr.* (1928). Mr. Fuller used the novel form because he felt that he could present a more faithful picture of Fisk in this form than if he wrote a biography. Perhaps he was right, for Jim Fisk's career will match any picaresque novel ever written. Circus owner, peddler, merchant, war contractor, speculator, Broadway play-boy, Fisk was a typical American of his day. He had the business acumen of his New England forbears, and a true genius for making money. Unlike his associates Drew and Gould, he wanted money for the pleasure of spending it. Because of his sexual immorality, he has come to represent the lowest stratum of American life in the Gilded Age. He has acquired more vices than he really had because he chose to ignore the proprieties behind which most of his associates and contemporaries entrenched themselves as pillars of society and morality. He did less harm to others than did either Drew or Gould. The remark which he is said to have made at the time of the gold-corner scandal in September 1869—"Nothing is lost save honor"—is characteristic of the business and social morality of the period. Others thought it; he said it. In spite of his character, his reputation, and the facts of his life, James Fisk was more of a man than the majority of those who achieved fame or notoriety in that "grim generation."

In matters of finance Jim Fisk was an amateur compared to his associate, Jay Gould. Gould was the most unscrupulous and treacherous, the least human of the men who amassed great fortunes in this period. His latest and only competent biographer, Robert I. Warshaw, has presented a coldly factual account of this colorless individual, whose only purpose in life was the accumulation of gold. *Jay Gould; the Story of a Fortune* (1928) gives us this man as he really was. It was not necessary for Mr. Warshaw to use any of the modern devices for bringing out the high lights in the character of his subject. There were none. A plain narrative of Gould's career was sufficient, for, outside of his financial activities, he had no life.

No one of these four books is a good biography, but each of them is essentially true. They present these four men as completely, perhaps, as they will ever be presented, and they give us a picture of men and life in America at a time when the "American system" was in one of its periods of "glory."

Biographies of the second generation of financiers and industrialists have been rather numerous during the last decade. With a few exceptions, they are official or authorized biographies. E. H. Harriman, John H. Patterson, John Muir of Wall Street, James B. Duke, Jacob H. Schiff, Henry C. Frick, Gustavus F. Swift, and Cyrus H. McCormick have been memorialized and eulogized by carefully chosen biographers. These and other books of the same type tell only a part of the story of the careers of their subjects. In deliberately suppressing facts concerning the manner in which these men became owners of railroads and banks, and monopolists in the tobacco, steel, and other industries, the biographers have presented accounts which are not only misleading but untrue. The country is supposed to be unaware of the methods by which railroads were acquired and competition in industry stifled.

In two instances biographies of this sort have been prepared by professional writers. Miss Ida M. Tarbell's *Life of Elbert H. Gary; the Story of Steel* (1925) is a vastly different book—on a similar subject—from the *History of the Standard Oil Company*. The passing years seem to have softened the crusading spirit that inspired the latter book, which is one of the severest indictments of John D. Rockefeller and the oil industry that can be found in print. The life of Judge Gary is is not only a eulogy of the man whose legal ingenuity made possible the formation of the United States Steel Corporation and who was its first president, but it is an apology for the system which enabled him to create the then largest corporation in the world. Miss Tarbell has continued her defense of big business in *Owen D. Young, a New Type of Industrial Leader* (1932).

Burton K. Hendrick was awarded Pulitzer prizes for his biographies of Walter Hines Page. This fact alone makes it difficult to understand how he could write the *Life of Andrew Carnegie* (1932). He has given us a charming account of the rise of the Scotch weaver's son from the position of telegraph messenger in Pittsburgh to that of the richest man in the world at the time of his retirement early in this century. We learn much about his travels and his philanthropies, but very little about the methods that he and his partners used to make the Carnegie interests what they were. This "biography" resembles a modern moving-picture film after a particularly moral board of censors has previewed it. As far as it goes, this book is interesting and delightful, but it is not true. It is not the life of Andrew Carnegie; it is those parts of his life that may properly accompany his smiling portrait. Fortunately, such reactionary accounts of famous men are fewer today than they were fifty years ago, for the very good reason that they are no longer accepted at face value.

The two latest books on men who have made great fortunes are John T. Flynn's *God's Gold; the Story of Rockefeller and His Times* (1932) and *Mellon's Millions; the Biography of a Fortune. The Life and Times of Andrew W.*

Mellon (1933), by Harvey O'Connor. Mr. O'Connor's book can hardly be called a biography of Andrew W. Mellon, for it is really a history of American industry and finance. Beginning with Mr. Mellon's father, Judge Thomas Mellon, the author traces most completely the means by which the Mellon family has come to be the richest family in the world. As a good newspaper man, Mr. O'Connor has collected facts and allowed them to speak for themselves. The very impersonality of the book intensifies the indictment brought against the moral, social, and political system which countenanced and encouraged the business practices which are detailed. *Mellon's Millions* is truly "the biography of a fortune."

Mr. Flynn has written a different kind of book on John D. Rockefeller. Mr. Rockefeller's public life closed more than fifteen years ago. Mr. Flynn has examined the enormous mass of source material to be found in books, magazine articles, and the reports of various state and federal investigation agencies which concerned themselves with inquiries into the business methods of Mr. Rockefeller and his associates. Mr. Flynn has written an historical biography of Rockefeller in which he sets forth the facts and gives his own interpretation of them. *God's Gold* presents the least biased and most complete picture of the world's greatest monopolist that has been written. If we read it, we shall learn a great deal about American business for the last seventy-five years, and we shall get a clear and fair interpretation of a most remarkable man. This is not an official biography. The author has tried to present Rockefeller's career from a purely objective point of view, and he has succeeded. A more personal biography of the oil magnate will be written, but it will not affect the value or the accuracy of Mr. Flynn's book.

6

Modern biographers have taken their subjects from every field of life in America and in Europe. Art and architecture, education and science, politics and feminism have been levied upon, and the yield has been remarkably high. Charles Moore's *Life and Times of Charles Follen McKim* (1929) and Elizabeth R. Pennell's *Life and Letters of Joseph Pennell* (1929) are among the best biographies of the last five years. Charles F. McKim was one of America's great architects, and this biography, by a fellow artist, is a completely executed portrait of the man and the artist. Mr. McKim's personality is clearly limned in this book, and his position in American art is definitely settled. The author had that rare combination of knowledge and understanding of his subject, and his own experience as an architect enabled him to appreciate properly the great work that McKim left.

Family biographies are rarely complete or true, but there are exceptions to all rules. Mrs. Pennell's biography of her famous husband is an exception to this rule. In the two volumes of this biography, she tells the simple and undramatic story of one of America's few great artists. Joseph Pennell's life was a rich and full one, and the fact that she shared most of it enabled his wife to present him as he really was. Geniuses are not easy people to live with, and Joseph Pennell was a genius. Mrs. Pennell does not gloss over his faults or the difficulties of their life together, nor does she hesitate to give him the credit and honor which he won for himself. No other person could have written this book, and no other biography of Pennell will supersede it. It has one fault, excessive length, and this may well be condoned in the unflagging interest of the narrative.

Women have played important parts in the political and social life of America. A few of the more famous ones have been the subjects of recent biographies. Rheta L. Dorr's *Susan B. Anthony, the Woman Who Changed the Mind of a Nation* (1928) and Alice S. Blackwell's *Lucy Stone, Pioneer of Women's Rights* (1930) are very partisan accounts of the two foremost American advocates of women's rights. These lives are biographical memorials, presenting only one side of the careers of these women, and only one side of the question for which they crusaded.

.In the *Lady of Godey's: Sarah Josepha Hale* (1931) Ruth Finley has written a most interesting account of the famous editor of *Godey's Lady's Book* and a true feminist. A rational reformer, a masterly publicist, Mrs. Hale˙was one of the most prominent figures in America in the nineteenth century, the founder of that peculiarly American institution, the woman's magazine.

The Susan Anthonys, Lucy Stones, and Sarah Hales wanted a voice in the government that ruled them; Peggy Eaton overturned the first cabinet of President Jackson. The romantic story of this remarkable woman is completely told in Queena Pollock's *Peggy Eaton, Democracy's Mistress* (1931). For almost a century Mrs. Eaton was one of the legendary figures in American history, and it was not until the appearance of Miss Pollock's book that the whole story was told. This is an excellent biography and a distinct contribution to American political history, for Mrs. Eaton was partly responsible for the frustration of John C. Calhoun's ambition to be President of the United States and for Martin Van Buren's success in securing the same office.

Modern American biography has made contributions to the political history of Europe as well as of America. Two of the most interesting and important of these contributions are Anna Bowman Dodd's *Talleyrand; the Training of a Statesman, 1754–1838* (1927), and Francis Hackett's *Henry VIII* (1929). An almost ideal combination of history and biography, presented in the best modern manner and with a most graceful style, makes *Talleyrand* the most complete and the best biography of one of the most famous and notorious figures of the French Revolution, the First Empire, and the Restoration. Despite the necessity of a wide and detailed historical background, the author keeps her subject always in the foreground of her picture, and we can readily follow the devious paths through which this wiliest of politicians made his way, indifferent and false to everyone but himself and his own success.

In his *Henry VIII*, Mr. Hackett was equally successful with an even more difficult subject. The literature on Henry VIII is enormous, but Mr. Hackett made the best use of the best of it. I should say that it is impossible for any writer to present an impartial study of Henry VIII. Mr. Hackett is not impartial, but he is fair. He built his book on a solid foundation of a definite point of view: that Henry VIII was something more than a "marrying man"; that it was not lust alone but an almost insane desire for a dynasty that started him on his career of brutality and bloodshed that led to separation from the Church of Rome and the founding of the Church of England. Woven into the bright and the dark colors of the tapestry of Henry's life are the many strands of the history of continental Europe that had so much to do with the shaping of Henry's career. This biography is not a defense of Henry VIII; it is an essay in interpretation. We may not accept the author's point of view, but we cannot ignore it, nor can we deny the fact that *Henry VIII* is one of the best historical biographies in English.

When a great subject is presented by a master, the result is literature. We have two unusual instances of this in modern American biography. The authors of the *Life of Sir William Osler* (1925) and *Charles W. Eliot, President of Harvard University, 1869–1909* (1930) are not professional biographers. Dr. Harvey Cushing, Osler's biographer, is a great brain surgeon, while Henry James is a writer. Each succeeded in writing a life that has added luster to the literature of biography, to his own name, and to the already famous name of his subject. Each of these biographies received the Pulitzer Award for their respective years.

Detailed analyses of these books would be futile. Each represents the very essence of perfect biographical method, complete understanding of the subjects, and styles that are perfectly attuned to the great physician who loved literature and wrote it, and to the equally famous university administrator whose greatest gift of expression was brevity. Each biography is complete and presents each man as he really was. Both books are in two large volumes, but neither is too long, for both men led very active and very full lives. An analysis of the methods used by Dr. Cushing and Mr. James could not present the intangible qualities of these books that place them among the very best in biographical literature. They are great biographies because when we have finished them we know Sir William Osler and Dr. Charles W. Eliot better, perhaps, than anyone knew them while they lived. No phase of their lives and characters is omitted, no flaw glossed over, no virtue overemphasized. They live and move and have their being from birth to death.

XI

TODAY

IT would seem that the high point of interest in modern biography came in 1932. The financial depression may have had some influence on the biographical flood, though I am inclined to think that public taste and more careful consideration of manuscripts by publishers were responsible for the decrease in the quantity of biography published during the last two years.

Though the rewrite and tabloid schools of biography are still in evidence, they have been superseded by that type of modern biography which, using the methods that have been in vogue for fifteen years, presents a complete, fair, and dignified treatment of its subject. We are no longer primarily interested in watching our prominent men being hurled from the pedestals which they may or may not have adorned. We want the truth, but we want it interestingly and fairly presented. We want to see both sides of the picture, to see the man as he really was.

In the material covered in this chapter, the principal lives published in 1934 and those biographies of 1933 which I had not seen when the earlier chapters were written, there is one remarkable fact: the number of men whose biographies have been written for the first time. The appearance of these lives indicates that modern biographers are not satisfied with rewriting; they are investigating the almost unlimited resources of biography in American life and are getting their material from original sources rather than from earlier accounts in print. I consider this movement one of the best indications that biographical writing in America is making steady progress in the right direction: the creation of a new field of literature. It is most significant that there has been but one major biography of Washington published in this period (1933–1934) and that Lincoln has been allowed to rest in peace entirely.

In *George Washington Himself* (1933) John C. Fitzpatrick has made a very important contribution to history and biography. As the editor of Washington's Diary and of the collected writings of Washington, Mr. Fitzpatrick has examined every known manuscript of our first President, and it is not strange that he should wish to present the Washington found in his own writings. That Mr. Fitzpatrick has accomplished his purpose is evident to anyone who reads this book; that he has corrected many of our misconceptions of the man is equally evident. To anyone who has not the time or the inclination to read Rupert Hughes's much more detailed biography of Washington, this life by Mr. Fitzpatrick is recommended as the best short account of Washington that we have. Its excellence rests on sound scholarship, a keen appreciation of modern biographical methods, and a style eminently readable.

When there is such a unanimity of opinion regarding the life and character of a man as there has been in the case of James Wilkinson, the biographer's task is greatly simplified. He has merely to select his material and tell his story, for his case is already proved. Royal O. Shreve could have only one point of view for the presentation of his subject, the one expressed in the full title of the book: *The Finished Scoundrel General James Wilkinson, sometime Commander-in-Chief of the Army of the United States, who made intrigue a trade and treason a profession* (1933). It was not necessary for Mr. Shreve to make use of any of the tricks of modern biography. The facts were plain for anyone who had the interest and the industry to collect and present them. In the words of the author, General Wilkinson was "a man who was without a doubt the most clever and persistent if not the most dangerous of that small company for whom history reserves the infamous name of traitor."

In an account based on primary sources of unimpeachable authenticity, Mr. Shreve proves his case. The book is a fascinating narrative of a man who has every claim to the title which the biographer bestowed upon him. This biography was badly needed, for General Wilkinson was an important figure in the Revolution, the early republic, and the Burr conspiracy. We have here a connected record of the activities of a man who really deserves the place in our history that has been occupied by Benedict Arnold.

The American Revolution produced many men of a character quite different from that of James Wilkinson. Some of them have been greatly neglected because their characters do not appeal to the modern temper. John Adams belongs in this class. A staunch patriot, within the restricted meaning of that much-abused word, a statesman of the first rank, the second President of the United States had to wait for more than a century for a biography that does him full justice as a man and a statesman. In *Honest John Adams* (1933) Professor Gilbert Chinard has given us a biography worthy of his subject and of himself. Based on a wide and thorough knowledge of history and a thorough investigation of the life of Adams himself, this life is an invaluable contribution to the literature of American biography and history.

Of equal importance with Professor Chinard's life of Adams, though their subjects never achieved Adams' prominence, are Nathan Goodman's *Benjamin Rush, Physician and Citizen* (1934) and Dorothie Bobbé's *DeWitt Clinton* (1933). Dr. Rush, a signer of the Declaration of Independence, surgeon-general of the Middle Department of the Continental army, the first professor of chemistry in the Medical School of the University of Pennsylvania, and a physician of national fame in his day, has been very competently treated by Mr. Goodman in this first complete biography. Because of his theories regarding the origin and spread of yellow fever, Dr. Rush became the center of a violent controversy which has tended to detract from his prominence as a citizen, a medical teacher, and a scientist. Mr. Goodman has attempted to preserve the balance by which Rush should be evaluated, accomplishing his purpose to a marked degree and firmly establishing Dr. Rush's position in our early medical and political history.

Dr. Rush was primarily a medical scientist; DeWitt Clinton was entirely a politician, one of the first "bosses" in New York politics. Mrs. Bobbé's book is an admirable interpretive narrative of Clinton's political career and the intricacies of New York politics in the days of Hamilton and Burr. This biography is a radical departure from Mrs. Bobbé's previous excursions into life-writing (see p. 243), though it is an excellent book of its kind.

The West has always been and will continue to be a fruitful field for the modern biographer. The men who settled and developed it were men of adventure and daring, men who, if they failed in their original purposes, carved their names deeply in the history of the country. Among such men were Father Junipero Serra, Captain Meriwether Lewis, Captain John Sutter, and John McLoughlin.

Continuing her researches in the history of the religious pioneers of North America (see p. 186), Miss Agnes Repplier has given us an admirable and complete account of the work done by the Franciscan friar, Junipero Serra, in settling the eighteenth-century missions in California, from the Mexican border to what is now San Francisco. Father Serra was past fifty before he was able to embark upon this work, but he brought to it such courage, such tenacity of purpose, such executive ability, that at his death some twenty years later the California missions were the only civilized communities in what is now the United States west of the Mississippi River. *Junipero Serra, Pioneer Colonist of California* (1934) is equal if not superior to anything that Miss Repplier has done in the field of American biography. Its only fault lies in the fact that, to make a sufficiently large book for commercial purposes, Miss Repplier adds two chapters on the fate of the California missions following Father Serra's death and the coming of relatively large groups of Americans to California.

Just about a generation after Serra's work in California, Captain Meriwether Lewis opened the Northwest through his famous pioneering trip from St. Louis to the head of the

Columbia River and the Pacific Coast, an adventure known in our history as the Lewis and Clark expedition. In *Meriwether Lewis, of Lewis and Clark* (1934), Charles M. Wilson has given us, for the first time, the complete story of one of the greatest adventures in our history. The most remarkable feature of the book is the manner in which Mr. Wilson develops Meriwether's character from his own writings, showing the melancholic trend of Meriwether's temperament. Shortly after his return from his march to the coast, Captain Meriwether committed suicide.

In the *White Headed Eagle, John McLoughlin* (1934) and *Sutter of California* (1934), Richard G. Montgomery and Julian Dana offer fascinating narratives of empire builders. John McLoughlin extended the power of the Hudson's Bay Company to the Pacific Coast, and John Sutter made the first permanent settlement in the interior of California. Their stories are so much a part of the greater story of the West that both of these biographies are necessarily presented from the historical point of view, though we never lose sight of either man. Mr. Dana is more modern in his method and style, accelerating his narrative with dialogue and imaginative description which may or may not have bases in fact. Mr. Montgomery makes his book equally interesting and, perhaps, more trustworthy by adhering strictly to facts in his narrative. Both are interesting and valuable as history and biography.

From the point of view of romantic interest it is difficult to distinguish between the subjects of these biographies. John McLoughlin was the most famous man in the Oregon country in the days when this vast territory was a pawn in a political game played by the United States and England. Captain John Sutter, a Swiss immigrant, acquired an empire under Spanish grants, became something of a benevolent despot, and finally lost his empire when, ironically enough, gold, which he despised for itself, was found on his property. Though the days of Sutter and McLoughlin are gone, these biographies enable us to live with these men.

Within the last few years considerable attention has been paid to the less well-known men who achieved military prominence or fame in the Civil War. This is particularly true in the case of southern general officers. In keeping with its traditions, the Confederacy produced a larger group of romantic figures, civil as well as military, than did the North.

Hamilton Basso and Howard Swiggett have taken advantage of their opportunities in this respect in their lives of P. T. Beauregard and John Hunt Morgan. In my judgment *Beauregard, the Great Creole* (1933) is an overly sympathetic account, a eulogy rather than a biography of the Confederate general. There is no attempt at a critical evaluation of Beauregard as a soldier, and little attention is paid to the basic reasons for his lack of success as one of the principal general officers of the Confederacy.

Mr. Swiggett planned a biography of John Hunt Morgan, because the latter was one of his boyhood heroes. It was not until he had his material collected that the author fully realized that the famous Confederate raider was anything but a hero. *The Confederate Raider. A Life of John Hunt Morgan* (1934) is an honest evaluation of the activities of a guerilla chieftain rather than a general officer of the Confederate army. Morgan's most famous exploit, the raid into Ohio, was the culmination of a series of forays, raids, and personal encounters which were decidedly unorthodox from the military point of view and little calculated to advance the Confederate cause. Individualism was a marked characteristic of many Southern officers; it was the dominating factor in Morgan's career. He either ignored the orders of his superiors or carried out his raiding plans without authority. It is not a pretty picture that Mr. Swiggett draws of his one-time hero, a picture that developed itself from the records. Honesty compelled his biographer to present Morgan as he found him, not as he would have liked to have him.

George Armstrong Custer is another one of those half-legendary figures with which our history is studded. A general officer in the Union army before he was twenty-five,

Custer created a reputation second to none for courage and military ability. It was, however, his activities as an Indian fighter after the Civil War and the circumstances surrounding his death—he was killed in battle with the Sioux at Little Big Horn—that made him a hero to most of us. Apparently Frederic F. Van de Water became tired of hearing of this intrepid warrior, for in *Glory Hunter: a Life of General Custer* (1934) he seems to have knocked Custer from his pedestal and destroyed the pedestal as well.

It is a difficult matter to pass judgment on a biography of this kind. The author started out to prove a thesis: that Custer was a glory hunter from his birth to his death, and that in seeking that glory he was a bully as a boy, insubordinate as a cadet at West Point and a subaltern in the army, incompetent and frequently cruel as a commander, and criminally negligent in the insignificant battle in which he lost his life. Mr. Van de Water seems to prove the various points of his thesis from primary sources. There is no question of the author's honesty, and the truthfulness of the book can be controverted only by those who are as familiar with the material as the author. Setting aside the author's thesis, I found *Glory Hunter* a fascinating account of a romantic, an exotic figure who was his own worst enemy.

The influence of character on material success is a problem which frequently confronts the biographer. It was certainly a major problem for William S. Myers when he came to write *General George Brinton McClellan* (1934). Professor Myers spent many years studying the character of McClellan and its effect on his career. He tried very hard to give a true explanation of McClellan's failure as commander-in-chief of the Union army in the early years of the war. The biographer's failure came from his inability or reluctance to separate the personality from the character. He wanted to justify McClellan's position and his acts; he succeeded only in substantiating the opinion that has been held generally: that McClellan lacked the ability to coöperate with his military and civil superiors, that he refused to accept advice on any subject, that he was totally lacking in military foresight, and that hesitation had assumed the proportion of a major deficiency. That there is much to be said in favor of Mc-Clellan Professor Myers proves, but he does not succeed in his primary purpose, the rehabilitation of McClellan's reputation as a great military leader.

Occasionally there appears on the literary horizon a book which is so superior to anything else published on the subject that comparison is impossible. This is exactly the case of Douglas S. Freeman's *R. E. Lee; A Biography* (1934-1935). When the first two volumes appeared in the fall of 1934, it was very evident that the definitive biography of the great Virginian had been written. Mr. Freeman exhibits every qualification of the ideal biographer: a thorough knowledge of the subject, a constructively critical point of view, a definite method of approach and treatment, and an impartial yet absorbing interest in his subject. If we add to these qualifications of the biographer a lifelong study of military history, a profound understanding of the southern point of view, and a style that is not only distinguished but perfectly adapted to the complexities of the subject, we can readily understand the unanimity of critical praise that followed the publication of the two parts of this long study of the man who, next to Washington and Lincoln, is considered the ideal American.

Though three-fourths of the book is concerned with the Civil War, there is a perfect balance, for Lee's life before the Civil War was preparation; the period after 1865 anticlimax. Throughout this long book we never lose sight of General Lee. That Mr. Freeman was able to keep his subject always in the foreground of his book—a difficult task for any biographer—is merely another indication of his mastery of the biographer's art.

Though a detailed analysis of the method developed in this book is impossible here, there is one feature of it that deserves mention. Mr. Freeman adopted a single point of view when he came to the military narrative. We see the war as Lee saw it, for we are never absent from his side. As Lee could be in only one place at one time, we are given the same vantage point. In this manner Mr. Freeman enables the reader—if he can—to pass judgment on Lee the strategist and tactician. This unique method not only clarifies the subject; it permits the reader to keep Lee in constant view.

There are many things in *R. E. Lee* of which the individual reader may not approve, but it seems to me that the biography as a whole marks one of the high points in the literature of biography in English. There will be other books written on General Lee—appreciations, interpretations, criticisms—but I doubt if any future writer will find much material that escaped the twenty years of research that made this life possible.

In the opinion of George Fort Milton the Civil War could have been avoided. At least that is his thesis in *The Eve of Conflict. Stephen A. Douglas and the Needless War* (1934). From Mr. Milton's book on Andrew Johnson I expected a full-length biography of Stephen A. Douglas, a very important but much neglected figure in our history. *The Eve of Conflict* is only incidentally a life of Douglas; it is primarily a political history of the United States in the decade before the Civil War, the period of Douglas' greatest activity and fame. Despite Douglas' prominence in the narrative, it does not provide us with any extensive account of his life, apart from the important role he played in the history of the period.

Thaddeus Stevens was as prominent a figure during and immediately following the Civil War as Douglas was in the decade which preceded it. The leader of the radical element in the North, Stevens dominated Congress by the sheer force of his personality. It is largely because of the unpleasantness of that personality that Stevens has never been completely revealed by his biographers. The latest life, *Thaddeus Stevens* (1934), is no more satisfactory than the two earlier ones, for Thomas Woodley has not succeeded in presenting an impartial portrait of his subject. Stevens was the kind of man whom one either admires or hates with equal intensity. Mr. Woodley seems to have fallen under the fascination which, it must be admitted, is inherent in Stevens' character. He tried to present every phase of the subject, but I think he failed. We see Stevens as a young lawyer fighting to destroy the influence of Masonry in politics, to create and preserve public schools in Pennsylvania; we do not get an equally clear impression of his relentless hatred of the South or the motives that lay behind his demands for political and social equality for the Negro unless they were, as I believe them to have been, the means by which he intended to perpetuate the supremacy of the Republican party.

The Republican party did maintain its supremacy, for, excepting Cleveland, every President from 1860 to 1912 was a Republican. The political history of this period is fascinating in itself and because of the men who were leaders of both parties, statesmen, politicians and spoilsmen. In *James G. Blaine, a Political Idol of Other Days* (1934) and *Chester A. Arthur; a Quarter Century of Machine Politics* (1934), Professors David A. Muzzey and George F. Howe have demonstrated that it was possible for men to achieve such success as spoilsmen and politicians that they almost reached the position of statesmen. In each of these additions to the "American Political Leaders" series (see p. 330), the author has been successful in proportion to the interest and importance of his subject. Arthur was President of the United States through the accident of President Garfield's assassination; Blaine was a possible or actual candidate from 1876 until his death in 1893. In telling the story of Blaine's life and explaining his fame and failure, Professor Muzzey has done full justice to the man and the period in which he loomed so large. This study of Blaine is superior to the earlier book by Charles E. Russell (see p. 222) because it is written from a more impartial point of view, with a better historical perspective, and in a more graceful style. I believe it is the definitive and perhaps the final biography of the "plumed knight" who, like W. J. Bryan, could capture audiences but not votes.

President Arthur's biographer had a more difficult task than Blaine's. Until he was named as Garfield's running mate in 1880, Chester A. Arthur was a political boss in New York City. A machine politician with an unenviable reputation as a spoilsman, Arthur's rise to the Presidency was considered a public calamity by many members of his own party. In the White House he disappointed the fears of his enemies and the hopes of his friends, by rising to the dignity of his position and refusing to become a pliable instrument in the hands of the "practical politicians" of his party. He was not able to secure the nomination in 1884, but he left the presidential chair a much greater man than he was when he succeeded to it. Professor Howe has narrated these events adequately, though *Chester A. Arthur* is written without particular distinction of manner or style. It is doubtful if anyone will write another biography of President Arthur. Professor Howe has presented the facts, and there is nothing in Arthur's character that would attract a more artistic biographer.

The difficulties facing the biographer of such a figure as President Arthur are no more serious than those which face the writer who tries to resurrect a forgotten figure in American public life. Professor William N. Brigance had opportunities and difficulties in *Jeremiah Sullivan Black, A Defender of the Constitution and the Ten Commandments* (1934). Black was one of the great constitutional lawyers of the mid-nineteenth century, a period when particularly vicious attacks were made upon the Constitution. A common pleas judge at thirty-two, Chief Justice of the Supreme Court of Pennsylvania at forty-one, Attorney-General and later Secretary of State in Buchanan's cabinet, one of the leading lawyers of the country in the turbulent days of Reconstruction, Black was a constant upholder and defender of government by law, whether that law was state or federal.

This biography could have been much more interesting than it is, had the author the opportunity to develop completely the various phases of Black's life and career. Originally prepared as a doctoral dissertation, the biography is concerned principally with Black's legal career and his place in American history. Despite its limitations, *Jeremiah Sullivan Black* presents a fairly complete interpretation of its subject and is particularly well done in those chapters dealing with the more important legal cases in which Black achieved fame as lawyer and statesman.

Occasionally we are reminded of the dictum of Johnson and Carlyle, that the life of any man would be interesting if properly presented. We have this dictum proved in Rachel Field's *God's Pocket. The Story of Captain Samuel Hadlock, Junior, of Cranberry Isles, Maine* (1934). This little book is truly an adventure in the art of biographical re-creation. With nothing more tangible than the memories of an aged grandson, "a gold snuff-box; a silhouette cut in London in 1824; an old compass, maps, and a chart; a marriage certificate in German script and two tattered copybooks crowded with faded entries in a vigorous Spencerian hand," Miss Field has re-created the person and the personality of Captain Hadlock as they must have been. An earlier Barnum, Captain Hadlock toured Europe with a show composed of a pair of Esquimaux, Arctic flora and fauna, and any other curiosity he could find. The story of his whirlwind courtship and marriage of a German girl who could speak no English, of his European travels, of his return to America with his bride, and his last trip to the North from which he never returned, reads like a tale out of the *Arabian Nights*. The most remarkable part of the book is the art with which Miss Field pieced together, without resorting to any questionable method, the fragmentary information in her possession to make one of the most fascinating biographical narratives that I have read. *God's Pocket* belongs among the classics of American biography.

The romantic adventurer is not confined to any period or any country. The end of the nineteenth century produced just as many as the beginning, though the opportunities were not so numerous. The reporter turned war correspondent is an example of the romantic adventurer in modern times, and Richard Harding Davis was, perhaps, the most famous war correspondent before the World War. Fairfax Downey's *Richard Harding Davis; His Day* (1933) is an account of Davis' life and career that Davis himself would have thoroughly enjoyed. It is not a great biography, this life of one reporter written by another, but it is toned exactly to the nature of its subject and written with a kindly tolerance for the foibles of the man who was a modern "Richard the Lion-Hearted," the living model of the "Gibson man" as he was the actual model, the boy who never grew up. There is here too a sincere appreciation and kindly criticism of the author of "Gallegher," "Soldiers of Fortune" and the "March Into Brussels," a classic description of the entrance of the German army into Brussels in August 1914.

During the years of his greatest fame and success Davis must have frequently seen and talked with a huge, smiling man who generally dined alone and in state at Delmonico's, where Davis himself was a constant visitor. James Brady was as famous as Richard Harding Davis, but in a different way. His fame rested on his collection of diamonds, his love of the theatre—he was one of the most famous of all first-nighters—and finally on his appetite. A salesman of railroad supplies and later a financier, "Diamond Jim" Brady was by avocation a connoisseur of food and drink, though he never indulged in the latter. His story and the story of Broadway in the nineties—they were almost the same thing—has been brilliantly if somewhat smartly narrated by Parker Morell in *Diamond Jim; the Life and Times of James Buchanan Brady* (1934). The tricks of modern biography which Mr. Morell uses in *Diamond Jim* are excusable or at least explainable: it would be impossible to write a plain unadorned narrative of

Brady's life. It must be presented as dramatically as it was lived if we are to catch the spirit of the man and the times that made him.

It is doubtful if Davis or Brady ever heard of Thorstein Veblen as they wandered up and down Broadway, though he too was making quite a name for himself in those days. In *Thorstein Veblen and His America* (1934) Joseph Dorfman has tried to explain what Veblen's ideas of economics and sociology and politics were, and how his theories have come to be facts. To the student of these subjects the book is valuable and perhaps interesting, though it is not well organized nor is the writing particularly clear. It fails as biography because we get only an occasional glimpse of the man. There are whole chapters in which he never appears. This method would be proper in a textbook; it is fatal in what purports to be a biography. There is an occasional sketch of Veblen which indicates that his personality must have been as fascinating as it was disturbing, but we get no clear picture of the author of the *Theory of the Leisure Classes*.

England and the Continent continue to provide interesting subjects for biographical treatment, subjects ranging from William the Conqueror to Cardinal Mercier. Phillips Russell's *William the Conqueror* (1933) (see p. 214) is an excellent narrative of William's life and conquests. From this book William, Duke of Normandy, emerges as a real personage, not a shadowy figure of the so-called dark ages of history. This is, as far as I know, the first attempt to present William, the man, against the background of his period. By cutting away the mass of history and legend which has heretofore concealed the character and personality of William, Professor Russell has enabled us to see and understand the claims which William had to the crown of England and the reforms he instituted after the conquest.

With the same purpose in view and with equal success, Henry Dwight Sedgwick has made the life and writings of Geoffrey Chaucer interesting to the average reader. *Dan Chaucer* (1934) is an extremely valuable addition to Mr.

Sedgwick's contribution to American biographical literature (see p. 201). There are numerous books on Chaucer, the greatest name in our literature before Shakespeare, but the great majority of them are interesting only to the scholar. Mr. Sedgwick has brought Chaucer close to all of us by the simplicity of his presentation and the clarity of his style. Among other things, this biographer makes us realize that Chaucer would perhaps be more at home in the modern world, although he lived entirely within the fourteenth century, than, let us say, Milton or Dryden or Swift. Excellent as biography, this book will serve as an admirable introduction to the study of one of the greatest of English poets.

It was quite natural that Francis Hackett should follow his biography of Henry VIII (see p. 347) with a companion study of Francis I (1935). They were not only exact contemporaries; both were rivals for the imperial crown, as well as for the balance of power in Europe. In my judgment, *Francis I* is a better biography than *Henry VIII*, though it will not be so popular as the former. It lacks the interest that *Henry VIII* had for us, not because it is less interesting *per se*, but because we are not so familiar with the history of France of the Renaissance as we are with England during the same period. There is perhaps more history in *Francis I* than in *Henry VIII*, for Francis was more deeply involved in continental affairs than was Henry. There is a decided improvement in character portrayal in this book, and in distinction of style. It is another chain in the development of a dignified literature of biography which is taking the place of the popular rewrite school of the last fifteen years.

Willard Connely had the same incentive for his second biography that Hackett had. In 1930 Mr. Connely published a rather racy and not particularly valuable life of William Wycherley, one of the most famous of the Restoration wits and dramatists. He has followed this with *Sir Richard Steele* (1934), a really distinguished account of the most important dramatist of eighteenth-century England and one of the great prose masters of our literature. This biography is totally different from and vastly superior to the book on Wycherley. Where the latter was a decidedly informal and casual treatment of a really important subject, *Sir Richard Steele* is a carefully documented and ably written interpretive narrative of one of the most important and certainly one of the most interesting literary figures of the eighteenth century. If Mr. Connely continues to work in this most fertile field with the same skill that he has shown in his latest work, he bids fair to take an important place in literary biography in English.

In a quite different field, Avraham Yarmolinsky is achieving equal success in literary biography. When *Turgenev* appeared in 1926 (see p. 298), Mr. Yarmolinsky gave ample evidence of his qualifications for critical biography. In *Dostoevsky* (1934) he has been even more successful. In this study of one of the greatest of the Russian novelists, the author has so carefully blended biography and criticism that we are able to understand how the massive and sometimes terrible novels of Dostoevsky came to be written. *Dostoevsky* is superior to *Turgenev* because it is a more complete analysis of a much more complex character and an illuminating criticism of a body of work more inherently Russian, and therefore less comprehensible to us, than Turgenev's work.

It is quite probable that Ralph Roeder's *Man of the Renaissance* (1933) is a natural outgrowth of the author's studies for *Savonarola* (1930). *Man of the Renaissance* is a composite biography in which Mr. Roeder has taken four great figures of Renaissance Italy—Savonarola, Machiavelli, Castiglione, and Aretino—to represent the Renaissance spirit. Superficially these four would seem to have little in common; actually each one embodies the Renaissance as it affected religion, politics, society, and the press.

One of the most fascinating features of biography is its variety. Every age and every field of human endeavor is represented in modern biography. We can turn from Italy of the Renaissance to England of the seventeenth and eighteenth centuries in *Isaac Newton; a Biography* (1934) by

Louis T. More. In this long and detailed study Professor More has presented the first full-length portrait of one of the greatest of all mathematicians and scientists, along with a detailed explanation of his epoch-making discovery of the law of gravitation and his equally important work in optics. I am not qualified to pass judgment on the scientific sections of this book, but I can say that it presents a complete account of Newton's life and character from a biographical point of view.

Cardinal Newman has been the subject of many biographies since his death in 1890, three of which have been written by Americans. Professor Atkins studied Newman as a religious leader; Professor Reilly presented him from a literary point of view. It remained, however, for Father J. Elliot Ross to write the best biography of Newman that has appeared. In *John Henry Newman; Anglican Minister, Catholic Priest, Roman Cardinal* (1933), we have a carefully considered interpretation of Newman's life and work from every point of view. I think we get closer to the man, as well as the priest and writer, in this book than in any other account of Newman that has been written. We accompany him step by step on that long and difficult road that was Newman's life. We become intimate not only with Newman but with the other leaders of the Oxford Movement and later with his most formidable adversary, Manning. Into just a little over three hundred pages, Father Ross has succeeded in compressing the very essence of Newman, the minister, the priest, and the cardinal. It is a masterpiece of biographical interpretation, written in a style and with an artistic economy that would have greatly pleased the subject.

BIBLIOGRAPHY

BIBLIOGRAPHY

I

THE following bibliography contains all the titles mentioned in the text, together with others of less importance. These latter have been inserted to indicate the temporary importance of some of the figures in American life, or to provide further material for the extended study of a particular literary or public figure.

Explanation of abbreviations used after some of the titles:

A. S.—American Statesmen
A. M. L.—American Men of Letters
E. M. L.—English Men of Letters
A. C. B.—American Crisis Biographies
L. A. B.—Library of American Biography

The Adams Family. By James Truslow Adams. 1930.

Prologue. John Adams. John Quincy Adams. Charles Francis Adams. John Quincy, Charles Francis, Henry, and Brooks Adams.

Abigail Adams and her Times. Laura E. Richards. 1917.

Abigail Adams, the Second First Lady. Dorothie Bobbé. 1929.

Charles Francis Adams, the First. Charles Francis Adams, Jr. 1900.

Henry Adams. James Truslow Adams. 1932.

The Works of John Adams, Second President of the United States: with a Life of the Author. John Quincy Adams and Charles Francis Adams. 10 vols. 1856.

Vol. I is the biography.

John Adams. John T. Morse, Jr. 1884, 1898. (A. S.)

This Man Adams; the Man Who Never Died. Samuel D. McCoy. 1928.

Honest John Adams. Gilbert Chinard. 1933.

Memoir of the Life of John Quincy Adams. Josiah Quincy. 1858.

John Quincy Adams. John T. Morse, Jr. 1883. (A. S.)

John Quincy Adams. Worthington C. Ford. 1902.

Mr. and Mrs. John Quincy Adams; an Adventure in Patriotism. Dorothie Bobbé. 1930.

John Quincy Adams, "Old Man Eloquent." Bennett C. Clark. 1932.

The Life and Public Services of Samuel Adams. William V. Wells. 3 vols. 1865.

Samuel Adams, Promoter of the American Revolution; a Study in Psychology and Politics. Ralph V. Harlow. 1923.

Samuel Adams. J. K. Hosmer. 1884, 1898. (A. S.)

Father of Little Women (Bronson Alcott). Honoré W. Morrow. 1927.

Louisa May Alcott. Her Life, Letters, and Journals. Ednah D. Cheney. 1889.

May Alcott; a Memoir. Caroline Ticknor. 1928.

Nelson W. Aldrich; a Leader in American Politics. Nathaniel W. Stephenson. 1930.

The Life of Thomas Bailey Aldrich. Ferris Greenslet. 1908.

Life of Ethan Allen. Jared Sparks. (L. A. B.)

Ethan Allen. John Pell. 1929.

Ira Allen, Founder of Vermont, 1751–1814. James B. Wilbur. 2 vols. 1928.

The "Also Rans"; Great Men Who Missed Making the Presidential Goal. Don C. Seitz. 1928.

    Aaron Burr, William H. Crawford, John C. Calhoun, Henry Clay, Lewis Cass, Daniel Webster, Winfield Scott, John C. Frémont, Stephen A. Douglas, William H. Seward, George B. McClellan, Horatio Seymour, Horace Greeley, Samuel J. Tilden, Winfield S. Hancock, James G. Blaine, Benjamin F. Butler, W. J. Bryan.

American Biography. Jeremy Belknap. 2 vols. 1794–1798. 1843. 3 vols. 1857.

    Contains forty-two sketches of the lives of early explorers, settlers, and governors of America.

Library of American Biography. Jared Sparks (ed.). First Series, 10 vols. 1834–1838. Second Series, 15 vols. 1844–1847. 25 vols. 1864.

An American Biographical and Historical Dictionary; Containing an Account of the Lives, Characters and Writings of the Most Eminent Persons in North America from its First Discovery to the Present Time. William Allen (ed.). 1809, 1832, 1858.

    This is our first biographical dictionary. First edition has about 700 items; second, about 1800, and third, nearly 7000.

Some American Ladies. Meade Minnigerode. 1926.

Martha Washington, Abigail Adams, Dolly Madison, Elizabeth Monroe and Louisa Adams, Rachel Jackson, and Peggy Eaton.

American Portraits, 1875–1900. Gamaliel Bradford. 1920–1922.

Mark Twain, Henry Adams, Sidney Lanier, James McNeill Whistler, James G. Blaine, Grover Cleveland, Henry James, and Joseph Jefferson.

Famous Americans of Recent Times. James Parton. 1867.

Henry Clay, Daniel Webster, John C. Calhoun, John Randolph, Stephen Girard and his College, James Gordon Bennett and the New York *Herald,* Charles Goodyear, Henry Ward Beecher and his Church, Commodore Vanderbilt, Theodosia Burr, and John Jacob Astor.

Strenuous Americans. Roy F. Dibble. 1923.

Jesse James, Admiral Dewey, Brigham Young, Frances E. Willard, James J. Hill, P. T. Barnum, and Mark Hanna.

Uncommon Americans. Don C. Seitz. 1925.

Joseph Smith, Brigham Young, Martin Scott, Lord Timothy Dexter, Peter Cartwright, Charles G. Finney, Israel Putnam, Nathan B. Forrest, John S. Mosby, Susan B. Anthony, Red Jacket, George Francis Train, Tecumseh, Ethan Allen, James A. McN. Whistler, Edmund Fanning, John Ledyard, Hinton R. Helper, Henry George, Mary Baker G. Eddy, Edwin Forrest, and David Crockett.

Susan B. Anthony, the Woman Who Changed the Mind of a Nation. Rheta L. Dorr. 1928.

Life and Treason of Benedict Arnold. Jared Sparks. (L. A. B.)

Life of Benedict Arnold; his Patriotism and his Treason. Isaac N. Arnold. 1880.

The Real Benedict Arnold. C. Burr Todd. 1903.

Benedict Arnold, the Proud Warrior. Charles C. Sellers. 1930.

Benedict Arnold, Patriot and Traitor. Oscar Sherwin. 1931.

Benedict Arnold, Military Racketeer. Edward D. Sullivan. 1932.

Chester A. Arthur: a Quarter-Century of Machine Politics. George F. Howe. 1934.

A Methodist Saint; the Life of Bishop Asbury. Herbert Asbury. 1927.

As God Made Them: Portraits of Some Nineteenth Century Americans. Gamaliel Bradford. 1929.

Daniel Webster, Henry Clay, John C. Calhoun, Horace Greeley, Edwin Booth, Portrait of a Scholar: Francis James Child, and Portrait of a Scientist: Asa Gray.

Life of John Jacob Astor. James Parton. 1865.

John Jacob Astor. Arthur D. Howden Smith. 1929.

John Jacob Astor, Business Man. Kenneth W. Porter. 2 vols. 1931.

Audubon, the Naturalist; a History of his Life and Time. Francis H. Herrick. 2 vols. 1917.

Audacious Audubon. Edward A. Muschamp. 1929.

Life of Stephen F. Austin. Eugene C. Barker. 1925.

Sir Francis Bacon, the First Modern Mind. Byron Steel. 1930.

Memoir of Nathaniel Bacon. William Ware. (L. A. B.)

Vasco Núñez de Balboa. F. A. Ober. 1906. (Heroes of American History)

Life and Letters of George Bancroft. M. A. de Wolfe Howe. 2 vols. 1908.

Bare Souls. Gamaliel Bradford. 1924.

Clue to the Labyrinth of Souls, Voltaire, Thomas Gray, Horace Walpole, William Cowper, Charles Lamb, John Keats, Gustave Flaubert, and Edward Fitzgerald.

James Nelson Barker, 1784–1858. Paul Musser. 1929.

Life and Letters of Joel Barlow . . . Charles B. Todd. 1886.

Barnum. M. R. Werner. 1923.

Unknown Barnum. Harvey W. Root. 1927.

Builders of the Bay Colony. Samuel E. Morison. 1930.

John White, Governor Winthrop, Thomas Shepard, John Hull, Henry Dunster, Nathaniel Ward, Robert Child, John Winthrop, John Eliot, and Mistress Anne Bradstreet.

Life of Chevalier Bayard. William Gilmore Simms. 1847.

Beauregard, the Great Creole. Hamilton Basso. 1933.

Beecher and his Accusers . . . Francis P. Williamson. 1874.

Life and Works of Henry Ward Beecher. T. W. Knox. 1887.

A Biography of Rev. Henry Ward Beecher. William C. Beecher, Rev. Samuel Scoville, and Mrs. Henry Ward Beecher. 1888.

Henry Ward Beecher: the Shakespeare of the Pulpit. J. H. Barrows. 1903. (American Reformers)

Henry Ward Beecher; an American Portrait. Paxton Hibben. 1927.

Beethoven, the Man Who Freed Music. Robert H. Schauffler. 2 vols. 1929.

Life of Jeremy Belknap with Selections from His Writings . . . J. Belknap. 1847.

Alexander Graham Bell, the Man who Contracted Space. Catherine D. Mackenzie. 1928.

James Gordon Bennett and His Times. Isaac C. Pray. 1855.

The James Gordon Bennetts. Don C. Seitz. 1928.

Thomas Hart Benton. Theodore Roosevelt. 1886. (A. S.)

Beveridge and the Progressive Era. Claude G. Bowers. 1932.

Ambrose Bierce; a Biography. Carey McWilliams. 1929.

Bitter Bierce; a Mystery of American Letters. C. Hartley Grattan. 1929.

Life of Ambrose Bierce. Walter Neale. 1929.

Big Frogs. Henry F. Pringle. 1928.

Herbert Hoover, Jimmy Walker, Rev. S. Parks Cadman, Kenesaw M. Landis, Ivy L. Lee, Bernarr McFadden, Samuel Untermeyer, Frank Hedley, William H. Anderson, Will H. Hays, Robert F. Wagner, Curtis D. Wilbur, Theodore Roosevelt, Jr., and John S. Sumner.

Saga of Billy the Kid. Walter Noble Burns. 1926.

Authentic Life of Billy the Kid. Pat F. Garrett. 1882. New edition by Maurice G. Fulton. 1928.

Biographical Sketches of the Signers of the Declaration of Independence . . . B. J. Lossing. 1860.

Biographies of Lady Russell and Madame Guyon. Lydia M. Child. 1832.

Biographies of Madame de Staël and Madame Roland. Lydia M. Child. 1832.

Biographies of Good Wives. Lydia M. Child. 1833.

Biography and the Human Heart. Gamaliel Bradford. 1932.

Biography and the Human Heart, Henry Wadsworth Longfellow, Walt Whitman, Charlotte Cushman, William Morris Hunt, An American Pepys: John Beauchamp Jones, Jones Very, Letters of Horace Walpole, and Biography by Mirror.

Biography of the Signers of the Declaration of Independence. John Sanderson. 5 vols. 1828.

Biography of the Signers of the Declaration of Independence. L. C. Judson. 1839.

Life and Dramatic Works of Robert Montgomery Bird. Clement E. Foust. 1919.

Jeremiah Sullivan Black. William N. Brigance. 1934.

An American Career and its Triumph; Life of James G. Blaine; with the Career of J. A. Logan. W. R. Balch. 1884.

Biographies of James G. Blaine and J. A. Logan . . . T. V. Cooper. 1884.

James G. Blaine; Sketch of his Life: with Record of the Life of J. A. Logan. C. W. Balestier. 1884.

Life and Public Services of James G. Blaine; also, Life of J. A. Logan. Russell H. Conwell. 1884.

Pine to Potomac; Life of James G. Blaine; with Sketch of the Life of Gen. J. A. Logan. E. K. Cressey. 1884.

Life of Hon. James G. Blaine. James W. Pierce. 1893.

Life of Hon. James G. Blaine. T. C. Crawford. 1893.

Life and Work of James G. Blaine. John C. Redpath and others. 1893.

Biography of James G. Blaine. Gail Hamilton. 1895.

James Gillespie Blaine. E. Stanwood. 1905. (A. S. 2d Ser.)

Blaine of Maine; his Life and Times. Charles E. Russell. 1931.

James G. Blaine; a Political Idol of Other Days. David S. Muzzey. 1934.

Life of Giovanni Boccaccio. Thomas C. Chubb. 1930.

George Henry Boker, Poet and Patriot. Edward S. Bradley. 1927.

Bonnie Prince Charlie (Charles Edward Stuart). Donald B. Chidsey. 1928.

Biographical Memoir of Daniel Boone, the First Settler of Kentucky. Timothy Flint. 1833.

The First White Man; or, the Life and Exploits of Col. Daniel Boone. Timothy Flint. 1849.

Life of Daniel Boone. John M. Peck. (L. A. B.)

Darling of Misfortune, Edwin Booth: 1833–1893. Richard Lockridge. 1932.

Young Boswell. Chauncey B. Tinker. 1922.

Life and Writings of Hugh Henry Brackenridge. Claude M. Newlin. 1932.

Diamond Jim; the Life and Times of James Buchanan Brady. Parker Morell. 1934.

Memoirs of the Rev. David Brainerd, Missionary to the Indians . . . Jonathan Edwards. 1749, 1822.

Life of David Brainerd. W. O. B. Peabody. (L. A. B.)

Life of Joseph Brant and History of the Border Wars of the American Revolution. William L. Stone. 2 vols. 1846.

Chief of the Pilgrims; or, the Life and Times of William Brewster. Ashbel Steele. 1857.

Phillips Brooks. M. A. de W. Howe. 1899. (Beacon Biographies)

The Life and Letters of Phillips Brooks. Alexander V. G. Allen. 3 vols. 1900.

Life of Charles Brockden Brown . . . William Dunlap. 2 vols. 1815.

Life of Charles Brockden Brown. William H. Prescott. (L. A. B.)

Captain John Brown. Life and Letters. F. B. Sanborn (ed.). 1891.

John Brown, 1800–1859; Biography Fifty Years After. Oswald G. Villard. 1910.

John Brown, Soldier of Fortune; a Critique. Hill P. Wilson. 1913.

John Brown; the Making of a Martyr. Robert P. Warren. 1929.

The Brownings; a Victorian Idyll. David G. Loth. 1929.

Bryan, the Great Commoner. J. C. Long. 1928.

Peerless Leader, William Jennings Bryan. Paxton Hibben. (Completed by C. Hartley Grattan.) 1929.

Bryan. M. R. Werner. 1929.

The Life, Character, and Writings of William Cullen Bryant. George William Curtis. 1879.

Life of William Cullen Bryant. Parke Godwin. 2 vols. 1883.

William Cullen Bryant. D. J. Hill. 1879. (American Authors)

William Cullen Bryant. John Bigelow. 1890. (A. M. L.)

William Cullen Bryant. W. A. Bradley. 1905. (E. M. L.)

Life of James Buchanan. R. G. Horton. 1856.

Life of James Buchanan. George Ticknor Curtis. 1883.

The Dukes of Buckingham; Playboys of the Stuart World. Robert P. T. Coffin. 1931.

Romantick Lady (Frances Hodgson Burnett); *the Life Story of an Imagination.* Vivian Burnett. 1927.

Life of Robert Burns. Franklin B. Snyder. 1932.

Life of Aaron Burr. Samuel L. Knapp. 1835.

Memoirs of Aaron Burr, with Miscellaneous selections from his correspondence. Matthew L. Davis. 2 vols. 1838.

The Life and Times of Aaron Burr. James Parton. 1858. 2 vols. 1872.

Aaron Burr. H. C. Merwin. 1899.

True Aaron Burr. A Biographical Sketch. Charles B. Todd. 1903.

An American Patrician: Aaron Burr. Alfred H. Lewis. 1908.

Aaron Burr: a Biography Written in Large Part from Original and Hitherto Unused Material. Samuel H. Wandell and Meade Minnigerode. 2 vols. 1927.

Aaron Burr; a Romantic Biography. Johnston D. Kirkhoff. 1931.

Life and Letters of John Burroughs. Clara Barrus. 2 vols. 1925.

Burton, Arabian Nights Adventurer. Fairfax Downey. 1931.

The Life and Public Services of Major-General Butler, the Hero of New Orleans. 1864.

Samuel Butler; a Mid-Victorian Modern. Clara G. Stillman. 1932.

William Byrd of Westover. Richmond C. Beatty. 1932.

George W. Cable; his Life and Letters. Lucy Cable Bikle. 1928.

Life and Letters of George Cabot. Henry Cabot Lodge. 1878.

Life of Sebastian Cabot. Charles Hayward, Jr. (L. A. B.)

John and Sebastian Cabot. F. A. Ober. 1908. (Heroes of American History)

Julius Caesar & the Grandeur that was Rome. Victor Thaddeus. 1927.

Life of John C. Calhoun . . . R. M. T. Hunter. 1843.

Life of John Caldwell Calhoun. J. S. Jenkins. 1850.

John Calhoun. H. von Holst. 1882, 1899. (A. S.)

Life of John C. Calhoun. G. M. Pinckney. 1903.

Life of John Caldwell Calhoun. William M. Meigs. 2 vols. 1910.

Life of Leonard Calvert. George W. Burnap. (L. A. B.)

Canfield: the True Story of the Greatest Gambler. Alexander Gardiner. 1930.

Al Capone; the Biography of a Self-Made Man. Fred D. Pasley. 1930.

Captains of Industry. James Parton. 1855.

John G. Carlisle, Financial Statesman. James A. Barnes. 1931.

Carlyle. Emery E. Neff. 1932.

The Incredible Carnegie. John K. Winkler. 1931.

Life of Andrew Carnegie. Burton J. Hendrick. 2 vols. 1932.

The Life of Charles Carroll of Carrollton, 1737–1832 . . . Kate Mason Rowland. 2 vols. 1898.

Life and Times of the Most Reverend John Carroll, Bishop and first Archbishop of Baltimore. John Gilmary Shea. 1888.

Life and Times of John Carroll, Archbishop of Baltimore (1735–1815). Peter Guilday. 1922.

Kit Carson; the Happy Warrior of the Old West; a Biography. Stanley Vestal. 1928.

Peter Cartwright: Pioneer. Helen H. Grant. 1931.

Casanova; his Known and Unknown Life. S. Guy Endore. 1929.

Life of Lewis Cass. Andrew C. McLaughlin. 1891, 1899. (A. S.)

Catherine the Great. Katharine S. Anthony. 1925.

Life and Times of Cavour. William R. Thayer. 2 vols. 1911.

Certain Rich Men. Meade Minnigerode. 1927.

    Stephen Girard, John Jacob Astor, Jay Cooke, Daniel Drew, Cornelius Vanderbilt, Jay Gould, and Jim Fisk.

Samuel de Champlain. Henry Dwight Sedgwick. 1903.

Memoir of William Ellery Channing. William H. Channing (ed.). 3 vols. 1848.

Charlemagne, the First of the Moderns. Charles E. Russell. 1930.

Life and Public Services of Salmon Portland Chase. Jacob W. Schmucker. 1874.

Private Life and Public Services of Salmon P. Chase. Robert B. Warden. 1874.

Salmon Portland Chase. Albert Bushnell Hart. 1899.

Cross in the Wilderness; (Life of Mother Julia Chatfield) *a Biography of Pioneer Ohio.* Sister M. Monica. 1930.

Studies in Chaucer; his Life and Writings. Thomas R. Lounsbury. 3 vols. 1891. Vol. I contains a short biography.

Dan Chaucer. Henry Dwight Sedgwick. 1934.

Lives and Times of the Chief Justices of the Supreme Court. H. Flanders. 2 vols. 1855–1858.

    John Jay, John Rutledge, William Cushing Oliver Ellsworth, and John Marshall.

Sketches of the Lives, Times and Judicial Services of the Chief Justices of the Supreme Court of the United States. George Van Santwood. 1854. 2d ed. by W. M. Scott. 1882.

    John Jay, John Rutledge, Oliver Ellsworth, John Marshall, and Roger Taney.

History of the Supreme Court of the United States; with Biographies of all the Chief and Associate Justices. Hampton L. Carson. 2 vols. 1904.

Letters of Lydia Maria Child with a Biographical Introduction. John G. Whittier (ed.). 1883.

Thomas Holley Chivers, Friend of Poe . . . a Strange Chapter in American Literary History. Samuel F. Damon. 1930.

Rufus Choate, Wizard of the Law. Claude M. Fuess. 1928.

Life of Gen. George Rogers Clark; with Sketches of Men Who Served under Clark. W. H. English. 2 vols. 1896.

George Rogers Clark; his Life and Public Services. Temple Bodley. 1927.

Life of George Rogers Clark. James A. James. 1928.

Clark of the Ohio; the Life of George Rogers Clark. Frederick Palmer. 1929.

Hero of Vincennes; the Story of George Rogers Clark. Lowell J. Thomas. 1929.

Biography of Henry Clay. G. D. Prentice. 1831.

Life and Speeches of Henry Clay between 1810 and 1842. James B. Swain. 1842. 2 vols. 1843.

Life and Speeches of Henry Clay. D. Mallory (ed.). 2 vols. 1843.

The Life of Henry Clay. Nathan Sargent. 1844.

Life and Times of Henry Clay. Calvin Colton. 3 vols. 1845, 1856.

The Life and Public Services of Henry Clay . . . Epes Sargent and Horace Greeley. 1859.

Memoir of Henry Clay. R. C. Winthrop. 1880.

Henry Clay. Carl Schurz. 2 vols. 1887, 1899. (A. S.)

The True Henry Clay. Joseph M. Rogers. 1902.

Life of Grover Cleveland. Deshier Welsh. 1884.

Life and Public Services of Grover Cleveland and T. A. Hendricks. C. F. Black. 1884.

Life and Public Services of Grover Cleveland. Pendleton King. 1884.

Life and Public Services of Grover Cleveland and John Thurman. W. U. Hensel and G. F. Parker. 1888.

Life of Grover Cleveland; with Sketch of Adlai E. Stevenson. G. F. Parker. 1892.

Grover Cleveland. J. L. Whittle. 1896.

Grover Cleveland, the Man and the Statesman. Robert McElroy. 2 vols. 1923.

Grover Cleveland; a Man Four-Square. Denis Tilden Lynch. 1932.

Grover Cleveland; a Study in Courage. Allan Nevins. 1932.

DeWitt Clinton. Dorothie Bobbé. 1933.

Jacques Coeur, Merchant Prince of the Middle Ages. Albert B. Kerr. 1927.

A History of the Life and Voyages of Christopher Columbus. Washington Irving. 3 vols. 1828.

The Life and Voyages of Christopher Columbus. Washington Irving. Abridged by the Author. 1829.

The Life of Christopher Columbus. Edward Everett Hale. 1891.

Christopher Columbus . . . Justin Winsor. 1891.

Columbus, the Discoverer. F. A. Ober. 1906. (Heroes of American History)

Anthony Comstock: His Career of Cruelty and Crime. D. M. Bennett. 1878.

Anthony Comstock, Roundsman of the Lord. Heywood C. Broun and Margaret Leech. 1927.

Confederate Portraits. Gamaliel Bradford. 1914.
      Joseph E. Johnston, J. E. B. Stuart, James Longstreet, P. G. T. Beauregard, Judah P. Benjamin, Alexander H. Stephens, Robert Toombs, and Raphael Semmes.

Russell H. Conwell and his Work; one Man's Interpretation of Life. Agnes R. Burr. 1917.

Road to the Temple; the Life of George Cram Cook. Susan Glaspell. 1927.

Memoirs of George Frederick Cooke. William Dunlap. 2 vols. 1813, 1815.

Jay Cooke, Financier of the Civil War. Edward P. Oberholtzer. 2 vols. 1907.

Legend of Calvin Coolidge. Cameron Rogers. 1928.

James Fenimore Cooper. Thomas Lounsbury. 1883. (A. M. L.)

James Fenimore Cooper. Henry W. Boynton. 1931.

Fenimore Cooper: Critic of His Times. R. E. Spiller. 1931.

Cope: Master Naturalist; the Life and Letters of Edward Drinker Cope. H. F. Osborn and H. A. Warren. 1932.

Cortes the Conqueror; the Exploits of the Earliest and the Greatest of the Gentlemen Adventurers in the New World. Henry Dwight Sedgwick. 1926.

Stout Cortez; a Biography of the Spanish Conquest. Henry M. Robinson. 1931.

The Life and Death of the deservedly Famous Mr. John Cotton, the late Reverend Teacher of the Church of Christ at Boston in New England. John Norton. 1657.

Troupers of the Gold Coast; or, the Rise of Lotta Crabtree. Constance M. Rourke. 1928.

Stephen Crane; a Study in American Letters. Thomas Beer. 1923.

Davy Crockett. Constance M. Rourke. 1934.

Richard Croker. Alfred H. Lewis. 1901.

Master of Manhattan; the Life of Richard Croker. Theodore L. Stoddard. 1931.

Life of Caleb Cushing. Claude M. Fuess. 2 vols. 1923.

Custer, the Last of the Cavaliers. Frazier Hunt. 1928.

Glory Hunter. A Life of General Custer. Frederic F. Van de Water. 1934.

Cyrano (Cyrano de Bergerac). Cameron Rogers. 1929.

Damaged Souls. Gamaliel Bradford. 1923.

> Damaged Souls, Benedict Arnold, Thomas Paine, Aaron Burr, John Randolph of Roanoke, John Brown, Phineas Taylor Barnum, and Benjamin F. Butler.

When Dana Was the Sun; a Story of Personal Journalism. Charles J. Rosebault. 1931.

Francis Dana; a Puritan Diplomat at the Court of Catherine the Great. W. P. Cresson. 1930.

Darwin. Gamaliel Bradford. 1926.

Charles Darwin; the Man and his Warfare. Charles H. Ward. 1927.

Daughters of Eve. Gamaliel Bradford. 1930.

> Eve in the Apple-Orchard, Ninon de Lenclos, Madame de Maintenon, Madame de ·Guyon, Mlle. de Lespinasse, Catherine the Great, George Sand, and Sarah Bernhardt.

Daughters of Genius; a Series of Sketches of Prominent Women. James Parton. 1886.

Sir William Davenant. Alfred B. Harbage. 1934.

Memoir of Lucretia M. Davidson. (L. A. B.)

Biography and Poetical Remains of the Late Margaret Miller Davidson. Washington Irving. 1841.

Life of William R. Davie. Fordyce M. Hubbard. (L. A. B.)

The Life and Adventures of Jefferson Davis. 1865.

Life of Jefferson Davis. F. H. Alfriend. 1868.

Life of Jefferson Davis; with a Secret History of the Southern Confederacy. Edward A. Pollard. 1869.

Jefferson Davis, a Memoir. Varina H. Davis. 2 vols. 1890.

Jefferson Davis, President of the South. H. J. Eckenrode. 1923.

Jefferson Davis; his Rise and Fall; a Biographical Narrative. Allen Tate. 1929.

Jefferson Davis, Political Soldier. Elizabeth J. Cutting. 1930.

High Stakes and Hair Trigger; the Life of Jefferson Davis. Robert W. Winston. 1930.

Richard Harding Davis; his Day. Fairfax Downey. 1933.

Life of Stephen Decatur. (L. A. B.)

Decatur. Irvin Anthony. 1931.

Life of Timothy Dexter. S. L. Knapp. 1858.

Lord Timothy Dexter of Newburyport, Mass. J. P. Marquand. 1925.

The Man Charles Dickens; a Victorian Portrait. Edward C. Wagenknecht. 1930.

The Life and Letters of Emily Dickinson. Martha Dickinson Bianchi. 1924.

Emily Dickinson: The Human Background of Her Poetry. Josephine Pollitt. 1930.

The Life and Mind of Emily Dickinson. Genevieve Taggard. 1930.

Life and Times of John Dickinson. Charles J. Stillé. 1891.

Trails, Rails and War; the Life of General G. M. Dodge. Jacob R. Perkins. 1929.

Dostoevsky. Avraham Yarmolinsky. 1934.

Life of Stephen A. Douglas. Henry M. Flynt. 1860.

Life of Stephen A. Douglas. James W. Sheahan. 1860.

The Eve of Conflict: Stephen A. Douglas and the Needless War. George Fort Milton. 1934.

Lorenzo Dow, the Bearer of the Word. Charles S. Sellers. 1929.

Dowie, Anointed of the Lord. Arthur Newcomb. 1930.

Forgotten Frontiers; Dreiser and the Land of the Free. Dorothy Dudley. 1932.

Book of Daniel Drew; Glimpse of the Fisk-Gould-Tweed Régime from the Inside. Bouck White. 1910.

James B. Duke, Master Builder. John W. Jenkins. 1928.

Dumas, the Incredible Marquis. Herbert Gorman. 1929.

Life of Timothy Dwight. (L. A. B.)

Peggy Eaton, Democracy's Mistress. Queena Pollack. 1931.

Life of William Eaton. Cornelius Felton. (L. A. B.)

The Life of Mary Baker Eddy. Sybil W. O'Brien. 1908.

The Life of Mary Baker Eddy . . . Georgine Milmine. 1909.

Memoirs of Mary Baker Eddy. Adam Dickey. 1927.

Mrs. Eddy: The Biography of a Virginal Mind. E. F. Dakin. 1929.

Mary Baker Eddy; a Life-Size Portrait. Lyman P. Powell. 1930.

According to the Flesh; a Biography of Mary Baker Eddy. Fleta C. Springer. 1930.

Mary Baker Eddy; the Truth and the Tradition. E. S. Bates and J. V. Dittemore. 1932.

Life of Edward the Black Prince, 1330–1376. Henry Dwight Sedgwick. 1932.

The Life and Character of the late Mr. Jonathan Edwards, president of the College of New-Jersey . . . Samuel Hopkins. 1765.

Memoirs of the Rev. Jonathan Edwards. John Hawksley. 1815.

Life of Jonathan Edwards. Sereno E. Dwight. 1829.

Life of Jonathan Edwards. Samuel Miller. (L. A. B.)

Jonathan Edwards. A. V. G. Allen. 1889, 1890, 1896.

Jonathan Edwards . . . David Turpie. 1893.

Jonathan Edwards; the Fiery Puritan. Henry B. Parker. 1930.

Jonathan Edwards. Arthur C. McGiffert. 1932.

Life of Charles W. Eliot. E. H. Cotton. 1926.

Charles W. Eliot, President of Harvard University, 1869–1909. Henry James. 2 vols. 1930.

Life of John Eliot, Apostle to the Indians. (L. A. B.)

Queen Elizabeth. Katharine S. Anthony. 1929.

Tudor Wench (Queen Elizabeth). Elswyth Thane. 1932.

Life of William Ellery. Edward T. Channing. (L. A. B.)

Ralph Waldo Emerson: His Life, Writings, and Philosophy. George W. Cooke. 1881, 1900.

Ralph Waldo Emerson. W. Hague. 1884.

Ralph Waldo Emerson. Oliver W. Holmes. 1884. (A. M. L.)

A Memoir of Ralph Waldo Emerson. James E. Cabot. 2 vols. 1887.

Ralph Waldo Emerson. George E. Woodberry. 1907.

Emerson; a Study of the Poet as Seer. Robert M. Gay. 1928.

Emerson, the Wisest American. Phillips Russell. 1929.

Life of Emerson. Van Wyck Brooks. 1932.

Life and Times of John England, First Bishop of Charleston (1786–1842). Peter K. Guilday. 2 vols. 1927.

Erasmus; a Study of his Life, Ideals and Place in History. Preserved Smith. 1923.

Life, Character & Influence of Desiderius Erasmus of Rotterdam; Derived from a Study of his Works and Correspondence. John J. Mangan. 2 vols. 1927.

Edward Everett, Orator and Statesman. Paul R. Frothingham. 1925.

Famous American Authors. S. K. Bolton. 1887.

Famous American Statesmen. S. K. Bolton. 1888.

Famous Families of Massachusetts. Mary C. Crawford. 2 vols. 1930.

Famous Men of Science. S. K. Bolton. 1889.

Great Mouthpiece; a Life Story of William J. Fallon. Gene Fowler. 1931.

William Few, Lieutenant General of Georgia Militia in the Revolutionary Service. Charles C. Jones, Jr. 1883.

Eugene Field's Creative Years. Charles H. Dennis. 1924.

Life of Eugene Field; the Poet of Childhood. Slason Thompson. 1927.

Stephen J. Field, Craftsman of the Law. Carl B. Swisher. 1930.

History of Henry Fielding. Wilbur L. Cross. 3 vols. 1918.

A Life of James Fisk, Jr. . . . Marshall P. Stafford. 1871.

The Life and Times of Col. James Fisk, Jr. . . . . R. W. McAlpine. 1872.

The Life of James Fisk, Jr. . . . Willoughby Jones. 1872.

Jubilee Jim: The Life of Colonel James Fisk, Jr. R. H. Fuller. 1928.

Life of John Fitch. Charles Whittlesey. (L. A. B.)

"Ruby Robert," alias Robert Fitzsimmons. Robert H. Davis. 1926.

Timothy Flint, Pioneer, Missionary, Author, Editor, 1780–1840. John E. Kirkpatrick. 1911.

Forgotten Ladies; Nine Portraits from the American Family Album. Richardson L. Wright. 1928.

The Savage Maid; Ann, Fanny, and Maria Storer, Sophy Hopkey, Deborah Sampson, Maria Monk, Anne Royal, Sarah

Josepha Hale, Margaret and Katherine Fox, and Belle Boyd.

Bedford Forrest, the Confederacy's Greatest Cavalryman. Eric W. Sheppard. 1930.

Bedford Forrest and his Critter Company. Andrew N. Lytle. 1931.

Life of Edwin Forrest: The American Tragedian. William R. Alger. 1877.

The Fabulous Forrest. The Record of an American Actor. Montrose J. Moses. 1929.

Stephen Collins Foster; a Biography of America's Folk-Song Composer. Harold V. Milligan. 1920.

Stephen Foster, America's Troubadour. John F. Howard. 1934.

Four Famous New Yorkers. D. S. Alexander. 1923.

The political careers of Cleveland, Platt, Hill and Roosevelt.

Francis I. Francis Hackett. 1935.

Francis Joseph, Emperor of Austria—King of Hungary. Eugene Bagger. 1927.

Emperor Francis Joseph of Austria. Joseph Redlich. 1929.

The Life of Benjamin Franklin; with many Choice Anecdotes and Admirable Sayings of the Great Man . . . Mason Locke Weems. 1817.

Memoirs of the Life and Writings of Benjamin Franklin . . . Written by himself to a late period and continued to the time of his death, by his Grandson. William Temple Franklin. 1818.

The Works of Benjamin Franklin; with Notes and a Life of the Author. Jared Sparks (ed.). 10 vols. 1836–1840.

Vol. I contains the biography.

Benjamin Franklin. Samuel Hutchins. 1852.

Life of Dr. Franklin. J. N. Norton. 1861.

Life and Times of Benjamin Franklin. James Parton. 2 vols. 1864.

Benjamin Franklin. A Biography. G. C. Hills. 1865, 1884.

Life of Benjamin Franklin. O. L. Holley. 1866.

Life of Benjamin Franklin. John Bigelow. 3 vols. 1874.

Benjamin Franklin . . . John S. C. Abbott. 1876.

The Life of Benjamin Franklin. Jeremiah Chaplin. 1876.

Life and Times of Benjamin Franklin. Joseph Franklin and J. A. Headington. 1880.

Benjamin Franklin. E. M. Tomkinson. 1885.

Benjamin Franklin as a Man of Letters. John Bach McMaster. 1887. (A. M. L.)

Benjamin Franklin. John T. Morse, Jr. 1889. (A. S.)

Benjamin Franklin, Printer, Statesman, Philosopher, and Practical Citizen. Edward Robins. 1896.

The True Story of Benjamin Franklin. E. S. Brooks. 1898.

The True Benjamin Franklin. Sydney G. Fisher. 1899.

The Many-Sided Franklin. Paul L. Ford. 1899.

The Works of Benjamin Franklin . . . with a Life. A. H. Smith. 1905.

Benjamin Franklin, Self-Revealed. William Cabell Bruce. 2 vols. 1917.

Benjamin Franklin, the First Civilized American. Phillips Russell. 1926.

Frederick the Great. Margaret Goldsmith. 1929.

Frederick the Great, the Philosopher King. Victor Thaddeus. 1930.

Life, Explorations and Public Services of John Charles Frémont. Charles W. Upham. 1856.

Frémont and '49. Frederick S. Dellenbaugh. 1914.

Man Unafraid. The Story of John C. Fremont. Herbert Bashford and Harr Wagner. 1927.

Frémont; the West's Greatest Adventurer. Allan Nevins. 2 vols. 1928.

John Charles Frémont; an Explanation of his Career. Cardinal L. Goodwin. 1930.

Henry Clay Frick, the Man. George B. Harvey. 1928.

Life of Robert Fulton. James Renwick. (L. A. B.)

Life of Robert Fulton . . . J. F. Reigart. 1856.

Robert Fulton, his Life and its Results. R. H. Thurston. 1891.

Memoirs of Margaret Fuller Ossoli. R. W. Emerson, J. F. Clarke, and W. H. Channing. 2 vols. 1852.

Margaret Fuller: A Psychological Biography. Katharine Anthony. 1920.

Margaret Fuller. Margaret Bell. 1930.

Life of Albert Gallatin. Henry Adams. 1879.

A Gallery of Eccentrics . . . Morris Bishop. 1928.

    Elagabalus, Brusquet, Jan Baptista van Hebmont, Sir Thomas Urquhart, Sir Jeffry Hudson, François Timoleon de Choisy, Duke Mazarin, Capt. Bartholomew Roberts, Bampfylde-Moore Carew, Edward Wortley Montagu, Lorenzo da Ponte, and Edward Porson.

The Life of Gen. James A. Garfield. James M. Bundy. 1880.

Life of James A. Garfield. J. R. Gilmore. 1880.

Life of James A. Garfield, Late President of the United States ... William R. Balch. 1881.

Life, Speeches and Public Services of James A. Garfield. Russell H. Conwell. 1881.

Life and Work of James A. Garfield. J. C. Redpath. 1881.

Biography of James A. Garfield. B. J. Lossing. 1882.

Life and Letters of James Abram Garfield. Theodore C. Smith. 2 vols. 1925.

James A. Garfield, Party Chieftain. Robert G. Caldwell. 1931.

William Lloyd Garrison. Wendell P. Garrison and Francis J. Garrison. 4 vols. 1885–1889.

Life of Elbert H. Gary; the Story of Steel. Ida M. Tarbell. 1925.

Bet-a-Million Gates; the Story of a Plunger. Robert I. Warshaw. 1932.

Genghis Khan; the Emperor of All Men. Harold Lamb. 1927.

The Life of Elbridge Gerry... James T. Austin. 2 vols. 1828–1829.

Life of James, Cardinal Gibbons. Allen S. Will. 1911.

Life of Cardinal Gibbons, Archbishop of Baltimore. Allen S. Will. 2 vols. 1922.

Sir Humphrey Gilbert. Donald B. Chidsey. 1932.

John Gilley. Charles W. Eliot. 1904.

Life and Times of Stephen Girard, Mariner and Merchant. John B. McMaster. 2 vols. 1918.

Simon Gerty, the White Savage. Thomas A. Boyd. 1928.

Goethe. Thomas Calvin. 1917.

Goldoni: a Biography. Hobart C. Chatfield-Taylor. 1913.

Oliver Goldsmith: a Biography. Washington Irving. 1849.

William Crawford Gorgas, his Life and Work. Marie D. Gorgas and Burton J. Hendrick. 1924.

Life of Samuel Gorton. John M. Mackie. (L. A. B.)

Life of Jay Gould, How He Made His Millions. Murat Halstead and J. F. Beale, Jr.

The Life and Achievements of Jay Gould, the Wizard of Wall Street . . . Henry D. Northrop. 1892.

The Wizard of Wall Street and His Wealth; or, The Life and Deeds of Jay Gould. Trumbull White. 1892.

Jay Gould; the Story of a Fortune. Robert I. Warshaw. 1928.

Life and Services of U. S. Grant, as a Soldier. 1864.

Life of U. S. Grant. F. W. H. Stanfield. 1865.

Grant and his Campaigns: a Military Biography. H. Coppée. 1866.

Campaign Lives of U. S. Grant and S. Colfax. J. S. Brisbin. 1868.

Grant and Colfax: their Lives and Services. L. P. Brockett. 1868.

Life and Services of U. S. Grant. H. Coppée. 1868.

Life of U. S. Grant. W. A. Crafts. 1868.

Life of U. S. Grant. H. C. Deming. 1868.

Life of Ulysses S. Grant. Charles A. Dana and J. H. Wilson. 1868.

Life, Campaigns and Battles of Gen. Ulysses S. Grant. B. J. Lossing. 1868.

A Popular and Authentic Life of U. S. Grant. E. D. Mansfield. 1868.

A Personal History of Ulysses S. Grant . . . A. D. Richardson. 1868.

Life and Services of General U. S. Grant, Conqueror of the Rebellion and Eighteenth President of the United States. 1868.

Original and Authentic Record of the Life and Deeds of General Ulysses S. Grant. Frank A. Burr. 1885.

The Life of Gen. U. S. Grant . . . L. T. Remlap (ed.). 1885.

Ulysses S. Grant . . . W. C. Church. 1897.

Ulysses S. Grant: His Life and Character. Hamlin Garland. 1898.

Life and Military Services of Gen. U. S. Grant. W. H. Van Orden. 1899.

Ulysses S. Grant. Owen Wister. 1900.

Ulysses S. Grant. William Allen. 1901.

True Ulysses S. Grant. Charles King. 1914.

Ulysses S. Grant. Franklin S. Edmonds. 1915. (A. C. B.)

Ulysses S. Grant. Louis A. Coolidge. 2 vols. 1917. (A. S. 2d Ser.)

Meet General Grant. W. E. Woodward. 1928.

Rise of U. S. Grant. Arthur L. Conger. 1931.

The Life of Horace Greeley . . . James Parton. 1855, 1872.

The Life of Horace Greeley . . . L. D. Ingersoll. 1873.

Horace Greeley, Founder of the New York Tribune. Don C. Seitz. 1926.

Hetty Green, a Woman Who Loved Money. Boyden Sparks and Samuel T. Moore. 1930.

Memoirs of the Life and Campaigns of the Hon. Nathaniel Greene, Major General in the Army of the United States . . . Charles Caldwell. 1819.

Sketches of the Life and Correspondence of Nathaniel Greene. William Johnson. 2 vols. 1822.

Life of Nathaniel Greene. George W. Greene. (L. A. B.)

Life of Nathaniel Greene. William G. Simms. 1849.

Life of Nathaniel Greene, Major-General in the Army of the Revolution. George W. Greene. 3 vols. 1867–1868.

Life of William Guthrie. William Dunlap. 1796.

Lady of Godey's: Sarah Josepha Hale. Ruth Finley. 1931.

God's Pocket. The Story of Captain Samuel Hadlock . . . Rachel Field. 1934.

Dr. Lyman Hall, Governor of Georgia in 1783. Charles C. Jones, Jr. 1891.

G. Stanley Hall; a Biography of a Mind. Lorine Pruette. 1926.

The Life and Letters of Fitz-Greene Halleck. James G. Wilson. 1869.

Fitz-Greene Halleck; an Early Knickerbocker Wit and Poet. Nelson F. Adkins. 1930.

The Life of Alexander Hamilton. J. C. Hamilton. 2 vols. 1834.

Life and Times of Alexander Hamilton. S. M. Smucker. 1856.

The Life of Alexander Hamilton. John T. Morse, Jr. 1876.

Life and Epoch of Alexander Hamilton. George Shea. 1881.

Alexander Hamilton. Henry Cabot Lodge. 1882, 1898. (A. S.)

Alexander Hamilton, the Constructive Statesman. L. H. Bontell. 1890.

Alexander Hamilton. William G. Sumner. 1891.

Alexander Hamilton, Nevis–Weehawken. J. E. Graybill. 1898.

Alexander Hamilton. Charles A. Cognant. 1901.

The Intimate Life of Alexander Hamilton. Allan M. Hamilton. 1910.

The Greatest American, Alexander Hamilton. Arthur H. Vandenburg. 1921.

Alexander Hamilton. Henry J. Ford. 1924.

Alexander Hamilton, First American Business Man. Robert I. Warshaw. 1931.

John Hancock, the Picturesque Patriot. Lorenzo Sears. 1912.

Marcus Alonzo Hanna; his Life and Work. Herbert D. Croly. 1912.

Hanna. Thomas Beer. 1929.

John Hanson, Our First President. S. S. Smith. 1932.

Thomas Hardy, Poet and Novelist. Benjamin Chew. 1928.

Edward H. Harriman. John Muir. 1912.

E. H. Harriman; a Biography. G. E. Kennan. 2 vols. 1922.

Life and Letters of Joel Chandler Harris. Julia E. Harris. 1918.

Life of Gen. Benjamin Harrison. Lew Wallace. 1888.

The Life of Major-General William Henry Harrison . . . 1840.

The Life of W. H. Harrison; the People's Candidate for the Presidency. 1840.

The Life of Bret Harte. H. C. Merwin. 1911.

Bret Harte: Argonaut and Exile. George R. Stewart. 1931.

Nathaniel Hawthorne. Henry James, Jr. 1879. (E. M. L.)

Nathaniel Hawthorne; a Memoir. R. H. Stoddard. 1879.

Life of Nathaniel Hawthorne. Moncure D. Conway. 1890.

Nathaniel Hawthorne and His Wife. Julian Hawthorne. 2 vols. 1884, 1891.

Nathaniel Hawthorne. George E. Woodberry. 1902.

Life and Genius of Nathaniel Hawthorne. F. P. Stearns. 1906.

Hawthorne, a Study in Solitude. Herbert Gorman. 1927.

The Rebellious Puritan; Portrait of Mr. Hawthorne. Lloyd R. Morris. 1927.

Hawthorne. Newton Arvin. 1929.

The Life and Letters of John Hay. William R. Thayer. 2 vols. 1915. (A. S. 2d Ser.) 1 vol. ed. 1929.

John Hay, from Poetry to Politics. Tyler Dennett. 1933.

Gov. Rutherford B. Hayes. Life and Public Services. Russell H. Conwell. 1876.

The Life, Public Services and Select Speeches of Rutherford B. Hayes. J. Q. Howard. 1876.

Sketch of the Life and Character of Rutherford B. Hayes. William D. Howells. 1876.

Rutherford B. Hayes, Statesman of Reunion. Hamilton J. Eckenrode and Pocahontas W. Wight. 1930.

Life and Letters of Lafcadio Hearn. Elizabeth Bisland. 2 vols. 1906.

W. R. Hearst; an American Phenomenon. John K. Winkler. 1928.

That Man Heine; a Biography. Lewis Browne and Elsa Weihl. 1927.

Henry of Navarre. Henry Dwight Sedgwick. 1930.

Henry VIII. Francis Hackett. 1929.

Caliph of Bagdad; Being Arabian Night Flashes of the Life, Letters and Work of O. Henry. Robert H. Davis and Arthur B. Maurice. 1931.

Sketches of the Life and Character of Patrick Henry. William Wirt. 1817.

Life of Patrick Henry. Alexander H. Everett. (L. A. B.)

Patrick Henry. Moses Coit Tyler. 1887. (A. S.)

Patrick Henry: Life, Correspondence and Speeches. William W. Henry. 3 vols. 1891.

The True Patrick Henry. George Morgan. 1907.

Life of Francis Higginson. Thomas W. Higginson. 1891.

Life of James J. Hill. Joseph G. Pyle. 2 vols. 1917.

Life of Oliver Wendell Holmes. Emma E. Brown. 1884.

Life and Letters of Oliver Wendell Holmes. John T. Morse, Jr. 2 vols. 1896.

Life of Francis Hopkinson. George R. Hastings. 1928.

Life of Isaac T. Hopper. Lydia M. Child. 1853.

Life of Samuel Houston of Texas. 2 vols. 1884.

Sam Houston, Colossus in Buckskin. George Creel. 1928.

The Raven; a Biography of Sam Houston. Marquis James. 1929.

Julia Ward Howe. Laura E. Richards and Maud H. Elliott. 2 vols. 1915.

Sir Billy Howe. Bellamy Partridge. 1932.

Varina Howell, Wife of Jefferson Davis. E. O. Rowland. 2 vols. 1927.

Life of Henry Hudson. Henry R. Cleveland. (L. A. B.)

Adventures of Henry Hudson. Francis L. Hawkes. 1852.

John Huss: his Life, Teachings, and Death, after Five Hundred Years. David S. Schaff. 1915.

Life of Anne Hutchinson. George E. Ellis. (L. A. B.)

An American Jezebel; the Life of Anne Hutchinson. Helen Augur. 1930.

Anne Hutchinson; a Biography. Edith Curtis. 1930.

Unafraid; a Life of Anne Hutchinson. Winifred K. Rugg. 1930.

Ibsen, the Master Builder. Adolph E. Zucker. 1929.

Biography and History of the Indians of North America from its first Discovery to the Present Time . . . Samuel G. Drake. 1837.

Colonel Bob Ingersoll; a Biographical Narrative of the Great American Orator and Agnostic. Cameron Rogers. 1927.

Life and Letters of Washington Irving. Pierre M. Irving (ed.). 4 vols. 1862.

Memoir of Washington Irving. Charles Adams. 1870.

Washington Irving. D. J. Hill. 1879.

Washington Irving. Charles Dudley Warner. 1881. (A. M. L.)

The Life of Washington Irving. R. H. Stoddard. 1883.

Washington Irving. H. W. Boynton. 1901.

Washington Irving, Esquire, Ambassador at Large from the New World to the Old. George S. Hellman. 1925.

Isabella of Spain; the Last Crusader. W. T. Walsh. 1930.

Chronicles of Andrew Jackson, and Biographical Sketch of his Life. Isaac Hillyard. 1822.

Life of Andrew Jackson. John H. Eaton. 1824.

Biography of Andrew Jackson. Philo Goodwin. 1832.

Life of Andrew Jackson. Amos Kendall. 1843.

Life of Andrew Jackson. Alexander Walker. 1857.

Life of Andrew Jackson. James Parton. 3 vols. 1860.

Life and Public Services of General Andrew Jackson . . . John S. Jenkins. 1880.

Andrew Jackson and Martin Van Buren. W. O. Stoddard. 1887.

General Andrew Jackson; Hero of New Orleans and Seventh President of the United States. Oliver Dyer. 1891.

Andrew Jackson As a Public Man. William G. Sumner. 1882, 1897. (A. S.)

History of Andrew Jackson, Pioneer, Patriot, Soldier, Politician, President. A. C. Buell. 2 vols. 1904.

Life and Times of Andrew Jackson. Arthur S. Colyer. 2 vols. 1904.

True Andrew Jackson. Cyrus T. Brady. 1906.

When Men Grew Tall; or, the Story of Andrew Jackson. Alfred H. Lewis. 1907.

Life of Andrew Jackson. John S. Bassett. 2 vols. 1911. 1 vol. 1928.

Life and Times of Andrew Jackson. Thomas E. Watson. 1912.

Andrew Jackson: an Epic in Homespun. G. W. Johnson. 1927.

Andrew Jackson, the Gentle Savage. David Karsner. 1929.

Andrew Jackson, Border Captain. Marquis James. 1933.

The Life and Military Career of Stonewall Jackson. Markinfield Addy. 1863.

The Life of Stonewall Jackson. John Esten Cooke. 1863.

Life of T. J. (Stonewall) Jackson. Ex-Cadet. 1864.

Stonewall Jackson: A Military Biography. John Esten Cooke. 1866.

The Life and Campaigns of Lieut.-Gen. Thomas J. (Stonewall) Jackson. R. L. Dabney. 1866.

Story of Stonewall Jackson: the Career of Thomas Jonathan (Stonewall) Jackson. W. C. Chase. 1903.

Stonewall Jackson, the Good Soldier. Allen Tate. 1928.

Pilgrimage of Henry James. Van Wyck Brooks. 1925.

Henry James, Man and Author. Pelham Edgar. 1927.

Three Jameses; a Family of Minds. C. Hartley Grattan. 1932.

Rise and Fall of Jesse James. Robertus Love. 1926.

Life of John Jay. William Jay. 2 vols. 1833.

John Jay. George Pellew. 1890. (A. S.)

Life of Thomas Jefferson, with Letters. B. L. Rayner. 1834.

The Life of Thomas Jefferson. G. Tucker. 1837.

Life of Thomas Jefferson. Henry S. Randall. 1858.

Private Life of Thomas Jefferson. H. W. Peirson. 1862.

The Life of Thomas Jefferson. James Parton. 1874.

Sketch of the Life, Character, and Public Service of Thomas Jefferson. T. J. Davis. 1876.

Thomas Jefferson. John T. Morse, Jr. 1883, 1898. (A. S.)

Thomas Jefferson. James Schouler. 1893.

The True Thomas Jefferson. William E. Curtis. 1901.

Thomas Jefferson. David S. Muzzey. 1918.

Jefferson. Albert Jay Nock. 1926.

Thomas Jefferson, the Apostle of Americanism. Gilbert Chinard. 1929.

Sarah Orne Jewett. Francis O. Matthiessen. 1929.

Sword of God: Jeanne d'Arc. S. Guy Endore. 1931.

Joan of Arc, Maid of France. Albert Bigelow Paine. 2 vols. 1925.

Life, Speeches and Services of Andrew Johnson. 1865.

Life and Speeches of Andrew Johnson. Frank Moore. 1865.

Life and Speeches of Andrew Johnson . . . Lillian Foster. 1866.

Life of Andrew Johnson. John Savage. 1866.

Andrew Johnson, Plebeian and Patriot. Robert W. Winston. 1928.

Andrew Johnson; a Study in Courage. Lloyd P. Stryker. 1929.

Age of Hate; Andrew Johnson and the Radicals. George Fort Newton. 1930.

Life of Samuel Johnson. Thomas B. Chandler. 1805.

Dr. Johnson & Mr. Boswell. Harry Saltpeter. 1929.

The Life and Times of Sir William Johnson, Bart. William L. Stone. 2 vols. 1865.

Johnson of the Mohawks; a Biography of Sir William Johnson, Irish Immigrant, Mohawk War Chief, American Soldier, Empire Builder. Arthur Pound and R. E. Day. 1930.

Life and Correspondence of John Paul Jones. Robert Sands. 1830.

Life of Paul Jones. William G. Simms. 1845.

Life of Paul Jones. Alexander S. Mackenzie. 1846.

Life and Character of John Paul Jones. J. H. Sherburne. 1851.

Life and Exploits of Paul Jones. O. J. Victor. 1861.

Paul Jones. Molly E. Seawell. 1892.

Commodore Paul Jones. Cyrus T. Brady. 1900.

Life of Paul Jones. James Otis. 1900.

Paul Jones. Hutchins Hapgood. 1901.

Story of Paul Jones. Alfred H. Lewis. 1906.

Paul Jones, Founder of the American Navy. A. C. Buell. 2 vols. 1900.

Life and Letters of John Paul Jones. Anna F. DeKoven. 2 vols. 1913.

John Paul Jones, Man of Action. Phillips Russell. 1927.

O Rare Ben Jonson. Byron Steel. 1927.

Josephine, Empress of the French. F. A. Ober. 1895.

James Joyce, his First Forty Years. Herbert Gorman. 1924.

John Keats. Amy Lowell. 2 vols. 1925. 1 vol. 1929.

Fanny Kemble. Dorothie Bobbé. 1931.

The Life of John Pendleton Kennedy. H. T. Tuckerman. 1871.

Simon Kenton, his Life and Period, 1755–1836. Edna Kenton. 1930.

Thomas Killigrew; Cavalier Dramatist, 1612–83. Alfred Bennett Harbage. 1930.

Kings of Fortune; or, Triumph of Self-Made Men. Walter R. Haughton (ed.). 1885.

Life of Samuel Kirkland. Samuel K. Lathrop. (L. A. B.)

Gallant Ladies. Cameron Rogers. 1928.
  Mata Hari, Mary Read and Anne Banny, Calamity Jane, Adrienne Lecouvreur, and Lola Montez.

Life of General Lafayette. H. D. Holstein. 1824.

Life of Lafayette. Robert Waln. 1827.

Life of General Lafayette. P. C. Headley. 1851.

Lafayette. John Bigelow. 1882.

Life of Lafayette . . . Lydia H. Farmer. 1888.

Life of General Lafayette. Bayard Tuckerman. 2 vols. 1889.

Lafayette. Henry Dwight Sedgwick. 1928.

Lafayette. Brand Whitlock. 2 vols. 1929.

Lafitte, the Pirate. Lyle Saxon. 1930.

Sidney Lanier. Edwin Mims. 1905. (A. M. L.)

Sidney Lanier; a Biographical and Critical Study. Aubrey H. Starke. 1933.

Life of Robert Cavalier De La Salle. Jared Sparks. (L. A. B.)

Laud, Storm Center of Stuart England. Robert P. T. Coffin. 1930.

Biography of James Lawrence, late Captain in the Navy of the United States . . . Washington Irving. 1813.

Henry Charles Lea. Edward S. Bradley. 1931.

Memoirs of the Life and Travels of John Ledyard. Jared Sparks. 1828. Reprinted in L. A. B. as *Life of John Ledyard.*

Life of Arthur Lee. R. H. Lee. 2 vols. 1829.

Memoirs of the Life of the late Charles Lee, Esq. . . . Second in Command in the service of the United States of America during the Revolution . . . Edward Langworthy. 1792, 1813.

Life of Charles Lee. Jared Sparks. (L. A. B.)

Light-Horse Harry Lee. Thomas A. Boyd. 1931.

Life and Campaigns of Gen. Robert E. Lee. James D. McCabe, Jr. 1867.

Lee and his Lieutenants; comprising the Early Life, Public Services and Campaigns of General Robert E. Lee and His Companions in Arms . . . Edward A. Pollard. 1867.

A Life of Gen. Robert E. Lee. John Esten Cooke. 1871.

Robert E. Lee. John Esten Cooke. 1893.

Memoirs of Robert E. Lee . . . A. L. Lang and M. J. Wright. 1887.

General Lee. Fitzhugh Lee. 1895.

Robert E. Lee: Man and Soldier. Thomas Nelson Page. 1911.

Lee, the American. Gamaliel Bradford. 1912.

Marse Robert, Knight of the Confederacy. J. C. Young. 1930.

Lee of Virginia; a Biography. William E. Brooks. 1932.

R. E. Lee. A Biography. Douglas S. Freeman. 4 vol. 1934–1935.

Administration of Jacob Leisler. Charles F. Hoffman. (L. A. B.)

Meriwether Lewis, of Lewis and Clark. Charles M. Wilson. 1934.

Life of Abraham Lincoln. J. L. Scripps. 1860.

The Life of Abraham Lincoln . . . J. Q. Howard. 1860.

Life and Speeches of Abraham Lincoln and Hannibal Hamlin. W. D. Howells and J. L. Hayes. 1860.

The Life and Public Services of Abraham Lincoln . . . D. W. Bartlett. 1860.

The Private and Public Life of Abraham Lincoln. O. J. Victor. 1864.

The Martyr President. 1865.

Life and Martyrdom of Abraham Lincoln. 1865.

Life of Abraham Lincoln . . . Joseph H. Barrett. 1865.

Life and Times of A. Lincoln. L. P. Brockett. 1865.

Abraham Lincoln; his Life and Public Services. Phoebe Hanaford. 1865.

Life and Public Services of Abraham Lincoln . . . Henry J. Raymond. 1865.

The Life of Abraham Lincoln. J. G. Holland. 1866.

The History of Abraham Lincoln and the Overthrow of Slavery. I. N. Arnold. 1866.

Real Life of A. Lincoln. G. A. Townsend. 1867.

Sketch of the Life of Abraham Lincoln. I. N. Arnold. 1869.

Life of Abraham Lincoln: from his Birth to his Inauguration as President. Ward Hill Lamon. 1872.

Abraham Lincoln and the Abolition of Slavery in the United States. Charles Godfrey Leland. 1879.

Abraham Lincoln. John G. Nicolay. 1882.

Life of Abraham Lincoln. I. N. Arnold. 1885.

Abraham Lincoln. Ernest Foster. 1885.

Abraham Lincoln: True Story of a Great Life. W. O. Stoddard. 1885.

The History of the Life, Administration, and Times of Abraham Lincoln. J. R. Irelan. 2 vols. 1888.

Life of Abraham Lincoln. William H. Herndon and Jesse W. Weik. 3 vols. 1889. 2 vols. 1892, 1928. 1 vol. 1930.

Abraham Lincoln: A History. John G. Nicolay and John Hay. 10 vols. 1890.

Abraham Lincoln, the Liberator. C. W. French. 1891.

Abraham Lincoln. A Biographical Essay. Carl Schurz. 1892.

Abraham Lincoln. C. C. Lincoln. 1893.

Abraham Lincoln. John T. Morse, Jr. 2 vols. 1893. (A. S.)

Abraham Lincoln and the Downfall of American Slavery. Noah Brooks. 1894.

Abraham Lincoln, the First American. D. D. Thompson. 1894.

Truth is Stranger than Fiction; the True Genesis of a Wonderful Man. J. H. Cathey. 1899. As: *The Genius of Lincoln.* 1904.

Abraham Lincoln, the Man of the People. Norman Hapgood. 1899.

Life of Abraham Lincoln. Ida M. Tarbell. 2 vols. 1900, 1917, 1928.

Abraham Lincoln, his Youth and Early Manhood. With a Brief Account of his Later Life. Noah Brooks. 1901.

The Real Lincoln. C. L. C. Minor. 1901.

Abraham Lincoln; a Short Study. I. N. Phillips. 1901.

Life of Abraham Lincoln. Joseph H. Barrett. 1902.

The Story of Abraham Lincoln. Eleanor Gridley. 1902.

The True Abraham Lincoln. William E. Curtis. 1903.

Abraham Lincoln and his Presidency. J. H. Barrett. 1904.

Life of Abraham Lincoln. H. B. Binns. 1908.

Abraham Lincoln. Brand Whitlock. 1909.

Abraham Lincoln. An Interpretation in Biography. Denton J. Snider. 1909.

Lincoln. A. M. Bullock. 1913.

Lincoln the Politician. T. A. Levy. 1918.

The Real Lincoln; a Portrait. Jesse W. Weik. 1922.

Lincoln; an Account of his Personal Life, Especially its Springs of Action as Revealed and Deepened by the Ordeal of War. Nathaniel W. Stephenson. 1922.

Life of Abraham Lincoln. William E. Barton. 2 vols. 1925.

Abraham Lincoln: The Prairie Years. Carl Sandburg. 2 vols. 1926. 1 vol. 1927. Also 1 vol. abridged.

Abraham Lincoln, 1809–1858. Albert J. Beveridge. 2 vols. 1928.

Abraham Lincoln; the Politician and the Man. Raymond Holden. 1929.

Abraham Lincoln; Profusely Illustrated with Contemporary Cartoons, Portraits and Scenes. Albert Shaw. 2 vols. 1930.

Lincoln, the Man. Edgar Lee Masters. 1931.

Lincoln and His Cabinet. C. E. Macartney. 1931.

Abraham Lincoln; a New Portrait. Emanuel Hertz. 2 vols. 1931.

Lincoln, the Politician. Don C. Seitz. 1931.

Set My People Free; a Negro's Life of Lincoln. William E. Lilly. 1932.

President Lincoln. William E. Barton. 2 vols. 1933.

Lincoln. A Psycho-Biography. L. Pierce Clark. 1933.

Life of Benjamin Lincoln. Francis Bowen. (L. A. B.)

Mary, Wife of Lincoln. Katherine Helm. 1928.

Mary Todd Lincoln; an Appreciation of the Wife of Abraham Lincoln. Honoré Willsie Morrow. 1928.

Mrs. Abraham Lincoln; a Study of her Personality and her Influence on Lincoln. William A. Evans. 1932.

Mary Lincoln, Wife and Widow. Carl Sandburg and Paul Angle. 1932.

Jenny Lind. Edward C. Wagenknecht. 1931.

Lives of Distinguished Naval Officers. James Fenimore Cooper. 2 vols. 1846.

Lives of Great English Writers; from Chaucer to Browning. Walter S. Hinchman and Francis B. Gummere. 1908.

Lives and Times; Four Informal American Biographies. Meade Minnigerode. 1925.
> Stephen Jumel, William Eaton, Theodosia Burr, and Edmund C. Genet.

The Life of George Cabot Lodge. Henry Adams. 1911.

Lonely Americans. Rollo W. Brown. 1929.
> Charles W. Eliot, James McNeill Whistler, Edward Macdowell, George Bellows, Charles Eliot Norton, Raphael Pumpelly, Emily Dickinson, and Abraham Lincoln.

Life of Henry Wadsworth Longfellow, with Extracts from his Journals and Correspondence. Samuel Longfellow. 2 vols. 1886. A third vol. (1888) contains further extracts. 3 vols. 1891.

Henry Wadsworth Longfellow. Thomas W. Higginson. 1902. (A. M. L.)

A Victorian American, Henry W. Longfellow. Herbert Gorman. 1926.

Lope de Vega, Monster of Nature. Angel Flores. 1930.

The Son of Marie Antoinette (Louis XVII); *a Biography.* Meade Minnigerode. 1934.

Life of James Russell Lowell. Emma E. Brown. 1887.

James Russell Lowell. Edward Everett Hale. 1899.

James Russell Lowell: A Biography. H. E. Scudder. 1901.

James Russell Lowell: His Life and Work. Ferris Greenslet. 1905. (A. M. L.)

Ignatius Loyola; an Attempt at an Impartial Biography. Henry Dwight Sedgwick. 1923.

Ignatius Loyola; the Founder of the Jesuits. Paul Van Dyke. 1926.

Man of the Renaissance. Four Lawgivers; Savonarola, Machiavelli, Castiglione, Aretino. Ralph Roeder. 1933.

Martin Luther: the Man and his Work. A. C. McGiffert. 1911.

Life and Letters of Martin Luther. Preserved Smith. 1911.

Martin Luther. Elsie Singmaster. 1917.

Epoch; the Life of Steele Mackaye, Genius of the Theatre in Relation to his Times & Contemporaries. Percy Mackaye. 2 vols. 1927.

History of the Life and Times of James Madison. William C. Rivers. 3 vols. 1859–1868.

James Madison. Sydney H. Gay. 1884. (A. S.)

Ferdinand Magellan. F. A. Ober. 1906.

Magnalia Christi Americana; Or the Ecclesiastical History of New England, from its First Planting in the Year 1720 (sic) *until the Year of our Lord, 1698.* Cotton Mather. London, 1702. Reissued in 2 vols. 1820, 1853.

　　Contains sixty sketches, of varying length, of the principal clergymen and public figures of New England.

Mahomet and His Successors. Washington Irving. 2 vols. 1849–1850.

Sir Thomas Malory, his Turbulent Career; a Biography. Edward Hicks. 1928.

Mère Marie of the Ursulines; a Study in Adventure. Agnes Repplier. 1931.

Marie Antoinette. Katharine Anthony. 1933.

Life of General Francis Marion. Mason Locke Weems and General Horry. 1805.

Life of Francis Marion. William G. Simms. 1844.

Marlborough: The Portrait of a Conqueror. Donald B. Chidsey. 1929.

Julia Marlowe, her Life and Art. Charles E. Russell. 1926.

Life of Father Marquette. Jared Sparks. (L. A. B.)

Père Marquette. Agnes Repplier. 1929.

John Marshall. Allan B. Magruder. 1885, 1898. (A. S.)

Life of John Marshall. Albert J. Beveridge. 4 vols. 1916–1919. 2 vols. 1929.

Life of George Mason. Kate Mason Rowland. 2 vols. 1892.

Life of John Mason. George E. Ellis. (L. A. B.)

The Life of the Very Reverend and Learned Cotton Mather, D. D. and F. R. S. Samuel Mather. 1729.

The Mathers (Cotton and Increase) Weighed in the Balance and Found Not Wanting. D. A. Goddard. 1870.

Cotton Mather: Puritan Priest. Barrett Wendell. 1891.

Life and Times of Cotton Mather; or, a Boston Minister of Two Centuries Ago, 1663–1728. A. P. Marvin. 1892.

Cotton Mather: Keeper of the Puritan Conscience. Ralph and Louise Boas. 1928.

Memoirs of the Life of . . . Increase Mather. E. Calamy. 1725.

Increase Mather, the Foremost American Puritan. Kenneth B. Murdock. 1925.

The Life and death of that reverend man of God, Mr. Richard Mather, Teacher of the Church in Dorchester in New-England. 1670. Reissued as *Life and Death of Mr. Richard Mather.* 1850.

Guy de Maupassant; a Biographical Study. Ernest A. Boyd. 1926.

Catherine de Médici. Paul Van Dyke. 2 vols. 1922.

Lorenzo the Magnificent (Medici). David G. Loth. 1929.

Herman Melville: Mariner and Mystic. Raymond D. Weaver. 1921.

Herman Melville. Lewis Mumford. 1928.

Men of Art. Thomas Craven. 1931.

Giotto, Leonardo Da Vinci, Michael Angelo, Titian, Rubens,

Rembrandt, Greco, Velasquez, Goya, Hogarth, Blake, Turner, Ryder, Delacroix, Daumier, and Cézanne.

Men Against Death. Paul De Kruif. 1932.

Semmelivers, Banting, Minot, Spenser, Finsen, and Rollier.

Sketches of Men of Progress. James Parton. 1870.

Men of Our Times. Harriet Beecher Stowe. 1868.

Life of Cardinal Mercier. John A. Gade. 1934.

Microbe Hunters. Paul De Kruif. 1926.

Lieuwenhoek, Spallanzani, Pasteur, Koch, Roux, Bering, Metchnikoff, Theobald Smith, David Bruce, Roland Ross, Battista Grasse, Walter Reed, and Paul Ehrlich.

Life of Donald G. Mitchell. (Ik Marvel). Waldo H. Dunn. 1922.

John Mitchell, Miner; Labor's Bargain with the Gilded Age. Elsie Gluck. 1929.

Weir Mitchell: His Life and Letters. Anna Robeson Burr. 1929.

A Modern Plutarch. John Cournos. 1928.

Mark Twain and Anatole France; Paul Gauguin and Henry Thoreau; Herman Melville, Arthur Rimbaud, and Charles M. Doughty; Ferdinand La Salle, Charles Stewart Parnell, and Honoré de Balzac; John Brown and Giuseppe Garibaldi; Henry Frederic Amiel and Henry Adams; George Sand and George Eliot; Robert E. Lee and Simon Bolivar; Cecil Rhodes and Ferdinand de Lesseps.

Mohammed. Roy F. Dibble. 1926.

Molière; his Life and his Works. Brander Matthews. 1910.

James Monroe. Daniel C. Gilman. 1883, 1899. (A. S.)

Life of James Monroe. George Morgan. 1921.

Life of Richard Montgomery. John Armstrong. (L. A. B.)

The Life of Dwight Lyman Moody. W. R. Moody. 1900.

D. L. Moody. William R. Moody. 1930.

D. L. Moody: Worker in Souls. Gamaliel Bradford. 1927.

The Confederate Raider. A Life of John Hunt Morgan. Howard Swiggett. 1934.

Life Story of J. Pierpont Morgan. Carl Hovey. 1912.

Morgan, the Magnificent; the Life of J. Pierpont Morgan (1837–1913). John K. Winkler. 1930.

House of Morgan; a Social Biography of the Masters of Money. Lewis Corey. 1930.

Imperial Brother; the Life of the Duc De Morny. Maristan Chapman. 1931.

Life of Gouverneur Morris; with Selections from his Correspondence and Miscellaneous Papers. Jared Sparks. 3 vols. 1832.

Gouverneur Morris. Theodore Roosevelt. 1888. (A. S.)

Samuel F. B. Morse; his Letters and Journals. Edward L. Morse. 2 vols. 1914.

Levi Parsons Morton. Robert M. McElroy. 1930.

Memoir of John Lothrop Motley. Oliver Wendell Holmes. 1879.

Mozart. Marcia Davenport. 1932.

John Muir of Wall Street. O. M. Fuller. 1927.

Muldoon, the Solid Man of Sport. Edward Van Every. 1929.

Alfred de Musset, 1810–1857; a Biography. Henry D. Sedgwick. 1931.

General George Brinton McClellan. William S. Myers. 1934.

Cyrus Hall McCormick; Seed Time, 1809–1856. William T. Hutchinson. 1930.

Life and Times of Charles Follen McKim. Charles Moore. 1929.

One of the People; Life and Speeches of William McKinley; with a brief Sketch of Garret A. Hobart. Bryan Andrews. 1896.

Life of William McKinley, Soldier, Lawyer, Statesman. Robert P. Porter. 1896.

Life and Distinguished Services of William McKinley . . . with a Sketch of the Life of Garret Hobart. Murat Halstead. 1896

The White Headed Eagle. John McLoughlin, Builder of an Empire. Richard G. Montgomery. 1934.

Life of Napoleon Bonaparte. William M. Sloane. 4 vols. 1896–1897.

Short Life of Napoleon Bonaparte. Ida M. Tarbell. 1896.

Napoleon. An Intimate Biography. Walter Geer. 1921.

Napoleon and his Family. The Story of a Corsican Clan. Walter Geer. 1927.

Napoleon and Josephine; the Rise of the Empire. Walter Geer. 1925.

Napoleon and Marie-Louise; the Fall of the Empire. Walter Geer. 1925.

Napoleon; a Sketch of his Life, Character, Struggles and Achievements. Thomas K. Watson. 1903.

Th. Nast, His Period and His Pictures. Albert Bigelow Paine. 1904.

Carrie Nation. Herbert Asbury. 1929.

A Naturalist of Souls. Gamaliel Bradford. 1917, 1926.

Psychography, Walter Pater, The Poetry of Donne, A Pessimist Poet (Giacoma Leopardi), Anthony Trollope, An Odd Sort of Popular Book (Anatomy of Melancholy), Alexander Dumas, A French Lamb (Jules Lemaître), A Great English Portrait Painter (Edward Hyde, Earl of Clarendon), A Gentleman of Athens (Xenophon), Letters of a Roman Gentleman (Pliny), Ovid Among the Goths, and the Portrait of a Saint (Francis de Sales).

The Life of Nelson, the Embodiment of the Sea Power of Great Britain. Alfred T. Mahan. 2 vols. 1897.

John Henry Newman; Anglican Minister, Catholic Priest, Roman Cardinal. J. Elliot Ross. 1933.

Isaac Newton; a Biography. Louis T. More. 1934.

Frank Norris; a Biography. Franklin Walker. 1932.

Life of General Oglethorpe. W. B. O. Peabody. (L. A. B.)

The Life of Sir William Osler. Harvey Cushing. 2 vols. 1925.

The Great Physician. A Short Life of Sir William Osler. Edith G. Reid.

Life of James Otis. Francis Bowen. (L. A. B.)

Life and Letters of Walter Hines Page. Burton J. Hendrick. 3 vols. 1925–1926.

Training of an American; the Earlier Life and Letters of Walter Hines Page. Burton J. Hendrick. 1928.

Life of Thomas Paine . . . Moncure D. Conway. 2 vols. 1892.

Life of Thomas Paine. William Van der Weyde. 1925.

Thomas Paine; Prophet and Martyr of Democracy. Mary Agnes Best. 1927.

Life of William Palfrey. John G. Palfrey. (L. A. B.)

Life of Alice Freeman Palmer. George H. Palmer. 1908.

Theodore Parker: A Biography. O. B. Frothingham. 1874.

Francis Parkman. Henry Dwight Sedgwick. 1904. (A. M. L.)

Life of Francis Parkman. C. H. Farnham. 1901.

Walter Pater. Ferris Greenslet. 1905.

John H. Patterson; Pioneer in Industrial Welfare. Samuel Crowther. 1923.

Pauline, Favorite Sister of Napoleon. W. N. C. Carlton. 1930.

A Sketch of the Life of John Howard Payne. Theodore S. Fay. 1833.

The Life and Writings of John Howard Payne. Gabriel Harrison. 1875.

Life of Thomas Love Peacock. Carl Van Doren. 1912.
The Life of William Penn . . . Mason L. Weems. 1819.
Life of William Penn. George E. Ellis. (L. A. B.)
The Life of William Penn . . . Samuel M. Janney. 1852.
The True William Penn. Sydney G. Fisher. 1900.
William Penn as the Founder of Two Commonwealths. A. C. Buell. 1904.
The Penns of Pennsylvania and England. Arthur Pound. 1932.
Life and Letters of Joseph Pennell. Elizabeth R. Pennell. 2 vols. 1929.
Power and Glory; the Life of Boies Penrose. Walter Davenport. 1931.
People's Book of Biography . . . James Parton. 1869.
Soul of Samuel Pepys. Gamaliel Bradford. 1924.
Philip II of Spain. David G. Loth. 1932.
David Graham Phillips and His Times. Isaac F. Marcosson. 1932.
Life of Sir William Phips. Francis Bowen. (L. A. B.)
The Life of Franklin Pierce. Nathaniel Hawthorne. 1852.
Franklin Pierce; Young Hickory of the Granite Hills. Roy F. Nichols. 1931.
Life of Zebulon M. Pike. Henry Whiting. (L. A. B.)
Life and Times of Lydia E. Pinkham. R. C. Washburn. 1931.
Life of William Pinckney. Henry Wheaton.
Pizarro and the Conquest of Peru. F. A. Ober. 1906.
Incredible Pizarro, Conqueror of Peru. Felix Shay. 1932.
The Works of the late Edgar Allan Poe: With Notices of his Life and Genius. Nathaniel P. Willis, James Russell Lowell, and Rufus W. Griswold. 2 vols. 1850. 3 vols. 1855.
Memoir of Edgar Allan Poe. R. H. Stoddard. 1856.
The Life and Poems of Edgar Allan Poe. E. L. Didier. 1877.
A Defense of Edgar Allan Poe. Life, Character and Dying Declarations of the Poet. J. J. Moran. 1885.
Edgar Allan Poe. George E. Woodberry. 1885. (A. M. L.)
Life and Letters of Edgar Allan Poe. James A. Harrison. 2 vols. 1903.
Life of Poe. Susan A. Weiss. 1907.
The Life of Edgar Allan Poe. George E. Woodberry. 2 vols. 1909.
Edgar A. Poe; a Psychopathic Study. J. W. Robertson. 1923.
Edgar Allan Poe; a Study in Genius. J. W. Krutch. 1926.

Edgar Allan Poe, the Man. Mary E. Phillips. 2 vols. 1926.

Israfel; the Life and Times of Edgar Allan Poe. Hervey Allen. 2 vols. 1927.

Juan Ponce de Leon. F. A. Ober. 1908.

Commodore David Porter, 1780–1843. A. D. Turnbull. 1929.

Portraits of American Women. Gamaliel Bradford. 1917–1919.

　　Abigail Adams, Sarah Alden Ripley, Maty Lyon, Harriet Beecher Stowe, Margaret Fuller Ossoli, Louisa May Alcott, Frances Elizabeth Willard, and Emily Dickinson.

Portraits of Women. Gamaliel Bradford. 1916.

　　Lady Mary Wortley Montagu, Lady Holland, Miss Austen, Madame D'Arblay, Mrs. Pepys, Madame de Sévigné, Madame du Deffand, Madame de Choiseul, and Eugénie de Guérin.

Memoir of Thomas Posey. James Hall. (L. A. B.)

Life of Edward Preble. Lorenzo Sabine. (L. A. B.)

Life of William H. Prescott. George Ticknor. 1864.

William Hickling Prescott. Rollo Ogden. 1905. (A. M. L.)

William H. Prescott. Harry T. Peck. 1905. (E. M. L.)

Life of Count Pulaski. Jared Sparks. (L. A. B.)

Joseph Pulitzer: His Life and Letters. Don C. Seitz. 1924.

Life of Israel Putnam. O. W. B. Peabody. (L. A. B.)

The Quick and the Dead. Gamaliel Bradford. 1931.

　　Theodore Roosevelt, Woodrow Wilson, Henry Ford, Nikolai Lenin, Benito Mussolini, and Calvin Coolidge.

Book of Rabelais. Jake Falstaff. 1928.

François Rabelais, Man of the Renaissance; a Spiritual Biography. Samuel Putnam. 1929.

Francis Rabelais; the Man and his Work. Albert Jay Nock and C. R. Wilson. 1930.

Life of Sebastian Rale. Convers Francis. (L. A. B.)

Sir Walter Raleigh. F. A. Ober. 1909.

Sir Walter Raleigh; That Damned Upstart. Donald B. Chidsey. 1931.

Raleigh and His World. Irvin W. Anthony. 1934.

The Life of John Randolph of Roanoke. H. A. Garland. 2 vols. 1850.

John Randolph. Henry Adams. 1882. (A. S.)

John Randolph of Roanoke, 1773–1833. William C. Bruce. 2 vols. 1922.

Randolph of Roanoke; a Political Fantastic. G. W. Johnson. 1929.

Henry J. Raymond and the New York Press. Augustus Maverick. 1870.

Rebel Saints. Mary Agnes Best. 1925.
George Fox, Margaret Fell, Thomas Lurting, Mary Fisher, Katherine Evans, Sarah Chivers, William Penn, Edward Burroughs, Mary Dyer, and Elizabeth Haddon.

Life of Joseph Reed. Henry Reed. (L. A. B.)

Life of Thomas B. Reed. Samuel W. McCall. 1914.

Thomas B. Reed, Parliamentarian. W. A. Robinson. 1930.

Life of Whitelaw Reid. Royal Cortissoz. 2 vols. 1921.

R. v. R.; Being the Last Years and Death of One Rembrandt Harmenszoon van Rijn. Hendrik W. Van Loon. 1930.

Ernest Renan. Louis F. Mott. 1921.

Life of Paul Revere. Elbridge H. Goss. 2 vols. 1891.

True Story of Paul Revere, His Mid-Night Ride, His Arrest and Court-Martial, His Useful Public Services. C. F. Gettemy. 1905.

Paul Revere. Emerson G. Taylor. 1930.

James Ford Rhodes, American Historian. M. A. De W. Howe. 1929.

Life of John Ribault. Jared Sparks. (L. A. B.)

The Youth of James Whitcomb Riley. Marcus Dickey. 1919.

The Maturity of James Whitcomb Riley. Marcus Dickey. 1922.

Life of David Rittenhouse. James Renwick. (L. A. B.)

Hero of the Filipinos, the Story of José Rizal, Poet, Patriot and Martyr. Charles E. Russell. 1923.

John D; a Portrait in Oils. John K. Winkler. 1929.

God's Gold; the Story of Rockefeller and His Times. John T. Flynn. 1932.

Take the Witness (Life of Earl Rogers). Alfred Cohn and Joe Chisholm. 1934.

Madame Roland; a Biographical Study. Ida Tarbell. 1896.

Theodore Roosevelt and his Time, Shown in his own Letters. Joseph Bucklin Bishop. 2 vols. 1920.

Theodore Roosevelt. Walter C. McCaleb. 1931.

Theodore Roosevelt. Henry F. Pringle. 1931.

Betsy Ross, Quaker Rebel. Edwin S. Parry. 1930.

Jean-Jacques Rousseau. Matthew Josephson. 1931.

Royal Charles, Ruler and Rake. David G. Loth. 1930.

Benjamin Rush, Physician and Citizen. Nathan G. Goodman. 1934.

Charles-Augustus Sainte-Beuve. George M. Harper. 1909.

Sainte-Beuve. Louis F. Mott. 1925.

Saints and Sinners. Gamaliel Bradford. 1932.
    Caesar Borgia, Saint Francis of Assisi, Casanova, Thomas à Kempis, Talleyrand, Fenelon, and Byron.

Haym Salomon and the Revolution. Charles E. Russell. 1930.

George Sand, the Search for Love. Marie H. Howe. 1927.

Seven Strings of the Lyre; the Romantic Life of George Sand, 1804–1876. Elizabeth W. Schermerhorn. 1927.

Santa Anna; the Napoleon of the West. Frank C. Hanighen. 1934.

Savonarola; a Study of Conscience. Ralph Roeder. 1930.

Jacob H. Schiff: His Life and Letters. Cyrus Adler. 2 vols. 1928.

Schopenhauer, Pessimist and Pagan. V. J. McGill. 1931.

Carl Schurz, Reformer. Claude M. Fuess. 1932.

Scottish Queen (Mary Stuart). Herbert S. Gorman. 1932.

Junipero Serra; Pioneer Colonist of California. Agnes Repplier. 1933.

Seven Iron Men. Paul De Kruif. 1929.

Samuel Sewall and the World He Lived In. N. H. Chamberlain. 1897.

William Henry Seward. Thornton K. Lathrop. 1896.

Seymour and Blair: Their Lives and Services. D. G. Croly. 1868.

Life of William Shakespeare. W. J. Rolfe. 1902.

Life of William Shakespeare. Joseph Q. Adams. 1923.

Shelley; his Life and Work. Walter G. Peck. 2 vols. 1927.

Life of Gen. Philip H. Sheridan: its Romance and Reality. F. A. Burr and R. J. Henton. 1888.

Sheridan; a Military Narrative. Joseph Hergesheimer. 1931.

John Sherman. Theodore E. Burton. 1906. (A. S.)

Sherman, Fighting Prophet. Lloyd Lewis. 1932.

The Life and Letters of Stuart P. Sherman. Jacob Zeitlin and Homer Woodbridge. 2 vols. 1929.

Immortal Sidney. Emma M. Denkinger. 1931.

Mrs. Sigourney, the Sweet Singer of Hartford. Gordon S. Haight. 1930.

Edward Roland Sill; his Life and Work. W. B. Parker. 1915.

William Gilmore Simms. W. P. Trent. 1892. (A. M. L.)

Alfred E. Smith. Henry Moskowitz. 1924.

Up From the City Streets, Alfred E. Smith; a Biographical Study in Contemporary Politics. Norman Hapgood and Henry Moskowitz. 1927.

Alfred E. Smith: A Critical Study. Henry F. Pringle. 1927.

Life of Captain John Smith. George S. Hillard. (L. A. B.)

Adventures of Captain John Smith. Francis L. Hawks. 1843.

Life of Captain John Smith, the Founder of Virginia. William Gilmore Simms. 1846.

Captain John Smith . . . Charles Dudley Warner. 1881.

Life of Captain John Smith, Planter of Virginia. C. K. True. 1882.

John Smith—also Pocahontas. John G. Fletcher. 1928.

Biographical Sketches of Joseph Smith, the Prophet, and his Progenitors for Many Generations. Lucy Smith. 1853.

The Life of Joseph Smith, the Prophet. George Q. Cannon. 1888.

Prophet of Palmyra; Mormonism Reviewed and Examined in the Life and Character of its Founder . . . (Joseph Smith.) T. Gregg. 1890.

Joseph Smith and His Mormon Empire. H. M. Beardsley. 1931.

Colonel William Smith and Lady. Katherine M. Roof. 1929.

Some Noted Princes, Authors and Statesmen of Our Times. James Parton. 1885.

The Life and Writings of Jared Sparks. H. B. Adams. 2 vols. 1893.

Life and Public Services of Edwin M. Stanton. George C. Gorham. 2 vols. 1899.

Edwin McMaster Stanton, Autocrat of Rebellion, Emancipation, and Reconstruction. F. A. Flower. 1905.

Life of John Stark. Edward Everett. (L. A. B.)

Statesmen of the Old South. William E. Dodd. 1911.

Thomas Jefferson, John C. Calhoun, and Jefferson Davis.

Sir Richard Steele. Willard Connely. 1934.

Little Alec; a Life of Alexander H. Stephens. Eudora R. Richardson. 1932.

Life and Times of Laurence Sterne. Wilbur L. Cross. 1909. 2 vols. 1925. 2 vols. in 1, 1929.

Life of Baron Steuben. (L. A. B.)

John Stevens; an American Record. A. D. Turnbull. 1928.

Thaddeus Stevens: Commoner. E. B. Callender. 1882.

Thaddeus Stevens. Samuel W. McCall. 1899. (A. S.)

Thaddeus Stevens. Thomas F. Woodley. 1934.

Life of Thaddeus Stevens. James A. Woodburn. 1913.

The True Stevenson. George S. Hellman. 1925.

Life of Ezra Stiles. James L. Kingsley. (L. A. B.)

Portrait of a Banker; James Stillman, 1850–1918. Anna Robeson Burr. 1927.

The First Billion; the Stillmans and the National City Bank. John K. Winkler. 1934.

Lucy Stone; Pioneer of Women's Rights. Alice S. Blackwell. 1930.

William Wetmore Story and His Friends. Henry James. 2 vols. 1903.

Story of Philosophy; the Lives and Opinions of the Greatest Philosophers. Will Durant. 1926.

Story of Religion As Told in the Lives of Its Leaders . . . Charles F. Potter. 1929.

Life-Work of the Author of Uncle Tom's Cabin. T. F. McCray. 1889.

Life of Harriet Beecher Stowe. Charles E. Stowe. 1890.

Life and Letters of Harriet Beecher Stowe. Annie Fields (ed.). 1897.

Harriet Beecher Stowe: The Story of Her Life. Charles E. Stowe and Lyman B. Stowe. 1911.

Harriet Beecher Stowe. Martha F. Crow. 1913.

Sketch of the Life, Personal Appearance, Character and Manners of Charles S. Stratton . . . General Tom Thumb . . . N. Y. 1847.

August Strindberg, the Dedeviled Viking. V. J. McGill. 1930.

Jeb Stuart. John W. Thomason. 1930.

Life and Times of Pieter Stuyvesant. Hendrik Van Loon. 1928.

Grand Turke; Suleyman the Magnificent, Sultan of the Ottomans. Fairfax Downey. 1929.

Life of John Sullivan. O. W. B. Peabody. (L. A. B.)

John L. Sullivan; an Intimate Narrative. R. F. Dibble. 1925.

Life and Times of Charles Sumner. Elias Nason. 1874.

Memoir and Letters of Charles Sumner. Edward L. Pierce. 4 vols. 1878–1894.

Charles Sumner. Moorfield Storey. 1900. (A. S.)

William Graham Sumner. Harris E. Starr. 1925.

Sutter of California. A Biography. Julian Dana. 1934.

Yankee of the Yards; the Biography of Gustavus F. Swift. Louis F. Swift and Arthur Van Vlissingen. 1928.

Swift. Carl Van Doren. 1930.

Swinburne. George E. Woodberry. 1905.

Swinburne. Samuel C. Chew. 1929.

John Addington Symonds. Van Wyck Brooks. 1914.

William Howard Taft. Herbert S. Duffy. 1930.

Talleyrand; the Training of a Statesman, 1754–1838. Anna B. Dodd. 1927.

Tamerlane, the Earth Shaker. Harold Lamb. 1928.

Memoir of Roger Brooke Taney, Chief Justice of the Supreme Court of the United States. Samuel Tyler. 1872.

The Life and Services of Commodore Josiah Tatnall. Charles C. Jones, Jr. 1878.

Bayard Taylor. Henry W. Longfellow. 1879.

Life and Letters of Bayard Taylor. Marie H. Taylor and Horace E. Scudder. 2 vols. 1884.

Bayard Taylor. Albert H. Smith. 1896. (A. M. L.)

Frederick W. Taylor, Father of Scientific Management. Frank B. Copley. 2 vols. 1923.

Life of Major General Zachary Taylor . . . C. F. Powell. 1847.

Life and Times of Tennyson from 1809 to 1850. Thomas R. Lounsbury. 1916.

American Orchestra and Theodore Thomas. Charles E. Russell. 1927.

Life of Benjamin Thompson, Count Rumford. James Renwick. (L. A. B.)

Hizzoner, Big Bill Thompson; an Idyll of Chicago. John Bright. 1930.

Henry D. Thoreau. F. B. Sanborn. 1882. (A. M. L.)

The Life of Henry David Thoreau . . . F. B. Sanborn. 1917.

Henry David Thoreau. H. S. Salt. 1896.

Henry Thoreau, the Cosmic Yankee. J. B. Atkinson. 1927.

Three Men of Letters; Berkeley, Dwight, Barlow. Moses Coit Tyler. 1895.

Life, Letters, and Journals of George Ticknor. George Hillard and Anna Ticknor (eds.). 2 vols. 1876.

Life and Public Services of Samuel J. Tilden . . . and Sketch of T. A. Hendricks. T. P. Cook. 1876.

Life of Samuel J. Tilden of New York. John Esten Cooke. 1876.

The Life of Samuel J. Tilden. John Bigelow. 2 vols. 1895.

Beloved Physician: Edward Livingston Trudeau. Stephen Chalmers. 1916.

Trumpets of Jubilee. Constance M. Rourke. 1927.

> Lyman Beecher, Henry Ward Beecher, Harriet Beecher Stowe, Horace Greeley, and Phineas T. Barnum.

Albion W. Turgee. Roy F. Dibble. 1921.

Turgenev, the Man—his Art—and his Age. Avraham Yarmolinsky. 1926.

Mark Twain. His Life and Works. A Biographical Sketch. Will M. Clemens. 1892.

My Mark Twain. William Dean Howells. 1910.

Mark Twain. A Biography. Albert Bigelow Paine. 3 vols. 1912.

A Short Life of Mark Twain. Albert Bigelow Paine. 1920.

Ordeal of Mark Twain. Van Wyck Brooks. 1920.

"Boss" Tweed; the Story of a Grim Generation. Denis Tilden Lynch. 1927.

Two Spies: Nathan Hale and John André. B. J. Lossing. 1886.

Moses Coit Tyler. Howard M. Jones. 1933.

Union Portraits. Gamaliel Bradford. 1916.

> George B. McClellan, Joseph Hooker, George G. Meade, George Henry Thomas, William Tecumseh Sherman, Edwin M. Stanton, William H. Seward, Charles Sumner, and Samuel Bowles.

In One Man's Life; Being Chapters from the Personal and Business Career of Theodore N. Vail. Albert Bigelow Paine. 1921.

The Life of Martin Van Buren, Heir Apparent to the "Government" and the appointed successor of General Andrew Jackson . . . David Crockett. 1835.

Biography of Martin Van Buren, Vice President of the United States. William Emmans. 1835.

The Life and Political Opinions of Martin Van Buren, Vice President of the United States. W. M. Holland. 1835.

The Life and Times of Martin Van Buren. W. L. Mackenzie. 1846.

Life of Martin Van Buren. Thomas M'Elhiney. 1853.

Martin Van Buren: Lawyer, Statesman and Man. William A. Butler. 1862.

Martin Van Buren. Edward M. Shepard. 1888. (A. S.)

An Epoch and a Man: Martin Van Buren and His Times. Denis Tilden Lynch. 1929.

The Vanderbilts and the Story of their Fortune. W. A. Croffut. 1886.

Commodore Vanderbilt; an Epic of American Achievement. Arthur D. H. Smith. 1927.

Life of Sir Henry Vane. Charles W. Upham. (L. A. B.)

Thorstein Veblen and His America. Joseph Dorfman. 1934.

Amerigo Vespucci. F. A. Ober. 1907.

Mind of Leonardo da Vinci. Edward McCurdy. 1928.

The Virginia Plutarch. Philip A. Bruce. 2 vols. 1929.
    Short studies of famous Virginians from Powhatan to Woodrow Wilson.

Life of Voltaire. James Parton. 2 vols. 1881.

Voltaire, Genius of Mockery. Victor Thaddeus. 1928.

Life, Travels and Books of Alexander Von Humboldt. R. H. Stoddard. 1859.

Life of Benjamin F. Wade. A. G. Riddle. 1886.

Life of Francis Amasa Walker. James P. Munroe. 1923.

Romantic Rise of a Great American. (John Wanamaker.) Russell H. Conwell. 1924.

John Wanamaker. Herbert A. Gibbons. 2 vols. 1926.

Life of Artemus Ward, the First Commander in Chief of the American Revolution. Charles Martyn. 1921.

Artemus Ward (Charles Farrar Browne.) Don C. Seitz. 1919.

A Memoir of the Rev. Nathaniel Ward, A. M., Author of the Simple Cobbler of Agawam in America . . . John W. Dean. 1868.

Life of Samuel Ward. William Gammell. (L. A. B.)

Life of Joseph Warren. Alexander H. Everett. (L. A. B.)

Mercy Warren. Alice Brown. 1896.

A Short Sketch of General Washington's Life and Character. In Charles H. Wharton's *Poetical Epistle to his Excellency George Washington* . . . John Bell. 1779.

The American Patriot and Hero. A Brief Memoir of the Illustrious Conduct and Character of his Excellency General Washington . . . John Maxwell. 1785.

True and Authentic History of his Excellency George Washington. Thomas Thornton. 1790.

The Life of General Washington, present president of the United States. Also of the brave General Montgomery . . . 1794.

A History of the Life and Death, Virtues and Exploits of General George Washington. Mason Locke Weems. 1800.

Life of George Washington . . . John Marshall. 5 vols. 1804–1807. Rev. ed. 2 vols. 1832.

The Life of George Washington. Aaron Bancroft. 1807.

The Life of George Washington . . . David Ramsay. 1807, 1811.

A Life of Washington. James K. Paulding. 2 vols. 1835.

Life of George Washington. Francis Glass. 1835.

   Written in Latin prose!

The Life and Writings of George Washington. Jared Sparks. 12 vols. 1834–1837.

The Life of George Washington. Jared Sparks. 1839. 2 vols. 1842.

Life of George Washington. Washington Irving. 5 vols. 1855–1859.

Washington and the Generals of the American Revolution. Rufus Griswold. 2 vols. 1847.

Washington and his Generals. J. T. Headley. 1847.

Life of George Washington. J. T. Headley. 1856.

The Life of George Washington. Edward Everett. 1860.

Public Life of Washington . . . H. W. Bellows. 1866.

Washington and the American Republic. B. J. Lossing. 3 vols. 1879.

Life of Washington. Virginia F. Townsend. 1887.

The Life of George Washington, Studied Anew. Edward Everett Hale. 1888.

Life and Times of George Washington. S. S. Schmucker. 1890.

Life of George Washington. S. G. Arnold. 1890.

George Washington. C. C. King. 1894.

George Washington. Henry Cabot Lodge. 2 vols. 1889. (A. S.)

General Washington. Bradley T. Johnson. 1894.

George Washington. Horace E. Scudder. 1895.

George Washington. Woodrow Wilson. 1896.

Washington, the Soldier. H. B. Carrington. 1898.

George Washington. Worthington C. Ford. 2 vols. 1900.

George Washington. Norman Hapgood. 1901.

Washington's Life and Military Career. M. H. Hancock. 1902.

George Washington. Alonzo M. Bullock. 1904.

George Washington, Patriot, Soldier, Statesman . . . J. A. Harrison. 1906.

Seven Ages of Washington. Owen Wister. 1907.

The True George Washington. Paul L. Ford. 1909.

George Washington. Worthington C. Ford. 1911.

George Washington; the Human Being and the Hero. Rupert Hughes. 3 vols. 1926–1930.

George Washington; the Image and the Man. W. E. Woodward. 1926.

Washington. Joseph D. Sawyer. 2 vols. 1927.

George Washington. Shelby M. Little. 1929.

Unknown Washington; Biographic Origins of the Republic. John Corbin. 1930.

Washington, Commander-in-Chief. T. B. Frothingham. 1930.

George Washington, Son of his Country. Paul Van Dyke. 1931.

George Washington Himself. A Common-Sense Biography Written from His Manuscripts. John C. Fitzpatrick. 1933.

Memoirs of the Lives, Characters and Writings of . . . Dr. Isaac Watts and Dr. Philip Doddridge. Jeremy Belknap and Andrew Kempis. 1793.

James Watt. Andrew Carnegie. 1905.

Life of Anthony Wayne. John Armstrong. (L. A. B.)

Mad Anthony Wayne. Thomas A. Boyd. 1929.

Gentleman Rebel; the Exploits of Anthony Wayne. John H. Preston. 1930.

Life of Daniel Webster. Samuel L. Knapp. 1831.

Private Life of Daniel Webster. Charles Lanman. 1852.

Daniel Webster, His Life and Character. B. F. Tefft. 1852.

Life . . . of Daniel Webster. Fletcher Webster. 2 vols. 1856.

Life of Daniel Webster. George T. Curtis. 2 vols. 1870.

Daniel Webster. Joseph Bainvard. 1875.

Life of Daniel Webster. B. F. Tefft. 1880.

Daniel Webster. Henry Cabot Lodge. 1883. (A. S.)

Daniel Webster. Norman Hapgood. 1899.

The True Daniel Webster. Sydney G. Fisher. 1911.

Real Daniel Webster. E. R. Kennedy. 1924.

Daniel Webster. Allan L. Benson. 1929.

Godlike Daniel. Samuel H. Adams. 1930.

Daniel Webster. Claude M. Fuess. 2 vols. 1930.

Noah Webster. Horace E. Scudder. 1881. (A. M. L.)

Parson Weems of the Cherry Tree. Harold Kellock. 1928.

Life of the . . . Duke of Wellington. Francis L. Clarke. With Supplementary Chapters by William Dunlap. 1814.

John Wesley; a Portrait. Abram Lipsky. 1928.

John Wesley. John D. Wade. 1930.

Whitman. John Burroughs. 1896.

Walt Whitman; his Life and Work. Bliss Perry. 1906.

Whitman; an Interpretation in Narrative. Emory Holloway. 1926.

Magnificent Idler; the Story of Walt Whitman. Cameron Rogers. 1926.

Life of James McNeill Whistler. Elizabeth R. and Joseph Pennell. 1908.

Henry White; Thirty Years of American Diplomacy. Allan Nevins. 1930.

J. William White, M.D. A Biography. Agnes Repplier. 1919.

John Greenleaf Whittier . . . W. S. Kennedy. 1882.

Life and Letters of John Greenleaf Whittier. S. T. Pickard. 2 vols. 1894.

John Greenleaf Whittier. G. R. Carpenter. 1903. (A. M. L.)

Quaker Militant; John Greenleaf Whittier. Albert Mordell. 1933.

Memoir of the Rev. Michael Wigglesworth, Author of the 'Day of Doom.' John Ward Dean. 1871.

Life, Literary Labors and Neglected Grave of Richard Henry Wilde. C. C. Jones, Jr. 1885.

The Finished Scoundrel. General James Wilkinson, sometime Commander-in-Chief of the Army of the United States . . . Royal O. Shreve. 1933.

Life of Frances E. Willard. Anna A. Gordon. 1914.

William the Conqueror. Phillips Russell. 1933.

Memoir of Roger Williams, the Founder of the State of Rhode Island. James D. Knowles. 1834.

Life of Roger Williams. William Gammell. (L. A. B.)

Life of Roger Williams. Romeo Elton. 1853.

Roger Williams, the Pioneer of Religious Liberty. Oscar S. Strauss. 1894.

Roger Williams, Prophet and Pioneer. Emily Easton. 1930.

Roger Williams, New England Firebrand. James E. Ernst. 1932.

Nathaniel Parker Willis. Henry A. Beers. 1885. (A. M. L.)

Life of Alexander Wilson. W. B. O. Peabody. (L. A. B.)

Woodrow Wilson and his Work. William E. Dodd. 1920.

Woodrow Wilson; a Character Study. Robert E. Annin. 1924.

Life of Woodrow Wilson. Josephus Daniels. 1924.

Woodrow Wilson, the Man, his Times, and his Task. William Allen White. 1924.

Woodrow Wilson: Life and Letters. Ray S. Baker. 4 vols. 1927–1931.

Woodrow Wilson, the Man Who Lives On. John K. Winkler. 1933.

Life and Letters of John Winthrop. R. C. Winthrop. 1864.

John Winthrop . . . J. H. Twichell. 1891.

Life and Poems of Theodore Winthrop. Laura Winthrop Johnson (ed.). 1884.

Memoirs of the Life of William Wirt. John P. Kennedy. 2 vols. 1849. 1 vol. 1851.

Life of Henry A. Wise. Barton Wise. 1899.

Wives. Gamaliel Bradford. 1925.

Confessions of a biographer, Mrs. Abraham Lincoln, Mrs. Benedict Arnold, Theodosia Burr, Mrs. James Madison, Mrs. Jefferson Davis, Mrs. Benjamin Butler, and Mrs. James G. Blaine.

Eminent Women of the Age. James Parton. 1869.

A Biography of Fernando Wood. A History of the Forgeries, Perjuries, and Other Crimes of our Model Mayor. Abajiah Ingraham. 1856.

Biography of Hon. Fernando Wood. Donald MacLeod. 1856.

Leonard Wood; a Biography. Herman Hagedorn. 2 vols. 1931.

Terrible Siren; Victoria Woodhull (1838–1927). Emanie L. Sachs. 1928.

William Wordsworth; his Life, Works, and Influence. George McLean Harper. 2 vols. 1916.

Brawny Wycherley. Willard Connely. 1930.

Life of Brigham Young. Edward H. Tullidge. 1876.

Brigham Young and His Mormon Empire. Frank J. Cannon and George L. Knapp. 1913.

Brigham Young. M. R. Werner. 1925.

Life of Brigham Young. Susa Gates and Leah Widstoe. 1930.
Owen D. Young. Ida M. Tarbell. 1932.
Zola and his Time. Matthew Josephson. 1928.

II

A partial list of books and articles on the subject of biography.
The articles have been confined to those written by Americans.

BOOKS

Cross, Wilbur L. *An Outline of Biography. From Plutarch to Strachey.* N. Y. 1924.

Dunn, Waldo H. *English Biography.* N. Y. 1916.

Johnston, James C. *Biography, the Literature of Personality.* N. Y. 1927.

Longaker, Mark. *English Biography in the Eighteenth Century.* Phila., 1931. *Contemporary Biography.* Phila., 1934.

Maurois, André. *Aspects of Biography.* N. Y. 1929.

Merrill, Dana K. *Development of American Biography.* Port., Me., 1932.

Nicolson, Harold G. *The Development of English Biography.* N. Y. 1928.

Stauffer, Donald A. *English Biography Before 1700.* Camb., 1930.

Stuart, Duane R. *Epochs of Greek and Roman Biography.* Berkeley, Calif., 1928.

Thayer, W. R. *The Art of Biography.* N. Y. 1920.

ARTICLES

Adams, James T. "New Modes in Biography" and "Biography as an Art" in *The Tempo of Modern Life.* N. Y. 1931.

Bowerman, George F. "The New Biography." *Wilson Bulletin* 4:107–111, 153–159. Nov. 1929.

Boyd, Ernest. "Sex in Biography." Harpers 165: 752–759. Nov. 1932.

Bradford, Gamaliel. "Biography and the Human Heart." *Century* 120: 180–191. Spring 1930. Also in volume of same title, Bost., 1932. "Confessions of a Biographer" in *Wives,* N. Y., 1926. "Psychography" in *A Naturalist of Souls,* N. Y., 1917, 1926. "The Art of Biography" in *Sat. Rev. of Lit.* 1: 769–770, May

23, 1925. "The Art of Psychography," *Lit. Rev.* 3: 641–642, April 28, 1923.

Carter, John. "The Rewrite School of Biography." *Independent* 118: 389–390, 403. April 9, 1927.

Crothers, Samuel M. "Satan Among the Biographers" in *Cheerful Giver,* Bost., 1923.

DeVoto, Bernard. "The Skeptical Biographer." *Harpers* 166: 181–192. Jan., 1933.

Field, Louise M. "Biographical New Dealing." *North Amer. Rev.* 238: 546–552. Dec., 1934.

Fuess, Claude M. "The Biographer and His Victims." *Atlantic* 149: 62–73. Jan., 1932. "Debunkery and Biography." *Atlantic* 151: 347–356. March, 1933.

Howe, M. A. DeWolfe. "Biography Drifts Toward the Novel." *Independent* 115: 359–361. Sept. 26, 1925.

Johnston, George A. "The New Biography; Ludwig, Maurois, and Strachey." *Atlantic* 143: 333–342. April, 1929.

Lewin, Walter. "Bowdlerized Biography." *Forum* 10: 658–666. 1890–1891.

Notestein, W. "History and the Biographer." *Yale Review* n. s. 22: 549–558. March, 1933.

Thayer, W. R. "Biography." *North Amer. Rev.* 180: 261–278. 1905. "Biography in the Nineteenth Century." *North Amer. Rev.* 211: 632–640, 826–833. 1920.

INDEX

Italics indicate published biographies.

S